HERITAGE STUDIES 6
ANCIENT CIVILIZATIONS
Fourth Edition

bju press®
Greenville, South Carolina

Note: The fact that materials produced by other publishers may be referred to in this volume does not constitute an endorsement of the content or theological position of materials produced by such publishers. Any references and ancillary materials are listed as an aid to the student or the teacher and in an attempt to maintain the accepted academic standards of the publishing industry.

HERITAGE STUDIES 6: Ancient Civilizations
Fourth Edition

Writers
Carol Arrington Ardt, MEd
Jill Blackstock, MEd
Pam Frank

Third Edition Writers
Peggy S. Alier, MEd
Marnie Batterman, MEd
Eileen M. Berry, MA
James R. Davis, MA
Annittia Jackson
Debra White

Consultants
Dennae White, EdD
Dennis Bollinger, PhD

Biblical Worldview
Brian C. Collins, PhD
Bryan Smith, PhD

Academic Oversight
Jeff Heath, EdD

Editors
Elizabeth Turner, MA
Joanna Lynch, MA

Designer
Michael Asire

Illustrators
Vladimir Aleksic
Jonathan Bartlett
Seb Camagajevac
Paula Cheadle
Rudolf Farkas
Zach Franzen
Josh Frederick
Emily Heinz
Jennifer Hudson
Frank Ordaz
Kathy Pflug
Lynda Slattery
Del Thompson
Courtney Wise

Content Image Curator
James Frasier

Cover Illustration
Ben Schipper

Page Layout
Carrie Walker
Faith Bupe Mazunda
Bonnijean Marley

Permissions
Sharon Belknap
Tatiana Bento
Sylvia Gass
Ashleigh Schieber

Project Coordinator
Heather Chisholm

Photo credits appear on pages 390–91.

Text acknowledgments appear on-page with text selections.
The bicycle illustration of Taoist nonaction on page 127 comes from Bryan W. Van Norden, *Introduction to Classical Chinese Philosophy* (Indianapolis: Hackett, 2011), 127.

All trademarks are the registered and unregistered marks of their respective owners. BJU Press is in no way affiliated with these companies. No rights are granted by BJU Press to use such marks, whether by implication, estoppel, or otherwise.

© 2018 BJU Press
Greenville, South Carolina 29609
First Edition © 1986 BJU Press
Second Edition © 1998, 2008 BJU Press
Third Edition © 2012 BJU Press

Printed in the United States of America
All rights reserved

ISBN 978-1-62856-228-6

15 14 13 12 11 10 9 8 7 6 5 4 3

CONTENTS

Chapter

1	In the Beginning	2
2	Mesopotamia	20
3	Ancient Egypt	48
4	Ancient Israel	74
5	Ancient India	98
6	Ancient China	116
7	Ancient Persia	138
8	Ancient Greece	158
9	Ancient Rome	184
10	The Byzantine Empire	210
11	Mesoamerica	234
12	Ancient Africa	256
13	Ancient Japan	276
14	The Middle Ages in Europe	292
15	A Kingdom from Shore to Shore	316

Resource Treasury

Atlas	334
Primary Source Documents	348
Biographical Dictionary	369
Gazetteer	372
Glossary	374

Index

381

WHY STUDY HERITAGE STUDIES 6?

The goal of HERITAGE STUDIES 6 is to develop student historians. The Creation Mandate, found in Genesis 1:28, provides the basis for Christian involvement in the various academic disciplines. The Creation Mandate teaches that we are to rule God's world and make culture from His creation. Fulfilling the Creation Mandate requires knowledge and skill in many areas, including in the study of history.

Our goal is not merely to teach students the facts of history. We strive to teach students to think like historians and with a biblical worldview. To accomplish this goal, we use questions to prompt students to think on a deeper, more critical level. We also emphasize having students participate in creating history and culture rather than simply reading about it. Another goal is to expose students to vocations of history and social sciences and to encourage them to consider pursuing one of these vocations in their future. The world needs historians with a biblical worldview who love God and other people.

1 IN THE BEGINNING

FOCUS
The Bible is completely accurate as the source for how history began.

| 5000 BC | 4000 BC | 3000 BC | 2000 BC | 1000 BC |

- Noah's birth ca. 4000 BC
- Abraham's birth ca. 2200 BC
- Genesis written ca. 1440s BC
- ca. 5000 BC Creation
- ca. 3400 BC Flood
- 1526 BC Moses' birth

Have you learned a skill or learned a lot about a certain subject? For example, do you play an instrument, participate in a sport, or collect something? How long have you been doing that? Who helped you learn?

Tubal-cain was the first person skilled at metallurgy. Most people before the Flood lived a long time. Imagine how much Tubal-cain would have discovered about metal working in, say, 250 years. He would have known how and where to get ores such as iron; he would have designed and built the forge, and he would have invented and fashioned tools.

When hammering iron into shape, a smith pays close attention to the color of the metal. White or yellow means the metal is very hot and easier to shape, while red and dull orange mean it is cooler—although not cool—and less pliable. Today we know that iron is worked with best when it is between red (1500°F) and bright yellow (2200°F). No wonder the onlookers at this forge are standing back.

The Bible also tells about Jubal, Tubal-cain's half-brother, who was the father of all those who play the pipe and lyre.

Why is the evolutionary thinking about prehistory inaccurate?

Where Does History Come From?

How do historians know what happened in the past? Most often they look for writings about what happened in earlier times. And sometimes they look for clues that can be dug out of the earth. By excavating an old city, historians might be able to tell how people ate, what kind of jobs they had, what they wore, and more.

But where did the very first people come from? What did they do? These are questions that many historians think are impossible to answer. No tomb has been discovered with a skeleton identified as "the first man." A written record that tells about the beginning of history would be very valuable.

Fortunately, that document does exist. The Bible is the only completely reliable source that reveals how history began.

Of course, the Bible is more than just a historical source. It is the Word of God. Every word is true, and it stands above anything written by a mere human being. Some historians think the Bible is just a religious book. They think it might be useful for Christians, but they do not think it contains helpful historical information. Many people fail to see how important the Bible is for studying history.

But Christians know that there is no better source for how history began than the Bible, which was given by the God who knows and controls all things.

The first book of the Bible, Genesis, was written by **Moses** about 3,500 years ago. As God's prophet, Moses wrote exactly what God wanted him to write.

The first words of the Bible are "In the beginning God created" (Genesis 1:1). A Christian view of history is founded on this Creation. Without the Creation described in the first chapter of Genesis, there would not be "history" in a meaningful sense. God provides a historical account of what happened on each of the first seven days. Genesis 1 also introduces time divisions. God ordered the heavenly bodies "for signs, and seasons, and for days, and years" (Genesis 1:14). God alone is eternal. Everything else, at some point, began.

Much of the Bible is a historical narrative. Genesis is a historical narrative, as is part of Exodus. Some of the Old Testament prophets were historians of a sort, recording God's view of Israel's history.

Moses Hebrew whom God used to lead the Israelites out of slavery; wrote the first five books of the Bible.

INSPIRATION OF THE BOOKS OF THE LAW

The Bible asserts that all Scripture was given by **inspiration** of God (2 Timothy 3:16). This inspiration means that the Holy Spirit guided the men who wrote the Bible, breathing out God's words through them so that what they wrote was the Word of God.

The first five books of the Bible are known as the books of the Law. Other names for this section of the Bible are the *Pentateuch* and the *Torah*. Many verses in the Bible indicate that Moses wrote these books. In the New Testament, Jesus Himself referred to Moses as their author when He said,

> These are the words which I spake unto you, while I was yet with you, that all things must be fulfilled, which were written in the law of Moses . . . concerning me (Luke 24:44).

---

inspiration (of Scripture) God breathing out the Scriptures, using holy men to record them.

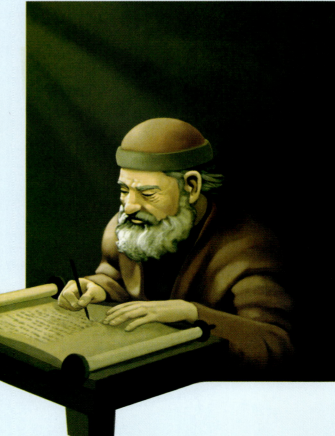

Moses wrote the books of the Law by inspiration of God. What materials may Moses have used to record Scripture?

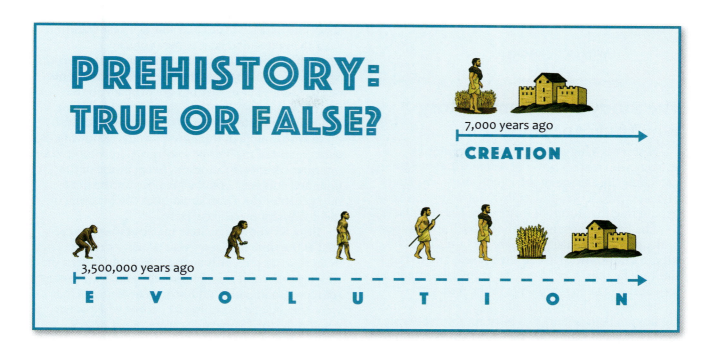

In the Bible, God narrates and explains His creative and redemptive work in history. He did not create the world with a fully formed society. Society develops over time. Nations, governments, schools, businesses, banks, airlines, technology, trade groups, and other institutions developed over the course of history. Each generation builds on the insights and skills of those that preceded it. This building on the work of previous generations has led to human accomplishments such as pyramids, literature, Bach's music, and the *Saturn V* rocket.

Prehistory

Most history textbooks begin by talking about how humans evolved. To evolve means to develop gradually. The period when humans supposedly evolved is called **prehistory**. This term is used because no written records from that time exist. In fact, evolutionists believe that mankind had not yet developed the ability to write.

The story, as evolutionists tell it, begins with early humanlike creatures that lived in East Africa about 3,500,000 years ago. These creatures learned how to make simple stone tools. Then they evolved more and could stand upright and develop tools that were more advanced.

Supposedly, around 250,000 years ago, these creatures evolved into the earliest humans. The early humans continued to develop. Some began to bury the dead. Evolutionists think that the burying of the dead might be the first evidence of religion among humans.

Other early humans began to paint the walls of the caves they lived in. During all this time, the early humans gathered fruits and nuts or hunted for their food. But about 12,000 years ago, as the story of evolution goes, humans learned they could plant seeds and grow plants that they could eat. This discovery allowed them to settle down and build homes. They also began to tame animals to help them work. Eventually, about 6,000 years ago, the first cities developed. Soon humans learned to write. They created written records, and modern history began.

However, there is no "prehistory" in the evolutionary sense because the Bible contains a written record that tells the history of the beginning of the world. In Genesis, Moses records the eyewitness testimony of the divine eyewitness, God.

The Bible indicates that people were created directly by God about 6,000 or 7,000 years ago. It also says that humans could speak from the very beginning. It is quite possible that humans could also write in the very beginning. In addition, agriculture and cities did not take thousands of years to develop; they appeared in the first generations of people.

 Why is the Bible a reliable historical record for the origin of mankind?

---

prehistory The period when humans supposedly evolved and when there were no written records.

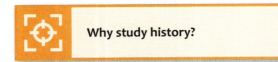

Why study history?

The Study of Ancient History
Why Study Ancient History?

History is a big story full of smaller stories. Anyone who reads a novel or watches a movie understands the enjoyment of a good story. The study of history holds the same enjoyment with the added benefit that the stories of history are based on facts.

The goal of most historians is to tell true stories of the past. People can use these accounts from history to know how to live in the present and in the future. They can learn from the accomplishments as well as the mistakes of people in the past.

History teaches people about themselves. What are human beings like? The most important way to answer this question is to see what God says in the Bible. That is the one sure way to know. Another way to learn about people is to study how they have acted for thousands of years.

History is also important because it provides an opportunity to praise God. Throughout history, God has used people and events to complete His sovereign plan. Recorded history shows the struggle of mankind against God. Mankind, in its selfishness, continues to strive for power and to resist God.

A good example of such a man is King Nebuchadnezzar. The book of Daniel tells of Nebuchadnezzar, who was a great and powerful ruler of Babylon. At one time, this king even declared himself to be a god and expected everyone to worship him. God taught him who really controls the world. This king learned that God is the sovereign ruler over everything. He also learned that no one can stop God from doing His will both in heaven and on earth. By studying history, people can see the mighty acts of God through events and in the lives of people.

How Do People Study History?

How do historians learn about the past? The historian begins by gathering facts. There are three major sources for facts about the past.

First, the historian studies *artifacts*, physical manmade objects from the past. These objects could include ancient pottery or artwork that an archaeologist finds at a site. Historians also study important buildings of the past and the ancient ruins of cities. These all provide valuable clues about the past.

A second source for the historian is *tradition*, or the passing of information from generation to generation. In some societies, people did not preserve memories of the past in writing. Instead they told about the past in stories and songs. These traditions were then passed to later generations.

A third source for the historian is *written records*. Many people in the past recorded historical events of their time. These writings are primary sources, or firsthand accounts, and are valuable to historians. When using written records for historical study, there are a couple of things to consider. Knowing the background of the author may reveal how the author interprets events. In addition, being aware of the intended audience and the purpose for the document enables the historian to infer the meaning of the document more accurately.

Primary sources include material that was created at the time in history that is being studied. They include written records such as firsthand letters, diaries, legal documents, newspapers, and art. Primary sources also include oral histories or journals that were created at a later time by people who participated in historical events or were eyewitnesses.

Secondary sources include material that was created by someone who was not a participant in or an eyewitness to a historical event; examples include an encyclopedia entry or biography.

In the 1970s, thousands of clay tablets were found in Ebla, an ancient city in what is now Syria. They were a collection of records kept near the central court. Some translators of these primary sources believe that the tablets prove the name *Canaan* was in use in ancient Ebla. Critics had previously claimed that the Bible used the name *Canaan* incorrectly, but the tablets may prove them wrong.
Do Christians need such an artifact to know that the Bible is true?

Below: The Roman theater in Ephesus (modern-day Turkey) seated almost 25,000 spectators. What does the theater suggest about how ancient civilizations used leisure time?

Bottom: This glazed brick relief of the Lion of Babylon represents Nebuchadnezzar II's reign. What might a historian infer about Nebuchadnezzar's reign from the image of a lion?

Which Roman surgical tools look similar to tools doctors use today?

Ancient Greeks used animals in design motifs to decorate everyday items like this clay jug.

The gathering of information is just the beginning. A historian needs to evaluate the accuracy of the artifacts, traditions, and written records. Some historical accounts may present only one side of a story. For example, a written record by a Greek about a war with Persia may not accurately tell the Persian side of the story. But if the historian can find some Persian records that confirm the Greek record, then he will have more confidence in the accuracy of both sources.

Research presents challenges for the historian. Sometimes historians disagree about how to interpret evidence. These disagreements often result from historians having different worldviews. A Christian historian's **worldview** begins with the Bible. Someone who does not believe in the Bible will view evidence differently. Some non-Christian historians believe that early humans were primitive, ape-like creatures. They do not believe that these early humans were advanced or had much intellect. The Christian historian believes that mankind was created in God's image and has always been intelligent. For example, shortly after Creation, people were inventing things such as musical instruments and metal tools (Genesis 4:21–22).

The historian also needs to understand what is important and what is not. If he is telling the story of how empires rose and fell in China, the design of Chinese dishes would probably not be relevant.

---

worldview How a person sees and interprets the universe and everything in it.

PRODUCING A HISTORICAL ACCOUNT

The historian gathers primary written sources about his subject, compares the written records, **chooses the most reliable sources,** **evaluates the material** for strengths and weaknesses, **combines information** from several sources, **produces a narrative** that represents the majority of his research, **interprets and explains** why an event happened and why it remains important, and **presents the completed historical account** for others to study and evaluate.

As the historian examines the sources, he begins to see a picture of what happened in the past. He looks at written records and artifacts to explain what life may have been like at that time. He looks at the sequence of events in history to see how some events affected others. He looks for reasons for how and why events happened. Many of a historian's questions may be answered, but many others may not. A Christian historian remembers that God, the Creator, knows and controls all things, including history (Colossians 1:16–17).

 What should a historian keep in mind when he chooses sources?

ACTIVITY

Evaluating Historical Resources

Sources can be classified as primary or secondary.

A primary source gives a firsthand, eyewitness account of an event. A secondary source usually contains information taken from a primary source.

Historians use these two kinds of sources to gain insight into the major events in history. Different authors have varying viewpoints of the same events. By gathering multiple sources and combining the information, historians can gain a more accurate picture of what occurred.

1. Examine the sources provided by your teacher. Complete the chart to determine which are primary sources and which are secondary sources.
2. Determine each author's viewpoint or possible bias and record examples in the chart to support your opinion.
3. Discuss the strengths and weaknesses of your sources. Record them in the chart.

Stonehenge is a famous archaeological site in Wiltshire, England. How did ancient people build Stonehenge?

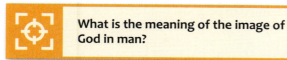

What is the meaning of the image of God in man?

Creation, Fall, Redemption
Creation

In the beginning, there was nothing but God. He created the world out of nothing, just by speaking it into existence. It was a perfect world. There was no pain or suffering or death. Everything was good. But God created His masterpiece last. He took the soil He had already created and with His own hands made the first man. He breathed life into that man. Then He created the first woman. The creation of mankind was the climax of God's creation. God's creation of everything was the first week of history.

God created humans in His own image. This means that people are a picture of what God is like. The sense of right and wrong that humans have is rooted in the image of God. Like God, people have the ability to think, love, use language, know right and wrong, and enjoy relationships. God created humans in His image so that they would be capable of ruling over the world He created.

God created people with a purpose. Genesis 1:28 records that God told man and woman to fill, subdue, and have **dominion** over the earth:

> Be fruitful, and multiply, and replenish the earth, and subdue it: and have dominion over the fish of the sea, and over the fowl of the air, and over every living thing that moveth upon the earth.

Civilization began in an environment suited to providing for the needs of mankind and for giving them opportunities to carry out God's **Creation Mandate**. Civilizations are built in geological locations with environments that can sustain people. For example, God placed the first man and woman in a garden with rivers that would take them out into the wider world and to places with the resources they would need to advance human **civilization** (Genesis 1:26–28). People carry out God's mandate by using resources and adapting their environment to meet their needs.

History is about people living out the Genesis 1:28 mandate. When people work together in a civilizaton, **culture** results.

The development of culture must be governed by God's Word in an attempt to carry out God's plan for the world. Culture is not a human invention. It is a gift from God. God created people to make culture in civilizations. The history of civilizations is something Christians should study.

The Creation Mandate also gives people power. Power is an important theme of civilization that allows mankind to exercise some control over nature and to command communities of people. God intended people to have dominion over the world, but only as they submit to God. People are stewards in the world. Those who rule over the world must be tempered by remembering the image of God. People subdue, or rule over, the earth in many different ways. These ways include language, science, technology, and art. History tells the story of how people have developed these fields.

The Fall

Sadly, the story of history is not a story of people providing a beautiful picture of God. People have not used the abilities God gave them to rule wisely over the earth. Instead, history includes wars, oppression, diseases, and false religions.

What did the artist include in this painting of the Garden of Eden that would be necessary to create a civilization?

dominion The authority to rule.

Creation Mandate The first command given by God to mankind; God's instruction to people to have children and to fill and rule over the earth.

civilization A group of people who establish cities, governments, social classes, specialized jobs, arts, sciences, written language, and religion.

culture A system of customs including language, religion, government, economy, and arts that groups of people use to develop their world.

The Bible explains why the story of history is often so sad. The first humans, Adam and Eve, were created in God's image but were not equal to Him. God is the Creator, and Adam and Eve were His creation.

Although God gave them dominion over all the earth, He was still the ruler over all things. God forbade Adam and Eve from eating from the tree of the knowledge of good and evil.

One day, Satan, in the form of a serpent, tempted Eve to break God's law. Satan told her that if she and Adam ate the fruit, they would be like God in a new and special way. Adam and Eve tried to become like God, and the **Fall** occurred when they chose to break God's law. But they did not become like God. Instead, their disobedience brought sin, suffering, and death into the world.

For a civilization to flourish, there must be a form of justice. People are expected to do right and to respect the rights of others. Governments ensure justice by punishing evildoers. God Himself carried out justice by driving Adam and Eve from the garden.

All the people after them were born sinners. People were supposed to picture what God is like, but sin distorted that picture. The ability God gave people to rule over the earth was twisted for evil purposes. Not only does pain accompany the work of filling the earth, the subduing of the earth is thwarted by suffering and death. Suffering, disease, and death are primary issues in the history of civilization. The cause of all humanity's woes is sin.

History is filled with stories of people who sought to rule the earth as if they were gods. Some even claimed to be gods. But their rule was not the good and caring rule that God intended. They ruled unjustly, harshly, and selfishly. The human race has wandered from its Lord and repeatedly built civilizations opposed to God.

For a civilization to prosper, it needs people who share the same values to work together. People have citizenship within a social structure. They have certain rights, privileges, and duties that equip them to help shape their civilization. Problems arise when people do not do right and do not respect the rights of others. For example, Cain went out from God's presence to build the city of Enoch in the land of Nod. On the surface, it looks like Cain and his descendants obeyed God. But a closer examination of the account reveals that when Cain built the city, he disregarded God's command for him to be a wanderer.

As time passed, more and more people demonstrated lawlessness, injustice, and disregard for God. Lamech, who was in the line of Cain, committed murder and celebrated by composing a poem about it. People lived out the Creation Mandate, but their rule was not one of love toward God or neighbor. Later, at Babel, the people ignored God's command to refill the earth. Instead, they congregated on the plain of Shinar and built a city with a tower in defiance of God.

As a consequence of the Fall, the earth rebelled against people's efforts to subdue it, just as people had rebelled against God's authority. They planted crops to grow food, but the ground made this difficult by growing weeds and thorns. They built roads and cities, only to have them destroyed by floods, earthquakes, and volcanoes. They built great civilizations, but wars, diseases, and plagues killed many people.

Worst of all, people turned away from loving and worshiping the one true God. They worshiped gods made in their own image.

God's Promise of Redemption

History is not all bad news. Much of the Bible reveals a special kind of history, the history of **redemption**. God is not working to replace what He made. He is working to restore what He made.

Fall (of mankind) The breaking of God's law by Adam and Eve with the consequence of sin for them and all people.

redemption Christ's act of rescuing and freeing people from sin; salvation.

How was justice carried out in the Garden of Eden?

What things will need to be changed when God restores the earth?

The history of redemption began in the Garden of Eden when God told Satan that there would be hatred between Satan and Eve and between Satan's offspring and Eve's offspring. In the future, one of her offspring would defeat Satan entirely. Genesis 3:15 promises that God will provide salvation through a man (Jesus Christ) who will defeat Satan. It also outlines history as the struggle between God's people (the seed of the woman) and Satan's people (the seed of the serpent).

God is working to restore His people to bear God's image as God had intended it to be. The Bible tells how God has provided salvation from sin. After people accept God's gift of salvation, they should live differently (Colossians 3:5–8; 1 John 2:15–17). By submitting to God, they will produce the fruit of the Spirit in their lives and become the kind of people God created them to be (Colossians 3:12–17; Galatians 5:22–23).

Christians should be citizens who exercise the power they have as image bearers of God to promote justice in their communities and countries. In a fallen world, these efforts are often frustrated. But one day, Jesus Christ will return in power to rule over the entire earth. He will be a king who rules with righteousness and justice (Psalm 72:1–2). Only those whom He has made righteous will be citizens of this kingdom. The environment will be changed. Thorns and thistles will no longer affect the ground. Instead, the world will be filled with abundant fruitfulness (Amos 9:13). As king, Christ will reign from the great city of Jerusalem.

God's original plan for people to build a just and righteous civilization will be fulfilled in the new Jerusalem (Revelation 21–22).

KEY THEMES OF CIVILIZATION

▶ **Justice**
Justice is the idea that people should do right and respect the rights of others (Genesis 1:26–27; Mark 12:30–31). Governments are obligated to ensure justice by encouraging people to do right and by punishing wrongdoers (Deuteronomy 1:10–18; 1 King 10:9).

▶ **Power**
Power is the ability to bring things under control. For civilizations, it includes the ability to command communities of people and to exercise some control over nature. The biblical mandate in Genesis 1:28 to exercise dominion over the earth implies a broad use of power.

▶ **Citizenship**
Citizenship is a status that people have within a society that gives them certain rights, privileges, and duties. Citizenship gives people the opportunity to shape their civilization, but it also imposes duties that call them to be sacrificial. Biblically, a Christian's view of citizenship should be shaped by the knowledge that people are made in the image of God and that they are called to have dominion over the earth.

▶ **Environment**
Environment is the physical geography in which civilizations are located. God made people to live on the earth and to rule over the world by adapting the environment to meet human needs. Knowing how people have changed and used their environment is essential to the study of world history.

At present, fallen humans continue to build Babel instead of Jerusalem. They build civilizations that ignore or defy God instead of adoring and serving Him. But one day every Babel will fall in judgment, and Christ will reign over all the earth from Jerusalem.

How do the image of God in man and the Creation Mandate relate to historical study?

Relate how the Fall affects the unfolding of history.

In what way does Genesis 3:15 provide the thesis for human history?

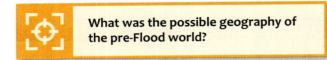

What was the possible geography of the pre-Flood world?

Geography and the Earliest Civilizations

The Flood was such a powerful event that it reshaped the geography of the entire world. Therefore it is difficult to determine the exact geography of the pre-Flood world. However, the Bible does provide clues about the pre-Flood geography, and scientists have found clues as well.

Geography of Eden

The garden in which God placed the first people is called the "Garden of Eden." The first chapters of Genesis indicate what the geography of the garden and the land around it was like.

The garden was a part of the region called Eden (Genesis 2:8). A river flowed out of Eden and into the garden (Genesis 2:10). Typically, branches of rivers come together, making a river larger as it flows. But the river that flowed out of Eden was different. It divided into four rivers called the Pishon, the Gihon, the Tigris, and the Euphrates. These four rivers flowed from the garden to different parts of the world. The Pishon flowed through the land of Havilah. The Gihon flowed through the region of Kush. And the Tigris and the Euphrates flowed through the region of Assyria, an ancient Mesopotamian civilization. In order for these rivers to flow to the different regions, the water would need to flow downhill due to the force of gravity. So historians can assume that the source of the rivers in the garden was at a higher elevation.

Today it is impossible to find Eden's exact location because of the changes the Flood made to the earth's surface. When **Noah** got off the ark, he was surrounded by land that was very different from where he grew up. The Tigris and Euphrates Rivers that exist today are not the same that flowed out of Eden. It is possible that Noah and his descendants used names they knew to identify what they saw around them. Many people have reused names in this manner throughout history. For example, when the Pilgrims settled the New World, they used names such as *York* and *Birmingham* from back in Europe to identify places. The familiar names helped them feel at home even though they had moved. It is logical to assume that Noah's family did the same thing. When exploring, they found a major river and named it the Tigris River. This was the name of a river they knew.

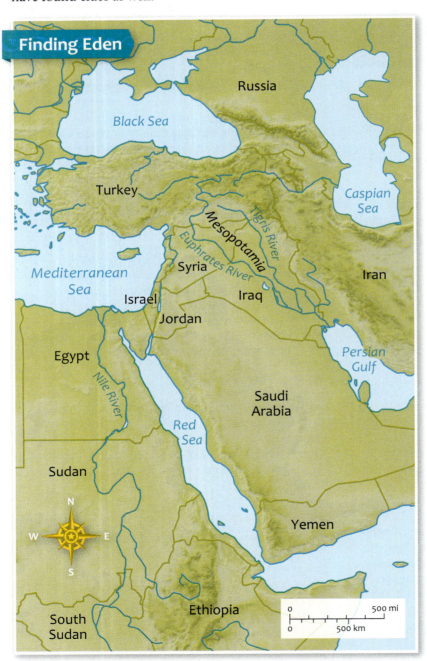

Finding Eden

Noah Man whom God saved from the Flood with his wife, three sons, and his sons' wives; directed by God to build an ark and put every kind of animal in it.

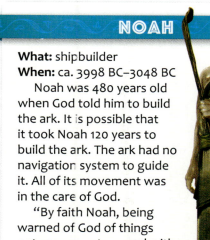

NOAH

What: shipbuilder
When: ca. 3998 BC–3048 BC

Noah was 480 years old when God told him to build the ark. It is possible that it took Noah 120 years to build the ark. The ark had no navigation system to guide it. All of its movement was in the care of God.

"By faith Noah, being warned of God of things not seen as yet, moved with fear, prepared an ark to the saving of his house; by the which he condemned the world, and became heir of the righteousness which is by faith" (Hebrews 11:7).

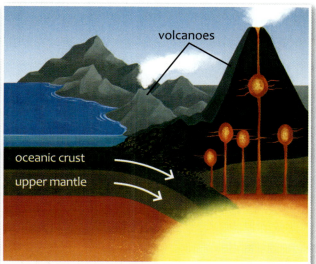

What effect did the Flood have on the plates that make up the earth's crust?

Geography of the World After the Flood

The **universal flood** made massive changes in the earth's geography. Think about the forces that were at work when the fountains of the deep opened up or when flood waters rose to cover the highest mountains. The force of the water was powerful enough to carve the Grand Canyon. It may have even moved the continents of the earth. Many scientists have noticed that the continents on either side of the Atlantic Ocean seem as though they could fit together. There are several pieces of evidence that the continents might have been joined together at one point. First, there are similar fossils at points where the different continents could have come together. For example, fossils of the extinct seed fern *Glossopteris* have been found in Asia, South America, Africa, Australia, and Antarctica.

Second, the plates that make up the earth's crust still continue to show some movement. The plates that form the continents are called continental plates. Plates that form the ocean floor are called oceanic plates.

Scientists who support evolution believe that the movement of the continental plates took place over long periods of time. But scientists who believe in Creation note that the plates could have been split during the Flood. This sudden split would explain why similar fossils of plants and animals are found on different continents. It would also explain why the continents look as though they could have fit together at some point.

Cultural Geography of the Earth After the Flood

After it rained for forty days and nights, the floodwaters lasted for 150 days. As floodwaters subsided, the ark stopped drifting and rested on mountains. Several months later, the land was dry enough for Noah and his family to leave the ark. They had the whole earth to themselves. God told them to be fruitful and multiply in order to refill the earth with people.

Genesis 10 details the **descendants** of **Ham**, **Shem**, and **Japheth** and where they relocated. This chapter is often called the Table of Nations. Each of the descendants had to find the resources necessary to support what would become villages, towns, and great cities.

---

universal flood A flood in which water covers the entire earth; often used to refer to the flood of Noah's time.

descendant A person whose family line can be traced to a certain person or group.

Ham A son of Noah; received a curse for his wickedness; his descendants founded nations in the Far East, Africa, and along the eastern coast of the Mediterranean Sea.

Shem A son of Noah; his descendants include the nation of Israel.

Japheth A son of Noah; his descendants moved into what is now Turkey and eastern Europe.

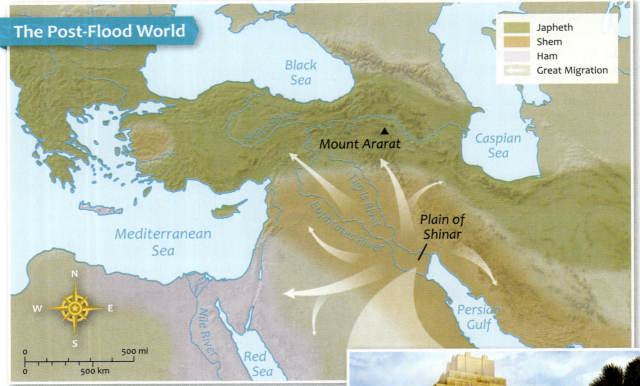

The Post-Flood World

Look at the regions where God directed Ham, Japheth, and Shem. What kind of landforms do each of these regions have?

Babel and the Rise of Nations

After the Flood, descendants of Noah's sons gathered in the plain of Shinar. These people began to build the city that would later be called Babel. They planned to build a great tower. Their reasons for building the tower are revealed in Genesis 11:4, which says, "Go to, let us build us a city and a tower, whose top may reach unto heaven; and let us make us a name, lest we be scattered abroad upon the face of the whole earth."

God stopped these people from carrying out their plan. At that time, all the people of the world spoke the same language. But then God caused the people of Babel to speak multiple languages, so they could not understand each other. Because they could no longer communicate as one group, they could not work together. The people were forced to abandon the construction of the tower. They formed groups that spoke the same languages, and these groups scattered throughout the earth.

Mediterranean Sea The sea surrounded by Europe, Asia, Asia Minor, the Near East, and Africa.

migrate To move from one country or region to settle in another.

Why did God stop the people from building the Tower of Babel?

Genesis 10 records the descendants of Noah's sons and where their nations developed. Ham's descendants founded nations in the Far East, in Africa, and along the eastern coast of the **Mediterranean Sea**. Shem's descendants formed nations along the Persian Gulf and in the Middle East. Japheth's descendants **migrated** to what is now Turkey and Eastern Europe.

How was the geography of the earth altered by the Flood?

Where did the descendants of Shem, Ham, and Japheth relocate geographically?

Why did people form cities before and after the Flood?

How did civilizations develop after the Fall?

Features of Cain's Civilization

The Bible is the only primary source that tells about life before the Flood. It describes what happened after God sent Cain away. The Bible says Cain settled in the land of Nod, east of Eden. Cain named his settlement after his son, Enoch. The Bible records that the city of Enoch demonstrated the features of a civilization.

FEATURES OF A CIVILIZATION

As people began to fill the earth, families settled together in groups. Within these groups, individuals carried out God's mandate to subdue the earth. As these people worked together, certain elements emerged and played a part in the growth of a civilization. The word *civilization* comes from a Latin word that means "citizen of a city."

- **Organized Cities and Government**
  Cities are central locations for government, religion, and culture. A government manages resources and provides defense, an economic system, and rules of conduct.
- **Social Classes**
  People are often divided into social classes. Each class, or level, of people has a different function.
- **Job Specialization**
  Each person focuses on a specific job or trade. They then rely on trade with other people to supply goods and services to meet their other needs.
- **Arts, Sciences, and Written Language**
  As people work together in a civilization, they communicate through art, music, and written language. They also use sciences to develop technology and to learn about their world.
- **Religion**
  Religion is a system of basic values, beliefs, and behaviors that are directed in worship toward God and lived out in community with other people. False religion worships that which is not God, and this idolatry corrupts values, beliefs, and behaviors.

Cities and Government

The first chapters of Genesis share far more than just the story of Creation. They also show the characteristics of the first civilization. Other than mentioning the city of Enoch, the Bible is not specific about other cities before the Flood. But there are geographic locations mentioned in Genesis 2 that suggest areas where groups of people settled. The Bible also gives several indicators that support the idea that multiple cities were developed. For example, God commanded people to spread out from Eden. There were at least 1,500 years between the Creation and the Flood. This period of time was long enough for several million people to be on the earth to develop cities.

Many post-Flood cities clustered together. When cities group together, some type of government always forms. People naturally seek order because they were created in the image of an orderly God. Even in the Garden of Eden, Adam and Eve had direction by God, and God set up the rules.

The Bible does not specify all the types of government that these post-Flood cities used, but it does indicate some methods of governing. For example, Genesis 10:10 describes Nimrod as having a kingdom. This description shows that a **monarchy** was an early form of government. This type of government was repeated after the Flood as well.

Social Classes

In a civilization, people often divide into social classes. Each social class has a different purpose.

Historians have learned from some cultures that people were in social classes based on how much money they had. Sometimes social classes depended on religious beliefs. When describing the early people, the Bible gives information only about jobs that people held. The first chapters of Genesis mention occupations such as kings, artisans, and shepherds. However, it is unwise to assume people's jobs put them into certain social classes. Historians must be careful not to read more into the record than is actually there.

Job Specialization

Early humans were not dependent solely on hunting and gathering to get food as evolutionists believe. Genesis 4 reveals that people were involved in agriculture during the earliest period of human history. These early humans grew crops and kept

continued on page 18

---

monarchy A form of government with one ruler.

LIFE IN ENOCH

Cain built a city and named it after his son Enoch. Genesis 4:16–24 suggests certain themes and features of civilization that were found in Enoch.

Power

Cain was able to order a community of people to build the city. The community exercised control over nature by using natural resources to build the city and support the population through agriculture, trade, and commerce.

Justice

Lamech's actions show a wrong sense of justice. He neither respected the rights of others nor did he do right. He married two women. He also justified murder by saying that the man deserved more punishment for hurting Lamech than Cain did for killing Abel. Cain's punishment came from God, but Lamech took justice into his own hands. He punished the man by killing him, saying he did it in self-defense.

Arts, Sciences, and Written Language

Cain and his descendants must have had an understanding of the principles of physics in order to build the city.

People applied their knowledge of metals and chemistry to develop metallurgy. Artificers heated and shaped iron to make tools for building and gardening. They also combined copper and tin to make bronze for making tools.

Cain's descendents were also gifted in the arts. Jubal was the father of musicians who played the harp and the pipe. Artisans handcrafted these instruments.

Tubal-cain taught all the smiths how to fashion iron and bronze.

Environment
Enoch was east of Eden in the land of Nod. The city probably sat beside a river that branched from the river in Eden or near another water source. Pasture for grazing cattle likely lay on the outskirts of the city, along with fertile soil for growing crops. The natural resources in the area included iron ore, copper, and tin.

Religion
Little is known about religion in Enoch. Cain offered at least one sacrifice to God. But Cain wanted to be accepted by God on his own terms. He built the city of Enoch, a city that existed apart from God. But there was still a knowledge of God in the city, which is revealed by Lamech's knowledge of Cain's encounter with God.

Job Specialization
Cain engineered the building of a city. Stone masons probably helped lay the foundation and walls of the city. Miners dug for metals and possibly precious stones. Cain's descendants became cattlemen, metal workers, and musicians. Farmers raised food and livestock.

Key Themes of Civilization
- Justice
- Power
- Citizenship
- Environment

Features of a Civilization
- Organized cities and government
- Social classes
- Job specialization
- Arts, sciences, and written language
- Religion

Workers fueled ovens until they were hot enough to remove metal from ore.

Lamech's son Jubal originated the skill of playing the harp and flute.

continued from page 15

cattle. They focused on producing enough food to feed their families. They invented tools and methods that increased food production. Eventually, they produced more food than they needed for their families. This extra food allowed people to use their talents in areas other than farming. They could focus on carpentry or working with leather. These people then traded their products for the food they needed. This type of commerce grows and strengthens a civilization.

Job specialization occurs when a person devotes his time and talent to a specific type of work that becomes his occupation. Genesis 4 gives examples of job specialization. Cain was a farmer (Genesis 4:2), and Abel was a shepherd (Genesis 4:2). Later, Cain's descendants included shepherds, musicians, and metal workers (Genesis 4:20–22).

In addition to these jobs, other jobs also developed. For example, early people developed building skills. Noah used carpentry to build the ark. Each piece of wood had to be cut to exact dimensions. Once built, Noah waterproofed the ark. Furthermore, early people developed plans for the tower of Babel. Brick makers shaped and fired clay until it was as hard as stone. Then brick masons used a mineral substance to cement bricks together to build the tower (Genesis 11:3). There is no doubt that people were involved in a variety of job specialties before the Flood.

Arts, Sciences, and Written Language

The Bible indicates that people used technology to do different jobs and to build cities. Mathematical skills and carpentry would be invaluable to build a city, an ark, or a tower. The development of job specializations allowed some people to have more time to be involved in the arts and make advances in science.

Early people were involved in mining. Genesis 4 implies that they mined tin, copper, and iron. Tin and copper can be combined to make bronze. Genesis 4:22 mentions Tubal-cain, a forger of bronze and iron. Such metals were forged into useful tools and instruments. These passages of Scripture contradict the evolutionary teaching that metal-working skills were acquired much later in human development.

Early people also developed the arts. The Bible mentions Jubal as the father of those who played the lyre and pipe (Genesis 4:21). In addition, early civilizations enjoyed the beauty of language and even developed poems. Adam was the first human to write a poem. The Bible also records how Lamech puts his boast into poetry (Genesis 4:23–24).

Building of the Ark Encounter in Williamstown, Kentucky. How would Noah have built the ark without modern equipment?

What are some skills Noah and his family may have used while living on the ark?

TRUE RELIGION VS. FALSE RELIGION

Where do religions come from? Every civilization in this book has a religion.

As God's creatures, people have within them the sense that there is a God and that He deserves to be worshiped and obeyed. This internal sense explains why religions exist worldwide. Atheism, a belief that there is no God, is something people have to talk themselves into. It is not the natural response of humans.

Even though people have been created with the knowledge that God exists, they cannot know God unless He speaks to them. The speech of God to people is found in the Bible.

False religions form when people reject God and His Word. These people reject the parts of God's truth they do not like. Then they use the parts they do like to create false religions and gods. Some religions develop from sinful human imaginations. These religions sometimes mix worship with evil practices. The Bible repeatedly tells of false religions and how God desires for people to abandon their gods and worship Him alone (Deuteronomy 30:2, 17–18).

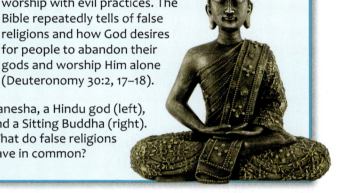

Ganesha, a Hindu god (left), and a Sitting Buddha (right). What do false religions have in common?

Religion

Adam and Eve and their descendants had religion even though they did not have the Bible. Their religion came from the knowledge God created in them, what He taught them, and what they saw in the creation around them.

Adam and Eve demonstrated their belief in one God. They acknowledged that He is the Creator of all things and that He alone is worthy of worship. Cain and Abel understood that God expected His people to obey and make sacrifices to Him in faith.

The Bible describes a few early people who had close relationships with God, including Abel, Noah, and Enoch.

Unfortunately, because people have sinful natures, sin corrupted the practice of true religion. For example, when Cain brought an offering of fruit to God, he demonstrated that he recognized God. But he refused to worship God in a way that was pleasing to God.

By the beginning of Genesis 6, religion was further corrupted. People were so wicked that their every thought was evil. They no longer worshiped God. God was grieved by mankind's sin. Because humans were so corrupt, God destroyed them with a flood. However, He preserved Noah, a man who He said walked with Him. God also spared Noah's family. Noah passed on his knowledge of God to his children and grandchildren. He lived long enough to pass his knowledge to several generations! But Noah was not a perfect man, and neither was his family. The corruption of sin was evident again.

At the tower of Babel, there is evidence again of a departure from true belief in God. When the people scattered, they took their beliefs with them. All of those beliefs had foundations in the truth, which is why there are similar stories in different cultures. Versions of the Creation story and the story of the Flood appear in many different cultures. But they are only corrupted versions of the true story that God revealed to Moses. The first chapters of Genesis record Creation and God's judgment of sin through the Flood. God preserved this record so that all future generations would know the true God.

How did people practice the arts and sciences in the pre-Flood and early post-Flood eras?

What job specializations occurred at this time?

How did people depart from the belief in one God to create world religions?

MESOPOTAMIA

FOCUS
Mesopotamian civilizations emerged after God multiplied people's languages.

Sumer ca. 3000 BC	Abraham called out of Ur ca. 2100 BC	Babylonian Empire ca. 2000 BC		Height of Assyrian Empire ca. 750 BC	
3000 BC	2500 BC	2000 BC	1500 BC	1000 BC	500 BC
	ca. 2350 BC Akkadian Empire	ca. 2000 BC Hittite Empire settled in Asia Minor			612 BC Chaldean Empire

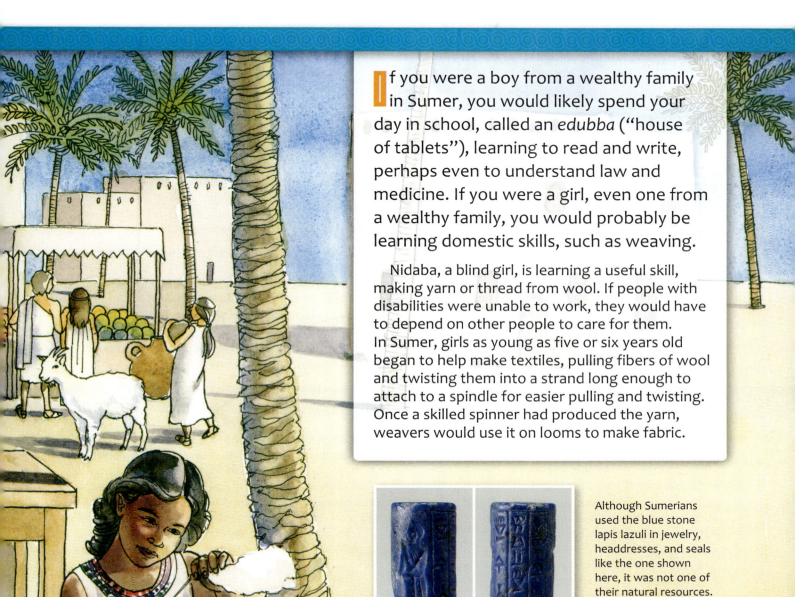

If you were a boy from a wealthy family in Sumer, you would likely spend your day in school, called an *edubba* ("house of tablets"), learning to read and write, perhaps even to understand law and medicine. If you were a girl, even one from a wealthy family, you would probably be learning domestic skills, such as weaving.

Nidaba, a blind girl, is learning a useful skill, making yarn or thread from wool. If people with disabilities were unable to work, they would have to depend on other people to care for them. In Sumer, girls as young as five or six years old began to help make textiles, pulling fibers of wool and twisting them into a strand long enough to attach to a spindle for easier pulling and twisting. Once a skilled spinner had produced the yarn, weavers would use it on looms to make fabric.

Although Sumerians used the blue stone lapis lazuli in jewelry, headdresses, and seals like the one shown here, it was not one of their natural resources. Merchants had to go as far as 1,500 miles to trade textiles or other goods for it.

Why was the Fertile Crescent an ideal place for a civilization to flourish?

Sumerian Civilization
Geography

This chapter begins after God multiplied the languages. Shem's descendants migrated along the **Tigris River** and the **Euphrates River**. These rivers flowed down from the mountains into a plain that historians call **Mesopotamia**. This name comes from a Greek word that means "between the rivers." Mesopotamia is considered the cradle of civilization. The earliest evidence of agriculture, written language, and cities was discovered there.

Mesopotamia was part of a larger region that historians call the **Fertile Crescent**. This was a curved area from the Persian Gulf to the Mediterranean Sea. Its fertile land was good for farming.

Over time, villages in Mesopotamia expanded into cities. The cities became the civilization that archaeologists and historians call **Sumer**.

Tigris River A river that flows from the Taurus Mountains through Turkey, Syria, and Iraq to the Persian Gulf; a border of Mesopotamia.
Euphrates River A river that flows from the Taurus Mountains through Turkey, Syria, and Iraq to the Persian Gulf; a border of Mesopotamia.

SIR LEONARD WOOLLEY

What: archaeologist
When: Apr. 17, 1880–Feb. 20, 1960
Where: Great Britain

Leonard Woolley was a world-famous archaeologist and an expert in Mesopotamian studies. He located sites that yielded an abundance of archaeological finds. He is best known for his excavation of a large cemetery in Ur where treasures of precious metals and gemstones were found. He discovered tools, weapons, art, and other artifacts that contributed to understanding the Sumerians. He was knighted in 1935 for his contributions to the field of archaeology.

Mesopotamia The ancient region between the Euphrates River and the Tigris River.
Fertile Crescent A curved area from the Persian Gulf to the Mediterranean Sea.
Sumer One of the first civilizations in Mesopotamia.

ARCHAEOLOGY AND THE OLD TESTAMENT

Archaeologists study artifacts to find clues about the Sumerian people. For instance, a woman's jewelry could give clues to whether she was rich and powerful or poor but creative. Many artifacts are found at a dig, a place where archaeologists excavate a historic site.

Every dig needs experts in history, archaeology, architecture, translation, photography, and drawing. These experts try to interpret and preserve what is found. Sometimes a dig is chosen by the presence of a **tell**. *Tell* comes from the Arabic word for "high."

Work at a dig begins with surveys of the site. Archaeologists use the information from these surveys to draw a map and divide the area into square sections. Today archaeologists often use computers to map the area, make calculations, and keep records. They dig slowly to avoid damaging fragile objects. When an object is found, it is photographed, labeled, and recorded.

In the 1850s, British archaeologists discovered Mesopotamian artifacts in Iraq. Most archaeologists believed that the site where the artifacts were found was the biblical city of Ur. In 1922 a British archaeologist named Sir **Leonard Woolley** began excavating the site. He found many treasures from Ur and from the land of Sumer. Evidence from archaeological digs indicates that Sumer was one of the earliest civilizations after the Flood.

Objects that were long hidden under the soil give insight into Sumerian life. For example, artifacts reveal that Ur was a grand place surrounded by high walls. It boasted huge palaces and plazas. People of Abraham's day used canals to irrigate their fields. They grew grain and vegetables and sold wool to other countries. Some people were weavers or metalworkers, and some studied medicine or the stars.

Many secular archaeologists and historians assume that Sumer was one of the first civilizations. They do not believe the Bible's account

---

tell A mound made up of layered dirt and the remains of buildings.
Leonard Woolley Archaeologist who, in the 1920s, uncovered many artifacts from Ur and the land of Sumer.

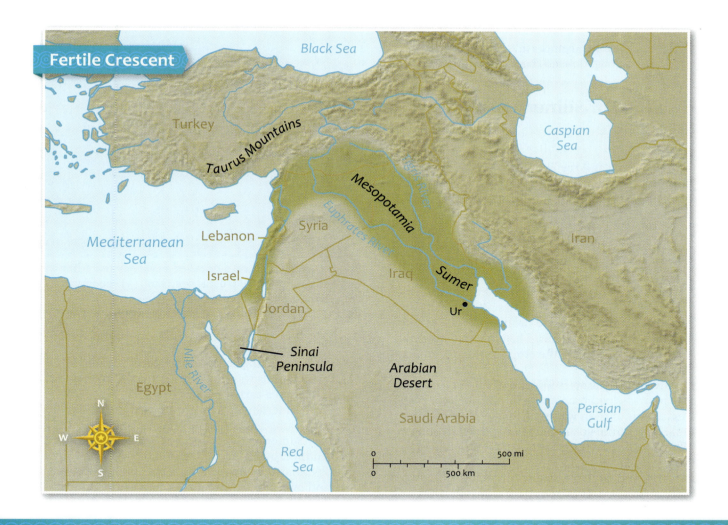

Fertile Crescent

of a worldwide flood destroying previous civilizations. No artifacts have been found from before the Flood. However, the Bible says that civilizations existed before the Flood. Genesis records that people built cities before the time of Noah. There were skilled musicians and workers in brass and iron. They knew much about agriculture.

Sometimes an archaeological find proves skeptics of the Bible wrong. For example, skeptics have said that the Bible was inaccurate because it states that Rebekah rode on a camel to meet Isaac. Researchers believed that camels were not used as beasts of burden during Abraham's time. But records from Sumerian tablets show that camels were indeed used as beasts of burden in Abraham's time.

Sometimes an archaeological discovery helps people understand the Bible better. Archaeologists discovered many skeletons in caves around Ur. Sumerians used the same burial caves for generations. This habit of burying people in the same area explains the biblical phrase "gathered to his people."

 What is the role of an archaeologist, and how does he excavate a site?

What advances in farming and irrigation did the Sumerians develop?

The Rise of Sumer
Agriculture
Planting

The Tigris and the Euphrates carried **silt** down from the mountains. During rainy seasons, the rivers flooded and spread silt across the plains. The silt made the land good for farming.

Early Sumerian farmers used sticks to poke holes in the ground. Then the farmers dropped seeds into each hole. This was hard, slow work. So the Sumerians developed plows as a better way of preparing the soil for planting. Early plows were pieces of wood that made long, shallow trenches in the soil. It was much easier for farmers to drop seeds into a trench than into individual holes. The plow also loosened the soil so the roots of the crops could grow more easily.

Eventually farmers found that hitching oxen to the plows helped prepare even more land for planting. A pair of oxen was hitched to a plow with a yoke. Use of the yoke was first recorded in Sumer. The yoke helped the oxen pull a plow or a heavy wagonload.

silt A sediment of very fine particles containing rock and minerals that is found at the bottom of bodies of water.

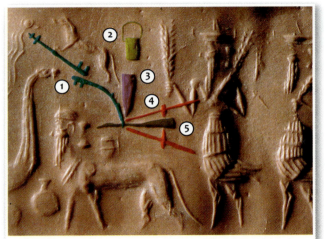

Agricultural tools on a detail of a cylinder seal from Mesopotamia: (1) yoke, (2) seed bag, (3) seed funnel, (4) handle, and (5) plow share

Sumerian farmers were also the first known people to use the wheel. Pulling a heavy load on a cart with wheels was much easier than dragging that same load on a cart without wheels.

The Sumerian farmers grew nearly all the barley, wheat, sesame seeds, flax, vegetables, and dates that the Sumerian people needed. The farmers who owned their own land sold their harvests in the city market. Many farmers did not own land but worked on land owned by the temple or by wealthy individuals. These farmers received part of the harvest to use or to sell.

EARLY RIVER CIVILIZATIONS

Early people settled in river valleys for several reasons. The land close to the rivers was flat, making it easier for farmers to plant crops. The rivers nourished the soil and made it fertile. The rivers also provided fish to eat and fresh water to drink. The rivers served as highways on which people could travel from one place to another, exchanging ideas and goods.

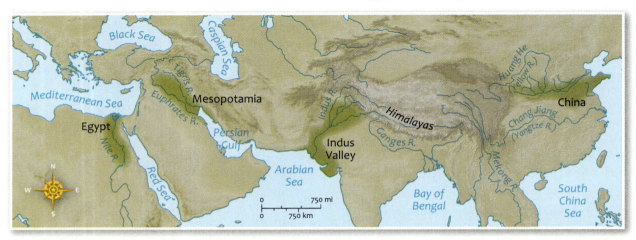

24

THE REGION TODAY

Mesopotamia

Location
Modern-day Iraq contains much of what is recognized as ancient Mesopotamia. Iraq is located in the Middle East at the head of the Persian Gulf. The following countries border Iraq: Turkey in the north, Kuwait and Saudi Arabia in the south, Jordan and Syria in the west, and Iran in the east.

Climate
Summers are usually hot and dry in the central or southern regions. Temperatures can reach as high as 118°F in July and August. Temperatures are cooler in northern Iraq, where the land is mountainous. The mountains receive more precipitation and colder winters than the lowlands. Rainfall in Iraq usually occurs between December and April, averaging about 4–7 inches of rain annually.

Topography
Southern Iraq is a low floodplain between the southern parts of the Tigris and the Euphrates. Northern Iraq has rolling hills and fertile soil. Mountains rise in the northeast, and desert spans the west.

Natural Resources
The region's natural resources include oil, natural gas, phosphates, and sulfur. The Tigris and the Euphrates provide water for irrigation.

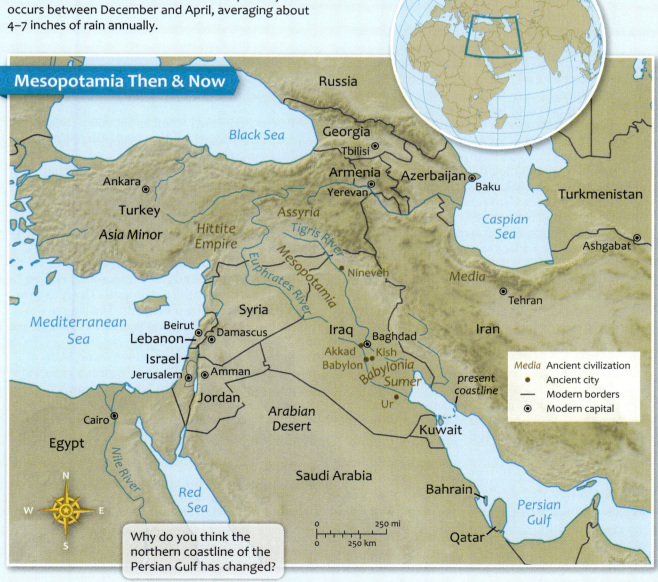

Mesopotamia Then & Now

Why do you think the northern coastline of the Persian Gulf has changed?

Legend:
- *Media* Ancient civilization
- • Ancient city
- — Modern borders
- ⊙ Modern capital

Flood Control

Outside the city of Ur, farmers worked in the fields. Mesopotamia had fertile soil, but the crops also needed water. Some years the right amount of rain fell. But more often, the region received either so little rain that the crops withered from the heat or so much rain that the crops were destroyed from flooding. Sometimes floods killed livestock and washed away homes.

Sumerians formed levees by building up dirt to hold back floodwaters. The levees protected the Sumerian homes as well as their crops.

Irrigation

Most of the area beyond the rivers was desert. During the summer, the ground became dry and hard under the hot sun. With no rain for months, plants died.

To help solve this problem, the Sumerians developed **irrigation** as a way of supplying water to crops. They built storage basins to hold water supplies. Then they dug canals, or manmade waterways, to carry water from the river. The canals allowed the farmers to plant crops in locations that were far from the river. A farmer could use irrigation to keep his crops alive throughout the dry summer.

Farmers were also able to use irrigation to give water to their animals. Cattle and sheep grazed in the fields. Donkeys and oxen worked in the fields and transported heavy loads. Pigs were raised for meat. Goats and sheep provided meat as well as hides and wool.

The Sumerians made good use of the water from the Tigris and Euphrates Rivers. The Sumerian civilization depended on irrigation for agriculture just as famers do today.

Sumerian City-States

The development of the plow and irrigation increased the amount of food the farmers could grow. They produced a food **surplus**. Because of the surplus, fewer people needed to farm. New occupations developed as people began working at specialized jobs and trades.

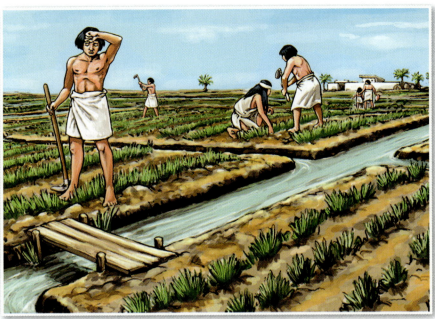

Sumerians practiced water management through the use of irrigation systems and levees. What water sources were available for the Sumerians to do this?

Priests performed religious activities. Rulers governed the people. Soldiers kept order. Craftsmen made goods. Job specialization allowed people to develop new skills. These skills helped to create and maintain the civilization.

Some farm settlements grew into villages, and villages grew into cities. Although most people worked on farms, cities became important places. Each Sumerian city developed into a **city-state**. A city-state was independent of other city-states. It had its own government and laws. Sumerians believed that their cities belonged to the gods. The ruler, usually a priest, represented the gods. The temple was both a place of worship and the center of government.

Some city-states wanted more power. They fought other city-states for more farmland and water. Because of these battles, the city-states formed strong armies. The people built thick walls around their cities for protection. During Abraham's lifetime, **Ur** was a powerful Sumerian city-state.

---

irrigation A way of supplying water to land or crops.
surplus An amount that is more than what is needed.
city-state A city and the surrounding land and villages it controls.
Ur A powerful city-state in Sumer.

 How do the effects of geography on Mesopotamia compare to the effects of geography on modern-day Iraq?

How did Sumer develop from farm settlements to city-states?

What were the names and significance of the Sumerian social classes?

Society

One feature of early civilizations was the development of **social classes**. The Sumerian civilization had three social classes. Each class had a different role. The upper class consisted of the city-state rulers, governmental officials, and priests. These people had the most power. The middle class was the largest class. It consisted of farmers, fishermen, merchants, traders, and skilled workers. Slaves were in the lowest class. They were common in Sumer. Slaves were forced to serve others and were thought of as property. Some slaves were prisoners of war; others were criminals. Some people became slaves to pay their debts. Despite being under the rule of masters, slaves had certain privileges. Slaves could hold property or go into business. Sumerian slaves could eventually purchase their own freedom.

social class A group of people in society with the same social position, often determined by economic status.
barter A system in which people exchange goods and services for other goods or services.

Fishermen, Merchants, and Traders

The Sumerians were among the first people to use sails to move boats. Many boats sailed on the Euphrates River. Some were trading ships that had come from faraway places. Others were fishing boats owned by local fishermen. Every day that fishermen went to the river, they returned home to sell their catches at the city market. Fish and bread were important foods in the Sumerian diet.

At the edge of the city of Ur, on the Euphrates River, stood the docks where trading ships and fishing boats were anchored. Dockworkers, merchants, traders, and sailors conducted their business there. Ships brought goods from as far away as India in the east and Egypt in the west. The ships were loaded with gems, wood, stone, and metal for the workshops of Ur. Early trade in Sumer was conducted by **barter**. For instance, a merchant might trade his grain for another item, such as lumber or copper. Often a food surplus in one city-state was bartered for a different kind of good in another city-state. Trade between city-states helped city-states grow in wealth and power.

Trading with other countries was essential to the growth of a civilization. Besides the people of Sumer, other groups of people in the world were organizing into civilizations. These groups of people traded with Sumer.

ECONOMY

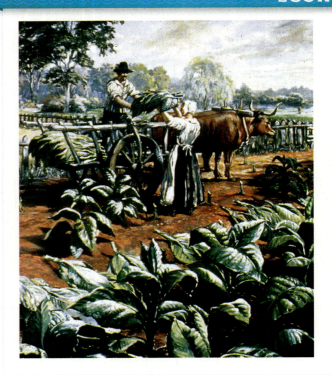

What was the economy like in Sumer? Farming was the main economic source. Farmers grew everything they needed and then sold their food surplus. Many people worked for owners of farms.

Trade was also important. Skilled artisans turned raw materials from foreign countries into finished goods. These goods were often exported to other countries.

When the United States was being settled, it had an economy similar to Sumer's. Colonists provided raw materials for countries in Europe. However, unlike the Sumerians who turned raw materials into finished goods themselves, the colonists shipped raw materials abroad. People in Europe turned the raw materials into goods that were shipped back to America to be sold.

The American people eventually began to cultivate wheat, corn, tobacco, indigo, and rice. These crops became the people's exports. Like Sumer, America used its resources to produce goods and grow crops. Both Sumer and the United States prospered through commerce with other countries.

The Sumerians kept careful records of their business dealings. Using a reed stylus, a pointed writing tool, **scribes** wrote down sales on soft clay tablets. After a scribe recorded a sale, he allowed the tablet to dry. Then he wrapped it in another piece of clay that served as an envelope. The tablet was stored in the temple with other legal records. From these careful records, archaeologists have learned much about Sumerian economics.

When two merchants finished a business deal and the scribe put his last marks on the tablet, each person had to sign it. They did not use the scribe's stylus to write their names. Rather, they used clay seals shaped like cylinders. This kind of **cylinder seal** was small, only about one to two inches long and about a half-inch in diameter. It had carvings that identified the owner. The carvings could include plants, animals, gods, and wedge-shaped symbols. Each merchant rolled his seal across the wet clay tablet to approve the sale. The cylinder seal was a fast, simple way to sign one's name. The mark of a cylinder seal stood either for approval, as on a legal document, or for ownership, as on goods ready to be shipped.

Artisans and Buyers

Workers gathered imported materials at the docks and took them into the city. These resources were delivered to the **artisans** to be made into products for export or goods for citizens to buy.

scribe A person whose job is to record information in writing.
cylinder seal A clay cylinder used to imprint one's signature.
artisan A skilled craftsman.

A clay cylinder seal with cattle relief. What might this seal have been used for?

In the center of Ur, artisans turned raw materials into finished goods. Archaeologists have found records and the remains of clothing, pottery, jewelry, and other objects made in the artisans' shops.

Many of the workshops in Ur produced goods for everyday use. Some of the busiest shops in the city were those that sold cloth. The cloth makers employed women to spin thread from flax or wool and then weave it into cloth. The people of Ur bought their cloth at one shop, had it dyed at another, and then took it home to make clothing.

After leaving a cloth maker's shop, a person in Ur might have stopped at a pottery shop. Clay was one of the few raw materials that was plentiful in the river valley. Artisans threw clay onto their potter's wheels and formed pots. Sumerians were possibly the first people to use the wheel to make clay pots. Before that time, pots were either molded or coiled by hand. The potter's wheel allowed a potter to produce pots of the same size and shape faster than before. Potters in Ur made all sorts of containers for storing and serving food. The potters added carvings and decorations to make the pots attractive as well as useful.

Over the centuries, the ancient method of making pottery has not changed much. The designs of pitchers, bowls, cups, and plates are also much the same. In this region, potters still work at their wheels. Today, tourists can buy the beautiful pottery as souvenirs. Ships transport these works of art to nations that did not even exist when Abraham left Ur.

The city of Ur also had shops that made luxury goods. The artisans trained for many years to learn the skills for making beautiful objects. They made jewelry and fine dishes from the copper, silver, gold, and precious jewels imported into Sumer. The finished pieces,

Gold pendants hang from a necklace made of carnelian (a red quartz) and lapis (a semiprecious blue stone).

intricately and beautifully designed, were either sold in Ur or shipped to other cities and lands.

A special craft in Ur was shell inlay. An artisan used white shells from the river and arranged them into a design. He made sure the pieces fit together, almost like pieces of a puzzle. Once satisfied with his design, he pressed the pieces into softened tar on another surface such as metal. After the main design was finished, he may have surrounded it with lapis lazuli. A shell-inlay artisan had to be patient and careful. Some works of sparkling white shells and lapis lazuli inlay still exist and show the high quality of Sumerian workmanship.

 Why was trade important to the development of Sumer?

How did the roles of Sumerian artisans and buyers differ?

LIFE IN SUMER

Power
Kings ruled the people, and soldiers kept order. Government officials, priests, and priestesses also had power over people. For example, priests and priestesses controlled much of the land.

Some city-states wanted more power and developed strong armies to fight for more farmland and water.

Justice
Sumerians had laws and contracts to ensure that business agreements were kept. There were written laws of retribution for people who broke laws or contracts. Citizens pressed charges against the offender, and the courts saw that retribution was exacted.

Arts, Sciences, and Written Language
Craftsmen made drums, tambourines, reed pipes, and stringed instruments. Potters created decorative pottery. Artisans fashioned gold jewelry that had blue gemstones.

The Sumerians developed the arch and the column. They included domes on towers. They built canals and dikes to irrigate crops, and they made sailboats. They used wheels, studied astronomy, developed a number system, and used geometry. They also practiced medicine.

Sumerians developed cuneiform writing. Written works included stories, proverbs, and poems.

Specialized Jobs
Sumerians farmed, fished, herded, mined, and traded. They also held positions as rulers, priests, government officials, scribes, and teachers. Other Sumerians were architects, mathematicians, scientists, sailors, or soldiers.

Environment
Sumer sat on a fertile plain with the Tigris and Euphrates Rivers flowing down from the mountains.

Mesopotamians bought goods through a barter system.

Citizenship
People lived in a monarchy, but they had some rights similar to living in a democracy. For example, slaves could hold property or start a business, even though they were in the lowest class. They could even purchase their own freedom.

Social Classes
A person's role in society was reflected by his social class. The king, government officials, and priests were the most powerful. Farmers, fishermen, merchants, traders, and skilled workers made up the middle class, which was the largest class of people. Slaves made up the lowest class of people.

Religion
Sumerians were committed to polytheism. They built ziggurats as temples. The ziggurat was thought to link heaven and earth. They thought it was a stairway that led up to the gate of the god's dwelling place in heaven.

Key Themes of Civilization
- Justice
- Power
- Citizenship
- Environment

Features of a Civilization
- Organized cities and government
- Social classes
- Job specialization
- Arts, sciences, and written language
- Religion

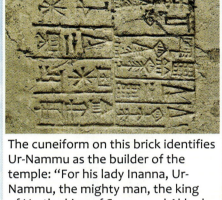

The cuneiform on this brick identifies Ur-Nammu as the builder of the temple: "For his lady Inanna, Ur-Nammu, the mighty man, the king of Ur, the king of Sumer and Akkad, built her temple."

This clay cylinder, found at the temple in Ur, records the rebuilding of the ziggurat.

A religious processional makes its way from the temple.

This relief depicts Ur-Nammu making an offering to the moon god Nanna.

31

THE STANDARD OF UR

Leonard Woolley excavated at the Tell el-Muqayyar, also known as the ancient city of Ur. In one of the largest graves in the Royal Cemetery, Woolley uncovered a wooden box. The weight of the soil had crushed the sides of the box together. The box was later restored to what was possibly its original appearance. Today it is on display in the British Museum. Although the box's original purpose is unknown, Woolley thought the box may have been carried on a pole as a standard, or a flag. That is why today the box is called the Standard of Ur.

The artisan who made the box used shell inlay with red limestone and lapis lazuli to create the scenes on the sides, or panels, of the box. The two larger panels are known as "War" and "Peace." The "War" panel shows a Sumerian army with cloaked infantry carrying spears and chariots being pulled by donkeys. This piece is one of the earliest representations of a Sumerian army. The "Peace" panel shows a banquet scene with a procession of people bringing animals and goods.

The shell inlay work of the Sumerian artisans is often echoed in modern-day products such as guitars, jewelry boxes, hair combs, and furniture.

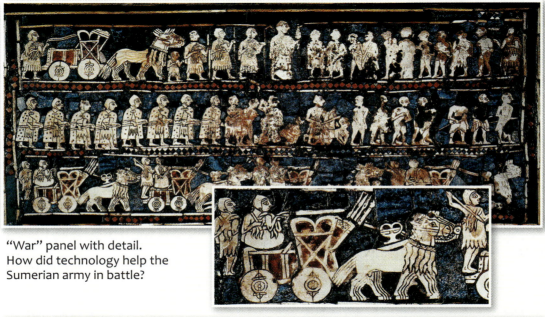

"War" panel with detail. How did technology help the Sumerian army in battle?

"Peace" panel. A story runs from bottom to top, ending with a royal banquet.

What characterized family life and clothing in Sumer?

Daily Life
School and Family

Education is an important part of a civilization. Sumerian schools, called tablet-houses, were attached to the temple. The "school father," or chief teacher, gave students lessons to practice. School fathers were very strict. The school also had a teacher called "the man in charge of the whip." He helped maintain school discipline. Usually only boys from wealthy families attended school. The instruction the boys received helped them learn to become scribes. Scribes were highly respected in Sumer. From sunrise to sunset, the students wrote lists on clay tablets, did mathematical problems, and learned grammar.

Parents in Sumer believed in strong discipline. They taught their children obedience and respect. A child who disobeyed could be disowned or sold into slavery. When children reached marrying age, the parents arranged marriages for them.

Men were at the head of their families. Some were priests. Others were farmers or tradesmen. Women were not considered equal to men, but women who were priestesses or born of royalty were allowed to learn to read and write. Some women held administrative positions. Women were allowed to conduct business and own property. Women of lower social classes typically raised children and kept the home.

Clothing

The Sumerians made their clothing from wool or flax, natural resources that were available to them. Men wore skirt-like garments or robes pinned at the right shoulder. Women wore similar robes or dresses but pinned their garments at the left shoulder. Fringe was a decorative adornment on clothing of both men and women. Both men and women wore jewelry, including bracelets, necklaces, and earrings. Hairstyles changed over time in Mesopotamia just as they do in the modern world.

Sir Leonard Woolley created this headdress from pieces of jewelry found at Queen Puabi's burial site.

Sumerian husband and wife

A bronze mirror found in an ancient Mesopotamian home. What other grooming tools might have been used by the Mesopotamians?

Describe a typical Sumerian school day.

Where was the center of religion in a Sumerian city-state?

Religion
Priests and Religious Beliefs

Religion played a role in almost every aspect of Mesopotamian life. The Mesopotamians worshiped their gods by praying to them, giving them gifts, and performing rituals. They believed that if the gods were pleased, the people would prosper. If the gods were not pleased, disaster would strike. Religious rituals and prayers accompanied all activities, no matter how ordinary.

The Mesopotamian religion was a clear rejection of the one true God. The people practiced **polytheism**, the worship of many gods. These gods were thought up by people. The people believed that the gods ate, slept, and married. But unlike people, the gods supposedly lived forever. The Mesopotamians created these gods in their image instead of recognizing that they themselves had been created in the image of the one true God.

In the center of Ur stood an impressive pyramid-like structure called a **ziggurat**. This temple could be seen by people approaching the city while they were still a long distance away.

polytheism The worship of many gods.
ziggurat A pyramid-like temple.

 MESOPOTAMIAN BELIEFS

Mesopotamians believed that humans were created to serve the gods. The Mesopotamians believed in many gods who were not all-powerful. These gods had to work hard, and their work frustrated them. The Mesopotamian gods were not morally perfect as the God of the Bible is perfect. These gods complained about having to fulfill their duties. But the Bible teaches that work is a blessing, not something to be avoided.

The Mesopotamian worldview is a corruption of the biblical worldview. God made people to work. When people work and rule over the earth, they show that they are made in God's image. But after the Fall, work did become hard and frustrating. So the Mesopotamians developed myths in which the gods were frustrated with work and created humans to do the work they did not want to do.

A ziggurat usually had three to seven terraced levels with a shrine or a tiny temple on top. A couch or bed was placed in the shrine for the god to rest on. Gardens were planted on each terrace. The bricks were often covered with tiles or painted to make the levels different colors. In an area beside the ziggurat, there were homes for the priests and the priestesses and others involved in the activities of the temple. There were storehouses, workshops, and additional chambers. Pens holding sacrificial animals were also kept near the temple.

The ziggurat in Ur was originally built by a king named Ur-Nammu. He built the ziggurat in honor of the moon god. A later king, Nabonidus, rebuilt the ziggurat and made some changes. Archaeologists learned about these kings when J. E. Taylor began an excavation at the temple site in 1864. He found four cylinders, one at each corner of the ziggurat. The text on one of these cylinders was a record of the ziggurat's architects.

> I am Nabonidus, king of Babylon, patron of Esagila and Ezida, devotee [follower] of the great gods. . . . Now that ziggurat had become old, and I undertook the construction of that ziggurat on the foundations which Ur-Nammu and his son Shulgi built following the original plan with bitumen and baked brick.

The Mesopotamians worshiped hundreds of gods. Each god had a name and a responsibility. The people believed that several gods controlled parts of the universe, such as the sky, the sun, and the air. They were considered the main gods. Every city-state had its own god or goddess. In Ur, one god the people worshiped was the moon god Nanna. His statue was kept in the ziggurat's shrine, and food was offered to him daily. The priests and priestesses who lived at the temple sacrificed animals and followed rituals, believing this devotion would keep the god happy.

People relied on the priests to help gain the favor of the gods. The priests also interpreted the wishes of the gods. The people were taught that only priests could communicate directly with the

Sumerian male worshiper statue made of alabaster with black limestone, shell, and bitumen decoration

SOME OF MESOPOTAMIA'S GODS

	Sumerian name	Akkadian name	City	Responsibility
Morning and evening star goddess	Inanna	Ishtar	Uruk	goddess of love and war
Sun god	Utu	Shamash	Larsa and Sippar	god of truth and justice
Freshwater god	Enki	Ea	Eridu	god of wisdom, magic, and arts and crafts
Storm god	Ishkur	Adad	several cities	god of thunder and rain

A people called the Akkadians later conquered Sumer. They worshiped many of the same gods as the Sumerians but called the gods by different names.

gods. This made the priests powerful in Mesopotamia. The priests and priestesses controlled much of the land.

The hundreds of gods required constant worship. Archaeologists think that the people may have placed statues of worshipers in temples. These statues would have stood in continuous prayer while their owners went about their daily lives. Placing the statues in the temple was a convenient way for the people to provide constant worship.

Kings and Government

A civilization needs a well-organized government to manage its resources. When the Mesopotamians began to live in cities, a large portion of the population stopped growing its own food. The people who continued to farm needed to grow enough food to trade with those who did not farm. A manager saw that the surplus food was made available to everyone.

Sumer was made up of several city-states that often fought each other for more land and power. At first, the priest of a city-state tried to pick the best military leader to defend that city-state in battle. After the fighting was over, the leader was expected to return to normal life. But some of these leaders held on to their positions and became rulers. This was the beginning of kings.

Eventually every city-state had its own king. The king was considered a god's highest representative on earth. The Sumerians believed that a god selected the king, giving him authority. To stay in power, the king needed the approval of the priest. A king respected the priest, and the priest acknowledged the king as the god's choice to rule the city-state.

The temple was important not only as the center of religion but also as the seat of the Sumerian government. The king took over some of the jobs previously done by the priests. He directed the building of new canals, temples, and roads. Each king served as the chief lawmaker and judge. Some kings wrote laws and ruled by them. In Ur, a lawbreaker often had to pay fines as a punishment. For example, a Sumerian code of law indicates that if a man cut off another man's foot or nose, he had to pay the injured man a certain amount of silver. Legal records were required for all business transactions, contracts, marriages, adoptions, and wills. Archaeologists have found many of Sumer's records, still in their clay envelopes, filed in the temples.

Bronze and copper sculpture of King Ur-Nammu carrying a basket

What role did religion play in people's lives in Sumer?

Compare biblical truth with the polytheism of ancient Sumer.

How did kings rise to power, and what was their impact on the city-states?

How did written language develop in Sumer?

Advances and Inventions

Sumerians developed many things that still affect life today. They made many noteworthy advances in writing, math and sciences, the arts, and architecture.

Writing

Written language is an important feature of a civilization. Sumerians developed one of the earliest writing systems. They used picture symbols or signs that were drawn on clay tablets. As time passed, the picture symbols were gradually replaced with wedge-shaped characters. This wedge-shaped writing was later known as **cuneiform**. *Cuneiform* comes from the Latin words for "wedge-shaped."

Over the centuries, the placement of written symbols also changed. They were written in boxes, rows, or columns. Evidence shows that a symbol could represent an entire word or only a syllable. Scribes combined symbols to express more complex ideas. For example, the Sumerian word for barley was *she*. The symbol for barley could then represent the sound "she" in any word. In the Sumerian word for fig cake, *she-er-ku*, the barley symbol represented the word's first syllable.

Different people groups used the cuneiform script to record information. Cuneiform was used in the Sumerian, Akkadian, Hittite, and Urartian languages. Some people carved cuneiform on a cylinder to make a seal. These cylinder seals were used to sign documents and to record information.

PROGRESSION OF THE BARLEY SYMBOL

Barley symbol used as a sound in the word *she-er-ku*

she　　er　　ku

WHEELS

The Sumerians used wheeled vehicles such as carts and wagons. They used the potter's wheel to spin clay into bowls, pots, and vases.

The ancient invention of the wheel still affects life today. Wheelchairs, inline skates, bicycles, cars, tractors, and airplanes all depend on the wheel.

This baked-clay pull toy shows early wheels.

Math, Science, and Technology

Mathematics were important in Sumer for supporting the economy of its agricultural society. Many cuneiform tablets that contain economic records have been found. The different civilizations of Mesopotamia developed mathematical ideas still used today. These people were the first to recognize the concept of zero and to give a number a place value. They developed a number system based on the number 60. From that system came the 60-minute hour, 60-second minute, and 360° circle. They also used geometry to measure fields and to build temples.

Sumerians created a system of standard weights for business transactions. Since barley was originally used for trade, the smallest unit of weight was the barley-corn, which equaled the weight of one grain of barley. Eventually small pieces of silver of the same weight replaced the barley-corn as a standard weight.

cuneiform Wedge-shaped writing.
astronomy The scientific study of the stars and heavenly objects.
astrology Studying the movements and position of the sun, moon, stars, and planets in the belief that they influence people's lives.

These stone duck weights were standard weights used for business transactions in Mesopotamia. What would each size weight be used for?

Mesopotamians studied science as well. They made important contributions to **astronomy**. By observing the heavenly bodies, they divided the year into two seasons: summer and winter. Using the cycles of the moon, they developed a twelve-month calendar. By observing the night sky, they knew when to plant crops.

They tried to interpret human events by the position of the stars and the planets. Interpreting events in this way is called **astrology**. However, the position of the stars does not determine what will happen. God determines what will happen. Unfortunately, they did not recognize the true God to whom the heavens declare glory.

Mesopotamians developed the seeder plow, which allowed farmers to drop seeds down a funnel on the center of the plow. A farmer could plant seeds in the furrow as he plowed.

They made improvements in carpentry and advanced glassmaking. They fashioned leather goods, made perfume, and built canals. They used kilns to bake pottery and practiced metallurgy to create copper, lead, gold, and silver objects.

People developed systems of irrigation and sanitation. They developed systems for water storage and drainage.

The invention of the wheel improved transportation, and the sail improved boat travel.

Finally, advances were made in medicine. For example, they would make a list of symptoms and then come up with a diagnosis and treatment for each of those symptoms.

What tools, materials, and skills were needed to keep records?
What advancements were made in math and science?

ACTIVITY

Writing Cuneiform and Making a Cylinder Seal

Sumerian scribes were important people. In addition to keeping track of items for merchants, they kept records for the temple and the government. From these careful records, we have learned much about life in Sumer.

A scribe would record transactions on a clay tablet in cuneiform and place it in a clay envelope. The envelope was marked with a cylinder seal for security so that the information inside could not be changed. When the tablet dried, it was stored in the temple with other legal records.

This clay tablet and envelope are the records of an official court ruling about a disputed estate.

Part 1: Writing Cuneiform
1. Get a styling tool, clay, and instructions.
2. Form the clay into a flat square about a half inch thick.
3. Find the letters of your initials on the instructions. Press the wedge-shaped marks that represent your initials onto your clay tablet. Allow it to dry.

Part 2: Making a Cylinder Seal
1. Create a design for a cylinder seal on your page. Keep in mind that small details will not show up very well.
2. Shape your clay into a cylinder about two inches long and one inch wide. With your styling tool, press the reverse of your design around the clay cylinder. Remember that the indentations you make will produce raised areas when the hardened cylinder is used on soft clay. Let the cylinder harden.
3. On another day, make small tablets with soft clay. Roll your cylinder seal over a clay tablet to imprint your design.

What do Mesopotamian arts and architecture reveal about the culture?

Music

The Mesopotamians enjoyed music. Musicians played drums, tambourines, reed pipes, and stringed instruments called lyres. Kings hired musicians to play at special occasions. Music was important to religious rituals and daily work. People sang to the gods and to the kings. Music provided entertainment in the homes and the marketplaces.

Literature

Cuneiform helped the Sumerians record stories, proverbs, and **epics**. Epics were written about Sumerian gods and about military victories. A well-known Mesopotamian poem is the *Epic of Gilgamesh*. This epic describes the adventures of the legendary hero Gilgamesh and his search for eternal life.

In one part of the epic, Gilgamesh meets Utnapishtim. Utnapishtim tells Gilgamesh about how the god Enlil had been angry and had decided to cover the earth with water. Another god, Ea, had helped Utnapishtim by delivering him and his family from the universal flood. Ea had given him these instructions:

> Tear down (this) house, build a ship!
> Give up possessions, seek thou life.
> Despise property and keep the soul alive!
> Aboard the ship take thou the seed of all living things.

Utnapishtim tells how he had built a ship and had gathered aboard his family, the craftsmen who had helped him, and the animals of the field. The rains and the flood had raged for six days and nights and had stopped on the seventh day.

Most ancient civilizations had similar stories. In all these stories, a great flood nearly destroys the human race, but it is saved by a person similar to Noah. These similarities reveal that various civilizations remembered Noah and the Flood. As time passed, and civilizations developed their own mythology, the memory of the Flood mixed with myths, creating different accounts. The account in Genesis 6–8 was revealed to Moses by God. This revelation makes it the historically accurate account of the Flood.

epic A long poem about the actions of a hero.
Epic of Gilgamesh A Mesopotamian poem describing the adventures and eternal life of Gilgamesh, a legendary hero.

Silver bull-headed lyre from Ur. What modern instrument is this similar to?

This core-formed glass pot from Mesopotamia was made by wrapping molten glass strands around a removable core.

In what ways is this house the same or different from houses today?

Arts

The Mesopotamians were wonderful artisans. They created statues of gods for their temples. Because the Mesopotamians did not have the natural resource of stone, they did not have large stone sculptures. They made beautiful things with the materials they did have. They made jewelry of gold and lapis lazuli. They created colorful mosaics in beautiful patterns using little pieces of painted clay. Archaeologists have found remains of mosaics, helmets, lyres, jewelry, and decorated tablets.

Architecture

The climate and natural resources available determined what types of buildings were constructed in Mesopotamia. Wood was in short supply and stone was not available, so buildings were constructed with bricks made of mud. Over the centuries, rains and shifting sands destroyed much of Mesopotamia's mud-brick architecture. Archaeologists have not found as many buildings in Mesopotamia as in other ancient civilizations.

The arch and the column were developed by the Mesopotamians. They were some of the first people to use domes. These elegant architectural features were found in temples and in wealthy homes.

Mesopotamians built thick walls around their cities for defense, and the walls had turrets and gates. If an enemy attacked, everyone moved inside the walls for protection. Temples and palaces were located inside the walls. Houses were located both inside and outside the walls.

Mesopotamian houses varied according to the owner's social status. Kings lived in palaces. Wealthy upper-class families lived in two-story houses. These houses had a large, central, open courtyard. The family cooked, rested, and worked in the courtyard as much as in the rest of the house. There was a special area for the family's statue of their personal god. Most common middle-class families lived in smaller, one-story houses that crowded the narrow, winding streets and alleys. These houses usually had one outside door and no windows.

The thick mud-brick walls kept houses cool in the hot Mesopotamian climate. Often a family slept or entertained guests outdoors on their home's flat roof, where the air was cooler in the evenings. The basic style of homes in the Near East today is similar to that of ancient Mesopotamian homes.

 What examples of art are attributed to the Mesopotamians?

Why is the *Epic of Gilgamesh* account of the Flood different from the Genesis account?

Why were the Amorites able to defeat the Akkadians?

Later Mesopotamian Civilizations

The Sumerian civilization began about 3000 BC. One of the reasons Sumer maintained its power was its military knowledge and might. The Sumerians used spears, axes, clubs, bows, and chariots to fight battles. Soldiers wore copper helmets and leather cloaks dotted with metal disks. For additional protection, the soldiers carried rectangular shields as they marched as a **phalanx**.

Despite their knowledge and might, other countries began to win battles against Sumer. These countries eventually rose to power in Mesopotamia.

Akkadian Empire

Around 2334 BC, the ruler **Sargon I** came to power in the Sumerian city-state of Kish. Sargon conquered other city-states as well. He built the city of Akkad and made it the capital of the first **empire**. The Akkadian Empire stretched from the Persian Gulf to northern Mesopotamia. The Akkadians borrowed many ideas from the Sumerians, including cuneiform writing, farming techniques, and religion.

About one hundred years after the death of Sargon I, the city-state of Ur grew in importance. This may have been the same Ur that is mentioned in Genesis 11:31 as the place Abraham was from. Abraham was born into a world of polytheism and idolatry. God revealed Himself to Abraham around 2100 BC. When God called Abraham to leave Ur, God was not simply telling Abraham to leave home but also telling him to leave a way of life.

SARGON I

What: emperor of Akkadian Empire
When: ruled ca. 2334–2279 BC
Where: Mesopotamia

Sargon came to power in the city-state of Kish. Tradition says that he was a cupbearer to the king of Kish in Mesopotamia but then seized power and took the throne.

He conquered city-states throughout Mesopotamia. Sargon established the first known empire and made Akkad its capital. His authority was greater than that of the priests, and the people were encouraged to view Sargon as a god.

Later, Sargon was succeeded by his sons Rimush and Manishtushu, who united much of Mesopotamia under the Akkadian Empire.

Troops in Sumer were trained to fight in a phalanx with six tight rows of eight men.

phalanx A group of warriors who stood close together in a formation.
Sargon I Ruler of the Sumerian city-state Kish around 2270 BC; established the first empire.
empire A group of nations under one government.

The End of Sumer

After the death of Sargon I, the Akkadian Empire began to weaken. Sumer was again united. Around 2050 BC, Ur-Nammu ruled over the Sumerian civilization. But after his death, Sumer weakened from a series of wars with its neighbors. In the same way God had ended previous civilizations, God decided to end the Sumerian civilization. Invaders began to battle for control of Mesopotamia, and the Sumerian civilization fell by 2000 BC.

Amorite Civilization (Babylonian Empire)

The Sumerian civilization fell to a people called the Amorites. The Amorites established the Babylonian Empire. The empire's capital was the city of **Babylon**, one of the oldest and greatest cities of the ancient world. Babylon was located on the Euphrates River near modern-day Baghdad, Iraq. Babylon quickly became a center of trade.

The city of Babylon began shortly after the Flood. Nimrod, the great-grandson of Noah, established a kingdom that included Babylon

Bronze rider in chariot pulled by four donkeys

Babylon One of the greatest cities of the ancient world; beside the Euphrates River near present-day Baghdad.

Akkadian & Babylonian Empires

NUMBERING THE YEARS

Nearly 1,500 years ago, people stopped using the Roman system for numbering years. Instead, European scholars decided to number years from the birth of Jesus Christ.

The years prior to Christ's birth are labeled **BC**. BC stands for "before Christ" and is written after the year. For example, a time three thousand years before Christ would be "3000 BC." Historical dates become smaller as they approach the year 1.

The years following Christ's birth are labeled **AD**. In this case, the letters are written before the year. Usually AD is not written unless there would be confusion without it. For example, if someone lived from 43 BC until AD 25, AD is included with the year 25. Otherwise it might appear that he died in 25 BC.

Several centuries after the labels *BC* and *AD* became popular, a new movement developed. Some scientists, historians, and religious leaders called the time after Christ's birth the Vulgar Era. At that time, *vulgar* meant *common*. These scholars decided to label dates as *BCE* and *CE*. *BCE* stands for "before the common era," and *CE* stands for "common era." Both abbreviations go after the year. *BCE* and *CE* have often been preferred by those who seek to reduce Christ's importance in history.

If the date of an event is not known with certainty, the term *circa* is used. *Circa* is Latin for "around." It can be abbreviated **ca.** or c. Either *circa* or one of its abbreviations is written before the approximate date.

Even though there are several labels used to number years, references to dates echo one of the most important events in history: Jesus Christ came to earth.

BC Abbreviation meaning "before Christ"; used after the number of a year to signify a year before the birth of Christ.

AD Abbreviation for *anno Domini*, meaning "in the year of our Lord"; used before the number of a year to signify a year after the birth of Chirst.

ca. Abbreviation for *circa*, meaning "around"; used before the number of a year to signify the approximate year.

```
10 BC                            1 BC   AD 1                            AD 10
```

HAMMURABI

What: king of the Amorites
When: ca. 1795–1750 BC
Where: Mesopotamia

Hammurabi succeeded his father to the throne and became the sixth king of the Amorite Empire. The empire was an important power in the region due to its strong military, its location, and its size. Hammurabi fought to control the Euphrates River, an important source of water for agriculture. He is credited for bringing Mesopotamia under one ruler. The last fourteen years of Hammurabi's rule were marked by continual warfare.

(Genesis 10:10). The tower of Babel was probably built in or near this city.

Hammurabi, king of the Amorites, united the land of Mesopotamia. He was a successful military leader. Under his rule, city walls and new canals were built and maintained. He sent out governors, tax collectors, and judges to the city-states.

Hammurabi is best remembered for his code, or collection, of laws. He did not create these laws, but he gathered, organized, and simplified existing laws. There were laws on almost every aspect of daily life, including marriage, trade, theft, and murder. **Hammurabi's Code** contained some ideas that are still found in laws today. This inscription introduced the 282 laws in his code:

> To cause justice to prevail in the land, to destroy the wicked and the evil, that the strong might not oppress the weak.

Hammurabi King of the Amorites and ruler of the Babylonian Empire.

Hammurabi's Code A collection of Mesopotamian laws written by Hammurabi.

GOD'S LAW & HAMMURABI'S CODE

The law given from God through Moses is known as the Mosaic law. Some people claim that Moses copied Israel's law from Hammurabi. Although there are several places in which Hammurabi's Code is similar to the Mosaic law, there are also many differences. Furthermore, the Bible says that Moses received the law directly from God.

However, the similarities between the Mosaic law and Hammurabi's Code point to an important truth. All people have a basic sense of what is just and unjust because of the law of God written on their hearts (Romans 2:14–15). Though humans often reject God's law, it is impossible to reject all of it all the time. Life in God's world just would not work. In addition, the Babylonians and Israelites had similar living conditions at that time, so it is not surprising that the specific applications of God's natural law were similar to those given to Moses.

The differences between the codes are also significant. Unlike Hammurabi's Code, the Mosaic law forbids giving special treatment to wealthy people. All people are equal before God, regardless of their economic status. Also, the Mosaic law is God-centered. Crime is not merely doing wrong to another person; it is a sin against God. God's concern is that people think, act, and feel rightly toward Him and others even in their hearts. This concern with the heart sets God's law apart from every other code of law.

Finally, the Mosaic law contains large sections about how to worship God. There are no religious sections in Hammurabi's Code.

The stele of Hammurabi shows Hammurabi being commissioned by the sun god Shamash to inscribe the laws that were written in cuneiform. Would a stele be an effective way of communicating laws today?

Hammurabi's Code was one of retaliation. Specific crimes brought specific penalties. However, the penalty for breaking Hammurabi's laws varied according to the social class of the offender. For example, if a wealthy man broke a bone of a member of his own social class, his own bone was to be broken. If a wealthy man broke the bone of a commoner, he just had to pay a fine. Hammurabi had the code engraved on stone pillars. They were placed throughout the kingdom so that everyone would know the law.

 Who was the most influential Akkadian ruler?

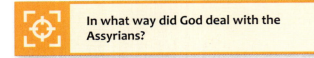

In what way did God deal with the Assyrians?

Hittite Empire

The Hittites were descendants of Heth, the grandson of Ham and great-grandson of Noah (Genesis 10:15). For a time, many historians did not think they existed. The Old Testament was the only source of information about these people until archaeological discoveries in the early 1900s confirmed their existence.

The Hittites began to settle in Asia Minor about 2000 BC. **Asia Minor** is the peninsula between the Black Sea and the Mediterranean Sea in what is now Turkey. The Hittites were not ruled by priests or gods as the Sumerians were. The Hittites had a king who was the commander of the army. His power depended upon the chief warriors. The Hittites excelled in the production of iron. They made the strongest weapons of the time and skillfully used horse-drawn chariots.

The Hittites extended their empire throughout Asia Minor, the Fertile Crescent region, and into Mesopotamia. Soon after they took control of the Amorite capital of Babylon, other nations invaded Hittite territory, and the rule of the Hittites ended.

Assyrian Empire

The Assyrians created the largest empire the world had seen up to that point. For centuries, they lived in northern Mesopotamia along the Tigris River. By 750 BC, they had built an empire that included the Fertile Crescent, Egypt, and part of Asia Minor. **Nineveh**, a city built earlier by Nimrod, became the capital city of the empire.

The Assyrians adopted gods, language, art, architecture, sciences, and literature from the Sumerian and Amorite civilizations. The Assyrians spread these cultural elements throughout the ancient world by their military invasions. One of the first libraries was in Nineveh. Modern historians have learned much about ancient civilizations from this library.

Asia Minor The peninsula between the Black Sea and the Mediterranean Sea in what is present-day Turkey.

Nineveh The capital city of the Assyrian Empire; beside the Tigris River.

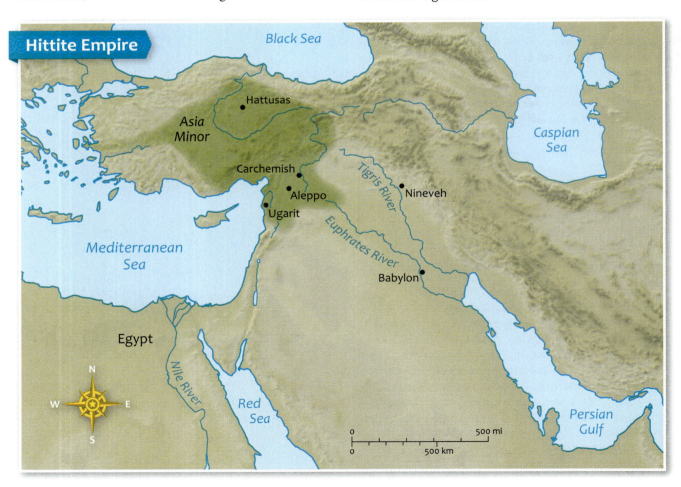

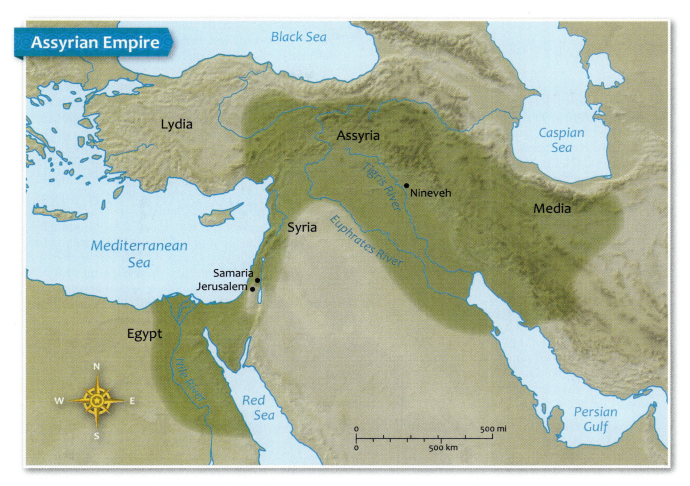

Assyrian Empire

The Assyrian military was unmatched by any other civilization of the day. The Assyrian army was equipped with iron weapons, siege towers, battering rams, and war chariots. It included foot soldiers, spearmen, archers, and a cavalry.

The Assyrians earned a reputation for fierceness. They terrorized the nations by making threats of destruction. They looted villages and burned crops. If the people resisted, the Assyrians sent in their forces. Soldiers tunneled under city walls or climbed over them on ladders. They used battering rams to knock down city gates. They removed the conquered people from their own lands and settled them in foreign countries.

The Assyrian Empire stretched from the Persian Gulf to the Nile River in Egypt. The kings chose officials to govern political areas called provinces. Each official collected taxes and enforced the laws. Roads were built to join parts of the empire. Soldiers were posted to protect travelers from thieves.

God used the Assyrians to chasten His disobedient people. In Isaiah 10:5–6, God described Assyria as a rod and staff in His hand that He would use to punish Israel. In 722 BC, the Assyrian army took captive the ten northern tribes of Israel. The Assyrians did not acknowledge God and were not aware of His workings.

Although the Assyrians were among the most ruthless people of the ancient world, God showed mercy on them. He sent **Jonah** to Nineveh to preach repentance. "Arise, go to Nineveh, that great city, and cry against it; for their wickedness is come up before me" (Jonah 1:2). As the people of this city "turned from their evil way" (Jonah 3:10), God mercifully turned away His wrath.

The people of Nineveh, however, eventually returned to their wicked ways, and God judged them (Nahum 1–3). In 612 BC, the Chaldeans and the Medes destroyed Nineveh, bringing the Assyrian Empire to an end.

Jonah Prophet whom God sent to Nineveh to tell the Assyrians to repent.

 What was the Hittite Empire like, and how was it different from the Sumerian Empire?

> Why do civilizations rise and fall?

Chaldean Empire

Shortly before 1000 BC, the Chaldeans began to settle around Babylon. They were constantly overrun by the Assyrian kings. In 612 BC, the Chaldeans joined with the Medes and helped destroy Nineveh. Babylon became the capital city of the Chaldean Empire. It is sometimes called the New Babylonian Empire.

During the reign of **Nebuchadnezzar II**, the empire reached its height. The Chaldeans' sudden rise to power amazed the ancient world. The Lord explained Nebuchadnezzar's success:

> I [the Lord God] have made the earth, the man and the beast that are upon the ground, by my great power and by my outstretched arm, and have given it unto whom it seemed meet unto me. And now have I given all these lands into the hand of Nebuchadnezzar the king of Babylon, my servant. . . . And all nations shall serve him (Jeremiah 27:5–7).

For much of his reign, Nebuchadnezzar did not show that he was God's servant. He was a proud king who made a golden image and required people to bow down to it. But late in his reign, Nebuchadnezzar was confronted by God. Instead of taking credit for Babylon's greatness, Nebuchadnezzar should have given glory to God. Daniel had shown Nebuchadnezzar the power of God. But Nebuchadnezzar viewed his own accomplishments with a heart of pride and failed to respond to God's warning.

As a result, he lived in the fields like an animal for seven years. He even thought like an animal for those years. But when Nebuchadnezzar recognized the foolishness of his pride and the greatness of God, God restored him as king. After Nebuchadnezzar's understanding returned, he wrote a letter that testifies that God rules over the kingdoms of the earth and gives them to whom He chooses. This letter is preserved in the book of Daniel.

Nebuchadnezzar is remembered for building up Babylon as "the glory of kingdoms, the beauty of the Chaldees' excellency" (Isaiah 13:19). The ancient Greek historian Herodotus said of Babylon, "In magnificence there is no other city that approaches to it." Babylon was surrounded by a brick wall. The wall was so wide that two chariots could pass on the road on top of it. A moat surrounding the wall also protected the city.

The Hanging Gardens of Babylon were one of the wonders of the ancient world. The gardens were probably built by Nebuchadnezzar for his wife, who missed the plants of her mountain homeland. The terraced gardens contained tropical palms, trees, and flowers. From the ground, the gardens seemed to hang in the air. The Euphrates River ran under the wall and through the middle of the city. It watered the gardens and provided a water supply for the city.

The book of Daniel indicates that "wise men," or astrologers, had an important position in the Chaldean Empire. They were called upon to advise the king. Although they claimed power to interpret dreams, they proved themselves unable to interpret the king's dreams (Daniel 2:10–11; 4:7).

Nebuchadnezzar was a powerful and effective leader. He grew the kingdom to be the largest in the world at that time. Nebuchadnezzar left the empire in better condition than he had found it.

Despite the glories of the Chaldean Empire, it did not last even one hundred years. There were several weak emperors who followed Nebuchadnezzar. Nebuchadnezzar's son ruled for only two years. Nebuchadnezzar's son-in-law managed to rule for four years, and Nebuchadnezzar's grandson was just a child when he came to the throne and ruled for only a few months.

It is unclear how the next ruler was related to Nebuchadnezzar. Some historians speculate that he was part of a group that killed Nebuchadnezzar's grandson in order to gain control of the throne. The new leader's name was Nabonidus. He ruled for seventeen years.

Nebuchadnezzar II The king of Babylon and the Chaldean Empire around 612 BC.

Chaldean Empire

CUNEIFORM INSCRIPTION

The cylinder displayed here is an official document inscribed in cuneiform. It records the efforts of King Nebuchadnezzar as he built his empire. The translation says the following:

I am Nebuchadnezzar, King of Babylon, lawful son of Napolassar. I the king of righteousness, the interpreter, the spoiler, filled with the fear of the gods and loving justice, have placed in the hearts of my people the spirit of reverence and have rebuilt their temples. My great god, Lord Merodach singled me out as the restorer of the city and the rebuilder of its temples, and made my name illustrious. I built temples, I rebuilt temples. The god hearkened to no king before me, so I built his temples. Let me state myself with glory, let me be an everlasting ruler.

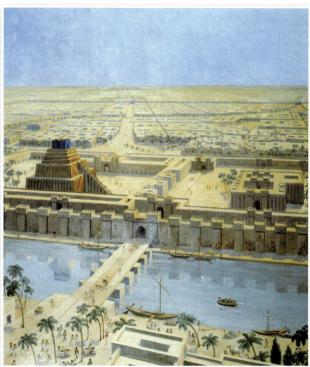

This painting by Maurice Bardin shows what Babylon may have looked like during the reign of King Nebuchadnezzar II.
What characteristics of a civilization are depicted in this painting?

Nabonidus did not like to stay in Babylon and spent most of those seventeen years traveling or staying in a small town in Arabia. He enjoyed learning about the accomplishments of those that had gone before him, and he suffered from physical ailments that he sought treatments for as he traveled. His son Belshazzar left a more notable mark on history.

Nabonidus left Belshazzar to rule the empire in his place. Historical records indicate that Belshazzar did not do much to improve the empire he was ruling. Not much is recorded about this man, but the historical record in the Bible (Daniel 5) describes one major event in Belshazzar's life.

Belshazzar decided to hold a feast in honor of the gods and to celebrate the empire's greatness. While Belshazzar and the nobles were feasting, Belshazzar commanded that the vessels Nebuchadnezzar had taken from the temple in Jerusalem be brought out. The party continued to feast and praise the false gods. The fingers of a man's hand appeared and wrote a message for Belshazzar on the wall.

Belshazzar was terrified and called for the astrologers, the Chaldeans, wise men, and the soothsayers (fortunetellers). But just like when God sent a message to Nebuchadnezzar, these men were unable to read or interpret the message on the wall.

The queen heard what was going on and suggested that Belshazzar call Daniel. Some scholars believe that the queen was probably Belshazzar's mother and the wife of Nabonidus. She would have remembered that Nebuchadnezzar had given Daniel a high position among the wise men.

Belshazzar promised Daniel wealth and power if he could interpret the writing on the wall. But Daniel did not want the glory for himself. Daniel proceeded to relate the serious message and its meaning. Belshazzar did not measure up to God's standard, and there was a price to pay.

Darius had already been marching an army toward Babylon. He swept in that night and conquered Babylon for the Persians. God had prepared and executed judgment against Belshazzar.

The story of Mesopotamia will begin again in a later chapter when the story of ancient Persia unfolds.

 What was the importance of the Chaldean Empire to the ancient world?

3 ANCIENT EGYPT

FOCUS
The Nile River was important to Egypt's economy and religion.

Joseph rises to second in command in Egypt
ca. 1880 BC

Moses leads Israelites out of Egypt
ca. 1446 BC

3000 BC — 2500 BC — 2000 BC — 1500 BC — 1000 BC

ca. 2700–2200 BC
Old Kingdom

ca. 2040–1650 BC
Middle Kingdom

ca. 1570–1075 BC
New Kingdom

Name five things you are grateful for today. Did you know that being grateful and expressing gratitude are good for you? Grateful people sleep better, do not get as stressed, and have more energy than people who focus on negative things. The Bible reminds Christians to give thanks to God in everything (I Thessalonians 5:18).

Ancient Egyptians had a tradition of being grateful in honor of a goddess named Hathor. All classes of people—from the pharaoh to the field laborers—observed a ritual called the Five Gifts of Hathor. In the ritual, Egyptians held out their left hands (the hand of work) and named five things in their lives for which they were grateful. Being ungrateful or complaining was considered the root of all other bad action.

What do you think Hepu and Adjo might be thankful for as they swim in the Nile River? Perhaps they are thankful that the person on the bank has alerted them to the cobra sunning itself on the rock!

49

Why was Egypt called the "Gift of the Nile"?

The Egyptian Civilization

As the Sumerian civilization was developing in Mesopotamia, other civilizations were growing in Europe, Asia, and Africa. Some people settled in northeastern Africa. These people were the descendants of Mizraim, a son of Ham and a grandson of Noah. In the original language of the Bible, the land is called Mizraim, but English translations usually call it **Egypt**. Many events recorded in the Old Testament took place in Egypt.

The Nile

An aerial view of Egypt would reveal a thin ribbon of green cutting a desert into two parts. Running through that green ribbon is a long blue thread, the **Nile River**.

The Nile River is the longest river in the world. It begins in central Africa and runs four thousand miles north to the Mediterranean Sea.

Imagine how the descendants of Mizraim felt when they saw the mighty Nile River for the first time. Egypt has been called "the Gift of the Nile." Without the Nile River, Egypt would have been very different. The Nile was a necessary part of ancient Egyptian life.

The geography of Egypt protected the people from most invasions. The vast and treacherous desert, the Sahara, provided protection from enemies in the east and the west. As the Nile flows through the Sahara, sections of the river become very shallow and rocky, causing dangerous rapids. These areas are called cataracts. Six cataracts appear along the path of the Nile. The cataracts slowed the advancement of invaders using the river to attack from the south.

The Nile River provided other benefits for the people. The Egyptians depended on the Nile for food and water. Wherever the Nile flowed, plants grew nearby. However, where there was no water, all was desert. At the edge of some Egyptian farms, a person could stand with one foot in green grass and the other foot in tan desert sand.

The Nile River became a useful highway for transportation. Travelers and traders navigated the river. Trade settlements developed near the cataracts, where river traffic slowed. Most major rivers flow north to south. The Nile, however, flows from south to north. The current allowed boats to float or sail northward. Winds blowing from the north moved boats with sails southward, against the current.

Egyptians throughout history honored and gave thanks to the Nile. They gave it the nickname *Hapi*, which means "well fed" or "fat." They worshiped the Nile as a god rather than acknowledging the true God who created the river. The following lines are from the Egyptian "Hymn to the Nile."

> Hail to thee, O Nile! Who manifests thyself over this land, and comes to give life to Egypt! . . . Lord of the fish, during inundation [flood], no bird alights on the crops. You create the grain, you bring forth the barley, assuring perpetuity [eternity] to the temples. If you cease your toil and your work, then all that exists is in anguish. . . . O Nile, come (and) prosper, come O Nile, come (and) prosper!

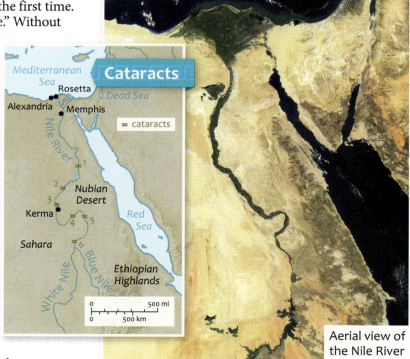

Aerial view of the Nile River

How did the Nile affect the survival, growth, and success of the Egyptian civilization?

What natural barriers discouraged invasion from other civilizations?

Egypt An ancient kingdom and later a modern country in northeastern Africa.

Nile River The river that flows from central Africa through Egypt; the longest river in the world.

How were taxes in ancient Egypt determined?

Flooding of the Nile

Each summer in ancient Egypt, the Nile overflowed its banks. Melting snows in African mountains and heavy spring rains in the south caused the river to rise significantly. The water would rush down the mountains and across the flat land of Egypt in a flood covering everything in its path. The flood typically lasted for four months. During those months the water soaked into the land. Silt would settle from the water. This silt became the life-sustaining feature of the flood. Without the annual fertilizing quality of the silt, the crops would not have thrived.

Farming Along the Nile

When the land was nearly dry from the flood, Egyptian farmers went to work in their fields. Because the soil was still soft, plowing was not necessary. The farmers simply scattered their seeds on the damp ground. Then they walked their farm animals back and forth across the field. The animals' hooves pushed the seeds into the soil.

Once the planting was done, the farmers had to keep the crops watered. The Egyptians dug irrigation canals for crops planted farther away from the river.

Many farmers used a **shadoof** to dip water from the Nile River into an irrigation canal. It was hard, daily work to keep the crops watered until harvest.

Some farmers used a water wheel that lifted water from the Nile to the irrigation canals. A donkey or an ox could be used to help turn the wheel. But few farmers could afford luxuries such as a water wheel. Most fathers relied on help from their sons.

The strip of fertile land along the Nile River is only about ten miles wide. However, it stretches the whole length of the river. As the river empties into the Mediterranean Sea, the Nile widens into a fan shape called a **delta**. A delta gets its name because it resembles the Greek letter *delta* (Δ). Early settlers

shadoof A device made from a long pole with a bucket on one end and a weight on the other; used to dip water out of the Nile River.

delta A fan-shaped area of fertile land at the mouth of a river.

What are the advantages and disadvantages of using a shadoof?

How did Egyptian farmers sow their seeds?

THE REGION TODAY

Egypt

Location
The Arab Republic of Egypt is located in northeastern Africa. Ancient Egypt was the land along the Nile River. Modern Egypt is bordered by Libya to the west, Sudan to the south, the Red Sea to the east, and the Mediterranean Sea to the north.

Climate
Egypt has hot, dry summers and moderate winters. Temperatures range from 107°F in the summer to 55°F in the winter.

Topography
The land is dominated by the Nile River and its valley. Desert lies to the east and west of the Nile. The Sinai Peninsula is in eastern Egypt.

Natural Resources
Egypt's greatest natural resource is water from the Nile River. Other natural resources include iron ore, petroleum, natural gas, phosphate, limestone, manganese, talc, zinc, asbestos, gypsum, and lead.

Egypt Then & Now

- Ancient city
- Modern borders
- Modern city
- Modern capital
- Old Kingdom (ca. 2700–2200 BC)
- Middle Kingdom (ca. 2040–1650 BC)
- New Kingdom (ca. 1570–1075 BC)

What body of water does the Nile flow into?

found the Nile Delta an ideal location to grow crops. They did not have to worry about having a water source because the land was low and well watered by the Nile. The people of Egypt planted a variety of crops. They grew wheat and barley, melons and cucumbers, onions and garlic, and dates and figs. The river supplied many kinds of fish and waterfowl. People also raised animals, but usually only the wealthy ate meat that was raised for food.

Egypt became the storehouse of the ancient world. The Nile provided Egypt with fertile land where an abundance of crops grew. Large harvests allowed Egyptians to store food for times of famine when the Nile River did not rise. Because of their careful planning, the Egyptians usually had more than enough to eat and were able to sell the extra to other regions.

Other civilizations learned of Egypt's bounty. Many people traveled to Egypt when they were in need of food. During a period known as the Middle Kingdom, a famine lasting seven years affected both Egypt and the surrounding lands. The book of Genesis records that God sent the pharaoh a warning of this famine in a vision. This dream was interpreted by Joseph, a Hebrew from Canaan who had been sold into slavery. Joseph told Pharaoh that the dream predicted seven years of abundant food followed by seven years of famine. He advised Pharaoh to store food during the seven plenteous years so that people would have food during the seven years of famine.

Pharaoh appointed Joseph to oversee this program. Because the Egyptians stored food for the famine, people from neighboring regions, such as Canaan, came to purchase food from Egypt during the famine. The Egyptians themselves also had to purchase food from Pharaoh, and this led to a change in how taxation worked in Egypt, at least for a while. When the Egyptians ran out of money to buy food, they sold themselves and their land to Pharaoh. They then owed a fifth of their harvest to Pharaoh.

The colorfully dressed people in the middle band of this Egyptian wall painting may be the Israelites being presented by Joseph to the pharaoh.

Right: Nilometers on Elephantine Island near the first cataract. How might the nilometer have worked?

Below: How might the Egyptians have calculated time with this water clock?

Taxes and Time

The people of Egypt depended on the Nile River not only for survival, but also as a means to pay their taxes. Governmental officials kept detailed records of when the river flooded and how high the water rose. The Egyptians used a **nilometer** to measure the Nile's water levels. The measurements affected how much the people owed in taxes because the more the Nile River flooded, the more fertile farmland there was to produce crops. The amount of taxes was determined by crop production.

Taxation in ancient Egypt was a part of life. Many things such as land, livestock, and crops were taxed each year.

Priests were not required to pay taxes. The earliest Egyptians did not have money; therefore, tax payments were made with a percentage of livestock or crops, but could also be paid by service in the military or work on the pharaoh's tomb.

Every family was required to pay a labor tax. A family member was chosen to serve in the military or to work on road construction or building projects.

Because of the importance of the Nile's floods, the Egyptians developed a calendar that told the exact days on which the Nile was expected to flood. This calendar had three seasons: Flood (Akhit), Planting (Perit), and Harvest (Shemu).

The Egyptian calendar was based on the phases of the moon. There were four months in each season. Each month had three weeks with ten days each. Since this calendar was five days short of a full year, the Egyptians added five more days to the calendar. They used these days to celebrate the birthdays of the gods.

The Egyptians used two types of clocks: the water clock and the sundial. Both kept time, but each had a disadvantage. The water clock had to be refilled often, and the sundial could be used only during the day. Ancient Egyptians used the stars to determine the time at night.

nilometer A device used to measure the Nile's water levels.

COMPARISON OF SEASONS AND CALENDARS

	Ancient Egypt	United States
Seasons in a Year	3	4
Months in a Season	4	3
Days in a Month	30	28–31
Weeks in a Month	3	4–5
Days in a Week	10	7

How did Joseph help the Egyptians and the Israelites?

How does the Egyptian calendar compare with the calendar in use today?

What artifacts of ancient Egypt do historians find most significant?

A Unified Egypt

The Egyptians began settling in two areas along the Nile River. The mountainous area to the south was called Upper Egypt, and the plains around the Nile Delta were called Lower Egypt. Around 3000 BC, Lower and Upper Egypt were unified under a leader named Menes who began the first **dynasty** of Egypt. At the time, people still identified Lower Egypt and Upper Egypt as two separate geographic regions, even though they were one kingdom.

Old Kingdom Pharaohs
(ca. 2700–2200 BC)

Most of Egyptian history is divided into three kingdoms. The first kingdom is known as the Old Kingdom. It started with Egypt's Third Dynasty. During this time, the **pharaohs** had great power. The Egyptians began to believe the pharaohs were gods.

Probably the most spectacular accomplishment of the pharaohs was the building of large tombs called **pyramids**. Each pyramid demonstrated the power and wealth that the pharaoh had gained during his reign.

Archaeologists have found evidence of at least eighty pyramids. Most of them were built during the Old Kingdom. Another name for the Old Kingdom is "the Age of Pyramids."

Pyramids

Today, people are amazed that the pyramids were built without modern technology. Step pyramids were the earliest type of pyramid. They were constructed with several flat, rectangular layers. Each layer was built gradually smaller going up. The step pyramids were made of mud bricks with the outer bricks arranged like stairs. The Egyptians believed that the pharaoh would climb the steps to reach the afterlife.

The design of pyramids changed over time. Later pyramids were made of large stones that were carefully cut into building blocks that fit snugly together. These pyramids had smooth sides of polished limestone.

Each pyramid contained more than just the buried body of a pharaoh. Food, clothing, furniture, and even games and toys were placed in the burial chamber. The pharaohs thought these things would bring them pleasure and ease in the next life. Statues were also placed in the tombs. These were thought to act as servants to the pharaoh in the afterlife. Detailed scenes of daily life were painted on the walls to make the pharaoh feel at home. Pyramids were usually built for royalty, but some wealthy Egyptians were able to afford such tombs as well.

The three pyramids in the valley of Giza are the most well known. The largest of these is the **Great Pyramid**, which was built for the pharaoh Khufu. Khufu ruled during the Fourth Dynasty. His magnificent pyramid covers thirteen acres and can still be visited today.

---

dynasty A line of kings or rulers who belong to the same family.

pharaoh A ruler of Egypt.

pyramid A large tomb constructed on a rectangular base with four sloping, triangular sides.

Great Pyramid The largest of the three pyramids in the valley of Giza; built for the pharaoh Khufu.

INSIDE THE GREAT PYRAMID

1. **entrance**
2. **underground chamber:** possibly the pharaoh's original burial chamber or a fake chamber to fool robbers
3. **Grand Gallery:** a large passageway that leads upward to the pharaoh's burial chamber
4. **queen's burial chamber:** possibly the location where the pharaoh's possessions were placed for the afterlife; the queen was actually buried in a smaller pyramid nearby.
5. **pharaoh's burial chamber:** the location of the pharaoh's sarcophagus
6. **air shafts:** likely provided ventilation for the workers

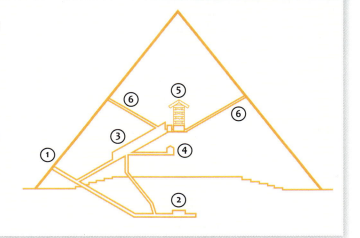

Artifacts

As with most civilizations, knowledge about the Old Kingdom comes from artifacts. Because the Egyptians were so careful to preserve things for the afterlife, a large number of objects survived. Egypt's hot, dry climate was also important in preserving artifacts. Regions with high humidity cause artifacts to decay more quickly. In Egypt, however, ancient food items, clothing, and colored paintings have survived. As a result, more has been learned about the ancient Egyptian civilization than any other.

The largest artifacts in Egypt are structures such as the great pyramids and the Sphinx. The paintings inside the pyramids reveal a great deal about the daily life of the Egyptians. In addition to pyramids, the pharaohs erected storehouses, beautiful palaces, and temples. Most of these buildings are located in the cities of Memphis and Thebes.

Historians have learned much about Egypt from records written on **papyrus**. The word *paper* comes from the word *papyrus*. The papyrus plant grew along the banks of the Nile and was used to make baskets, boats, and rope. Egyptian scribes and priests used it for thousands of years to keep records, write letters, and record stories. Papyrus was light and thin and could be stored easily. Many ancient civilizations used papyrus from Egypt until the Middle Ages.

papyrus Paper made from the stems of the papyrus plant.

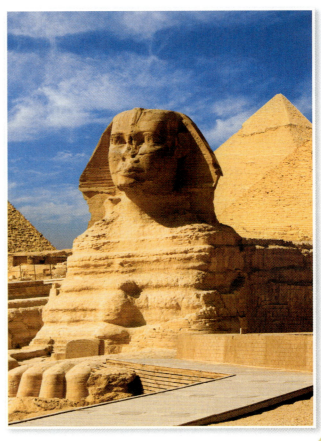

Archaeologists believe that the Sphinx was built to guard the pyramids.

Papyrus-Making Process

cut & harvest

peel

slice & soak

layer & pound

The Rosetta stone was the key to unlocking the Egyptian language.

JEAN-FRANÇOIS CHAMPOLLION

What: Egyptologist
When: 1790–1832
Where: France

Instead of attending a traditional school, Champollion was tutored by his older brother. This brother soon realized that Champollion had a gift for learning languages. By the age of nineteen, Champollion had received a Doctor of Letters degree. By age twenty, he had mastered thirteen languages. He was appointed the curator of the Egyptian department at the Louvre in Paris. He was a skilled French historian and linguist. He was also the founder of scientific Egyptology. His linguistic skills and the discovery of the Rosetta stone enabled him to read Egyptian hieroglyphics.

The Rosetta Stone

Ancient Egyptian writing is called **hieroglyphics**. People drew pictures of the ideas they wanted to express in language. The pictures became standardized, and some could be used as letters to spell names. This kind of writing was used from about 3000 BC to AD 1100, longer than any other form of writing used in ancient times.

For many centuries after the Egyptian civilization declined, no one was able to read hieroglyphics. But in 1799, a large black stone was found in the town of modern-day Rosetta, near the Mediterranean Sea.

hieroglyphics A system of writing made of picture symbols.
Rosetta stone An ancient rock stele or monument carved with Egyptian hieroglyphics, Greek, and another script; used as a key to decipher Egyptian hieroglyphics; discovered in the Egyptian town of Rosetta in 1799.
Jean-François Champollion Egyptologist who translated the hieroglyphics on the Rosetta stone in 1822.

The stone was the lower part of an upright monument called a stele. This stele had been engraved to record a decree of Pharaoh Ptolemy V. The inscription was written in Egyptian hieroglyphics, common Egyptian, and Greek.

The **Rosetta stone** became the key to unlocking the Egyptian language. Since Greek was a known language, it was used to translate the Egyptian symbols and words. However, it was not until 1822 that **Jean-François Champollion** successfully translated several of the hieroglyphics on the stone. The Rosetta stone made it possible for historians and archaeologists to read Egyptian hieroglyphics.

What are the names of the two areas where Egyptians settled along the Nile?

Explain how these areas get their name.

Why were the pyramids in the valley of Giza built?

What was the significance of the way the embalmer dressed?

Mummies

Because of their religious beliefs, the Egyptians carefully preserved the bodies of the dead through a process of mummification. The study of **mummies** has given archaeologists insight into the ancient Egyptians. For example, studying mummies has revealed what the people of Egypt actually looked like. Many civilizations buried or burned their dead, leaving nothing for archaeologists to study. However, the Egyptians dried the body, which halted decay. Archaeologists study the hair, bones, and skin to determine the age, health, and diseases of the mummy.

The Egyptians' preparation for the afterlife reveals that they did not believe in the true God. They believed that without a body, a person could not exist in the next world. So after a person died, his family paid an embalmer to preserve the body.

The embalmer wore the jackal-headed costume of the god Anubis. The Egyptians believed that Anubis was a guardian of the dead, and he became associated with the embalming process. In the embalming process, the embalmer first cleaned out the skull. Then he cleaned the abdominal cavities and dried the liver, stomach, lungs, and intestines. The embalmer placed each of these organs in special containers called **canopic jars**. He then filled the body with spices. The body was soaked for seventy days in a salt solution called *natron*. Once removed from the natron, the body was washed and wrapped in linen strips.

The embalmer returned the preserved mummy to the family for burial. The mummy was placed into a **sarcophagus**. Some wealthy families purchased several coffins that fit inside one another. The coffins were made of metal, wood, or stone. Some sarcophaguses were richly decorated. The mummy of a wealthy person was buried with many items to be used in the afterlife. Sometimes the deceased person's servants were buried with him so they could serve him in the afterlife.

Archaeologists have discovered much information about ancient Egyptians from mummies. What do you think archaeologists have learned from mummies?

mummy A dead body that has been preserved from decaying.

canopic jar A special container for organs of a dead body.

sarcophagus A stone coffin.

What were placed in canopic jars?

58

The Cartouche

A pharaoh often had the hieroglyphs of his name written inside an oval shape called a *shenu*. The word *shenu* came from the Egyptian word for "encircle." The Egyptians believed that the person whose name was encircled with a shenu would be protected.

A shenu served as a nameplate. Archaeologists have found shenus on monuments, tombs, amulets, and papyruses. These shenus contained hieroglyphs that represented a pharaoh's birth name, throne name, and sometimes other information.

Rameses II's cartouche

The shenu shape became very important to the Egyptians. The use of the shape extended beyond nameplates. Many sarcophaguses, burial chambers, and other structures were made in this long oval shape.

In the 1800s, Napoleon Bonaparte invaded Egypt. His French soldiers saw shenus on buildings and artifacts. They thought the shape of a shenu resembled the shape of their gun cartridges. Since the French word for "cartridge" is *cartouche*, the soldiers gave the name **cartouche** to the shenu symbols. Today archaeologists and historians continue to call the Egyptian nameplate a cartouche.

cartouche An oval shape containing hieroglyphs of a name written inside.

 What does the Egyptians' preparation for the afterlife reveal about their beliefs?

ACTIVITY

Deciphering Hieroglyphics

Have you ever seen a message written in code and wondered what it meant? To decipher a coded message, you need a key. Champollion used Greek as a key to interpret the hieroglyphics on the Rosetta stone. In this activity, you will use a key containing a hieroglyphic alphabet to decipher and write hieroglyphic words.

1. Turn to Activity Manual page 39.
2. Match the words and hieroglyphic spellings in Section A.
3. Answer the questions in Section B using words spelled in hieroglyphics.
4. Write your name in hieroglyphics in the blank cartouche in Section C.

vulture A	foot B	hand D	reed E (I)	horned viper F (V)	pot stand G
house H	cobra J (G)	basket K (C)	lion L	owl M	water N
lasso O	stool P	hillside Q	open mouth R	folded cloth S (C)	bread loaf T
quail chick U (W)	two reeds Y	doorbolt Z	hobble rope CH	lake SH	cow's belly TH

How did the three kingdoms of ancient Egypt differ?

Kingdoms of Egypt
Middle Kingdom
(ca. 2040–1650 BC)

The Old Kingdom thrived for over five hundred years. However, the later pharaohs were weak rulers, and their reigns resulted in disorder and war. More than a century of fighting took place. Then a new dynasty came into power, and Egypt became united again.

This new period is called the Middle Kingdom. During this time, the Egyptians experienced peace and stability. The pharaohs showed greater care for the people of the land. Under their leadership, larger canals and ponds were made to store the Nile's floodwaters for use during the dry season.

Egypt restored trade with its neighbors. The Egyptians built forts along the Nile River between the river's first and second cataracts. These forts helped control the trade routes. It was during this time that Joseph was brought to Egypt.

Temples, pyramids, palaces, and other buildings were also constructed during the Middle Kingdom. The people decorated these buildings with sculptures and paintings similar to those of the Old Kingdom. However, the pyramids built during the Middle Kingdom were smaller and less grand than those of the Old Kingdom. Instead of using stone, builders used mud bricks. Since the bricks were less durable, not many of the Middle Kingdom's pyramids have survived to the present day.

DATING ANCIENT EVENTS

The process of dating events in ancient history is complex. The dates given to ancient history are counted back from the time of Christ. But these dates were obviously not used prior to Christ.

Historians must study ancient methods of dating and find an event that has been dated by both the ancient and the modern systems. For Egypt, there was a star that rose on the first day of the Egyptian year every 1,460 years. Roman records reveal this happened in AD 139. Scholars can count backwards to know when this event occurred in ancient history. Since the Egyptians note that this event happened in year seven of one pharaoh's reign or year nine of another pharaoh's reign, scholars can connect ancient and modern dating systems.

Figuring out biblical dates is similar. From genealogy and king lists, scholars determine the time between events.

For example, historians know that Solomon began to build the temple in 967 BC. 1 Kings 6:1 says that there were 480 years from the year Israel left Egypt until Solomon began construction. Therefore, many scholars date the Exodus at 1446 BC. But even then, they cannot be sure because of the many factors in play when dating ancient events.

How is the Black Pyramid different from the Great Pyramid?

The Hyksos considered the hippopotamus to be sacred.

New Kingdom
(ca. 1570–1075 BC)

The peace of the Middle Kingdom did not last. The pharaohs neglected the security of the borders and failed to keep the forts in good repair. A people group called the **Hyksos** gradually migrated into Egypt and eventually took over. The word *Hyksos* means "foreign rulers." Historians believe these foreigners were from the Syria-Palestine area. The Hyksos ruled for about 150 years. From these people, the Egyptians learned to use weapons made of bronze and iron, as well as the horse-drawn two-wheeled chariot.

An Egyptian prince named Ahmose eventually drove out the Hyksos. He created a protective buffer south of the Upper Kingdom to prevent further invasions. He also expanded the kingdom farther east. Ahmose made Egypt mightier than it had ever been. This set the stage for what is called the New Kingdom. Shortly after the New Kingdom was established, the Egyptians enslaved the Israelites. Some scholars think that the enslavement was in connection to the expulsion of the Hyksos. Both the Hyksos and the Israelites were from the region of Canaan and Syria. So the Egyptians may have been concerned about foreigners growing powerful and gaining control over Egypt again.

Around this period, Moses, an Israelite child, was adopted by one of Pharaoh's daughters and raised in Pharaoh's household. Moses was taught to read and write. He studied history, arithmetic, and science. He learned all the wisdom of the Egyptians. But he knew he was an Israelite. At age forty, he killed an Egyptian who was beating an Israelite. When the murder became known, Moses had to flee to Midian. Forty years later, Moses returned with a command from God to Pharaoh to let the Israelites go. Pharaoh's refusal led to a series of ten plagues. These plagues were so severe that Egypt's leaders counseled Pharaoh to let the Israelites go. Pharaoh finally agreed, but he changed his mind after the Israelites left. He chased them with an army and six hundred chariots. But the Lord protected the Israelites. He destroyed all of Pharaoh's army in the waters of the Red Sea. The news of the plagues and this defeat spread throughout the surrounding region.

The New Kingdom was the greatest period in Egyptian history. Eventually, Egypt became a regional power. The pharaohs of the New Kingdom were warrior kings. They expanded Egypt's borders by conquering neighboring peoples. They also gained wealth by trading with other civilizations to obtain gold and ivory.

Queen **Hatshepsut** was one of the early rulers during the New Kingdom. She ruled with her husband until his death and was appointed regent over her young nephew, **Thutmose III**. She decided to crown herself pharaoh, giving herself more control.

Queen Hatshepsut's twenty-year rule was peaceful, and trade was developed with other nations.

Hyksos A people who invaded Egypt at the beginning of the New Kingdom; their technology included bronze and iron weapons and horse-drawn chariots.

Hatshepsut Queen of Egypt; ruled during the New Kingdom.

Thutmose III Became the ruling pharaoh of Egypt after Queen Hatshepsut's death.

Gold burial mask of Tutankhamun

What was the significance of Howard Carter's discovery?

After Hatshepsut's death, Thutmose III became the ruling pharaoh. He was the greatest Egyptian warrior king. He used chariots to invade Palestine and Syria. During his reign, the Egyptian empire stretched to the Euphrates River in the northeast.

Not all pharaohs began ruling as adults. **Tutankhamun** was about nine years old when he became pharaoh. He died when he was about eighteen or nineteen and was buried at Thebes in the Valley of the Kings. Tutankhamun is famous primarily for his tomb, which is described as one of the greatest archaeological discoveries of all time.

The British archaeologist **Howard Carter** discovered the tomb in 1922. The tomb was found in very good condition. It contained thousands of artifacts and much wealth. Carter spent over eight years cataloging all the statues, furniture, toys, pottery, and precious objects he found. Because of Tutankhamun's tomb, historians now have extensive information about how the pharaohs of the New Kingdom lived and died.

Rameses II was one of the last pharaohs who kept the empire strong. He defeated the Hittites, the greatest enemy of Egypt at the time. Later, he signed a lasting peace treaty with a new Hittite king. Rameses also built some of the greatest temples in Egypt. The temple at Karnak is the most famous. Rameses had many colossal statues of himself made.

Rameses II is also known as Rameses the Great. When he died, he was buried in a beautiful tomb. Although grave robbers broke into his tomb, his mummy was not destroyed. The mummy is currently in the Egyptian Museum in Cairo.

Egypt grew weaker after the death of Rameses II. The pharaohs were no longer able to protect the empire from invaders. Two hundred years after the death of Rameses, people from the west invaded Egypt. From then on, Egyptians were ruled by foreigners until the 1900s, when the modern nation of Egypt was formed.

Tutankhamun Pharaoh of Egypt at the age of nine; died around age eighteen or nineteen; sometimes referred to as King Tut; known for his tomb of treasures.

Howard Carter Archaeologist who discovered and cataloged Tutankhamun's tomb.

Rameses II One of the last pharaohs of Egypt; also called Rameses the Great.

 Why did the pyramids from the Old Kingdom outlast pyramids from the Middle Kingdom?

How did the Egyptians witness the power of the one true God?

What were some of the cultural developments in ancient Egypt?

Culture of Egypt
Social Classes

The social structure of ancient Egypt can be arranged in a triangle-shaped diagram called a **social pyramid**. An Egyptian's social class depended on his wealth or power. At the bottom of the social pyramid are the farmers, merchants, servants, and slaves. They represent the largest social class. On the next pyramid level are the priests, soldiers, scribes, and artisans. The next level includes the nobles and the pharaoh's generals and viziers. Viziers were the highest-ranking officials under the pharaoh. At the top of the pyramid is the pharaoh, who makes up the smallest social class.

Anyone from a lower class could rise to a higher class if he gained the pharaoh's favor. Even a foreign slave could rise to a higher class. For example, the Hebrew slave Joseph became very powerful and was second only to Pharaoh in authority.

Unlike many ancient civilizations, some women in Egypt held important roles. Women were able to buy and sell property. Many worked as farmers or merchants and at other jobs usually held by men in other cultures. Some women even served in the temples as priestesses.

Music

The ancient Egyptians loved music. It was part of their everyday life, including celebrations. Farmers sang while they worked in the fields. Children sang as they played. Craftsmen and traders sang as they worked in their shops or sailed up and down the Nile. The pharaoh and the nobles often had musicians entertain them. Even slaves made their chores less tedious by singing. Religious ceremonies used many songs in praise and prayer to the gods.

One of the main themes in Egyptian music was the Nile. The people sang thankful praises to the great river.

social pyramid A triangle-shaped diagram that shows the social structure of a society.

A scarab amulet was worn to ward off evil. Some were impressed with a seal or emblem representing a name or religious belief.

Daily Life

Egyptians ate bread made from either wheat or barley. They also ate melons, cucumbers, onions, dates, and figs. The river supplied them with many kinds of fish and waterfowl. They also raised animals for meat.

Each day, they wore clean clothing made of linen, cotton, or wool. The Egyptians also wove flax, a type of plant, into cloth to make some of their clothes. Men wore skirts that wrapped around their waists. This type of skirt was tied with a belt. Women wore long, sleeveless dresses. Young children did not wear any clothes until they were old enough for school. Then they dressed like the adults.

Egyptians were known for their cleanliness. Ancient washrooms have been found in some of the ruins. The plagues of frogs, lice, and flies sent by God were a terrible trial for the Egyptians.

Both men and women wore wigs made from human hair and beeswax. Women usually wore their hair long, and men were bald or cropped their hair just above their shoulders.

Men and women also wore cosmetics. They used black cosmetic powder called kohl to make their eyes look bigger. The kohl also protected their eyes from the glare of the sun. Egyptians loved strong-scented perfumes. On special occasions, a woman might wear a cone made of scented animal fat on her wig. As the fat melted, the perfume was released.

Both men and women wore necklaces that were often made of gold and beads. Many necklaces had **amulets**. The Egyptians believed that the amulet protected its wearer from evil spirits.

Boys of upper-class families started school at age four or five. Boys of the middle-class and lower-class families did not attend school. They learned the same trades as their fathers. Girls from all classes did not go to school but were instead trained by their mothers to run a household. Many girls were married around age thirteen.

Everyone worked for the pharaoh. Most people were paid with food and clothing rather than with money. Most of the people were farmers or other laborers.

Egyptians believed that after they died, they would be rewarded according to the good things they had done. The people put much time and effort into preparing for death and the afterlife.

---

amulet A large ornament worn on a necklace and thought to protect the wearer from evil spirits.

 What social classes existed in the Egyptian civilization?

Anubis   Osiris   Isis   Horus   Hathor

 What was the significance of religion in the daily lives of the Egyptians?

Religion

The Egyptians were polytheistic. They had hundreds of gods. There were gods of the land and of the sun, moon, and stars. There were gods who provided protection. There were even gods who represented daily activities. Families built altars in their houses to worship their favorite gods.

Egyptians believed that Ra, the sun god, created and ruled the world. During the Middle Kingdom, the priests of Thebes joined the god Amun to Ra. They called these gods as they were joined together *Amun-Ra*. They also told everyone how to worship. Having control over the worship system made the priests very powerful.

Osiris, the god of the underworld, was a favorite of the Egyptians. They believed that after burial, a dead person traveled by boat to the Hall of Judgment, where Osiris presided. Anubis, the jackal-headed god, weighed the dead person's heart against the Feather of Truth. Often, a papyrus copy of the *Book of the Dead* was buried with the person. This scroll provided instructions of what to do and say in the afterlife. The following translation is a portion of text from the book. It tells the person what to chant to declare his innocence during judgment.

> I have not committed sins against men. . . .
> I have not made any man to weep. I have not committed murder. I have not given the order for murder to be committed. I have not caused calamities to befall men and women. . . . I have not carried away the milk from the mouths of children. I have not driven the cattle away from their pastures. I have not snared the geese in the goose-pens of the gods. . . . I have not stopped water when it should flow. I have not made a cutting in a canal of running water. . . . I am pure. I am pure. I am pure.

continued on page 68

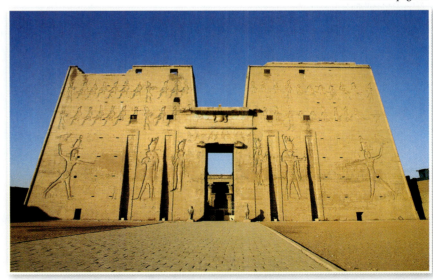

Temple of Horus in Edfu, Egypt. What are some differences between this temple and churches you have seen?

LIFE IN THEBES

Citizenship
Official documents reveal that both men and women were citizens. Most ancient Egyptians grew up, lived, and died in the area where they were born.

Justice
The Egyptians practiced law and order. There were judges and tax collectors. Honor was important and valued. It was expected that neighbors and their property be respected. Ancient hieroglyphs depict guards who defend public places and apprehend criminals.

Arts, Sciences, and Written Language
The hot, dry climate of Egypt preserved artifacts such as sculptures, paintings, official records, and religious documents. These artifacts allow historians to learn how Egyptians lived.

Egyptians used physics to move massive blocks of stone for the pyramids. They used math to figure taxes, keep records, and develop plans for machines and buildings.

The Nile provided a highway for travel and trade.

Job Specialization
Most people were farmers who raised animals and crops. There were many craftsmen such as carpenters and potters. There were also traders, doctors, scribes, and engineers.

Power
The pharaoh determined the law and carried out justice. Sometimes the pharaoh would delegate responsibilities to a representative.

Organized Cities and Government
Thebes was a political city where governmental officials lived and worked. The government created laws, taxed the citizens, constructed temples, oversaw trade, and defended Egypt's interests.

Religion
The priests performed rituals in the temples to the gods. They anointed the statues with oils and perfumes daily. The priest would clothe and paint the god. Offerings of food would be left for the statue.

Environment
Egyptians used mud to make bricks such as the ones that formed the wall around Thebes. They used the minerals in their land for activities such as preserving and adding flavor to food, making medicine, and tanning hides. They planted crops in the fertile soil by the Nile. The Nile also provided a source of fish, waterfowl, and water.

Key Themes of Civilization
- Justice
- Power
- Citizenship
- Environment

Features of a Civilization
- Organized cities and government
- Social classes
- Job specialization
- Arts, sciences, and written language
- Religion

A swim in the Nile provided relief from dry, hot weather.

Egyptians used the shadoof to move water to the irrigation canals.

EGYPTIAN BELIEFS

Ever since the Fall, every culture has had to deal with death. The Egyptians believed that they would be judged on whether they lived according to the justice and order that the gods had put into the world. If their works were good enough, they would spend the afterlife in a place of peace. Their burial practices were based on the belief that preservation of the deceased body would preserve that person's soul in the afterlife. But they did not believe that the body would ever live again.

The idea that people's souls will continue to live after death and the idea that people will face judgment for how they lived are true ideas. The Bible says, "It is appointed unto men once to die, but after this the judgment" (Hebrews 9:27; see also Revelation 20:12). But the Bible teaches that no one will be declared righteous before God on the basis of their works. No human works meet God's perfect standard of justice.

Stele showing Akhenaten and his family giving an offering to Aten, the sun god

continued from page 65

The Egyptians taught that Isis, the wife of Osiris, protected children. Horus, the son of Isis and Osiris, had the body of a man and the head of a falcon or a hawk. These three gods formed the model family that Egyptians tried to imitate. There were also gods of medicine, education, music, and even love. Hathor, the goddess of love, joy, and fertility, was sometimes depicted with the body of a woman and the head of a cow.

Egyptians believed that the pharaoh was the son of Horus. They believed the pharaoh was a god and the high priest of Egypt. Every morning, after washing and dressing, the pharaoh went to the temple to awaken the idol of Horus. He washed and clothed the idol, gave it food, and put makeup on it. After that ceremony, the people believed the day could proceed with the god's blessing.

One pharaoh of the New Kingdom tried to change the Egyptian beliefs. His name was Amenhotep IV. He believed there was only one great god, called Aten. The pharaoh even changed his own name to **Akhenaten** to show that he worshiped the god Aten.

The priests of the old gods did not like losing their influence. The Egyptian people did not want to give up the old gods either. After Akhenaten's death, young Tutankhamun and his advisers returned Egypt to the old religion.

Ancient Egypt was a great civilization for many centuries, but its greatness did not last forever. This greatness was also marred by false religion and injustice. In the Exodus of the Hebrews, God showed Himself triumphant over the gods of Egypt. Later, God allowed Egypt to fall to several other peoples, including the Kushites, the Assyrians, the Persians, the Greeks, and the Romans. Egypt was proud of its achievements, but it gave no glory to God for what it achieved. Ezekiel 29:3–4 says that Egypt fell because God judged it for its pride. But one day God will show mercy to Egypt. In Isaiah 19:21–22, the prophet tells of a time when Egypt will turn to the Lord and He will heal them.

Akhenaten Pharaoh during the New Kingdom; tried to change the Egyptians' beliefs about many gods and believed there was only one god, Aten.

 Why is it impossible to be declared righteous before God by good works alone?

How were the Kushites able to conquer the Egyptians?

Kush

Along the Nile River to the south of Egypt was a land called **Kush**. The name *Kush* is known from ancient Egyptian artifacts and writings and is also found in the Bible. During the Roman period, this area was referred to as *Nubia*, the Egyptian word for "gold."

Just as the Nile was vital to Egypt's survival, it was also very important to the survival of Kush. Many of the Kushite villages depended on the Nile for food, water, transportation, and trade.

Kushite Culture

The Kushites lived in farming villages where the people were either farmers or animal herders. Like the Egyptians, they used the shadoof and an irrigation system to be able to farm more land. A water wheel was introduced later from Asia. In the southern part of Kush, the villagers raised cattle on the savanna, a grassy plain.

The people of Kush had an abundance of natural resources, including gold, copper, fertile soil, ebony (dark, hard wood), and ivory. The Kushites' diet was more limited than the Egyptians' diet because Kush had less fertile ground for farming. The Kushites grew wheat, barley, sorghum, and a variety of vegetables. They ate fish, beef, and birds. Hippopotamus, ostrich, and turtle were delicacies that the people enjoyed on special occasions. The Kushites also grew cotton to make cloth.

The Kushites used palm wood and bricks for building. They fashioned pottery out of clay. They were also skilled hunters. They used the bow and arrow to hunt elephants, lions, leopards, and panthers. Elephants were tamed and used for work. Sometimes the Kushites traded animals with other civilizations.

Kush An ancient land along the Nile stretching from just south of Egypt to Khartoum in present-day Sudan.

Wall painting in the tomb of Amenhotep, viceroy of Kush, showing Nubians bringing tribute to the pharaoh

How do these pyramids compare with the Egyptian pyramids?

Kushites developed the Meroitic script that stemmed from Egyptian hieroglyphics.

Like women in the Egyptian civilization, women in Kush held a variety of roles. There were female warriors as well as queens and priestesses. But, as in Egypt, women were still the primary caregivers for the children and maintained the households.

The people of Kush developed two systems of written language. One system was a form of hieroglyphics similar to the Egyptian hieroglyphics. The other system was a form of script, or handwriting, with symbols that looked like letters. This script used a limited number of symbols to form words. The script language was later called **Meroitic**. It was named after the people of Meroë, the ancient city where the language was first used. Scholars have been able to decipher only a little of the Meroitic language.

The Kushites, like the Egyptians, were polytheistic in their religion. They pictured their primary god, Amun, with a head like a sheep's. The architecture of their pyramids and temples was also similar to those found in Egypt.

Meroitic A script language developed by the people of Kush.

History of Kush

Kush began as a strong village. As it gradually extended its power and conquered smaller villages around it, Kush developed into a civilization. The people of Kush established Kerma as a capital city. Kerma began trading goods with Egypt.

The three main settlements in Kush were Kerma, Napata, and Meroë. Napata was the capital of Kush for many years. Napata was the main trading center and was where many tombs were built.

Pyramids in ancient Kush were not built for just the pharaoh. Many pyramids were constructed for priests and high-ranking noblemen. Unfortunately, many tombs and temples of ancient Kush are covered by Lake Nasser.

As the Kushites became wealthier and more numerous, the Egyptians began to fear their growing power. During Egypt's Middle Kingdom, the pharaoh led his army to invade Kush. The Egyptians completely destroyed Kerma and conquered Kush. Over time, Kush adopted the Egyptian culture. The Kushites dressed like the Egyptians, worshiped Egyptian gods, and changed the Egyptian hieroglyphics to fit their own language.

THE REGION TODAY

Sudan

Location
Ancient Kush was located in northeastern Africa along the Nile River in northern Sudan. Sudan is bordered by Egypt to the north; the Central African Republic, the Democratic Republic of the Congo, Uganda, and Kenya to the south; the Red Sea, Eritrea, and Ethiopia to the east; and Libya and Chad to the west.

Climate
Sudan has hot, dry summers with moderate winters. Temperatures range from 100°F in the summer to 55°F in the winter. The northern part of the land has little or no rainfall, while the southern part has a rainy season.

Topography
The land is dominated by the Nile River and five of its six cataracts. To the east and west of the Nile is desert. The southern region is savanna.

Natural Resources
The land's greatest natural resource is water from the Nile River. Other resources include gold, ivory, ebony, and iron ore.

What helped sustain life in both Kush and Egypt?

THE ASWAN HIGH DAM

Floods and droughts have been a part of Egypt's entire history (Genesis 41:35–36). When the Nile River flooded, it often destroyed the land and the crops. Throughout history, Egyptians desired to control the water of the annual floods. In the late 1890s, while Egypt was under British rule, construction on a dam began. This dam was completed in 1902. It was located near the border of Egypt and Sudan. The dam helped control the annual flooding and held water in a reservoir for later release.

Over the next thirty years, the height of the dam was raised, and hydroelectric generators were added. By the 1940s, the height of the dam needed to be raised again. Instead, the decision was made to build a second dam further upstream. After ten years of construction, the **Aswan High Dam** was completed in 1970. The first dam, known as the Old Aswan Dam, remains but has limited function.

The Aswan High Dam formed a large manmade lake, **Lake Nasser**. The water in this reservoir began covering many of the temples, tombs, and villages of ancient Kush. Archaeologists from other countries helped save as many artifacts as they could before the area was completely flooded. The temples at Abu Simbel were moved to higher ground. Many other monuments were documented before the lake waters covered them.

Not everyone approves of the dam. Silt gets caught behind the dam, so the area below the dam no longer receives rich nutrients for farming. Fertilizers have to be used instead. The dam has also affected fishing because some fish fed on the silt in the water. Therefore, the dam has caused the fish population to decrease, which has affected people downstream who depended on the fish for food.

Aswan High Dam The manmade dam across the Nile River that formed Lake Nasser.

Lake Nasser The manmade lake formed by the Aswan High Dam.

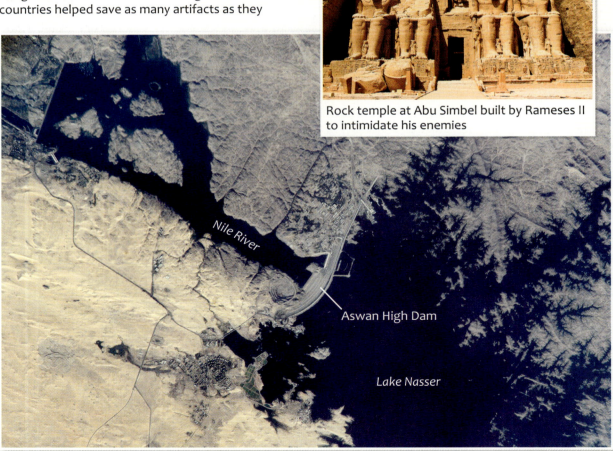

Rock temple at Abu Simbel built by Rameses II to intimidate his enemies

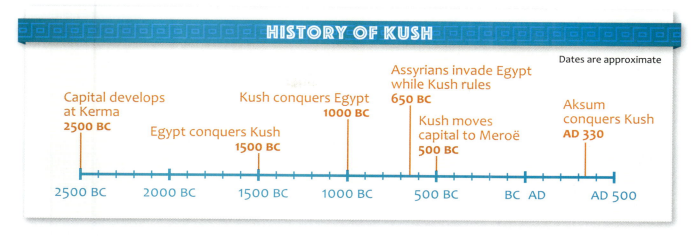

Egypt dominated the Kushites for about five hundred years. But toward the end of Egypt's New Kingdom, Kush became stronger. Egypt eventually lost control, and the Kushites established their independence. The Kushite king became known as a pharaoh, and Napata became the capital. Under the rule of Piye, Kush conquered Egypt. Kush ruled Egypt for about forty years.

In the mid-600s BC, the Assyrians invaded Egypt. The Assyrians had the advantage of iron weapons, and the Kushites were unable to defend Egypt. The Assyrians drove out the Kushites, who returned to their homeland.

The Kushites established a new capital at Meroë. In the surrounding areas, they discovered iron ore deposits. Iron became a valuable item to make weapons and tools for their own use as well as for trade with other civilizations. Kush exported gold, pottery, tools, ivory, leopard skins, ostrich feathers, and elephants. Slaves were also exported. The Kushites imported jewelry and other goods.

After a period of about four hundred years, the Kushite civilization began to decline. They had used nearly all their natural resources. Most of the trees had been burned as fuel. The savannas were overgrazed, and the cattle herds had diminished. Trade began to dwindle.

To the southeast of Kush, in what is Ethiopia today, the Aksum civilization had developed. Eventually the Aksum people destroyed Meroë and took over the land of Kush in AD 330. The Kushite kingdom had existed for more than one thousand years.

End of the Kushite Civilization

The Kushite civilization ceased to exist, but God used each civilization for His plan. Egypt was the place where Joseph rose from slavery to second in command to the pharaoh and provided for the Israelites during a famine. Egypt was the place where Moses became a son to the pharaoh and leader of the Israelites. God has a special plan for each civilization and person that He has created.

Tomb painting of trade in ancient Kush. What are some of the items Kushites traded?

Why was preserving the temples at Abu Simbel important?

What are two advantages and two disadvantages of the Aswan High Dam?

4 ANCIENT ISRAEL

FOCUS

The nation of Israel is God's chosen people through whom all the nations of the world are blessed.

Exodus ca. 1446 BC	Kingdom divides ca. 922 BC		Romans destroy Jerusalem AD 70	
1500 BC	1000 BC	500 BC	BC AD	AD 500
	ca. 1020 BC Saul anointed as first king	586 BC Babylonian Empire destroys Jerusalem		

Why would a king need 10,000 snails? Thousands of a special kind of snail from the deep waters of the Mediterranean Sea had to be caught, dried, boiled, and crushed to produce enough expensive and unfading red, blue, and purple dyes to color just one royal robe. These dyes were worth more than their weight in gold and were used only for the most important purposes. The Tabernacle, according to Exodus 26:1, was decked with red, purple, and blue curtains that may have been made with such dyes.

Do you think one girl in this illustration is royal? It is not likely, although Tirzah is wearing a blue veil. But she is probably wealthier than Mahlah, the girl she is running toward. Her blue headdress might have been made with linen thread dipped in dye made from lichens rather than the dye from snails. She is also wearing sandals. Most people went barefoot indoors, and some people went barefoot outside to save wear on shoes.

The process of producing clothing involved many people—from the herders of sheep and growers of flax, to the spinners of thread and yarn, to the dyers, to the weavers, to the makers of cloaks and tunics. Many women would use wool or linen thread to weave fabric for their own households. In addition, villages sometimes had groups of people skilled in the textile trade. For example, 1 Chronicles 4:21 refers to makers of fine linen in Ashbea.

Orchil, a purple dye, was produced from lichens of the genus *Roccella*. As the "poor person's purple," it was cheaper to produce than the dye made from snails but also more likely to fade.

How is the history of Israel different from the history of other nations?

Israel's Beginning

Israel's history is unlike the history of any other nation. Much of Israel's history was recorded by prophets. God's purposes and actions in history are revealed more clearly in Israel's history than in that of any other nation.

Around 2090 BC, God spoke to a man named Abram, who lived in Ur of the Chaldeans. The people there worshiped many gods. Abram believed in the same gods as those people. But God chose to reveal Himself to Abram. God told Abram to leave Ur and to travel to wherever God showed him. Abram then believed in the one true God.

God gave Abram many promises and changed his name to **Abraham**. These promises are called the **Abrahamic Covenant**. In this *covenant*, or binding agreement, God promised Abraham that his descendants would become a great nation. God promised to bless Abraham. God told him that all the nations of the world would be blessed through him.

Abraham showed that he believed God by doing what God said. He moved his family to Canaan, the land where God told him to go. Because Abraham believed God, God declared this former idolater to be a righteous man.

ABRAHAMIC COVENANT

Genesis 12:1–7

When God created Adam and Eve, He blessed them. He blessed their seed so that they would be fruitful and multiply. He blessed them by giving them rule over land. But when Adam and Eve sinned, the blessing on land and seed turned to judgment. As part of God's plan of redemption, God will turn the judgment into blessing again. God blessed Abraham's seed. God promised Abraham that his offspring would become a great nation. God also blessed Abraham regarding land. His offspring would live in the land that God gave them. Through Abraham, God would bless all the families of the earth. Jesus, a descendant of Abraham, would offer the blessing of redemption to all people.

Abraham Man whose descendants became the nation of Israel.

Abrahamic Covenant The agreement in which God promised Abraham that his descendants would become a great nation and that through him all the nations of the world would be blessed.

Israel The nation God made from the descendants of Jacob; named after God's special name for Jacob; the name of the Northern Kingdom after Israel split into two kingdoms.

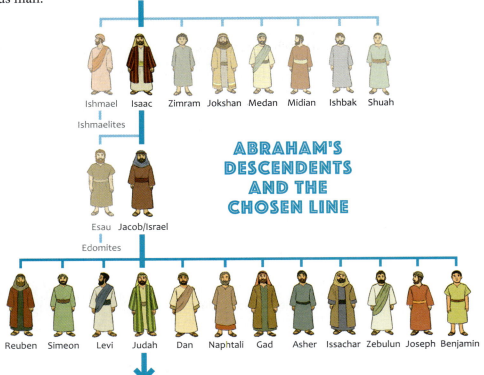

ABRAHAM'S DESCENDENTS AND THE CHOSEN LINE

Abraham → Ishmael (Ishmaelites), Isaac, Zimram, Jokshan, Medan, Midian, Ishbak, Shuah

Isaac → Esau (Edomites), Jacob/Israel

Jacob/Israel → Reuben, Simeon, Levi, Judah, Dan, Naphtali, Gad, Asher, Issachar, Zebulun, Joseph, Benjamin

Why did Jacob's family migrate to Egypt?

Abraham and His Sons

The nation of Israel was a result of God's promises. But it did not form right away. Abraham had several sons, but not all of them were included in all the promises of the Abrahamic Covenant. God chose only Isaac among Abraham's sons, and among Isaac's sons, only Jacob was chosen.

But then God chose all of Jacob's twelve sons to inherit the promises. The twelve tribes that came from them formed a new nation. This nation was called **Israel** because that was a special name that God had given Jacob.

The Israelites in Egypt

During Jacob's lifetime, a great famine struck Canaan. God had providentially moved Jacob's son Joseph to Egypt years before the famine. God enabled Joseph to interpret the pharaoh's dream, which predicted the famine. Joseph was then made the second highest ruler in Egypt. Joseph oversaw the building of storehouses to prepare for the famine. When the famine struck, people from many nations went to Egypt for food. In this way, Joseph was a blessing to many nations. Joseph's father and brothers and their families migrated to Egypt. Joseph made sure that they were given a portion of good land to live in.

After about four hundred years, the families of Jacob and his sons had grown into a large nation. A new pharaoh came to power, and the Egyptians became concerned about the growth of the Israelites. Afraid that they would become too powerful, the pharaoh enslaved the Israelites. But they continued to grow in number. So the pharaoh commanded that all the male babies be killed.

The people of Israel cried out to God. He heard their cry and called on a man named Moses to deliver the Israelites.

Moses' early life reveals God's protection. When Moses was a baby, his mother hid him so he would not be killed. The pharaoh's daughter found him and had compassion on him. She allowed the mother of Moses to care for him while he was a baby. When Moses was old enough, the pharaoh's daughter raised him as an Egyptian. But Moses knew he was an Israelite. One day, he saw an Egyptian taskmaster beating a fellow Israelite, so Moses killed the taskmaster. Because of this murder, Moses fled from Egypt. Later, God called him to return and lead the Israelites out of slavery, but Moses made many excuses. He did not feel qualified, yet God made it clear to Moses that He would deliver His people, and He wanted Moses to lead them.

Moses returned to Egypt and told the pharaoh to let God's people go. But the pharaoh's heart was hardened, and he did not let them go. Because of the pharaoh's stubbornness, God unleashed ten plagues on Egypt. God wanted the Israelites, the Egyptians, and all people to know that He is the one true God. The ten plagues ended with a final judgment on Egypt in which all the firstborn in the land were killed. God instructed the Israelites to spread the blood of a sacrificed lamb on each doorpost and on the beam above the door. Their obedience protected them from death when God judged Egypt. The Jews still remember this event during a holiday called **Passover**.

After the death of his firstborn, the pharaoh agreed to let the Israelites leave Egypt. This event in Israel's history is known as the **Exodus**, which took place about 1446 BC.

Moses, following God's direction, led the nation of Israel into the Sinai wilderness. The nation gathered at the base of Mount Sinai, and God declared that Israel was to be a nation set apart from all other nations. Israel was to point these nations to the true God. In this way, Israel would be a blessing to them.

MOSES

What: leader of the Israelites
When: ca. 1526 BC–1406 BC
Where: Egypt and the wilderness

Moses was born into a Hebrew slave family. After the daughter of Pharaoh found him in a basket on the Nile River, she raised him as her own son. Moses grew up with all the benefits of the highest class of people in Egypt. Having been taught all the wisdom of Egypt, he became mighty in his words and deeds (Acts 7:22).

But then Moses witnessed an Egyptian beating a Hebrew. Moses reacted and killed the Egyptian. Afraid because of what he had done, Moses fled to Midian, where he lived with a Midianite family and became a shepherd. There the Lord spoke to Moses from a burning bush and ordered him to lead God's people from slavery. So Moses became the leader of Israel.

God then took the Israelites out of slavery in Egypt. At Mount Sinai, God revealed His law to the Israelites through Moses. Moses continued to lead as God brought the Israelites to the Promised Land.

THE TEN PLAGUES OF EGYPT

1 **Water to blood** Exodus 7:14–25
2 **Frogs** Exodus 8:1–15
3 **Gnats** Exodus 8:16–19
4 **Flies** Exodus 8:20–32
5 **Plague on cattle** Exodus 9:1–7
6 **Boils** Exodus 9:8–12
7 **Hail** Exodus 9:13–35
8 **Locusts** Exodus 10:1–20
9 **Darkness** Exodus 10:21–29
10 **Death of the firstborn** Exodus 11:1–12:36

Passover A celebration that honors the Lord's deliverance of the Israelites from slavery in Egypt.
Exodus The Israelites' departure from Egypt.

 How did God fulfill His promise to bless all families of the earth through Abraham?

What symbolized God's presence with the Israelites?

The Mosaic Covenant

At Mount Sinai, God gave the nation of Israel His law through Moses. This law is known as the Mosaic law. God commanded the Israelites to obey His law.

In most ancient civilizations, the king or the ruler made the laws. In ancient Israel, God made the laws. The most well-known laws that God gave Israel are the Ten Commandments. Many of the laws applied the Ten Commandments to specific situations. For instance, one of the Ten Commandments is "Thou shalt not steal." But what if someone allows his oxen to graze in someone else's field? That is a kind of stealing. One of the Mosaic laws says that the offending person has to repay what is lost with the best of his own produce.

Other laws dealt with how Israel was supposed to worship God. They dealt with sacrifices and with how the tabernacle should be built. Finally, the Mosaic law had laws about what activities led a person to be considered clean or unclean. Being clean did not mean that a person was without sin, and being unclean did not mean that a person was a sinner. In fact, it was impossible to avoid becoming unclean because normal daily life led to uncleanness and the need to perform a ritual to become clean. These laws were like picture lessons. The need for continual cleansing from uncleanliness reminded the people of the continual need for cleansing from sin.

If the people of Israel obeyed the Mosaic law, God promised to bless them. But if the Israelites chose to disobey, God promised to punish the nation of Israel with famine, military defeat, and exile. The laws, with their promises and threatened judgments, are called the **Mosaic Covenant**.

MOSAIC COVENANT

Exodus 19:3–6

God gave Israel laws that told the people how to live to please Him. If they obeyed these laws, the nations around Israel would see the great and true God, and He promised to bless Israel. If the Israelites disobeyed, God promised to punish them. Israel's history under the Mosaic Covenant shows that it is impossible to keep all of God's law with one's own efforts.

TEN COMMANDMENTS

Exodus 20

1. Thou shalt have no other gods before me.
2. Thou shalt not make unto thee any graven image.
3. Thou shalt not take the name of the Lord thy God in vain.
4. Remember the sabbath day, to keep it holy.
5. Honour thy father and thy mother.
6. Thou shalt not kill.
7. Thou shalt not commit adultery.
8. Thou shalt not steal.
9. Thou shalt not bear false witness against thy neighbour.
10. Thou shalt not covet.

God told the Israelites that one of the reasons He gave them the Mosaic Covenant was so other nations could see the wisdom and righteousness of God. If Israel had obeyed God's laws, the other nations would have seen how wise God was in giving them such good laws that made their nation work so well.

Unfortunately, the Israelites broke the Mosaic Covenant repeatedly throughout their history. Even so, many nations have seen the wisdom in the Mosaic law, and these laws have shaped the laws of other nations.

Mosaic Covenant The agreement in which God gave the nation of Israel His law through Moses.

Worship in the Wilderness

When Adam and Eve first sinned, God withdrew His presence from them. The Garden of Eden was no longer available to people. God told the Israelites to build a place for worship. God wanted a **tabernacle** to be built as a symbol of God's presence with His people.

The priests offered a daily sacrifice for the sins of the Israelites. Then once each year, the high priest entered the most holy place in the tabernacle and sprinkled a sacrificed animal's blood on the ark of the covenant.

God gave Moses a plan for the materials, the size, and the placement of each part of the tabernacle. The workers took special care to follow God's plan as they built. The items in the tabernacle were symbols of God's holiness, justice, and other attributes. The tabernacle reminded the Israelites that God was providing a way for them to have a relationship with the one true God.

Religion

The main characteristic of the Israelite religion is **monotheism**. The Hebrew name for the one true God is **Yahweh**. The Bible is clear about there being only one God. The key text for this truth is Deuteronomy 6:4, which says, "Hear, O Israel: The Lord our God is one Lord." Jews call this important verse the *Shema*, which is a prayer they recite daily.

The covenants God gave His people were an important part of the Israelite religion. The Abrahamic Covenant gave the basis for Israel as a special, chosen nation. The Mosaic Covenant gave the guidelines for life that the Israelites were to follow. The Davidic Covenant and the New Covenant include a promised future for Israel despite her disobedience.

God commanded the Israelites to observe their deliverance by celebrating the Passover. The Jews still celebrate Passover each year to remember what God did for them. Passover occurs in March or April. Leviticus 23:5 tells us that Passover is celebrated "in the fourteenth day of the first month." The first month of the Jewish calendar is Nisan.

The tabernacle, later replaced by the temple, was the center of worship for God's people. Three times a year, all the men of Israel traveled to the capital city of **Jerusalem** for the Feast of Unleavened Bread (Passover), the Feast of Weeks, and the Feast of Tabernacles (Exodus 23:14–19). The Feast of Unleavened Bread lasted seven days. This feast was a time when the Israelites celebrated God's leading them out of bondage in Egypt. The Feast of Weeks was a time of celebration and thanksgiving for God's provision.

HEBREW MONTHS

Number	Name	Days	Equivalent
1	Nisan	30	Mar.–Apr.
2	Iyar	29	Apr.–May
3	Sivan	30	May–June
4	Tammuz	29	June–July
5	Av	30	July–Aug.
6	Elul	29	Aug.–Sept.
7	Tishri	30	Sept.–Oct.
8	Heshvan	29 or 30	Oct.–Nov.
9	Kislev	29 or 30	Nov.–Dec.
10	Tevet	29	Dec.–Jan.
11	Shevat	30	Jan.–Feb.
12	Adar	29 or 30	Feb.–Mar.

It lasted seven full weeks. The Feast of Tabernacles lasted seven days. It was a time to remember the forty years of wandering in the wilderness.

The Day of Atonement was another important time of worship for the Israelites. The Day of Atonement was the one day every year that the high priest could enter the most sacred room in the tabernacle or temple, the holy of holies. He would sprinkle sacrificial blood on top of the ark of the covenant. This act was a symbol of **atonement** for the people's sins. True atonement was made possible by Christ's sacrificial death on the cross.

Although many religious celebrations and ceremonies took place during the Old Testament period, most Israelites did not worship God as He commanded. The Israelites often abandoned the worship of Yahweh to worship the gods of other nations.

---

tabernacle The portable place of worship used by the Israelites in the wilderness; symbolized God's presence with the people.
monotheism The belief in one God.
Yahweh The Hebrew name for the one true God.
Jerusalem The capital of Israel.
atonement The restoration of the broken relationship between God and people.

The ark of the covenant was in the holy of holies and was a symbol of God on His throne. The lid was called the mercy seat.

The high priest was the only person who could enter the holy of holies. The colors he wore were the same colors as the curtains in the holy of holies, symbolizing his bringing the holy place to the people.

As a mediator, the high priest brought the people before God and he brought God before the people. Once a year, he entered the holy of holies to sprinkle the blood of a sacrificed animal on the mercy seat.

The incense altar stood directly across from the ark. It was made of acacia wood and covered with gold.

When the Israelites traveled through the wilderness, they placed the tabernacle in the center of their camp as a symbol of God's special presence with His people.

The lampstand probably symbolized the tree of life, which represented eternal life. The lampstand showed that God was providing a way for His people to have eternal life.

The table of showbread was for holding the bread of His presence. Twelve loaves of unleavened bread were placed in two rows of six on the table to represent the twelve tribes of Israel.

 Should God's laws and people's laws be considered equal?

What yearly act did the high priest perform to symbolize the atonement for sin?

What happened when the Israelites did not trust God to help them conquer the land of Canaan?

Dwelling in Canaan

God led the Israelites from Sinai to the edge of the land of Canaan. Along the way, the people complained about God's care of them. They lacked faith, forgetting the mighty acts God had done in leading them out of Egypt. They did not believe God's promise to help them take the land from the Canaanites. Because they did not trust God, they wandered for forty years in the desert before entering the Promised Land.

Entering the Promised Land

Before the Israelites could live in the land, they had to conquer it. Because the people of Canaan were very wicked, God commanded the Israelites to purge them from the land.

Moses' successor, Joshua, led the Israelites to obey God and conquer Canaan. God showed the people that when they obeyed Him, He would bless them and do miraculous works on their behalf. When the people disobeyed God, He punished them with defeat.

God helped the Israelites by parting the **Jordan River**. He also caused the walls of Jericho to fall. Under Joshua's leadership, the people of Israel conquered the land.

Judges and Kings

Although God enabled the Israelites to conquer the land of Canaan, the Israelites failed to obey. They allowed some of the people who lived there to remain alive. Furthermore, the Israelites did not show the nations the greatness of God by living according to His laws. Instead, the Israelites became more and more like the wicked nations around them. They began to worship the same false gods and to commit the same sins. As promised in the Mosaic Covenant, God punished them by sending other nations to rule over parts of Israel. When the Israelites cried out for help, God sent deliverers. But each time, the Israelites went back to doing evil and again suffered defeat from their enemies.

For more than three hundred years, there was a pattern of disobedience and punishment followed by God raising up a judge to lead Israel in repentance and deliverance. Finally, the people of Israel began to believe that the problems with their enemies could be solved in only one way. They asked the last judge, **Samuel**, to give them a king like the other nations.

Israel had several forms of government in its early history. Moses was the leader of the nation during the wilderness wanderings. He appointed overseers of thousands, hundreds, fifties, and tens. These overseers judged cases that the people brought before them. If one overseer was unable to resolve the case, he would refer it to an overseer above him.

When the people were settled in the land, cities and tribes were governed by elders. These were older, wiser men of the cities and tribes. It is not clear how they were chosen for their position.

God also raised up judges to deliver His people from oppressive nations, but the judges were not normal, long-term political leaders.

Beginning with Saul, Israel was governed by kings. Initially, God directly chose the kings, but the elders of the people also had a role to play in appointing the king. Eventually, however, a son of the king was expected to rule after his father's death.

Jordan River A river east of Israel that flows through the Sea of Galilee to the Dead Sea.

Samuel Last judge in Israel; anointed Saul to be king.

THE REGION TODAY

Israel

Location

Israel is located in the Middle East on the eastern shore of the Mediterranean Sea. The ancient territory of Canaan is now Israel, Lebanon, Jordan, and Syria.

Climate

The climate is temperate with mild winters and warm summers. Temperatures range from 48°F in the winter to 90°F in the summer. In the northern mountains, annual precipitation may reach 40 inches. In the southern deserts, there is little rainfall.

Topography

Five major land regions run north to south. The lowland coastal plain lies along the Mediterranean Sea. Rolling hills and valleys lead to the Lebanon Mountains in the northeast. The valley of the Jordan River lies to the east of these hills, and farther east is a large plateau. The desert lies in the southeast.

Natural Resources

Modern Israel has few natural resources. Petroleum and natural gas are available. Bromide and magnesium are extracted from the Dead Sea.

Israel's Twelve Tribes

Israel Then & Now

What places in this region have you heard about in the news?

- Ancient city
— Modern borders
⊙ Modern capital
 Extent of the kingdoms of David and Solomon
 Israel today
 Controlled by Israel

THE PHOENICIANS

Canaan contained several different civilizations. One was the Phoenicians. They were prosperous traders, craftsmen, and businessmen. Traders from other civilizations went to Phoenicia for a purple dye made from shellfish. People used this dye to color cloth. This purple cloth was very popular. It was worn only by royal or wealthy people.

The hills of Phoenicia were covered with forests. Many of the trees in these forests were the famous cedars of Lebanon. David used wood from these forests when he built his palace. Solomon also included Lebanon cedar in the construction of the temple in Jerusalem.

One of the Phoenicians' greatest achievements was the development of an alphabet. In fact, the modern English alphabet can be traced back to the Phoenician alphabet.

The leading city-state of Phoenicia was Tyre. It was located along the eastern coast of the Mediterranean Sea both on the mainland and on an island. Tyre grew wealthy and prosperous through trade. However, the prophet Ezekiel warned that Tyre would be destroyed. Nebuchadnezzar, the Babylonian king, destroyed the mainland section of Tyre in 571 BC. Years later, the city's rubble was thrown into the sea to make a land bridge to the remaining island city of Tyre. After that, it was never again a powerful city.

How were the stones of Tyre used after it was destroyed?

God warned the Israelites that a king would take their sons for his armies. The king would also take their daughters to work in his palace. He would take the people's land and crops to feed his servants and armies. But the people still wanted a king.

About 1020 BC, God told Samuel to anoint **Saul** as Israel's first king. At first, it seemed that Saul would defeat Israel's worst enemies, the Philistines. But Saul refused to obey God. Although Saul was king for many more years, he never led the Israelites to completely defeating the Philistines as the people had hoped.

Because Saul disobeyed God, God chose **David** to replace Saul. Under King David, the Philistine armies were finally defeated. David also captured the Canaanite city of Jerusalem and made it the capital. During his reign, the nation of Israel more than doubled in size.

David was the king of God's special choosing. He would serve as a model for all the kings who followed him. David was not a perfect king. He did some very bad things. But when confronted with his wrongdoing, David confessed his sin and repented.

DAVIDIC COVENANT

2 Samuel 7:8–17

As part of God's promises to restore the blessings of the Creation Mandate, God promised Abraham that kings would come from him. Later God revealed that a great king would come from the tribe of Judah, the tribe from which David came. This king would rule not only over Israel, but also over the whole world. This king would set right all that is wrong in the world. In the Davidic covenant, God promised David that he would always have a legitimate heir to his throne. God would establish David's throne forever. Jesus, David's descendant, will rule from David's throne forever, fulfilling this promise. Jesus is the promised king who will rule over the whole world and set right all that is wrong.

Saul First king of Israel.
David Second king of Israel; loved and obeyed God.

Most importantly, David led the nation in following the true God.

Just as God had made special covenants with Abraham and with Moses and the Israelites, God also made a covenant with David. In the **Davidic Covenant**, God promised that David would have a great name. David's dynasty would last forever, and God would be a father to the Davidic kings. If David's descendants disobeyed God, they would be punished. But God promised that He would fulfill all the promises of the Davidic Covenant eventually.

After David's death in 961 BC, his son Solomon became king. God gave Solomon wisdom and understanding that no other person has ever known. Israel became wealthy during Solomon's reign. Solomon's goblets were all made of gold because silver was so common that it was not valued (1 Kings 10:21–22). He built forts, palaces, and storehouses throughout Israel. His most impressive building project was the temple in Jerusalem. It was built from huge stones and cedar timbers from the Lebanon Mountains. The temple's decorations were made from gold, ivory, and precious stones.

During Solomon's reign, the people of Israel had peace. Yet Solomon disobeyed God and married the daughters of foreign kings to make treaties, or peace agreements, with their countries.

Solomon had seven hundred wives, including Ammonite, Phoenician, and Egyptian princesses. Each wife brought with her the false gods of her people. Even though Solomon worshiped the true God, he began to worship these false gods also. He even built places of worship for these false gods.

Although the kingdom was at peace, the people became discontent. They did not like the heavy burden laid on them by Solomon's building projects. God sent a prophet to tell Solomon of the future. He told Solomon that the peace in the kingdom would not last. The prophet said that after Solomon died, Israel would split into two kingdoms. However, God would keep His promise and permit David's dynasty to continue.

Davidic Covenant The agreement in which God promised to establish David's throne forever.

 Why were the people willing to give up so much to have a king?

ACTIVITY

Identifying Costs and Benefits

Throughout history, people have made decisions. A decision involves choosing between at least two things. As a decision is made, aspects of each choice must be considered. We may call these aspects the rewards and consequences, pros and cons, or benefits and costs.

As a person makes a decision, he must look at the choices or options available. Looking at costs and benefits can help you better understand history and the decisions people made. You can also relate the decisions to choices you have to make.

In this activity, you and a partner will look at a decision that was made in the history of Israel. Together you will list the costs and benefits of that decision. Then you will write about the decision and make a personal application.

1. Get your Bible and the Activity Manual page.
2. With your partner, choose a Bible account on the Activity Manual page.
3. Read the Bible passages. Identify the people involved and the choice that was made. List the options with their costs and benefits on the chart.
4. Write a paragraph summarizing the decision that was made. Include an application to your own life.

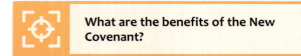 **What are the benefits of the New Covenant?**

Kingdom Divided

At Solomon's death in 922 BC, the twelve tribes of Israel asked Solomon's son Rehoboam if he would rule them more gently than his father had. He denied their request. Rehoboam said that he would rule them more severely. This caused the kingdom to split. The ten northern tribes followed Jeroboam, one of Solomon's officials. They formed the Northern Kingdom. The two southern tribes, Judah and Benjamin, remained under Rehoboam's rule. They established the Southern Kingdom.

The northern tribes kept the name *Israel*. Jeroboam established his capital at Samaria. To keep his people from returning to Jerusalem to worship, he made two golden calves and proclaimed them the gods of Israel. Later Ahab and Jezebel introduced the worship of Baal and Ashtoreth. The Northern Kingdom of Israel experienced some periods of great prosperity. For the next two hundred years,

NEW COVENANT

Jeremiah 31:31–40; 1 Corinthians 11:25

God announced a coming New Covenant in the book of Jeremiah. He promised to restore Israel and Judah from exile. He also promised Jews and Gentiles alike that those who are part of this covenant would receive the Holy Spirit. The Spirit would change their hearts from hard hearts to hearts that love and want to obey God. God also promised that He would forgive His people of all their sins. Jesus enacted this covenant in His death and resurrection. Christians remember this covenant when they partake of the Lord's Supper.

Israel prospered, and their culture continued to develop. Jeroboam continued the heavy taxation that Solomon established. These taxes funded a strong military that allowed Israel to advance economically. The geographical location allowed Israel to have better access to natural resources and to control trade routes. But alongside the prosperity, there was a great deal of injustice toward the poor.

The tribes of the Southern Kingdom took the name *Judah*. They kept the capital at Jerusalem. Judah's kings were all descendants of David. A few of Judah's rulers lived righteously before God, but many were wicked. The people of Judah did not worship the Lord in the way that He had commanded them. They had many places of worship away from the temple. In some of these places, archaeologists have discovered writings about Yahweh and Ashtoreth, a goddess who the writings indicate became Yahweh's wife. God's people had corrupted true worship of Yahweh by mixing it with the false worship of the peoples around them.

Prophets were appointed, or called, by God to deliver messages from God to His people. God used prophets to urge His people back to fellowship with Him. Prophets such as Obadiah, Joel, and Isaiah warned God's people to forsake idolatry. The prophets also spoke out against injustice. Amos prophesied against Israelites who used their wealth and power to oppress others. The warnings also included threats of punishment. The people did not listen to the warnings. In 722 BC, the judgment came. Israel was conquered by the Assyrian Empire, and the people were carried away as captives.

In 586 BC, King Nebuchadnezzar of the Chaldean (New Babylonian) Empire conquered Judah. He destroyed Jerusalem, including the temple. He also took more than ten thousand people away to

exile in Babylon. This time for the Israelites is known as the Babylonian captivity.

Many of those who were left behind fled to Egypt, Moab, or other countries. The dispersion of the Israelites is called the **Diaspora**. About this time, the Israelites became known as the *Jews*.

God had told the Israelites that if they did not keep the Mosaic Covenant, they would be scattered among other nations. The prophets had warned the people that God would be true to His word. But the prophets also had good news. God would make a **New Covenant** with His people. He would restore the Israelites to their land and change their hearts so they would love and obey Him. The New Covenant was God's promise of forgiveness of sin and restored fellowship. Christ's sacrificial death on the cross is the basis of the New Covenant.

God's People in Exile

When an empire made war and conquered a nation, it often forced the ruling class and the wealthy to relocate. This relocation was a way of controlling the conquered people. Generally, the commoners left in the land would not rebel without their leaders. Both the Assyrians and the Chaldeans relocated captives.

The Assyrians relocated the wealthy and important people from the northern tribes of Israel to the eastern part of Assyria. These Israelites were **assimilated** into the Assyrian culture. The Assyrians moved people from other conquered nations into the Northern Kingdom's region. Israelites who remained in the region eventually married these foreign people. Their descendants were called **Samaritans**, named after the former capital city of Samaria.

King Nebuchadnezzar relocated the southern tribes of Judah to Babylon. The Jews were allowed to retain their religion and cultural traditions. Some of the most important Jewish men were trained to serve in the Chaldean government.

In 539 BC, the Persian army, under the leadership of Cyrus the Great, conquered Babylon. Cyrus allowed the Jews to return to Judea, the former

---

Diaspora The scattering of the Israelites to many other nations at the time of the Babylonian captivity.

New Covenant The agreement in which God promised to give His Holy Spirit and to transform the hearts of His people to love and obey Him.

assimilate To absorb.

Samaritans A people in the Northern Kingdom of Israel; descendants of conquered peoples who intermarried with Israelites.

Esther A Jew who was chosen to be queen by King Xerxes (Ahasuerus) of Persia and whom God used to save the Israelites in Babylon from destruction.

The Babylonian Chronicles are a series of clay tablets that contain important events in Babylonian history. This tablet describes the destruction of Nineveh in 612 BC.

Southern Kingdom of Judah. Some Jews returned, but many chose to stay in Babylon, where they had already made their homes.

Later, King Xerxes (also known as Ahasuerus) ruled Persia. During his reign, a palace official named Haman grew angry with a Jew named Mordecai. Haman decided to take revenge on Mordecai by killing all the Jews in Babylon. Queen **Esther**, who also was a Jew, heard about Haman's plan. She risked her life and went to the king. Queen Esther pleaded with him to save her people from destruction. King Xerxes gave the Jews permission to defend themselves from anyone who would try to hurt or kill them. He also ordered the execution of Haman.

After Haman's death, the Jews held a great feast. They sent each other presents and gave gifts to the poor. This celebration became the holiday Purim. Purim is still celebrated today by Jews around the world.

 What is the significance of the New Covenant to Christians today?

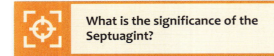 **What is the significance of the Septuagint?**

Return from Exile

The Jews returned from captivity in Babylon in groups. One group, led by Zerubbabel, rebuilt the temple. Ezra, a priest and prophet, returned to Judea with another group of Jews. He taught the people the law and worked to uproot sinful practices among the people. Nehemiah, also a prophet, returned with another group of returning Jews, and he led the rebuilding of the walls of Jerusalem. These three leaders, along with the prophets Haggai, Zechariah, and Malachi, helped the Jews become reestablished in their land.

Life in the Greek Empire

As the Persian Empire continued to expand, it tried to conquer the Greeks. But the Greeks repeatedly defeated the Persians. Under the leadership of Alexander the Great, the Greeks conquered the Persians. The land of Judea became part of the Greek Empire.

After Alexander the Great died, his kingdom was divided and distributed among his generals. Egypt was ruled by the Ptolemies, and Syria was ruled by the Seleucids. Judea lay on the border between the two kingdoms. As Egypt and Syria fought each other, Judea was often under the rule of one or the other.

While Judea was being ruled by the Ptolemies, a large number of Jews were relocated to Alexandria, Egypt. This move created a thriving Jewish community in Alexandria.

By this time, Greek had become a common language. It had spread under Alexander's leadership. Eventually the Old Testament Scriptures were translated into Greek. This translation was called the **Septuagint**. This was an important accomplishment. The Scriptures were now available to the **Gentiles** and to scattered Jews who no longer spoke Hebrew. The New Testament writers often quoted from the Septuagint. Most of the Gentile Christians in the early church used the Septuagint.

Septuagint Greek translation of the Old Testament.
Gentiles A name given to Greeks and other people who are not Jews.
Antiochus IV Seleucid king who became ruler of Judea in 176 BC.
Torah The first five books of the Old Testament; the Pentateuch.

Many of the Jews living under Greek rule began to adopt the customs and the lifestyle of the Greeks. The high priests, who were appointed by the Greek rulers, often promoted the sinful lifestyle of the Greeks more than the true worship of God. Some of the Jews were concerned by this. They began to insist on a strict, careful observance of the law in all its details.

In 176 BC, the Seleucid king **Antiochus IV** became ruler of Judea. During his reign, he personally entered the temple in Jerusalem and seized its treasures and sacred vessels to fund his military campaign. This action was a great offense to the Jews.

Later, while Antiochus was fighting in Egypt, the Jews attempted to overthrow his appointed leaders. When Antiochus returned from Egypt, he found Jerusalem at war.

Antiochus responded to this rebellion by tearing down the city's walls. He also placed idols in the temple and sacrificed pigs on the altar of God. He placed altars to false gods in many Jewish cities. Jews were put to death for keeping the Sabbath or for owning a copy of the **Torah**. Antiochus thought that if the Jewish religion were destroyed, the Jews would become like Greeks and not revolt anymore.

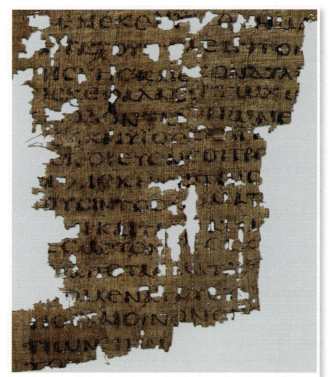

A portion of Amos 2 from the Septuagint found by archaeologists in an ancient garbage dump in Egypt. What material might this have been written on?

A 121-foot-long ancient Yemenite Torah scroll of the Pentateuch on gazelle skin. What did Antiochus think of the Jews and the Torah?

Coin of Antiochus IV

The Maccabean Revolt

The Jews who strictly followed the books of the Law were not willing to accept the destruction of their religion by Antiochus. Some Jews fled to the desert. In the small Judean town of Modin, some Jews began to rebel. A Jewish priest named Mattathias refused to worship the Greek idol that was placed in his town. He killed an official and destroyed the altar.

Mattathias raised an army and began a revolt. But he died of old age soon thereafter. His son, Judah, took leadership of the revolt. He was also called **Judas Maccabeus**, or Judah the Hammer. He led surprise attacks throughout the countryside. Though the Seleucids had superior forces, Judas defeated them several times.

After securing his victory, Judas led his army to Jerusalem. They cleansed and rededicated the temple 2,300 days after the first pagan sacrifice was offered, just as Daniel had prophesied (Daniel 8:11–14). The rededication of the temple was celebrated for eight days. Judas Maccabeus declared that this festival, **Hanukkah**, should be celebrated every year with gladness and joy.

With the temple cleansed, Judas wanted the Jews to be completely independent of the Seleucids. Judas continued the war against them. After he died, his brothers and their sons continued the fight. The Seleucid Empire was not able to keep the Jews under its rule, and the Jews were able to re-establish their kingdom.

The descendants of Judas's brother Simon established a dynasty that did not last long. This dynasty's kings proved to be both ruthless and highly influenced by Greek culture. During this time, two groups became important in Judea. They were the Pharisees and the Sadducees. The Pharisees were Jews who continued to stress purity of life and obedience to the Torah. They opposed the current rulers. The Sadducees were also Jews, but they supported the current rulers. The Sadducees were more

continued on page 92

Judas Maccabeus Leader of the Jewish revolt against the Seleucids in the second century BC.

Hanukkah The yearly Jewish celebration of the rededication of the temple after the victory over the Seleucids.

LIFE IN JERU

Social Classes
The Israelites were twelve tribes united under a monarchy. The levels of Israel's social structure were divided by importance and contribution to the society. The priests and soldiers were at the top. Merchants and farmers made up the middle level. The nomadic herders made up the lowest level.

Citizenship
During the Persian rule, the Israelites returned to Jerusalem. They were allowed to hold government positions, including the office of governor. The high priesthood was re-established, allowing the Israelites to practice their religious beliefs.

Power
The Israelites' authority was God, who gave the writings of Scripture for the people to follow. God sent leaders such as Moses and Joshua to lead them. After settling in Canaan, God sent judges to rule them. Eventually, God gave them a king and established a monarchy.

Religion
Israelites were monotheistic, believing in only one God. The temple was the center for worship and daily life in ancient Jerusalem. Zerubbabel began rebuilding the temple in 536 BC.

Arts and Written Language
The Bible records the building of altars and the tabernacle by the chief artisan Bezaleel (Exodus 31, 36–39). Regrettably, these altars and the tabernacle did not survive the exile.

Historians estimate that the Hebrew written language developed 2,500 to 3,500 years ago.

> Men are shown worshiping at the temple. Women worshiped separately in the Court of the Women.

SALEM

Key Themes of Civilization
- Justice
- Power
- Citizenship
- Environment

Features of a Civilization
- Organized cities and government
- Social classes
- Job specialization
- Arts, sciences, and written language
- Religion

Justice
The Pentateuch was the primary source for Israel's justice. God gave Moses the Ten Commandments for the Israelites to follow.

Job Specialization
The majority of the population were peasant farmers who grew crops for food and flax for clothing. Some Israelites were herders of sheep and goats. There were also tanners, masons, metalsmiths, weavers and dyers of cloth, merchants, doctors, and scribes.

Environment
Jerusalem is the capital city of Israel. It is sacred to Jews, Muslims, and Christians. The climate in Jerusalem usually has hot, dry summers and mild, wet winters.

Offering sacrifices was an important part of worship at the temple.

HANUKKAH

Hanukkah (or Chanukah) is an eight-day holiday that appears on most calendars. It is also referred to as the Festival of Lights. This holiday commemorates the cleansing and rededication of the temple in Jerusalem by Judas Maccabeus and his army.

The most familiar symbol of this holiday is the menorah. The menorah is lit on each night of the festival. According to Jewish tradition, when the menorah was lit at the temple's rededication, there was only enough oil for the lamp to burn for one night. However, the lamp stayed lit for eight nights!

One of the activities during Hanukkah includes spinning a top called a dreidel. Each of the four sides of the top has a Hebrew letter. They are the first letters of the Hebrew words for a "great miracle happened there."

An emblem of Israel, the Knesset Menorah in Jerusalem depicts scenes from Jewish history.

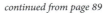

Dreidel is a popular game played during Hanukkah. Gelt is money given to children during Hanukkah.

This arm of the Knesset Menorah depicts the Maccabean Revolt.

continued from page 89

influential among the priests and the rulers of Judea than the Pharisees were. These different groups had differing ideas about how to be Jews in challenging circumstances. The descendants of the Maccabees wanted Jews to be independent from the Greek empires, but they were willing to adopt Greek culture. These Maccabean descendants were also willing to act violently, even against other Jews who threatened their power. The Sadducees too saw the importance of power in preserving the Jewish people and their worship at the temple. They worked with the new rulers, the Romans. But this work with the Romans sometimes involved corruption and injustice. In contrast to these other groups, the Pharisees stressed purity and obedience to the Torah. But Jesus taught that even the Pharisees could be unjust by laying heavy burdens on the people that they were not willing to bear themselves.

 What impact did Greek culture have on Israel's view of justice, power, and citizenship?

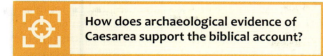
How does archaeological evidence of Caesarea support the biblical account?

Roman Rule

By 200 BC, the Roman Republic was the dominant power of the Italian peninsula and the western Mediterranean region. The republic continued to push eastward. It conquered what remained of the Seleucid Empire. Eventually the Roman Republic was ruled by Julius Caesar. Under his rule, the Romans took control of Judea. In 37 BC, Herod was made king over Judea. The Jews did not like Herod. He was a ruthless king. Herod continually worried about the security of his throne, so he was willing to kill anyone he thought was a threat to him. The Romans liked Herod because he was a faithful ally of the Roman Republic. They could depend on him to keep Judea under control. But the Romans eventually took over direct rule of Judea.

The Life of Jesus Christ

The Jews believed that the **Messiah** would be a descendant of David who would come to correct all the wrongs they had suffered. During Herod's reign, **Jesus** was born. He was a descendant of David and thus of the royal line. The angels who announced His birth identified Him as the King of the Jews. Jesus identified Himself as the Messiah, or the Christ, who was anointed to save His people. Neither the Jews nor anyone else could completely obey the law that God revealed in the Mosaic Covenant. This revealed the sinfulness of humanity and the need for a savior. Jesus came as that savior in fulfillment of the Old Testament covenants. Jesus is the descendant of Abraham who would bring blessing to all the nations of the earth as promised in the Abrahamic Covenant. He brought blessing by being the sacrifice for sins. Jesus paid the penalty for sin and offers forgiveness to those who trust Him. He also gives the Holy Spirit, who can change hearts. The Holy Spirit fulfills the promises of the New Covenant. As the Son of David, Jesus is King. One day He will return to reign on the earth and to put an end to all injustice.

Jesus performed many miracles and preached that the kingdom of God was near. He taught that He was a man, yet was also God. The followers of Jesus later examined the Hebrew Scriptures and saw how the prophecies about God's delivering His people through a Messiah were fulfilled by Jesus Christ.

The message of Jesus included an important element, the need for repentance. Like the ancient prophets, Jesus told the people that the root of their problems was sin. If they were to be included in the kingdom of God, they had to repent of their sins.

But the Jews did not recognize Jesus as their Messiah. Instead they rejected Him. The Pharisees and the Sadducees were rivals in Judea. But they conspired together to have Jesus executed. Jesus was brought before the Romans, and the Jewish religious leaders accused Jesus of being against Caesar. The Romans listened to the Pharisees and Sadducees and crucified Jesus.

Messiah The Old Testament name for the promised Redeemer, Jesus Christ.

Jesus God's Son; second person of the Trinity; the promised Messiah; came to earth as a man and died on the cross to pay the penalty for sin; rose from the dead and ascended to heaven.

What are the landforms of Bethlehem, the West Bank, and Palestine?

The followers of Jesus grieved at His death. But three days later, a great miracle happened. Jesus rose from the dead and appeared before His followers alive. All that had happened was part of God's sovereign plan. Jesus' death was the payment for the sins of the world. His death and resurrection made salvation possible for all people who repent and trust Him for eternal life.

Jesus ascended back into heaven, and His followers continued to spread His message of salvation. They preached the gospel to the people of Israel and to people all over the world. In this way, the Jews proved to be a blessing to all nations, just as God had promised in His covenant with Abraham.

Religion After Exile

The punishment of the exile to Babylon cured the Jews from the sin of idolatry. To this day, the Jewish religion of **Judaism** is a monotheistic religion. The loss of both the temple in Jerusalem and the ability to offer sacrifices there brought changes in Judaism. During the exile, when the Israelites had no temple, the **synagogue** became the center of Jewish worship.

When the Jews returned to Jerusalem after their exile in Babylon, they rebuilt the temple. It became known as the second temple. The Jews could offer sacrifices once again. However, the synagogue still remained a part of Jewish worship. Jesus taught in synagogues during His earthly ministry.

Later, after the Romans destroyed the second temple, Judaism underwent a further change. While the Sadducees lost influence, the Pharisees became strong. The Pharisees practiced rabbinic Judaism, which no longer focused on sacrifices to atone for one's sin. The focus was on careful obedience to the law so that a person lived a life that was as pleasing to God as possible.

The basic beliefs of Judaism include belief in only one God and the belief that His will is revealed in the

Judaism The monotheistic religion of the Jews.
synagogue A place where the Jews gather for worship.

CAESAREA MARITIMA

Caesarea Maritima was a port city located approximately sixty miles northwest of Jerusalem. King Herod employed Roman engineers to build the city and the harbor. The harbor had loading docks, storage areas, an inner harbor, and an outer harbor with a lighthouse. Caesarea Maritima became a main port for trade.

The harbor had been constructed over a geological fault line that runs along the coast of Israel. Seismic action and the sandy ocean floor caused the foundation to be unstable. There is also evidence that a tsunami struck the area sometime between the first and second centuries AD. Whether this tsunami only damaged the harbor or brought about its complete destruction is unknown. By the sixth century AD, the harbor lay in ruins below the ocean waves.

In June of 1961, Italian archaeologists led by Dr. Antonio Frova uncovered a limestone block at Caesarea Maritima. The block had an inscription that was part of a dedication to Tiberius Caesar from "Pontius Pilate, Prefect [governor] of Judea." The original artifact is now in Jerusalem in the Israel Museum.

The Bible says that, at the time of Jesus Christ, Pilate was the Roman governor of Judea. The limestone is one of the first artifacts discovered that states Pontius Pilate's actual name. It is also the first artifact to identify him as the Roman prefect who made his official residence in Caesarea.

The inscription of this limestone reads:
TIBERIEUM
(PON) TIUS PILATUS
(PRAEF) ECTUS JUDA (EAE)

Ancient synagogue ruins in Bar'am, Israel. Why did synagogues become centers of worship for the Jews?

Torah. The rabbis interpreted the Torah and applied it to all kinds of situations in life. These interpretations and stories that illustrate how the law is to be lived were gathered together in the Talmud. The rabbis believed that Jews were specially chosen by God for salvation. But because God is just, they also need to obey the law. They believed that perfection is not necessary because God is merciful.

The beliefs of Judaism contrast with the Christian view of the law. The New Testament teaches that God pronounces judgment on those who do not perfectly obey the law. Unfortunately, no one is able to perfectly keep the law. Paul described this problem in the book of Romans. He said that Israel had tried to keep the law but had been unsuccessful. The Jews had been so focused on keeping the law that they had not recognized Jesus as the Messiah (Romans 9:31–33). The Christian message teaches that salvation comes by grace. Jesus, the Messiah, kept the law and suffered the judgment that all people deserve for not keeping it. Because of the Messiah's life and suffering, God gives salvation by grace to all who repent of their sin and trust Jesus for salvation. Every person who calls on Jesus for salvation is no longer condemned for not keeping the law. God graciously forgives sins. Those who come to the Messiah for salvation also receive the gracious gift of the Holy Spirit, who helps them to love God and obey His laws. When Christians sin after salvation, God is faithful and righteous to forgive their sin and to continue to change them to be more like Jesus.

THE TALMUD

Under rabbinic Judaism, the focus on the law resulted in the production of religious writings. In the first and second centuries AD, the **rabbis** wrote down the interpretations of the law. This writing is called the Mishnah. Later, more traditions and stories about how the law had been applied were recorded in the Gemara. Together, the Mishnah and the Gemara are called the Talmud. The Talmud was completed by the fifth century AD.

rabbi Jewish religious teacher.

 What cured the Jews from their sin of idolatry?

What led to the destruction of Jerusalem?

Destruction of Jerusalem

During the time of Jesus, the rule of Israel began to shift from the Herodian dynasty to Roman rule. Eventually, Roman governors ruled the entire region. The governors enriched themselves by taking money from the people. This extortion, combined with the brutality of the Romans, made the Jews yearn for freedom.

Some Jews, known as *Zealots*, were already plotting the overthrow of Rome by military action. But the rest of the people were not ready for such drastic action. Their opinion changed, however, when the Roman governor, Florus, took money from the temple treasury for himself. Two Jews responded by mocking the governor as a penniless beggar who needed to steal to get money. Florus responded by having his troops beat, rob, and even crucify Jews. The city erupted, and Florus had a full-scale rebellion to deal with. He asked for help from his superior and received an entire **legion**, but the legion was not enough. The Romans were ambushed and suffered defeat.

The Roman emperor at the time was Nero. He called on Vespasian, a successful veteran commander, to go to Judea. Vespasian took more than three legions with him. Within a year, he had conquered the surrounding country and was preparing to take Jerusalem. At this point, in AD 68, the Roman Empire plunged into civil war. This delayed Vespasian's assault on Jerusalem.

The Jews thought that God had intervened on their behalf. They thought that the Roman Empire would shatter and that Jerusalem and the Jews would be freed once again. But Jesus had already predicted what would happen. He said that when armies surrounded Jerusalem, the people should know that its destruction was about to happen. God would pour out His wrath on His people. Many would be killed and those who remained would be scattered among the nations. Jerusalem itself would be "trodden down of the Gentiles, until the times of the Gentiles be fulfilled" (Luke 21:20–24).

Vespasian received word that an army had won him the position of emperor. He returned to Rome, leaving his son, Titus, in command of the Roman army in Judea.

---

legion An army consisting of three to six thousand soldiers.

JOSEPHUS'S ACCOUNT

The Burning of the Temple
Translated by William Whiston

While the holy house was on fire, every thing was plundered that came to hand, and ten thousand of those that were caught were slain . . . but children, and old men . . . and priests were all slain in the same manner . . . and as well those that made supplication for their lives, as those that defended themselves by fighting. The flame was also carried a long way, and made an echo, together with the groans of those that were slain. . . .

And now the Romans, judging that it was in vain to spare what was round about the holy house, burnt all those places, as also the remains of the cloisters and the gates. . . .

. . . And now all the soldiers had such vast quantities of the spoils which they had gotten by plunder, that in Syria a pound weight of gold was sold for half its former value.

A bas-relief on the Arch of Titus showing the Roman triumphal march carrying spoils from the Jerusalem temple

What characteristics made Masada a strong fortress?

In AD 70, Titus and the Roman army surrounded Jerusalem. They stayed in their camps and waited for months. The people of Jerusalem could not leave their city, and no one could enter. The Romans continued to wait until the city suffered from famine. Then the Romans broke down the walls and marched through Jerusalem. After about two months of difficult fighting, the city was firmly controlled by the Romans.

During the destruction of Jerusalem, the second temple was set on fire and destroyed. The Jewish historian **Josephus**, who was on the side of the Romans in this war, claimed the destruction of the temple was an accident. Another Roman account says that Titus ordered the temple's destruction in an effort to destroy the troublesome Jewish religion. Either way, the prophecy of judgment recorded in Matthew 24:2 came true. Jesus said of the temple, "There shall not be left here one stone upon another, that shall not be thrown down."

Masada

After the destruction of Jerusalem, three Jewish strongholds remained. The first two fell to the Romans by AD 72. The third stronghold, a mountaintop fortress called Masada, seemed impossible to capture. The Zealot Jews who had taken refuge there had plenty of food and water, and the winding narrow path to the top prevented the attacking army from reaching them.

But the Romans did not give up. For three years, they worked to move tons of earth to build a huge ramp. The ramp reached to the top of one of the walls of Masada. When the Jews inside saw that the Romans would break through, they committed mass suicide.

Israel ceased to exist as a nation in AD 70. However, throughout the centuries, the Jews maintained their identity as a people. In 1948 the nation of Israel was reborn. Although the Jewish people had rejected God's Messiah, God remained faithful to them. The apostle Paul, looking to the future, said the following:

> And so all Israel shall be saved: as it is written, There shall come out of Si'on the Deliverer, and shall turn away ungodliness from Jacob: For this is my covenant unto them, when I shall take away their sins (Romans 11:26–27).

Josephus Jewish historian; sided with the Romans during the destruction of Jerusalem in AD 70.

 How did Roman rule influence Israel?

5 ANCIENT INDIA

FOCUS Advanced Indian civilizations developed in the Indus Valley.

| 2500 BC | 2000 BC | 1500 BC | 1000 BC | 500 BC | BC | AD |

Harappan civilization ca. 2300 BC

Mauryan Empire ca. 320–184 BC

ca. 1500 BC Aryan civilization

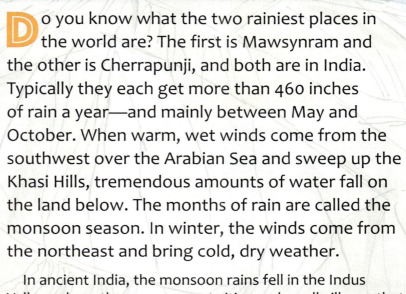

Do you know what the two rainiest places in the world are? The first is Mawsynram and the other is Cherrapunji, and both are in India. Typically they each get more than 460 inches of rain a year—and mainly between May and October. When warm, wet winds come from the southwest over the Arabian Sea and sweep up the Khasi Hills, tremendous amounts of water fall on the land below. The months of rain are called the monsoon season. In winter, the winds come from the northeast and bring cold, dry weather.

In ancient India, the monsoon rains fell in the Indus Valley, where there were great cities and small villages that depended on those rains to fill the rivers and drench the soil. Here, Nur is taking his flock to a more sheltered place, and he is happy that the grazing will be good because of the rain. Sheep and goats were among the first animals to be domesticated, which means that they were brought under control for work, food, or companionship. Their milk could be drunk or made into cheese; their skins could be made into clothing or tents; their horns could be used as cups or containers.

Jahan is running home before the heavy rain comes. She may help make a meal of fish, beef, or pork, served with chickpeas, lentils, and dates. She may even be hoping to make a flatbread with honey for a treat.

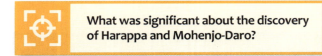

What was significant about the discovery of Harappa and Mohenjo-Daro?

Uncovering the Harappan Civilization

Throughout history, many great civilizations have come and gone. Some have left behind a wealth of information. Others, however, remain a mystery. For a long time, historians did not know much about the ancient civilizations of India. But that changed after a major discovery.

During the 1920s, **Sir John Marshall** and his team of archaeologists discovered the ancient city of **Harappa** and its sister city, **Mohenjo-Daro**. These cities were located in the Indus Valley in what is now Pakistan. They have been dated at approximately 2300 BC, and they existed at the same time as the Sumerian civilization and the Old Kingdom in ancient Egypt.

Harappa and Mohenjo-Daro

Archaeological digs do not always uncover secrets from the past. Archaeologists may spend years studying and searching for ancient civilizations. They may excavate site after site, only to end up empty-handed. However, John Marshall and his archaeologists were not disappointed. The discovery of Harappa and Mohenjo-Daro opened the door to a long-forgotten world. Archaeologists and historians could finally begin unraveling the mystery of India's past.

Although the cities of Harappa and Mohenjo-Daro are four hundred miles apart, historians believe that both were part of the same civilization. Excavations have uncovered similar artifacts, street plans, and architecture in both cities.

The people from these cities are called the **Harappan civilization**. For about eight hundred years, these ancient Indians flourished in the fertile Indus Valley. Because of the valley's closeness to the river, the land was good for farming and for raising animals.

Around 2300 BC, some of the first communities in ancient India formed in the Indus Valley. The people of the Harappan civilization were highly sophisticated. Archaeologists have found their well-organized cities. Both cities had two-story houses, indoor bathrooms, running water, and an advanced drainage system that ran throughout the entire city. Drains carried the sewage to pools away from where

Sir John Marshall British archaeologist who discovered and helped excavate Harappa and Mohenjo-Daro in the Indus Valley in the 1920s.

Harappa A city of one of the first civilizations in the Indus Valley; the sister city of Mohenjo-Daro.

Mohenjo-Daro A city of one of the first civilizations in the Indus Valley; the sister city of Harappa.

Harappan civilization People who settled in the Indus Valley and established the ancient cities of Harappa and Mohenjo-Daro.

The Great Bath at Mohenjo-Daro is made from baked bricks and sealed with bitumen to hold water. The Great Bath was likely used for religious ritual and for bathing.

Villagers carefully uncover a stone fort wall of an Indus Valley civilization.

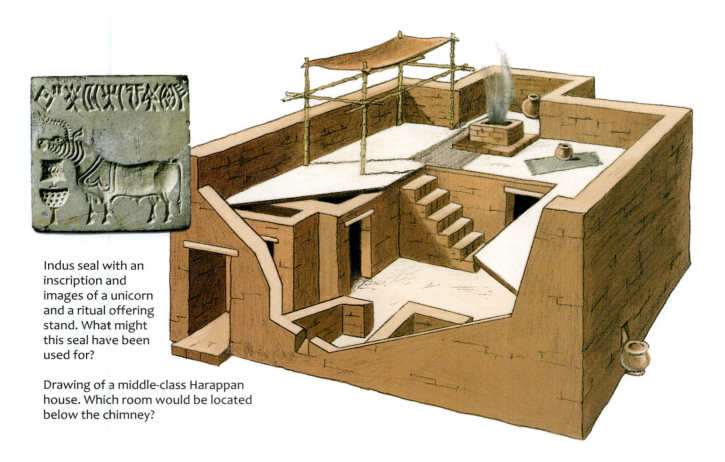

Indus seal with an inscription and images of a unicorn and a ritual offering stand. What might this seal have been used for?

Drawing of a middle-class Harappan house. Which room would be located below the chimney?

people lived. Eventually the sewage was conveyed to a river or out to the surrounding fields where it could fertilize the crops.

Mohenjo-Daro had a large public pool made of tightly fitted bricks waterproofed with a kind of tar called *bitumen*. Archaeologists call this structure the Great Bath. Many historians believe that it was used for religious ceremonies.

More artifacts, such as gold ornaments, bronze utensils, and bronze pots, showed archaeologists that the Indus people were artistic and skilled craftsmen. Many of these artifacts contain **pictographs**. These ancient writings remain an unsolved mystery even today.

An Advanced Civilization

The houses unearthed at Mohenjo-Daro show some interesting details about the Harappan way of life. Mohenjo-Daro appeared to have had two main streets. Many of the buildings along these streets seemed to be middle-class houses, probably owned by merchants and craftsmen.

A typical middle-class house had a floor made of red brick. Archaeologists believe the second story may have been made of wood. They found charred bits of wood along the tops of some brick walls. Each house had an open courtyard to let in light. Evidence shows that small rooms around the courtyard included a bathroom, a kitchen, and a room for the water well. The family's sleeping quarters were located in the back area and on the second floor of the house. The house also had rooms that may have been used for guests.

Archaeologists found artifacts in the houses and surrounding areas. These included jewelry and weights used for measuring equivalent amounts. The most common objects that have been found are seals made of clay or stone. It is likely that each merchant or family had a certain seal. The designs often included script and a picture of an animal or of a person surrounded by animals. Seals were sometimes pushed into soft clay that was used to close jars. Ancient Harappans also used seals to make clay tags for tradable goods such as bags of grain. Other common artifacts include pottery, utensils made of shells, small clay balls and toys, and statues. Historians are not certain whether the statues were used as idols or as pieces of art.

Many historians were surprised to learn how advanced the Harappans were. The Harappan civilization gives evidence that ancient minds were not inferior to the minds of today.

pictograph A picture or symbol used in early writing to represent a word, a group of words, or an idea.

THE REGION TODAY

India

Location
India is a large peninsula in southern Asia, jutting into the Indian Ocean above the equator. India is bordered by Pakistan to the northwest. China, Nepal, Bhutan, Myanmar, and Bangladesh are on the northeastern and eastern borders. The ancient Harappans lived in what is now Pakistan.

Climate
India's climate varies and can range from dry to tropical. The country is affected by yearly monsoons. Temperatures are above 70°F most of the year, except in the north. Annual precipitation ranges from zero to over four hundred inches, depending on the region.

Topography
India contains three major regions. The Himalaya Mountains stretch across northeastern India, forming a natural barrier that separates India and some neighboring countries from the rest of the continent. For this reason, India is often called the **Indian subcontinent**. To the south of the mountains is the northern plain, watered by three rivers: the Indus, the Ganges, and the Brahmaputra. Southern India is a large plateau called the Deccan.

Natural Resources
India's natural resources include large deposits of iron ore and some coal. India also has small amounts of other minerals such as gold, silver, uranium, diamonds, and emeralds. There is also much fertile land.

Indian subcontinent A peninsula in southern Asia that extends into the Indian Ocean, separated from neighboring countries by the Himalaya Mountains.

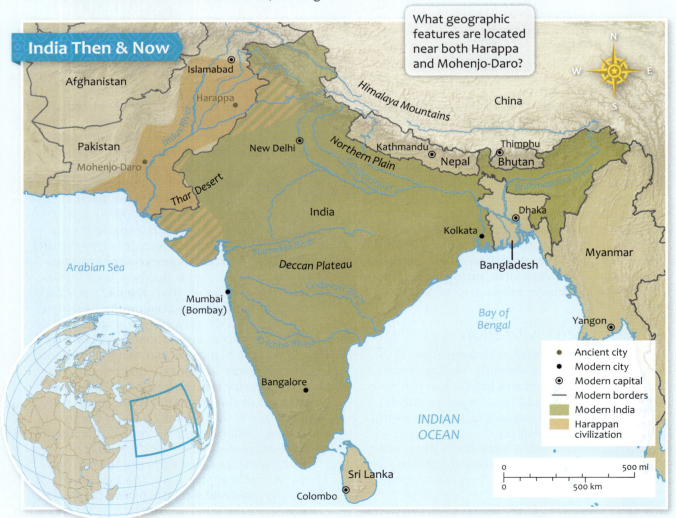

India Then & Now

What geographic features are located near both Harappa and Mohenjo-Daro?

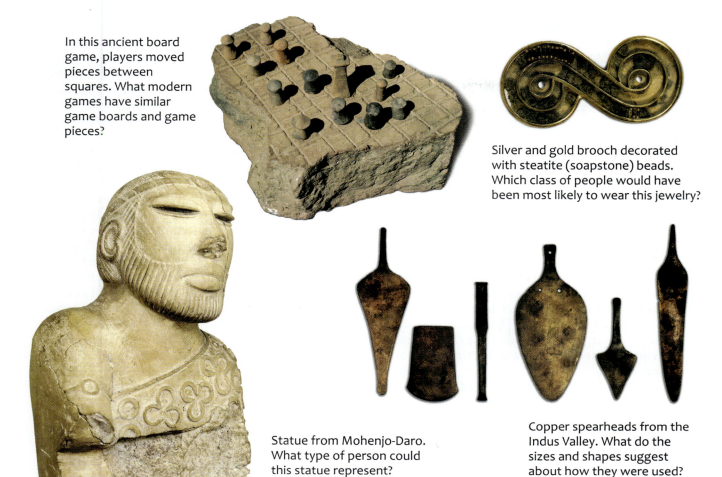

In this ancient board game, players moved pieces between squares. What modern games have similar game boards and game pieces?

Silver and gold brooch decorated with steatite (soapstone) beads. Which class of people would have been most likely to wear this jewelry?

Statue from Mohenjo-Daro. What type of person could this statue represent?

Copper spearheads from the Indus Valley. What do the sizes and shapes suggest about how they were used?

The Harappan Language

Ever since the excavation of India's ancient cities began, scholars have tried to decipher the writing on the Harappan artifacts. Many of the seals, pottery, and other artifacts display a language written in pictographs. Unfortunately, **linguists** have been unable to decipher the script. Jean-François Champollion deciphered Egyptian hieroglyphs by comparing them with a translation in a known language on the Rosetta stone. But since no artifact with a translation of Harappan writing exists, it is very difficult to crack the code.

Without knowing the Harappan people's language, historians have been unable to unravel much of the mystery surrounding their culture. Historians can make guesses about the Harappans' religious beliefs and customs by looking at the pictographs, but they cannot conclude anything definite.

---

linguist A scholar who studies languages.

The Disappearance of the Harappan Civilization

The mystery that surrounded the ancient Harappan people deepened as archaeologists uncovered more and more artifacts. One interesting discovery was a group of fourteen skeletons found in one room. Although the room may have been a burial place, it was more likely the scene of a tragedy. The Harappans may have been invaded by another people. Evidence suggests that the civilization came to a sudden halt between 1700 and 1500 BC. There could be a variety of reasons for its disappearance. If not an invasion, a flood or a famine could have driven the inhabitants of Harappa and Mohenjo-Daro from their homes.

What do the Harappan accomplishments suggest?

What are possible causes for the disappearance of the Harappan civilization?

How were the Aryans different from the Harappans?

The Aryan Civilization

A possible cause for the disappearance of the Harappans may have been an invasion by another people from the north. It is probable that a group of nomads moved into the Indus Valley after 1500 BC. One theory suggests that these people were blonde-haired, tall, and spoke ancient **Indo-European**. They worshipped the gods of the sky. These nomads herded cattle and became agricultural. They called themselves Arya, meaning "noble." The **Aryans** began a new period of civilization in the history of India.

The Aryans were a warlike people. They trained horses to pull lightweight chariots with two wheels. These chariots were faster than the Indian ox-drawn carts with four dense wheels. The Aryans likely came into India ready to conquer. The Aryan form of justice involved warring within their clan, warring with other clans of Aryans, and warring with non-Aryan people.

Disregarding the rights of the Indian people, they spread across northern India and took control over the non-Aryan people. Bands of Aryans also migrated east, south, and west. During their migrations, they married some of the people they had conquered. Most Indians today have hair and skin color similar to the original Indian people, rather than that of the fair Aryans.

The Aryans became less nomadic and began to settle into the Indus Valley. The Indus River and its tributaries nourished the fertile Indus Valley that supported the Aryan cattle herds and farming. Preferring not to live in large, established cities like the Harappans, they settled into villages with houses made of wood and stalks of river plants.

The family was the basis of Aryan society. Villages were comprised of related family groups. Men were leaders of their families. Women held a good position, but were subject to their husbands.

The Aryans in India did not form a strong central government but instead allowed each village to function independently. Each village was governed by a council of leading men and a **raja**. The raja was the most important man in the village.

Aryan tribes probably had a social structure even before coming to the Indus Valley. Some of their earliest hymns refer to nobility as well as to tribesmen. Later, religion would have a large impact on the social structure and life in the Aryan society.

Some villagers farmed for a living. Their success depended on the annual rains of the wet season. In

Indo-European A group of languages spoken by people of Europe and parts of Asia.

Aryans Nomads believed to have moved into the Indus Valley around 1500 BC; conquered the people of northwestern India.

raja A chief, prince, or ruler in India.

India, the rains come during the summer **monsoon** season. A monsoon is a wind that reverses direction with the change of season. India's summer winds blow from the southwest and bring moisture off the Indian Ocean. Once over land, the water vapor in the air condenses and falls as rain. If the rains are light or late, drought and famine may occur.

Aryans raised goats, cattle, and sheep. Cattle breeding was especially important to the farmer because cattle were a basis of the Aryan economy. Cattle were used to pay soldiers or priests for their services. Historians believe that cattle were not considered sacred animals at this time but that they were used as a type of money. A measure or pieces of gold were also used as money.

Each village also had craftsmen. Artificers made bronze tools and weapons. Some craftsmen made household items such as woven works and pottery. Carpenters built houses, and chariot makers provided transportation. Aryans also produced artwork. Much of their art reflected their religious beliefs. Sculptures of gods and goddesses were common and were probably used in worship.

---

monsoon A wind that reverses direction with the change of season.
Sanskrit Written language of the Aryans.

Agriculture and the production of goods made trade likely. Fruits, vegetables, grain, copper, tin, and precious metals could be carried by horse, donkey, or elephant. Cattle were also a large part of local commerce. The rivers served as highways to carry goods by boat to other nearby areas.

The Aryans appreciated music. They played the lute, harp, flute, drum, and cymbals. Aryans loved singing and dancing. They practiced science and medicine. Aryans were knowledgeable about astronomy and named many of the stars and planets.

The Aryans are famous for their hymns, poetry, and prayers. These were memorized and preserved orally. After a time, they were written down. The written language of the Aryans is called **Sanskrit**. Unlike the Harappan pictographs, Sanskrit has been translated. Because Sanskrit has been translated, more is known about the Aryans than about the Harappans. The Aryan way of life became the characteristic culture of both ancient and modern India.

> What were the major cultural accomplishments of the Aryans?
> How does India's geography relate to the development of the Aryan culture?
> How were Aryan villages governed?

ACTIVITY

Recognizing Sanskrit's Influence on English

Linguists are interested in how languages influence each other. When two different language groups frequently have contact with each other, both languages change. Each people group tends to adopt words and phrases from the other. The spellings or meanings of borrowed words can change slightly in the new language. Over time, the borrowed words may become so common that no one thinks about their being from another language.

English has been influenced by many other languages. One of those languages is Sanskrit, the ancient language of the Aryans. English is a much newer language than Sanskrit, so you might be surprised to discover how many commonly used English words have been borrowed from Sanskrit.

This Sanskrit text is on a temple wall in India.

1. Look up the following words in a dictionary.
   bandanna   loot   shawl
   guru   mantra   sugar
   jungle   orange   yoga

2. Examine the etymology of each word. The etymology is the word's origin or history, including what language the word came from. It is usually found in brackets at the beginning or the end of the dictionary entry. You will find that some Sanskrit words are related to Indian religions. Others are taken from daily Indian life and culture.

3. On the Activity Manual page, write out the Sanskrit word that each English word on the list comes from. If the meaning of the original Sanskrit word is given, write down that meaning as well. Compare the Sanskrit meaning with the English meaning.

4. Write a paragraph about your findings. Which Sanskrit words are related to Indian religions? How have the meanings of these words changed in English? What can you learn about daily life and culture in ancient India from the meanings of these words?

What is at the center of social relationships among Hindus?

Religions of Ancient India
Hinduism

The nomadic Aryans likely encountered different peoples and cultures as they traveled. As the Aryans settled in India, they adopted many beliefs and customs from other people groups. The Aryans developed varied groups of religions called **Hinduism**. Hinduism spread across India and still exists today. This religion was not fully formed until after the time of Christ. However, its beliefs and practices quickly grew to influence the Indians' entire way of life.

Beliefs and Practices

Hinduism is often used to describe the religion of India. Like many other ancient religions, Hinduism is polytheistic. Hindus worship thousands of gods, but they consider three gods to be the most important. These three gods are Brahma, the Creator; Shiva, the Destroyer; and Vishnu, the Preserver.

Hindu religions do not all share the same beliefs or practices. Sometimes the beliefs of various Hindu groups contradict each other. These contradictions do not bother Hindus. They think that what seems to contradict may actually harmonize in another dimension of reality. For instance, some Hindus believe that gods are persons. Other Hindus believe that god is a divine being that permeates everything.

Brahman, not to be confused with the Hindu god Brahma, is both the cause and the material of creation in Hindu beliefs. The concept of Brahman contradicts the biblical record of Creation where God created everything from nothing. Brahman is not a personal being, so he is often called the great soul, or the world soul. Hindus believe that everything in the world, including plants, animals, and gods, is part of Brahman. This belief is **pantheism**.

The majority of Hindus are very concerned about doing their duty. Their religious duties, or **dharma**, require them to always behave in a certain way. Most Hindus follow their religious practices diligently. They pray, perform rituals, worship at Hindu temples and shrines, and bring sacrifices and money to the priests. Some Hindus try to become holier by disciplining their bodies. They seclude, starve, and inflict pain on themselves in an attempt to make their souls purer. By following these practices, the Hindus hope to be good enough to eventually become one with Brahman, the world soul.

Hinduism A major Indian religion based on Vedic religious beliefs; belief in Brahman and reincarnation that serves as a unifying influence in India's diverse society.

Brahman Divine being of Hinduism believed to be the cause and material of creation; also called "the great soul" or "the world soul."

pantheism Belief that everything in the universe is part of a supreme being.

dharma Religious duties of a Hindu or a Buddhist.

A tiered tower with detailed decoration sits atop the gopura, an entrance building to a Hindu temple in India.

An Indian relief sculpture of Vishnu. What might Vishnu's four arms suggest?

HINDUISM

Something is wrong with the world. Every religion acknowledges this fact and seeks to provide a solution to the problem. The solution in Hinduism is to progress through the cycle of birth, death, and rebirth (reincarnation) until the person is finally released from the law of reincarnation and becomes one with Brahman.

In order to be released from the law of reincarnation, Hindus do good works to gain good karma. They also use meditation to understand Brahman better.

Christians also recognize that there is a problem with the world. But the problem is not being ignorant of Brahman. Nor is the problem being trapped in a cycle of reincarnation. The problem is sin. Because all people are sinners, there is much evil in the world and each person is under God's judgment. The Christian hope is not just to escape from this sinful world. The Christian hope is that Christ will redeem people and will fix this broken world.

Another part of Hinduism is **reincarnation**. How a person is reincarnated depends on the **karma** he has built up in his present incarnation. Karma is the result of one's good or bad deeds. A person who does good deeds will build good karma. Someone who has done evil or failed to do his duty builds bad karma. Because most Hindus believe in reincarnation, many of them seek to increase their good karma through good works. A Hindu usually accepts the social class into which he is born as the reward or punishment for his works in his past lives, and he tries to do good works so that his future lives will be better.

The Written Legacy

The ancient Hindus left a written legacy called the **Vedas**. These books were written in Sanskrit. The Sanskrit word *veda* means "knowledge."

The Rig-Veda is the oldest Veda. It was composed around 1500 BC. This Veda was passed orally from one generation to the next. The Rig-Veda was written down around 300 BC and is one of the earliest known books in the world. The Rig-Veda is a collection of hymns, prayers, and poems. It tells of the rituals and the philosophy of ancient Hinduism, and it shows that the ancient Indians enjoyed beauty and artistry.

PASSAGE FROM THE RIG-VEDA

Here is an English translation of a passage from the Rig-Veda. It is taken from a hymn addressed to Ushas, the Hindu goddess of dawn. The last two lines might seem similar to a psalm in the Bible. But a closer look at this passage reveals important differences. What false ideas are promoted in this Hindu hymn?

Dawn on us with prosperity, O [Ushas],
Daughter of the Sky,
Dawn with great glory, Goddess,
Lady of the Light, dawn thou with riches,
Bounteous One. . . .
For in thee is each living creature's breath and life.

"Dawn, Hymn XLVIII." In *Rig Veda: Mandala 1*, trans. by Ralph T. H. Griffith (n.p., 1889).

An Indian painting of Brahma receiving an offering

reincarnation The belief that after a person dies, he comes back in another form.
karma The Hindu belief that a person's deeds, good or bad, determine his state in reincarnation.
Vedas Collections of sacred hymn texts of Hinduism.

LIFE IN INDIA

Science and Language

People used tin and copper to make bronze. They forged tools and weapons, and they made lightweight, two-wheeled chariots.

They also practiced medicine and were knowledgeable about astronomy. They named many stars and planets.

Sanskrit was their written language. People created hymns, poems, and prayers.

Social Classes and Job Specialization

Ancient India had nobles and peasants. Later, the caste system divided people into groups that they would remain in for their entire lives. A person on a lower caste could not get a better job or marry someone in a higher caste.

There were many occupations in ancient India. The highest castes included positions such as religious leaders, warriors, and rulers. The middle castes included farmers, traders, and artisans. Laborers and servants belonged to the lowest castes of people. There were also outcastes. These outcastes included people who worked with meat and those who had been expelled from their own caste.

Justice

In many villages, the raja and a council of leading men carried out justice. Later, kings ruled over city-states and were responsible for punishing wrongdoers.

Outcastes live far outside the city.

A priest offers a sacrifice to the god Vishnu.

Laborers and servants do the difficult work.

Religion
Ancient Indians practiced animism. They worshiped spirits that they believed lived in stars, stones, rivers, animals, trees, and mountains. Over time, they developed Hinduism. Hindus do good works in the hope of being reincarnated to a better state in the next life. Buddhism also started in India.

Organized Cities and Government
Ancient India had a mix of villages and large cities. However, the villages did not form strong central governments like the large cities did. Each village was governed by a council of leading men and a headman. Under Hinduism, only those in the highest caste were allowed to rule or hold positions in government.

Arts
Ancient Indians wove cloth and made decorated pottery. They made statues and ornate towers such as the gopura that marks the entrance to a Hindu temple in southern India.

Environment
India has fertile land and abundant rivers. The Himalaya Mountains form a natural barrier from countries in the northeast.

Key Themes of Civilization
- Justice
- Power
- Citizenship
- Environment

Features of a Civilization
- Organized cities and government
- Social classes
- Job specialization
- Arts, sciences, and written language
- Religion

Soldiers practice military skills.

Two merchants finish bartering for livestock.

Craftsmen create weapons and pottery.

109

Families and Castes

In Hinduism, the belief in karma is very important to most Indians, but their relationships to other people are important as well. Because Hinduism teaches that everything is a part of Brahman, it emphasizes the group above the individual. Social relationships in Hinduism center on the group. The two basic groups in India since the rise of Hinduism have been the family and the **caste**.

The core of ancient Indian life was the family. When the Aryans settled in India, they encouraged large families. Families included more than just parents and their children. Grandparents, parents, sons, daughters-in-law, unmarried daughters, and grandchildren lived together in compounds made up of several huts or houses. The oldest man in the family had authority over the other members. Everyone had to follow his orders. Hinduism teaches that obedience in the family is an important duty.

The second important social group that Indians belonged to was the caste. Castes were the classes of Indian society. A person was born into a caste, which he would stay in for the rest of his life. Hindus believe that the higher a person is in the caste system, the closer he is to reuniting fully with Brahman. A Hindu hopes that when he is reincarnated, he will be reborn into a higher caste.

There were four main caste divisions in Indian society. The highest was the priestly caste. The priests held a great deal of power over the people. Hindus believed that when a member of the priestly caste died, he reunited immediately with the Brahman world soul and would no longer have a physical body.

The next caste was made up of warriors and rulers. The caste below that was made up of farmers, traders, and artisans. Finally, laborers and servants belonged to the lowest caste. Within the four main castes, there were hundreds of subcastes.

Some Indians were outside the caste system. They were called **outcastes**. Outcastes included any non-Hindu, anyone who worked with meat, and anyone who had been expelled from his own caste.

caste A strict social class a person is born into.
outcaste Anyone from outside the groups of the Hindu caste system; bound by strict social restrictions.

THE CASTE SYSTEM

Caste		Occupation
Brahmins		priests
Kshatriyas		warriors & rulers
Vaisyas		farmers, traders artisans/craftspeople
Sudras		laborers & servants

Outcastes		non-Hindus unclean laborers expelled caste members

Hindu priest

Each caste had rules for its members. The caste rules dictated whom one married, one's occupation, and one's clothing. Caste rules even determined whom a caste member could eat with. Part of dharma was keeping the rules of one's caste and being content to stay in it. In this way, a Hindu would gain good karma and have an opportunity to be reborn into a higher caste. A Hindu who did more or less than what his caste demanded was unlikely to be reborn into a higher level. The caste system made Indian society very rigid. Today the caste system still exists in India, although it is not as rigid as it once was.

Life Under the Caste System

People who were part of the higher castes were proud of their status in life. People in the highest caste had all their needs met by people in the lower castes. The lower castes grew food for them to eat, made clothes for them to wear, made furnishings for their homes, and defended them against their enemies.

Some people in the lower castes enjoyed their work. They were content with their place in society and did not want to change. However, others wished for better or different jobs. Some people may have wished to marry someone in a higher or lower caste. These people either had to accept their place in life and keep the rules or be expelled from their caste.

Many people were satisfied with the Hindu caste system. They believed that it kept order and peace in Indian society. Others suffered because of the strict caste rules. For example, the outcastes were rejected and excluded from normal life. Their only hope was to do their duty, die, and have a better life in a reincarnated state.

How do the religious beliefs and practices of Hinduism differ from biblical truth?

How does the caste system affect people's relationships and choices in life?

What are the advantages and disadvantages for members of different castes?

What differences are there between an ancient Indian family and a modern American family?

Why did Siddhartha Gautama change his beliefs from Hinduism to Buddhism?

Buddhism

Around 500 BC, a man began to question the teachings of Hinduism. His questions eventually led him to develop a new religion. His name was **Siddhartha Gautama**. He was born into a ruling family as a member of the warrior caste. He had a comfortable life in a wealthy family, but he was not happy in spite of the luxuries he enjoyed. The poverty and pain he saw in the world troubled him. He became dissatisfied with Hindu beliefs. At age twenty-nine, he left his home to find a remedy for his own unhappiness and that of the world.

Siddhartha Gautama disliked the caste system and the priests who ruled the people. The Hindus believed that only members of the priestly caste were ready to reunite with the Brahman. But Gautama could not accept that. Nor could he accept the poverty and pain he saw in the world around him. He decided that he was going to change his beliefs.

According to legend, one day while meditating beneath a tree, Gautama became **enlightened**. Siddhartha Gautama changed his name to **Buddha**. He thought that he had discovered the truth. He believed that he had found the solution to the problem of suffering in the world. He devoted the rest of his life to telling people what he believed to be the truth. He traveled around India teaching and gaining many followers for his new religion.

He introduced what he called the Four Noble Truths. These are the basic beliefs of Buddhist teaching. Buddha proposed that suffering can be overcome if a person does good works and ignores his desires. This religion became known as **Buddhism**.

Gautama, Siddhartha Founder of Buddhism.

enlightened Having received knowledge or understanding.

Buddha The name Siddhartha Gautama took for himself after he left Hinduism; "Enlightened One."

Buddhism A religion founded by Siddhartha Gautama; Buddhists follow the Eightfold Path and the Four Noble Truths.

nirvana The Buddhist belief in a state of complete enlightenment where a person has peace and freedom from desire.

BUDDHIST BEGINNINGS

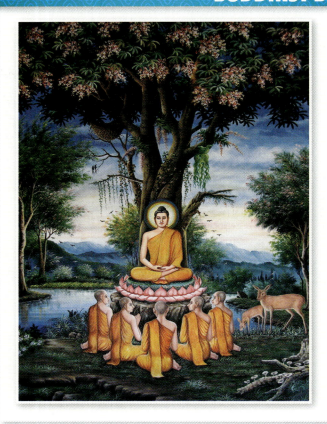

The Four Noble Truths
1. All people experience suffering.
2. Suffering is caused by desire for pleasures or things that a person cannot have.
3. A person can end suffering only by freeing himself from desire.
4. A person can free himself from desire and end suffering by following the Eightfold Path.

The Eightfold Path
1. Know and believe the Four Noble Truths.
2. Be good and kind to others.
3. Be truthful and refrain from gossip.
4. Live a moral life, avoiding evil actions such as stealing and harming others.
5. Work in a job that will help, not hurt, others.
6. Do good and oppose evil.
7. Think positive, healthy thoughts.
8. Practice meditation.

Painting of Buddha's first sermon to five companions at Deer Park in northern India. Buddha and the companions formed the first company of Buddhist monks. The company quickly grew to a thousand.

Tibetan Buddhist monastery built on a hilltop in the Indian Himalayas by the Spiti Valley and Spiti River

Wooden Buddha statue

Buddhist monk. How is his attire different from the Hindu priest's (p.111)?

BUDDHISM

Buddhism teaches that suffering affects everyone and that the reason for this suffering is desire. In order to escape suffering, a person must stop having desires. This is a logical teaching. If a person wants nothing, he will not suffer or be sad for not getting it. But even though this teaching is logical, it is false.

The Bible teaches that sin brings suffering to this world, but the goal of the Christian is not to escape suffering. Jesus suffered, and the Christian will suffer like Jesus. Nor should the Christian seek to escape his body or the physical world. Instead, the Christian should look forward to the resurrection of the body. The Christian endures suffering now as he looks forward to a new earth in which "God shall wipe away all tears from their eyes; and there shall be no more death, neither sorrow, nor crying, neither shall there be any more pain: for the former things are passed away" (Revelation 21:4).

The Eightfold Path was Buddha's list of good works. According to Buddhism, doing the things on the list is supposed to help a person achieve happiness and peace.

In Buddhism, a person's ultimate goal for salvation is to reach **nirvana** with peace and freedom from desires and wants. Only in this way will a person stop suffering. Like Hindus, Buddha believed in reincarnation. He believed that people would have another chance to reach nirvana if they did not achieve it in the present life.

Buddhism gained popularity in India. It was especially attractive to the outcastes and to the members of the lower castes. Buddhism was not based on a caste system. It gave everyone an equal opportunity to be enlightened. Buddhism gave the lower classes hope that they could change their circumstances. Some people in the higher classes also appreciated Buddha's ideas. Buddhism spread to other parts of the world over time.

 In what ways are Buddhism and Christianity different?

Why did Buddhism appeal to members of the lower castes and the outcastes?

How did Chandragupta Maurya develop the Mauryan Empire?

The Mauryan Empire

Chandragupta

In 326 BC, the army of the Greek leader Alexander the Great conquered portions of northwestern India. According to legend, while Alexander was in India, he met a young Indian warrior named **Chandragupta Maurya**. Like Alexander, Chandragupta decided to train a large army of his own.

Chandragupta conquered most of the Ganges River Valley. After Alexander died, Chandragupta and his army conquered the portion of India that Alexander had taken. Chandragupta added these small kingdoms to his empire and became the first ruler in the Mauryan dynasty. Almost all northern India was under his rule.

Chandragupta made many decisions that strengthened India as an empire. He chose **Pataliputra** as his capital city and established a centralized government there. He maintained a strong army of six hundred thousand soldiers. His military also included elephants and chariots. However, Chandragupta did not trust his subjects. He set up a network of spies throughout the empire to inform him of any rebellion.

TWO TYPES OF BUDDHISM

As Buddhism spread to other countries, it developed into two branches: Theravada Buddhism and Mahayana Buddhism. Theravada Buddhism is practiced primarily in southern Asia. It is the stricter of the two branches and sticks very closely to Siddhartha Gautauma's teachings. Mahayana Buddhism interprets Buddha's teachings more freely. Mahayana Buddhists do not believe it is as difficult to reach enlightenment as Theravada Buddhists do. Mahayana Buddhism is the larger of the two branches.

Asoka

Asoka, a grandson of Chandragupta, came to the throne in 273 BC. Asoka was one of the greatest rulers of the Mauryan Empire. He united most of the Indian subcontinent under his leadership.

However, after years of great military successes, Asoka began to hate warfare. He saw the bloodshed that resulted when he took over other cities, and he lost his desire to conquer. Instead, he devoted himself to Buddhism and its teachings.

Asoka worked diligently to promote Buddhism in his empire. He built thousands of dome-shaped shrines called **stupas**. His most well-known structure is the Great Stupa.

Chandragupta Maurya Indian warrior who conquered a large part of India and began the Mauryan dynasty.
Pataliputra The city chosen by Chandragupta to be the capital of the Mauryan Empire.
Asoka Ruler of the Mauryan Empire in ancient India; promoted Buddhism.
stupa A dome-shaped Buddhist shrine.

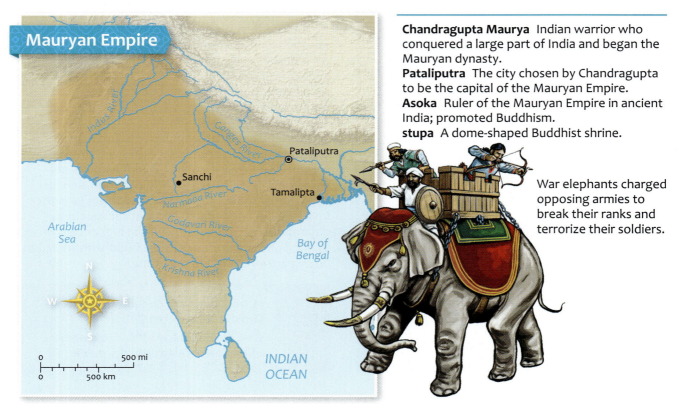

Mauryan Empire

War elephants charged opposing armies to break their ranks and terrorize their soldiers.

SIR JOHN HUBERT MARSHALL

What: British archaeologist
When: March 19, 1876–August 17, 1958
Where: Great Britain

John Marshall studied at King's College, Cambridge. Afterward he took part in excavations on Crete, a Greek island. In 1902 Marshall was named Director General of Archaeology in India. He excavated sections of Harappa and Mohenjo-Daro. He also helped uncover the ruins of the Mauryan Empire. Marshall restored the Great Stupa by rebuilding sections that were damaged after the fall of the Mauryan Empire. He was knighted in 1914 and received many other awards for his work.

The Great Stupa in Sanchi, India, is an ancient Buddhist monument that was originally built by the Mauryan emperor Asoka and later enlarged.

Since Buddhism emphasizes doing good works and relieving suffering, Asoka made many improvements to give his people better lives. He dug wells, planted trees, and constructed hospitals throughout his realm. Asoka did much to improve people's physical lives, but he could not address their most important need: knowledge of the true God.

Asoka had a major part in spreading Buddhism to other countries. His zeal led him to send Buddhist missionaries into areas outside his own borders. Many other Asian countries adopted Buddhism. Even today it is a popular religion in countries such as Myanmar, Thailand, Cambodia, Sri Lanka, China, Korea, and Japan.

Most people living in modern India, however, claim Hinduism as their religion. Ancient Hindu priests saw Buddhism as a threat to India's caste system. Asoka, however, tolerated people who opposed Buddhism and allowed them to practice other religions. He did not force people to become Buddhists. Perhaps this tolerance is one reason that Buddhism is not a major force in India today.

Asoka is believed by many to have been the greatest of the Mauryan kings. After the death of Asoka in 233 BC, the empire weakened. This was partly due to the poor leadership of Asoka's successors, internal rebellions, and invasions from foreigners. Invaders were able to overcome the last Mauryan king in 184 BC.

Nearly six hundred years later, around AD 400, a great empire called the Gupta was established in India. This empire began a period called the Golden Age of India.

Only in the last century has the mystery surrounding the ancient civilizations of India begun to unravel. As time goes on, more facts may be discovered. Perhaps one day people will even be able to read the Harappan language.

Much of India's history is shadowed by the false religions that its people created. But God has not forgotten India. Over the years, the gospel has spread into India, and many Indians have turned to Jesus Christ. One day, people of every language and nation will worship Christ. Many of India's people will be among them (Revelation 5:9–10).

What were the positive and negative aspects of Chandragupta Maurya's rule?

Why is Asoka often considered the greatest Mauryan ruler?

What accomplishments is Sir John Hubert Marshall known for?

ANCIENT CHINA

FOCUS
China's civilization developed and grew separate from the influence of other cultures.

| 1500 BC | | 1000 BC | | 500 BC | | BC AD | | AD 500 |

Shang dynasty ca. 1500–1000 BC
Zhou dynasty ca. 1000–221 BC
Qin dynasty 221–206 BC
Han dynasty 202 BC–AD 220

When someone mentions sharing ideas, finding information, and selling goods across the globe, do you think of the World Wide Web? More than two thousand years ago, there was a different kind of web that accomplished the same things—just in a slower, physical way.

The Silk Road was a web of trade routes stretching between China, India, Persia, Egypt, and Europe. Although named for the delicate and expensive fabric Chinese artisans made, the routes also carried things such as gems, spices, artwork, tools, vegetables, and grains. They also allowed the spread of information and philosophies from one culture to another. Travelers on these roads had to be prepared for robbers, harsh weather, and rough terrain.

Here nomadic tribesmen are attacking the caravan of the merchant Chen Yu. Since he had prepared well for the journey by hiring guards, he survived the robbery and made it to the next caravanserai (an inn for travelers), where the men and camels could eat and rest.

Chen Yu's men might have used bronze swords similar to this one from the late Eastern Zhou dynasty.

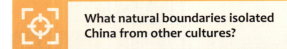

What natural boundaries isolated China from other cultures?

Geography

In the eastern part of the world, a civilization grew and thrived. Ancient China was separated from the rest of the world by mountains, deserts, and an ocean. These natural boundaries protected the Chinese people from foreign invaders for many centuries.

This isolation did not keep China's culture from flourishing. The Chinese were an advanced people. They were more skilled than many other civilizations of their day. The advanced skills of the Chinese support the fact that people have always been intelligent because they were created in God's image.

Geography played an important role in the development of ancient China. The Himalaya Mountains provided a natural southwest border, keeping invaders out. The Himalaya Mountains are the highest mountains in the world, with many peaks having an elevation of more than twenty-four thousand feet above sea level. The Gobi Desert and the Taklamakan Desert

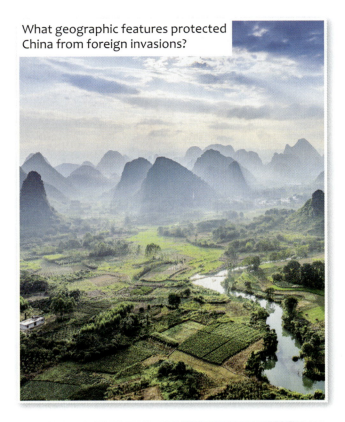

What geographic features protected China from foreign invasions?

The silt in the Huang He, or Yellow River, gives it a yellow color.

THE REGION TODAY

China

Location
China is the fourth-largest country in the world. It is located in East Asia, also known as the Far East. China shares its borders with fourteen countries: North Korea to the east; Russia and Mongolia to the north; Kazakhstan, Kyrgyzstan, Tajikistan, Afghanistan, and Pakistan to the west; and India, Nepal, Bhutan, Myanmar, Laos, and Vietnam to the south.

Climate
Most of China has a temperate climate similar to that of the United States. Both countries are close to the same lines of latitude. China's temperature varies from region to region. The climate is affected by yearly monsoons. Annual precipitation ranges from less than one inch to more than eighty inches. The northern regions are snowy in the winter, and the southeastern coast is rainy in the summer and autumn.

Topography
The eastern region is the lowlands, where the Yangtze River and the Huang He flow to the ocean. In central China, the land becomes rolling hills. The western part of China is hilly and mountainous. Tibet, in southwest China, has some of the highest mountain peaks in the world.

Natural Resources
China is one of the world's largest producers of iron ore. Large amounts of coal and oil exist there, but the industry for these resources needs further development. Other natural resources include deposits of tungsten, bauxite, aluminum, zinc, uranium, tin, lead, and mercury. The land has been heavily farmed, and many of the original forests have been destroyed.

China Then & Now

- ⊙ Modern capital
- — Modern borders
- Modern China
- Shang dynasty

What ocean borders China?

The Gobi Desert covers five hundred thousand square miles and is the world's fifth-largest desert.

Huang He (Yellow River) One of two major river systems in China that begins in northern China and flows to the Pacific Ocean; sometimes called "China's Sorrow."

border the north and the west of China. Extreme temperatures and poisonous snakes make these two deserts the world's most dangerous. The China Sea and the Yellow Sea are China's eastern and southern borders. Both seas are part of the Pacific Ocean. In ancient times, few civilizations had mastered shipbuilding. Being isolated from the rest of the world allowed the Chinese civilization to grow and thrive without western influence.

When the early Chinese migrated to East Asia, they settled near rivers. The Yangtze River and the **Huang He** are among the most important geographic features in China. These rivers provided fertile soil, food, fresh water, and transportation which allowed the ancient Chinese to thrive. Along these rivers, the Chinese built villages that eventually grew into a civilization. They named their land the Middle Kingdom because they thought it was in the center of the earth. The Chinese flourished as an advanced civilization.

 What is a natural boundary?
Why did ancient civilizations settle near rivers?

ACTIVITY

Making a Raised-Relief Map

The China Then & Now map on page 119 is a physical map of modern China. It is a flat representation that shows physical features, such as mountains, rivers, and valleys. In this activity, you will be making a kind of physical map, but your map will be a three-dimensional model. This kind of map is called a raised-relief map. It will show details of land features, such as the heights of mountains, the depths of valleys, and the paths of rivers cutting through the surrounding land.

1. Gather the following materials: the instruction page, a map pattern, cardboard, salt dough, a paintbrush, and paint.
2. Trace the outline of the map onto the cardboard.
3. Fill in the outline of your map pattern with the dough. Shape mountains, valleys, rivers, and other land features.
4. Let the dough dry.
5. Paint and label your map. Include a key.
6. Display your map.

How were tings and oracle bones used in the religion of the Shang dynasty?

The Rise of the Shang

China was ruled by several dynasties. One of the earliest was the **Shang**. This dynasty started ruling around 1500 BC. The Shang settled along the Huang He in northern China. Most of the people in the Shang dynasty were farmers. They grew vegetables and grains, especially rice, for food. The Huang He was called "China's Sorrow" because its floods killed thousands of people and ruined many harvests.

Religion

The Shang were polytheistic. They worshiped a supreme god who was over lesser gods. In addition, the Shang people, particularly the royal family, practiced a religion that involved **ancestor worship**. The Shang believed that the spirits of their departed ancestors lived on in the afterworld. They thought their ancestors had magical powers to punish or help people. When the weather was good, the Shang believed that their ancestors were pleased. If drought or famine came to the land, the Shang thought they had angered their ancestors.

To please their ancestors, the people used ornate bronze vessels, called **tings** (or dings), to cook meat for a sacrifice. Royal families had special ceremonies for preparing and serving their sacrifices. These sacrifices were offered as food to their ancestors.

The Shang religion centered on rituals and superstitions. Besides using tings in ancestor worship, the Shang also used **oracle bones**. The oracle bones show that the Shang had a system of writing. The king would have a priest write a question on the bone, such as "Will the rains flood the land?" Then the priest heated the bone with a hot metal rod. The heat caused the bone to crack. These cracks were believed to be the answers from the gods and ancestors. The priest interpreted these cracks. The king could make decisions based on these answers. Kings consulted oracle bones before making decisions about things such as planting, fighting, and building.

The priests were also governmental officials. They kept a close watch on political and economic affairs. Many interpretations of oracle bones were based on current events. Because the king and the people believed the priests could interpret oracle bones, the priests had great power in the Shang dynasty.

Arts

The ancient Chinese were skilled artisans. One of their skills was metalworking. Their special techniques in making bronze have not been equaled, even today. The Chinese kept their metalworking knowledge from other countries for centuries. The making of bronze required mining copper, tin, and

 ANCESTOR WORSHIP

The Chinese believed ancestors had power to influence the affairs of the living. Many Chinese still believe that descendants must perform rites to give ancestors the proper afterlife.

This duty hinders many Chinese from turning to Christ. They know that if a person becomes a Christian, he should no longer offer sacrifices to ancestors. He might feel that he is not honoring the family.

The Bible teaches that children should honor parents (Exodus 20:12). However, Luke 14:26 teaches that honoring parents must not be placed above honoring God. Nor should people give others credit for what only God can do. Only God controls all things (Daniel 4:34–35).

Shang The Chinese dynasty that began ruling around 1500 BC.

ancestor worship A belief that the spirits of ancestors live on in the afterworld and have powers to help or punish people who are still alive.

ting An ornate bronze vessel used in ancient China for cooking meat for sacrifices to the ancestors.

oracle bones Animal bones or turtle shells used in ancient China to predict the future.

Oracle bone

Bronze ting from the Shang dynasty. How did the Shang use tings such as this one in worship?

Mineral Resources of Modern China

In what part of China are the metals found to make bronze?

lead from different regions of China and transporting the three minerals to one location.

The Shang used bronze to make ornaments, statues, and vessels such as tings. They developed a difficult process of bronze casting that no other ancient people used. First, metalworkers made a mold in the shape of the object to be cast. The mold was made of several pieces of clay that fit tightly together. The detailed designs of the object were carved into the clay. After the mold was made, the metalworkers poured the molten bronze into the mold. When the bronze had cooled and hardened, the mold was carefully removed and saved for reuse. Once polished, the bronze object was ready to be used.

Although the Shang are best known for their works of bronze, they made advances in other arts as well. Farmers produced silk, which weavers made into colorful clothes. Artisans made vases and dishes from fine white clay. The Shang also carved statues from a green stone called jade.

Royal palaces and walled cities were part of the Shang heritage in architecture. The ruler's palace was at the center of the capital city. The houses of the artisans surrounded the palace. These houses were rectangular and built on flat earthen platforms.

Shang Tombs

Toward the end of their rule, the Shang moved their capital near the present-day city of Anyang. Much of what is known about the Shang dynasty comes from the tombs there. The Shang buried valuables and pottery with their rulers. Bronze cups, chariots, and oracle bones have been found in the tombs.

The Shang buried their dead in deep, cross-shaped pits. Each pit was covered with a wooden roof. Slanted ramps leading from the center of each grave allowed the body and burial offerings to be carried to the bottom. Some tombs contained the remains of human and animal sacrifices.

Government

The government was a monarchy. The king was assisted by officials with certain powers and duties. The officials were usually related to the king.

Archaeologists have found evidence that Shang was the capital city of the royal family line. This ancestral capital remained in the same location throughout the dynasty. The Shang kept family tablets, temples, and ceremonial dress there.

The king himself lived in and ruled from a political capital. The political capital was moved many times during the dynasty. These moves may have been due to struggles among the nobility. Artifacts and information on oracle bones suggest that Shang kings were at war with enemy forces. Sometimes the king sent out armies of thirteen thousand soldiers to fight for the empire.

The Shang kings developed a form of government that lasted about five hundred years. The Shang dynasty weakened and came to an end around 1000 BC. This sequence of events became a pattern throughout Chinese history. Each dynasty prospered for a period, then it declined and was overthrown.

What is a dynasty?

What is an oracle?

What other civilization had tombs similar to the Chinese tombs?

What were some of the achievements of the Zhou dynasty?

The Zhou

Around 1000 BC, the **Zhou** invaded the Shang from the west and overthrew their dynasty. The Zhou rule lasted longer than any other dynasty in Chinese history. There were thirty-seven kings in eight hundred years. The period in which the Zhou dynasty ruled is called China's **classical age**. Much of China's culture was established during this time.

Government

The Zhou believed that heaven, the supreme force of nature, gave the king his right to rule. This belief was called the **Mandate of Heaven**. According to the mandate, a king should be righteous and kind. If a king failed to act properly, he lost his right to rule. The mandate allowed the people to seize control from the king by force if necessary. If the new king they placed on the throne was successful, the people viewed his success as proof of heaven's support for his rule. The king was called the Son of Heaven. The Mandate of Heaven became a tradition of Chinese government. The Zhou leaders used this belief to justify their rebellion against the Shang.

The king was the highest authority in the Zhou dynasty. Beneath him were the nobles, and under them were the peasant farmers. The king gave his nobles land in exchange for their loyalty. Nobles also paid taxes and provided soldiers for the king. Nobles governed over the land that they owned. They gave plots of land to the peasant families to farm in return for a portion of the crops and goods produced.

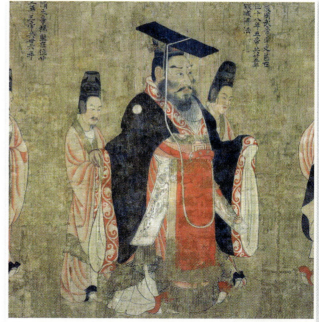
King Wu overthrew the Shang dynasty and became the first ruler of the Zhou dynasty.

The Family

China developed and preserved its culture by establishing strong family ties. The traditional family in China included many generations. A family usually occupied the same house or had houses around a common courtyard. The members of the family that lived together included children, parents, grandparents, aunts, uncles, and cousins. Older family members had more power and privileges than younger ones. Men were considered more important than women. Fathers were respected and obeyed by their wives and children.

On what river was the city of Luoyang located?

Zhou The Chinese dynasty that began ruling around 1000 BC.

classical age A time in a civilization's history that is thought to be its high point of cultural development and achievement.

Mandate of Heaven The Zhou belief that heaven gave the king his right to rule but required him to rule righteously.

The Writing System

The Chinese established their writing system during the Zhou dynasty. Like the writing of many other ancient peoples, it consisted of pictographs. The Chinese used brushes to make fine strokes when writing. This way of writing became a form of art.

Chinese pictographs changed over time. Some pictographs were combined to form new words or ideas. Unlike the English writing system, traditional Chinese writing is not based on a simple alphabet. Chinese writing consists of over sixty-five thousand characters that represent complete ideas, objects, and sounds. For example, the character for the word *good* is a combination of characters for the words *girl* and *boy*.

People learn to read Chinese by memorizing each of the characters. Those who master the written language have always had a place of distinction in Chinese society. Most Chinese people today know only about four thousand characters.

What did early Chinese writing consist of?

girl   boy   good

Currency

Like many ancient civilizations, the Chinese bartered or traded. Seashells and beans, as well as pieces of iron, gold, silver, and bronze have been used as money in many civilizations. Cowry shells were the earliest known form of **currency** used in China. These shells were easy to carry and count. During the Zhou dynasty, people used coins, small knives, and spades as currency. These were all made from metal mined in the region.

Classical Art

Artisans of the Zhou dynasty worked with bronze as the Shang had done. But the Zhou craftsmen developed a simpler method of making bronze. Many of their fine works still exist today. Artisans covered many of the bronze items with Chinese writing and intricate carvings of both real and imaginary animals.

The Zhou, like the Shang, used their bronze works mainly in religious ceremonies. The ceremonies often included placing the vessels in the tombs of ancestors. The Zhou also carved pieces of jade to create decorative pieces of art.

Music was important to the ancient Chinese. It was played during times of worship, work, and pleasure. Beautiful music and an elaborate ceremony were often part of archery tournaments attended by Zhou nobles.

What was the earliest known form of currency used in China? What do you think the small, square hole in the coin was for?

Bronze bells were used in social activities and political state ceremonies. The bells were struck with metal hammers.

Jade carvings were often used in rituals and represent the highest achievement of China's Bronze Age.

currency Money; any item of value that is exchanged for goods or services.

 What tradition of Chinese government did the Zhou leaders use to justify their rebellion against the Shang?

How does Confucianism compare and contrast to biblical truth?

Classical Education

Education was important during the Zhou period. A good education was highly prized by Chinese **philosophers** such as **Confucius,** who was also a teacher. His ideas greatly influenced China's classical age.

Confucius wrote many **proverbs** about everyday life. One of his proverbs was "Learning without thought is a snare; thought without learning is a danger." Confucius made education available to students from all social classes. A person from even the poorest background could have a better future if he had an education.

In China, education began at an early age and demanded total dedication of time and energy. Students spent many years learning the difficult Chinese language. They were also required to memorize classical Chinese literature.

In most ancient civilizations, soldiers, priests, and merchants held important positions among the people. Through much of Chinese history, however, no one exceeded the influence of the scholars.

Scholars during the Zhou dynasty wrote many books. These books are considered the classics of Chinese literature. Poetry, history, rituals, conduct, and music are some of the subjects of the books from that period. One had to have a thorough knowledge of these books to be considered a true scholar in China. Many ancient Chinese books were based on the teachings of Confucius.

CONFUCIUS

What: philosopher and teacher
When: 551–479 BC
Where: China

Confucius, who lived at about the same time as Buddha, was born with the name Kongfuzi. He grew up in poverty but worked a variety of jobs. He devoted his life to teaching and became the most honored teacher. The Chinese call him "the Master." His philosophy is contained in a collection of his sayings and activities called *The Analects*. Confucius's philosophy greatly influenced Chinese culture throughout history and into modern times. This philosophy became part of China's religious beliefs and practices.

philosopher A scholar who devotes himself to the pursuit of earthly wisdom.
Confucius Chinese philosopher whose teachings greatly influenced China's classical age.
proverb A wise saying that expresses a simple truth.

Confucius was a teacher during the Zhou dynasty. What are some differences between this scene and your school?

FIVE BASIC RELATIONSHIPS	
Duty: to set a good example of proper behavior	**Duty:** to show respect and obedience
father —— son	
elder brother —— younger brother	
husband —— wife	
elder friend —— younger friend	
ruler —— subject	

The Influence of Confucianism

Confucius was born into a poor but respected family. He lived during a time of social and political unrest. Confucius believed the people of a nation would be good only if the government set the right example of what goodness is. But if the people who worked in the government were not good, the government could not be good. Confucius tried to solve this problem by teaching his followers how to live a good life.

Confucius taught that a good life could be summarized as "What you do not want done to yourself, do not do to others." Because Confucius taught that true goodness is found in the way that a person treats other people, relationships were very important.

Confucius taught that there were five basic human relationships. In these relationships, a person's duty is to obey the elder person or the ruler. And the elder person or the ruler must set a good example for those under him. Confucius believed that if proper relationships in these five areas were kept, society would have harmony and order.

CONFUCIANISM

Confucius's definition of goodness was partly correct. He said that "What you do not want done to yourself, do not do to others." This is similar to Jesus' teaching that "Whatsoever ye would that men should do to you, do ye even so to them" (Matthew 7:12). Confucius knew that it would be impossible to live this kind of life. He knew that a person might sometimes live this way, but that it was impossible for a person to always treat others the way that he would want to be treated. The apostle Paul recognized this problem when he wrote, "The good that I would I do not: but the evil which I would not, that I do" (Romans 7:19). Confucius had no answer to this problem. He told his followers they should simply do their best.

Christianity teaches that trying one's best is not good enough. God is a righteous judge. A righteous judge must judge wrongdoing. To escape judgment, a person must be perfectly good. It is only through Jesus that a person can be declared right with God.

Even though Confucius identified five basic human relationships, he left out the most important relationship of all—people and God. He did not think there was a God who would judge all people. As a result, he simply told his followers to do their best in treating others well. But he neglected the greatest commandment of all: to love God with all of one's heart, soul, and mind (Matthew 22:37).

How did Confucianism develop? What did Confucius teach about relationships?

Built in 1302 to honor Confucius, the Temple of Confucius in Beijing was where advanced scholars took exams.

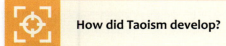

How did Taoism develop?

COMPARISON OF BELIEFS	
Confucianism	Taoism
active lifestyle	passive lifestyle
fulfillment of social obligations	freedom from responsibility
improvement of government, laws, and education	minimizing of government authority and involvement in society
focus on the human world	focus on the natural world

The Influence of Taoism

Second in importance to Confucianism was **Taoism**, which takes its name from the word *tao*, meaning "the way." Taoism taught that tao was the guiding force in nature. According to Taoist teaching, people ought to find peace and happiness by living in harmony with nature. People should not seek power, wealth, or learning. They should be content with a simple lifestyle. Everyone should live together in love and peace.

Followers of Taoism did not like the differences that Confucianism made between the social classes. Taoists also believed that people were not better than any other thing because people were just a part of nature. Taoists had little use for government. Instead, they felt that the government should leave the people alone to follow their own nature. According to Taoism, people could accomplish great things by "nonaction." Nonaction did not mean doing nothing. Instead, people should be like water and simply let things flow in a natural way. Nonaction is like riding a bicycle. When a person is good at riding a bicycle, he does not have to think about everything he is doing

A man named Lao Tzu has traditionally been considered to be the founder of Taoism.

TAOISM

Taoism (Daoism) is difficult to describe because Taoists taught that true philosophy was not something that depended on words. For example, a person can know how to ride a bike without being able to tell someone how to ride a bike. And a person who has heard a description of how to ride a bike may not be able to ride one. Riding a bike is something that people just do without thinking about the mechanics or expressing the process in words. Similarly, the Way must be followed through nonaction.

The Bible teaches that true religion is not a matter of words only. If people say that they have fellowship with God but live sinful lives, they are not telling the truth (1 John 1:6). But the Bible does give many words that describe who God is and what way of life pleases Him. These words tell of a problem: sin. And they tell how the Son of God became a man, lived, and died to save people from their sin. God shows grace to people by communicating to them clearly in the Bible.

to ride. Similarly, the best goodness is the kind that comes naturally, without even having to think about it.

Confucianism guided the thinking of China's educational, social, and political systems. Later, Taoism became the basis of magical and superstitious elements in Chinese culture. In many ways, Confucianism and Taoism are opposites.

Legalism

One group of thinkers in China did not believe that religion could solve society's problems. They believed that people were evil by nature and needed to be controlled by strict laws. This Chinese philosophy was known as **Legalism**. Legalists felt that those who disobeyed the law should be punished harshly. They thought a strong ruler was needed to maintain order. Confucianism, Taoism, and Legalism all became popular, but the Legalists were the first to put their ideas into practice throughout China.

Taoism A Chinese philosophy that promotes humility and submission to *tao*, "the way."

Legalism The belief that people are evil by nature and so must be controlled by strict laws.

What biblical truths refute Taoism?

What changes did Qin Shi Huang make to help unify China?

The Qin

The Zhou rulers established ultimate authority over the people, but they allowed nobles freedom in ruling local territories. As the nobles passed their power to their sons, loyalty to the king became less important. A time came when the king could no longer control the nobles. Fighting broke out between rival territories. Many people refused to defend themselves and their king against invasions. In 771 BC, invaders reached the capital. China endured an extended period of unrest. Instead of having a strong central government, powerful families struggled to govern. When a family became weak, a more powerful family would seize control.

China was divided into many **feudal** states, each with its own ruler. One of these feudal states, known as the Qin state, strengthened its military and began conquering neighboring states. Around 221 BC, the Qin dynasty was established. Under the rule of **Qin Shi Huang,** the Qin dynasty was founded. Qin Shi Huang's name means "first emperor." He was a fierce emperor who united China under one government.

Government

Qin Shi Huang established a Legalist government and set up a **bureaucracy.** The emperor divided his empire into thirty-six districts. He appointed a governor for each district.

QIN SHI HUANG

What: emperor during the Qin dynasty
When: ca. 221–210 BC
Where: China

Qin Shi Huang began his reign at the age of thirteen. He conquered his six rival states and united them by making changes in the government. He was the first emperor to unite China under one government. He brought order and protection to China through harsh and ruthless methods. He ordered the Chinese to use a standardized system for measurements and currency, allowing China's economy to progress. He required a standard writing system to aid communication. He is known for building the Great Wall for protection from invasions.

Changes in China

The government put in place by Qin Shi Huang gave him great power. His power allowed him to make changes to unify China, but his methods to implement the changes were often cruel and harsh. He took land from the nobles to limit their authority. Those who did not agree with him faced severe punishment, including hard labor or death.

Qin The dynasty that began ruling China around 221 BC.

feudal A political system where the ruler or government provides protection in exchange for service.

Qin Shi Huang Chinese emperor who began the Qin dynasty; name means "first emperor."

bureaucracy The managing of government through bureaus, or departments, with appointed officials.

Great Wall A series of fortified barriers over fourteen hundred miles long built across northern China to keep invaders out.

Compare the size of the Qin dynasty with the size of the Shang dynasty on the map on page 119.

Qin Dynasty

The irrigation system built during the Qin dynasty is still in use today.

China became more unified as Qin Shi Huang established the same laws and taxes for everyone. He standardized weights, measurements, and the money system. All Chinese people were required to use the same writing system.

Qin Shi Huang standardized the currency. He minted coins that were round and flat with a square hole in the middle that allowed people to carry them on a string. The coins were imprinted with the emperor's image.

The emperor's building projects also helped to unify China. The Chinese people built a network of roads. Each road was built to a standard width. The roads made traveling easier. The roads also allowed the Chinese army to move quickly to suppress revolts. Workers built canals to connect the rivers and improve transportation throughout the country. The rivers and canals made it easier to ship goods from the north to the south. They also built an irrigation system to provide water to more land for farming. To help protect the country, the Chinese built a wall in the north.

The Great Wall

The **Great Wall** is one of the best-remembered accomplishments of Qin Shi Huang. He ordered the wall to be built by linking a series of existing fortifications. The wall was actually designed as two walls with a space between them. Soil was piled and packed between the walls to form a road on top. The wall kept out invaders from the north, and the construction work kept discontented citizens busy.

Hundreds of thousands of people worked on the wall. They used stone, dirt, or whatever natural materials were available. The workers faced years of hardship, danger, and sometimes death. Qin Shi Huang thought it was better for a thousand people to die so that a million people could live. Legends say that thousands of dead laborers lie buried under the wall. Much of the Great Wall was constructed during the Qin period, but it was also worked on during later dynasties.

What were two reasons for building the Great Wall of China?

The terra-cotta army consists of thousands of life-sized soldiers, horses, and chariots. Why was the terra-cotta army made?

Censorship

Qin Shi Huang thought that scholars who knew philosophy and wrote books wanted to break up his empire. So he censored them, using the government to control their influence. He persecuted scholars and destroyed books. Over four hundred scholars who refused to turn in their books were either buried alive or sent to work on the wall. The emperor did not believe in education for the common people. He thought that common people were wasting time if they were not growing food. He ordered the destruction of all documents that contradicted his way of thinking. Qin Shi Huang especially disliked the teachings of Confucius and had the books about his teachings burned.

The people did not like the emperor's harsh punishments. Neither did they care for the way he spent large amounts of money on himself. For example, he built magnificent palaces and a tomb that covered twenty square miles.

A Terra-Cotta Army

Like other ancient people, the ancient Chinese often buried their dead with supplies such as food, weapons, and money. The Chinese believed in life after death, but not as the Bible teaches. Like the Egyptians, they thought that their dead ancestors would live on into the next world and need supplies to survive.

In 1974 some Chinese farmers were digging when they made an incredible discovery—a giant underground room filled with an entire army of statues. The army was keeping a silent guard at the tomb of Qin Shi Huang. Each life-sized statue was made of hard, waterproof clay called terra cotta. The statues were carved with unique detail. The terra-cotta army included over six thousand soldiers with weapons, horses, and chariots. Historians believe that this army was built to protect the emperor as he lived on into the next world. Artifacts like the terra-cotta army provide information about the way people in the ancient world lived and died.

The powerful Qin dynasty lasted less than thirty years, yet it left a lasting monument—the name *China* comes from the name *Qin*.

Does the United States have a bureaucracy?

How do you think building projects helped unify China?

What were some of the achievements made during the Han dynasty?

The Han

The **Han** dynasty rose to power around 202 BC. Emperor **Wu Ti** extended China to include present-day North Korea and parts of central Asia. Unlike the Qin dynasty, Wu Ti provided a strong, central government. Like some of the rulers before him, Wu Ti took land from the nobles, raised taxes, and placed the supply of grain under governmental control. Confucianism became the Chinese government's official philosophy. The philosophy was promoted through a university that Wu Ti began. The Han dynasty became so popular with the people that to this day some Chinese call themselves the "sons of Han."

Government

The Han rulers needed well-trained officials to help run the country, so they developed a civil-service system. This system trained people for governmental service. A person interested in becoming an official first needed a recommendation. Then he studied for many years. After his studies, he took three public exams. The first exam covered history and the principles of government. The second exam was on the teachings of Confucius. Palace guards supervised the first two exams. The emperor himself directly supervised the third, which was on poetry and political essays. Those who attained this level were given positions in the government.

Governmental officials were not just scholars. They had a vital role in government. They supervised activities such as the building of roads, the dealings of merchants, and the collecting of taxes.

WU TI

What: emperor during the Han dynasty
When: ca. 140–87 BC
Where: China

Wu Ti was the most famous Han ruler. He began his reign at the age of sixteen. He was known for extending China's borders from North Korea to central Asia. Under Wu Ti's leadership, a civil-service system was established to train government officials. The Pax Sinica, or Chinese Peace, was formed to promote trade with other civilizations. Wu Ti is known for establishing the Silk Road, which was named for the main item that China traded with other civilizations.

Han The dynasty that began ruling China around 202 BC.

Wu Ti A Chinese emperor during the Han dynasty who greatly expanded China.

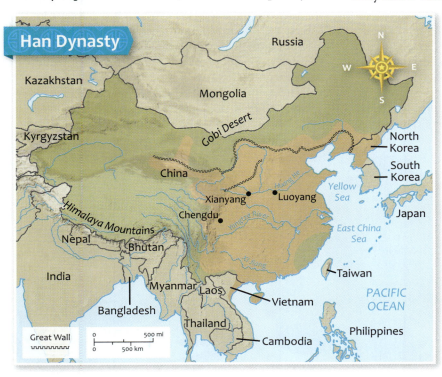

Han Dynasty

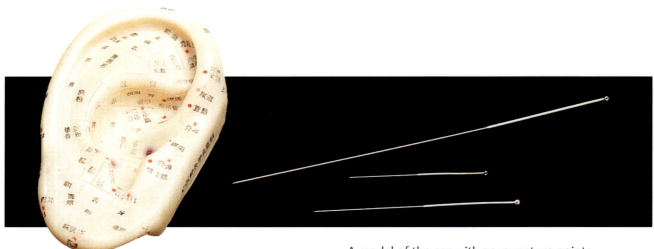

A model of the ear with acupuncture points labeled and different sizes of acupuncture needles. What is the purpose of acupuncture?

Achievements and Inventions

The Han dynasty was a glorious period in Chinese history. The Chinese made achievements in medicine, manufacturing, science, and literature. They even invented a way to make paper.

Medicine

The Han used special herbs as medicine. They also developed **acupuncture**. This procedure is done by poking needles into the skin at specific points on the body to prevent or treat pain and sickness. Some believed that acupuncture allowed a life force to move through the body to bring balance. Some people still use acupuncture today.

Manufacturing

China also advanced in manufacturing and increased the country's production of goods. The Chinese had become master metalworkers. The iron plow and the wheelbarrow increased production on farms. Swords and armor made the army more powerful.

The Chinese began using the rudder, a vertical blade attached to a ship. The rudder could be turned to change the ship's direction. Ships traveled farther, allowing China to establish trade connections with other countries.

The ancient Chinese are known for how they made silk. They raised silkworms and unwound the threads from the worms' cocoons. The threads were dyed and woven into beautiful fabrics. The Chinese kept these processes secret. Revealing the secret was punishable by death. During the Han dynasty, weavers used foot-powered looms to weave the silk threads into fabric. Clothing made from silk was very expensive. It was originally reserved for the emperor and other important leaders.

Science

A man named **Chang Heng** invented an important scientific instrument called the **seismoscope**. It was used to detect earthquakes. The Chinese called it an "earthquake weather-clock." Chinese seismoscopes were bronze jars with eight dragon heads. Each dragon held a small ball in its mouth and pointed in one of eight different directions. Under each dragon sat an open-mouthed frog.

---

acupuncture A procedure using needles to prevent or treat pain and sickness; originated in ancient China.
Chang Heng Inventor of the seismoscope.
seismoscope A scientific instrument used to predict earthquakes.

How did the development of the seismoscope help the Chinese?

What were some ways the early Chinese used hemp?

Inside the bronze jar was a pendulum. Whenever there was an earthquake, the pendulum would move, causing one of the balls to drop from the dragon's mouth into the frog's mouth. The Chinese determined the direction of the earthquake by which frog the ball fell into.

After an earthquake occurred, the Chinese leaders determined the earthquake's location. Then the leaders sent troops to that area. The troops carried food and supplies to help people, particularly the farmers, whose work supported the entire country.

Literature

During the Han dynasty, poets created long works of literature that combined poetry and prose. Another poetry style featured short lines of verse that could be sung. Poets were hired for the beauty of their verses.

Han writers also created important works of history. Sima Qian wrote a complete history of all the Chinese dynasties through the early Han. His writings were important, especially since Qin Shi Huang had destroyed many works during the Qin dynasty. Sima Qian's work was called the *Shiji* (*Records of the Grand Historian*). His style and format became the model for later historical writings.

Paper

Before paper was invented, the ancient Chinese used silk, bone, turtle shell, and other materials to keep written records. During the Han dynasty, the Chinese invented paper using **hemp**. They gathered plant fiber or tree bark and pounded it to a pulp. Water was added to the pulp and the mixture was spread into a thin layer to dry. The dried pulp formed a coarse sheet of paper. Not only was hemp used to make paper, but it was also used to make clothing and armor. Hemp fibers could be woven into a heavy cloth to make armor one to three inches thick. It was lighter and less expensive to make than metal armor. It was an effective protection from early weapons such as arrows.

hemp A plant fiber used to make paper, baskets, rope, and thick fabrics.

 How was the Chinese process of paper making similar to the Egyptian process of making papyrus?

LIFE IN THE HAN

Social Classes
Four classes of people developed as the Han civilization became established. The emperor's family was at the top. Under the emperor came soldiers, governmental leaders, and scholars. The next class of people included the producers of goods, such as peasant farmers, craftsmen, and artisans. The lowest level consisted of merchants, traders, servants, and slaves.

Environment
Even though China was geographically isolated from other civilizations, it thrived economically and culturally. The grasslands provided grazing for sheep, horses, and cattle. The sea and rivers provided ample fishing. Mining produced metals for tools. Fertile river valleys provided farmland for crops. China's geographic features allowed the civilization to flourish.

Justice
The Chinese emperor was the supreme ruler who determined the law. The emperor consulted the religious leader. As the civilization developed, the emperor delegated responsibilities to officials.

Job Specialization
Farming was the occupation of most Chinese people. There were also craftsmen who specialized in making tools or building structures. Merchants and traders sold or traded goods to other Chinese and along the Silk Road.

Few caravans traveled the entire length of the Silk Road. Instead, goods passed from one trader to another, with each trader adding his fee.

With the invention of inexpensive, lightweight paper, more people could own books, and ideas could spread.

DYNASTY

Arts, Sciences, and Written Language
Art and science can be seen in architecture. The Chinese constructed magnificent palaces and temples. They developed written language during the Zhou dynasty around 1000 BC. Writing was considered a form of art.

Organized Cities and Government
Cities developed along the Yangtze River and the Huang He, which provided water, food, and transportation. The emperors of the Han dynasty had control over all of China.

Citizenship
People became citizens at birth. It was expected that citizens obey and follow Chinese law. They were expected to act according to their position in society.

Religion
The earliest Chinese civilization practiced ancestor worship. Later civilizations adopted Taoism, Confucianism, and Buddhism.

Key Themes of Civilization
- Justice
- Power
- Citizenship
- Environment

Features of a Civilization
- Organized cities and government
- Social classes
- Job specialization
- Arts, sciences, and written language
- Religion

Gifts like food and drink were offered to ancestors in hopes that the ancestors would watch over the people.

Women and girls had the primary responsibility for silk production. Half of every year was devoted to the care of silkworms and the making of thread and cloth.

Why were boys valued more than girls?

Trade Routes

Emperor Wu Ti sent his general, Zhang Qian, to explore regions to the west of China. Wu Ti wanted him to find allies to help defend China from its enemies, especially the ones from the north.

Zhang Qian was unable to find allies for China; however, he brought back information from his travels. For example, he had discovered a breed of horse that would be useful in battle. These horses were larger and more powerful than the horses in China. Wu Ti encouraged trade with a foreign king to get these horses for China's cavalry.

Trade routes formed as the Chinese began trading with other regions. The main trade route was called the **Silk Road**. It stretched about four thousand miles from China to lands in the west. The Silk Road was named after the most famous item that was carried on it for trade—silk.

Traveling on the Silk Road was difficult and dangerous. Merchants traveled together in groups for protection. They hired armed guards to protect them from bandits who stole goods and water. Traders used the Bactrian camel to transport goods. This two-humped camel did well in both the extreme heat of the desert and the freezing cold of the mountains.

Silk and fine pottery from China were highly valued by people in other lands. Chinese merchants traded with those people and brought home horses and new products, such as fruits and cotton. Other civilizations eventually exchanged ideas and inventions with China.

Buddhism Comes to China

The Silk Road and other trade routes brought products and ideas from other lands. These new ideas included religion. Merchants and teachers from India brought Buddhism to China in the second century AD.

Silk Road The trade route that stretched about four thousand miles from China to the Mediterranean Sea; linked China to the nations in the West.

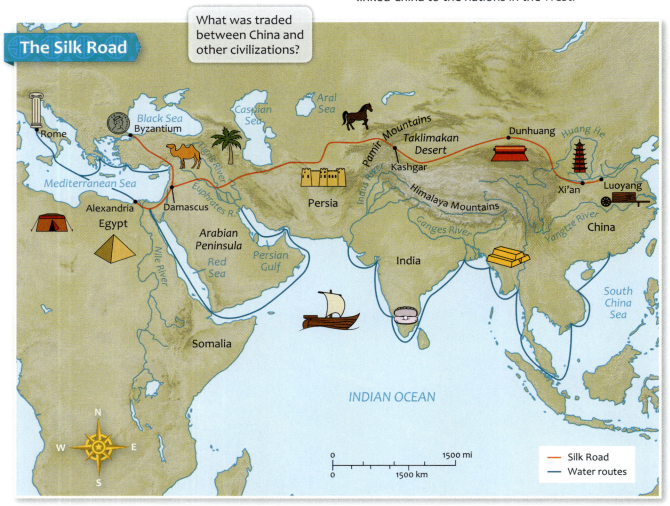

The Silk Road

What was traded between China and other civilizations?

MAHAYANA BUDDHISM

Mahayana Buddhism had to explain why some of its teachings differed from other versions of Buddhism. They said that Buddha knew that different people had different abilities to understand his teaching. So some Mahayana teachings were different from the original teachings, but they helped people of lesser ability come closer to the truths Buddha wanted to teach. Other teachings were given to those with better understanding. This mindset allowed Mahayana Buddhists to dismiss earlier Buddhist teachings and to accept later ones.

Some people think that this is the way the Old and the New Testaments of the Bible work. They think the Old Testament is no longer relevant and has been replaced by the New Testament. But this is not true. Both the Old and New Testaments teach truth, are still relevant, and are fully God's Word. One reason that Christians do not follow some of the practices of the Old Testament, such as sacrifices, is that they were symbols pointing forward to Christ. When Christ came, the symbols were no longer needed. In addition, some practices became irrelevant and outdated as society progressed and technology developed further.

As Buddhism spread from India to other countries, it developed into Theravada Buddhism and Mahayana Buddhism. **Mahayana Buddhism** was the branch that spread to China.

Unlike the Theravada Buddhists, Mahayana Buddhists believe it is a duty to help others reach nirvana, the state of peace or bliss. A Mahayana Buddhist hopes to become a **bodhisattva**, a person who has reached enlightenment but delays nirvana to help others reach enlightenment.

Society

During the Han dynasty, there was a time of social change. Social classes became more rigid. Confucianism divided people into four social classes. The upper class was made up of the emperor, his court, and scholars who held governmental positions. The second class was the largest and included the peasants. The third class was the artisans. Merchants made up the fourth class, which was the lowest because merchants did not produce goods for society.

A person's class was not tied to wealth or power. The peasants were poor yet made up the second-highest class. Merchants were often very wealthy but ranked as the lowest class. The lifestyles of the people, however, did vary according to their wealth.

The emperor and his court lived in a large palace. Many of the wealthy families lived on large estates. They filled their homes and their tombs with expensive and beautiful things. They hired laborers to farm their land and private armies to defend it.

Most people were poor and lived in the countryside. They wore plain clothes and lived simply. The peasants worked long days farming. In the winter, they were forced to work on governmental building projects.

The Han believed that the family should be strong. Children were taught to respect their elders. Disobeying parents was a crime. Children also honored dead parents with offerings and ceremonies. Boys were valued more than girls because sons carried on the family line and were responsible for the care of elderly parents.

The Fall of the Han Dynasty

By AD 220, the last of the Han rulers had been overthrown. For the next four hundred years, China suffered from internal wars and invasions. But the country would unify and flourish once again during a period known as China's golden age.

The influence of ancient China has continued across the centuries. Chinese inventions, such as paper and the seismoscope, made life more convenient. The Chinese laid the foundation for many advances that would later follow. Many things enjoyed today come from the ancient Chinese and their culture.

Pottery ladle from the Han dynasty

Mahayana Buddhism A branch of Buddhism that believes that everything that people see is an illusion and the ultimate goal is the state of nirvana.

bodhisattva A Buddhist who has reached enlightenment but delays nirvana to help others reach enlightenment.

 How are today's American social classes different from the Chinese social classes during the Han dynasty?

ANCIENT PERSIA

FOCUS
Persia rose from a humble beginning to become a powerful civilization.

Cyrus II rises to power ca. 559 BC | Wars with Greece 490–479 BC | Parthian period ca. 250 BC–AD 224

ca. 522 BC Darius the Great begins his reign | 334 BC Fall to Alexander the Great | ca. AD 224–651 Sassanid period

When you look at the night sky, you are looking at some of the same stars that Daniel, Queen Esther, and Nehemiah saw in ancient Persia. The constellation that is now called Orion, for example, would have been familiar to all of them. Perhaps they found comfort in looking at the stars, knowing that people in their homeland of Judea would see those stars too.

The study of the stars was important in the ancient Persian Empire, especially to men known as magi. Although our modern word *magic* comes from the same root as *magi*, these men were not magicians. They were respected scholars, famous even in other countries. They studied history, agriculture, music, poetry, astronomy, and many other subjects. They often advised kings. Daniel, well-trained and more discerning than all his fellow magi, was appointed Rabmag, chief of all the wise men, by Nebuchadnezzar of Babylon. When the Medes and Persians conquered Babylon, Daniel was kept in his powerful position.

The star that today's astronomers call Sirius was named Tir, Tishtrya, or Roozahang by Persians. In this picture, Amitis is learning about stars from her father, one of the magi. But they are living more than five hundred years after Daniel's time. Amitis's father tells her to find Tir by looking for three stars in a slanted row and then looking toward the horizon for a bright star in line with them. Because he has studied about Daniel and Queen Esther, he understands what their beliefs were. He wonders whether someday soon a star will herald the birth of the King of the Jews. So every clear evening, he goes to the rooftop and watches toward the east.

What can be inferred from the Cyrus Cylinder about Cyrus's treatment of the Jews?

An Empire Is Born

About two decades after the rise of the Babylonian Empire and only three years after the destruction of Jerusalem, two nomadic tribes called the Medes and the Persians moved into southwest Asia. They settled south of the Caspian Sea in the area that is now Iran. The Medes were stronger until a Persian leader named **Cyrus II** led a rebellion against the Medes and defeated them.

With Persia in control, the two nations combined armies and advanced westward into Asia Minor toward the kingdom of Lydia. This land was previously called Phrygia before coming under the control of Lydia. It was a wealthy civilization because of its gold and silver.

As the Medo-Persian army neared Lydia, Croesus, Lydia's king, came out to fight them. Cyrus and his army defeated Croesus and captured Lydia's capital city, Sardis. Instead of killing Croesus, Cyrus took him prisoner and allowed him to live in the Persian royal court.

Cyrus was a wise conqueror. He allowed his defeated enemies to maintain some measure of self-rule, tolerated their religious beliefs, and restored captive peoples to their homelands. The Persian Empire now extended west to the Aegean Sea.

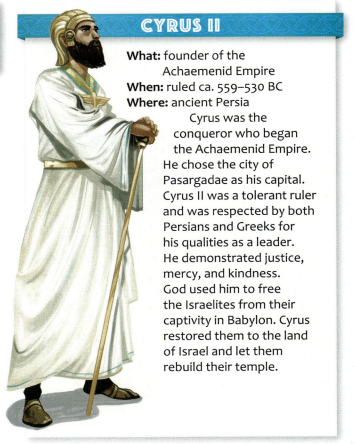

CYRUS II

What: founder of the Achaemenid Empire
When: ruled ca. 559–530 BC
Where: ancient Persia

Cyrus was the conqueror who began the Achaemenid Empire. He chose the city of Pasargadae as his capital. Cyrus II was a tolerant ruler and was respected by both Persians and Greeks for his qualities as a leader. He demonstrated justice, mercy, and kindness. God used him to free the Israelites from their captivity in Babylon. Cyrus restored them to the land of Israel and let them rebuild their temple.

Cyrus II A Persian leader who led a successful revolt against the Medes.

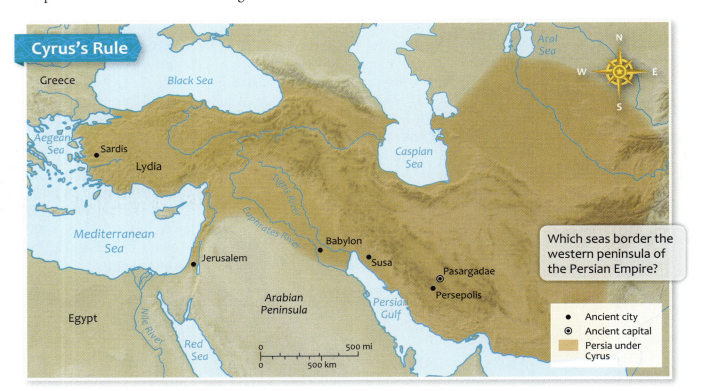

Which seas border the western peninsula of the Persian Empire?

THE REGION TODAY

Location
Ancient Persia was located in the Middle East in what is now Iran. At the height of Persia's power under Darius I, the Persian Empire extended from the Mediterranean and Aegean Seas in the west to the Indus River in the east.

Climate
The climate is mostly arid or semiarid. Cooler temperatures are found in the north with heavy snowfall in winter, especially in the mountains. Summers are hot and dry with temperatures exceeding 100°F. Most of Iran's rainfall occurs along the coast of the Caspian Sea.

Topography
The Zagros Mountains cut diagonally across the country from the northwest to the southeast. The Elburz Mountains line the Caspian Sea. In the central region is a

Iran
desert plateau. A coastal plain runs along the Caspian Sea, while another marshy plain lies in the southwest.

Natural Resources
The country's natural resources include petroleum, natural gas, coal, chromium, copper, iron ore, lead, manganese, zinc, and sulfur.

Geography and Culture
The mountainous terrain encouraged the Persians to develop a strong cavalry for warfare. The Persian road system allowed the East and the West to be in contact as never before.

Compare this map to the map on page 140, which shows the Persian empire under Cyrus. What new territory had been conquered since the reign of Cyrus?

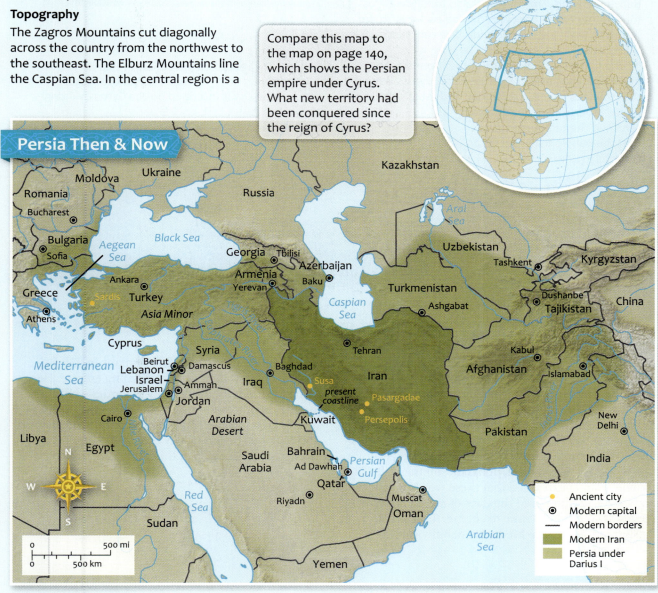

Persia Then & Now

ARCHAEOLOGY: THE CYRUS CYLINDER

The prophet Isaiah mentioned Cyrus by name 150 years before Cyrus's birth. Isaiah called Cyrus the Lord's anointed (Isaiah 45:1). Isaiah foretold that God would use Cyrus to free the Israelites from slavery in Babylon and let them rebuild their temple (Isaiah 44:28–45:6).

Like the Mesopotamians, the Persians used cylinder seals. One famous Persian cylinder seal is now in the British Museum. This artifact, known as the **Cyrus Cylinder**, tells about Cyrus's tolerant attitude toward his subjects.

In 1879 a scholar named Hormuzd Rassam found the cylinder seal at the site of the ancient Babylonian temple. The cylinder seal contained a message about Cyrus's respect for Marduk, a Babylonian god. The message also told how Cyrus freed some of the conquered peoples. He let them return to their homelands and make sanctuaries for their gods.

The Cyrus Cylinder does not mention Israel by name, but the book of Ezra says that Cyrus allowed the Israelites to return to Judah and rebuild God's house in Jerusalem. Cyrus also returned the temple treasures that the Babylonians had taken from Jerusalem.

Cyrus Cylinder A cylinder seal found at an ancient Babylonian temple; contains an account of Cyrus's conquest of Babylon and his restoration of the city.

From the Cyrus Cylinder:

> I am Cyrus, king of the universe, the great king, the powerful king, king of Babylon, king of Sumer and Akkad, king of the four quarters of the world. . . . I sought the welfare of the city of Babylon and all its sanctuaries. As for the population of Babylon, . . . I soothed their weariness, I freed them from their bonds(?). Marduk, the great lord, rejoiced at [my good] deeds, and he pronounced a sweet blessing over me. . . . I collected together all of their people and returned them to their settlements.

Translated from Persian by Irving Finkel, Curator of Cuneiform Collections at the British Museum © The Trustees of the British Museum, 2017

The record of the defeat of Babylon by Cyrus in 539 BC and his work to restore the city is inscribed on the Cyrus Cylinder.

Next, Cyrus led his army against the Babylonian Empire, which ruled the lands to the south. The book of Daniel records the fall of Babylon to the Persians. On the night the city fell, the ruler Belshazzar was having a feast for a thousand of his nobles. While they were drinking from vessels taken from the Jewish temple, a hand appeared and wrote the words "Mene, mene, tekel, upharsin" on the wall. The prophet Daniel explained that these words meant that God had numbered the days of the Babylonian kingdom, and it had come to an end. That night, Belshazzar died in the Medo-Persian invasion.

Cyrus conquered the Babylonians in 539 BC, adding the new land to his spreading empire. He continued to treat his defeated enemies well, allowing them to help make their own laws, to speak their own languages, and to keep their own customs and religious beliefs. Many believe the empire was strengthened because of this tolerance.

 How did the Persian Empire develop?

What contributions did the first rulers of the Persian Empire make?

The Empire Grows

The dynasty that Cyrus began is known as the **Achaemenid** period of Persia. Cyrus ruled the Persian Empire until his death in 530 BC. He was buried in a grand royal tomb in the capital city, **Pasargadae**. His son Cambyses took the throne after him.

Cambyses continued to extend Persia's empire. His most important success was conquering Egypt. But while in Egypt, he received news of a rebellion in Persia. Cambyses immediately headed for home. But on the way, he died of a wound caused by an accident with his own sword.

Darius I became the next king after he and some other nobles put down the rebellion. Darius was later known as Darius the Great because of his long and successful reign.

Under Darius, the Persian Empire reached its greatest size and power. Fewer than thirty years had passed since Cyrus rose to power among the nomads. Now people from many different lands were paying tribute to Darius. He needed a strategy for keeping his large empire organized.

Central Government

Darius formed a plan for governing the empire. He set up a place for government in one central city. Then he divided the conquered lands of his empire into twenty provinces. Each province was known as a **satrapy**. A governor, or a **satrap**, was assigned to each satrapy. The satrap's responsibilities included collecting tribute for Darius and reporting to him. A governmental system in which local governments are subject to a main authority is called a *centralized government*.

Darius moved the capital from Pasargadae to **Susa**. He also began building **Persepolis**, the ceremonial capital of the Achaemenid Persian empire.

Achaemenid The name of the Persian dynasty that began with Cyrus II.
Pasargadae The capital city of the Persian Empire under the rule of Cyrus II.
Darius I Also known as Darius the Great; king who expanded the size and power of the Persian Empire.
satrapy A province in ancient Persia.

satrap A governor in Persia who ruled a particular province; was responsible for collecting tribute and reported to the king.
Susa The capital city of ancient Persia after Darius I came to power.
Persepolis The capital city of Persia after Susa.

DARIUS I (THE GREAT)

What: third ruler of the Persian Empire
When: ruled ca. 522–486 BC
Where: ancient Persia

Darius I was not directly in line for the throne, but he rose to power after the death of Cambyses, Cyrus's son. Darius is famous for his Persian architectural style. He also established provinces and determined the amount of yearly tribute people paid to the satraps. He established standards for coin values, measures, and weights. He standardized routes by sea and land to promote commerce and trade. During Darius's reign, the Persian Empire reached the height of its size and power.

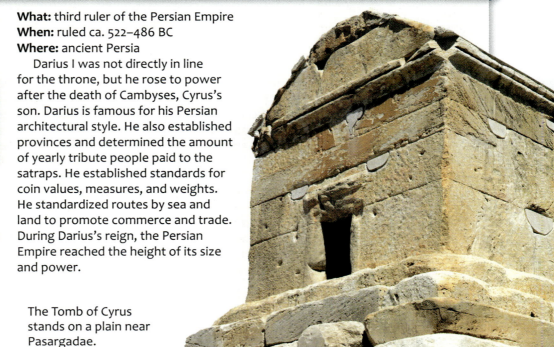

The Tomb of Cyrus stands on a plain near Pasargadae.

Darius's Rule

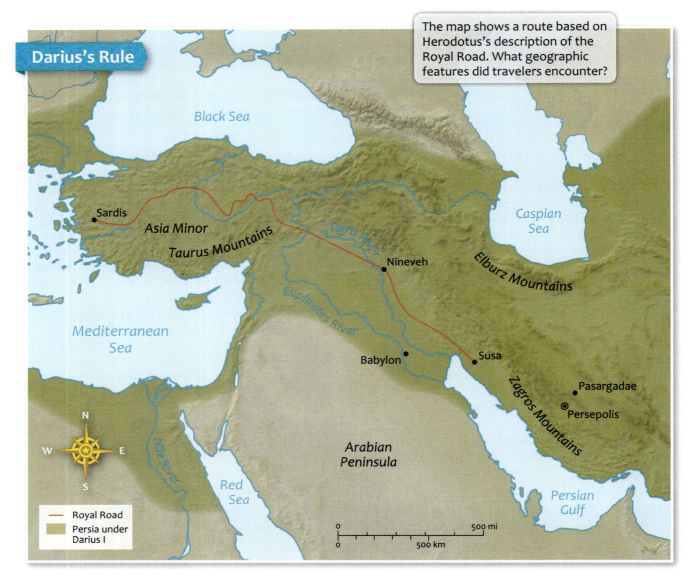

The map shows a route based on Herodotus's description of the Royal Road. What geographic features did travelers encounter?

The Road System

Darius needed the ability to communicate important messages to all parts of his kingdom. He also needed to receive news and collect wealth from distant areas. To keep his empire connected, Darius built and maintained a good road system. This system had about eight thousand miles of stone roads that connected the entire empire. The longest road, called the **Royal Road**, stretched over sixteen hundred miles from Susa to Sardis.

Darius had royal messengers stationed along this road to carry messages in relay style. **Herodotus**, a famous historian from Greece, describes the Royal Road and the king's messengers who traveled it.

> Nothing mortal travels so fast as these Persian messengers. . . . Along the whole line of road there are men, they say, stationed with horses, in number equal to the number of days which the journey takes, allowing a man and a horse to each day; and these men will not be hindered from accomplishing at their best speed the distance which they have to go, either by snow, or rain, or heat, or by the darkness of night. The first rider delivers his despatch to the second, and the second passes it to the third; and so it is borne from hand to hand along the whole line, like the light in the torch-race (Herodotus, *The History of Herodotus: Book VIII*, trans. George Rawlinson [NY: Tudor, 1928], 461).

Royal Road The longest stone road in the Persian Empire, stretching over sixteen hundred miles from Susa to Sardis.

Herodotus Greek historian; known as the Father of History.

Trade

The road system helped long-distance trade to flourish in the Persian Empire. The expanded empire gave Persia access to new resources and new ports for trade. People transported a variety of goods on the Persian roads. About once a year, ambassadors from all parts of the empire traveled the roads and carried goods to present as tribute to Darius. Some of these gifts are pictured in reliefs from the Apadana at Persepolis. These gifts likely included vessels made from precious metals and ivory. Gifts may have also included fragrances, dyes, cloth, ebony, objects made from cedar, and livestock. As the Persians saw the variety of goods produced in other lands, the demand for those goods grew.

The Lydians had used coins made from precious metals as an international means of trade. Some time after the Persians conquered the Lydians, the Persians adopted the use of coinage for trade. Darius introduced a common currency for his empire. The **daric** was a gold coin stamped with his image. The coin depicted the king kneeling while holding a bow.

daric The coin used in the Persian empire; named after Darius I.

Gold daric depicting a Persian king as an archer

It was used for foreign trade. A silver coin called a *siglos* or *shekel* was also commonly used in commerce. The emperors who followed Darius continued to use the gold daric and the silver shekel, but the coinage contained the image of the newest emperor carrying the weapon he chose.

HERODOTUS

What: Greek
When: 484–425 BC
Where: Asia Minor

Herodotus grew up as a subject of the Persian Empire during the fifth century BC. His writings indicate that he was well-educated and that he traveled widely. Herodotus became known as the Father of History.

Wherever he went, Herodotus listened and watched. He talked to people who remembered the past. He wrote down the interesting stories he heard. Over the years, he recorded the major events of his time in a lengthy work called *The History of Herodotus*. Herodotus spent most of his adult life working on this project. Much of what people know about ancient Persia comes from his writings. He describes the rise and fall of each of the Persian rulers. He also gives detailed accounts of the wars between Persia and Greece. Herodotus even records backgrounds and customs of foreign people he met during his travels.

Today scholars disagree on how accurate Herodotus was in his historical accounts. Some say that he did not always give objective details, especially when he recounted stories he had heard from others. Yet most scholars agree that he demonstrates some of the best qualities of a historian. Herodotus gathered information diligently, paid attention to details, and tried to bring people and places to life. He seems to have tried to present the material honestly and fairly.

Herodotus was an excellent writer. He had studied classical Greek prose, drama, and poetry. His reading had taught him to use language in a beautiful way. Many scholars compare The Histories to a work of poetry because of its graceful style.

Herodotus wrote in Greek, but scholars have translated his work into English and other languages.

DARIUS'S ORDER ABOUT THE TEMPLE

Cyrus had allowed the Israelites to return to Judah to rebuild the temple. The Israelites did so, but their work was stopped many times as other people tried to discourage them. Ezra 5 records that an official named Tattenai questioned the Jews' right to rebuild the temple. Tatennai wrote to King Darius to find out whether the Jews' work on the temple should continue.

Darius searched for and found Cyrus's decree. He wrote a letter back to Tattenai, telling him to allow the work on the temple. He also ordered that Tattenai help the Israelites with the project's expenses. Darius included a threat of death for anyone who tried to change his orders.

> And the God that hath caused his name to dwell there destroy all kings and people, that shall put to their hand to alter and to destroy this house of God which is at Jerusalem. I Darius have made a decree; let it be done with speed.
>
> Ezra 6:12

A Strong Military

Darius needed military strength to keep his empire under control. Persia had a strong force of paid soldiers who were professionally trained. Ten thousand of these soldiers were the king's own special force, called the **Immortals**. When one of the Immortals died, another immediately took his place. Darius himself had been one of the Immortals during the reign of Cambyses.

Persia also had a well-trained cavalry. Horses helped the soldiers travel quickly over Persia's mountainous terrain. When fighting an enemy, the Persian cavalry usually led the attack and was followed by foot soldiers.

The Persian military was well organized and loyal. Herodotus described it as the most valiant of all the armies he had seen. Darius used his army to end several rebellions during his reign. He also used the army to expand his empire. In the east, he conquered territory as far as the Indus River. In the west, he conquered a number of Greek city-states around the Aegean Sea. However, Darius never gained control over all the Greek city-states.

Immortals Special soldiers for the king in ancient Persia.

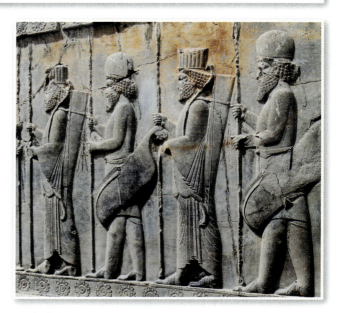

Relief showing a processional of Persian and Median soldiers from the Apadana at Persepolis

 Why did trade grow in the Persian Empire?

How valuable was Herodotus's work?

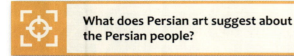

What does Persian art suggest about the Persian people?

Culture in Ancient Persia

Language

It is likely that there were many different languages spoken in ancient Persia. However, a language called Aramaic became the common tongue of the empire. A few parts of the Old Testament are written in this language rather than in Hebrew.

The kings of the Persian Empire wrote and spoke a language that became known as Old Persian. Old Persian was written in cuneiform that looked similar to the version used by the ancient Sumerians. Each symbol stood for a syllable.

Darius had an inscription and a bas-relief made on a cliff face near the base of the Zagros Mountains. The carvings were high on a cliff that could be seen along a trade route connecting the ancient capital of the Medes in northwest Iran with Babylon. The inscription and pictures tell about Darius's rise to power. The writing was made with cuneiform symbols carved in Old Persian, Babylonian, and Elamite. After Darius's scribes finished carving the inscription, they removed the rock ledge they had been standing on.

For centuries, no one could read this carving, called the Behistun Inscription, because it was too high on the cliff face to be read. In 1836 a British diplomat and scholar named Henry Rawlinson began studying the inscription. He risked his life to climb the cliffs and copy the cuneiform script. Afterward, he worked on deciphering the three languages.

The Behistun Inscription was just one of the sources used to decipher Persian cuneiform. Rawlinson and other scholars worked for years to solve the mystery of the wedge-shaped symbols. Their work resulted in a great breakthrough in understanding ancient civilizations. Many other cuneiform scripts could finally be read.

View showing the cliff face of the Behistun Inscription

The Behistun Inscription records Darius's rise to power. In what way did the inscription serve a purpose similar to the Rosetta Stone's?

LIFE IN PERSEP

Persepolis was the ceremonial capital of the Achaemenid dynasty. Inscriptions ascribe buildings to Darius I, Xerxes I, and Artaxerxes III. Alexander the Great destroyed the city in 330 BC, but the remains still exist in Iran.

Social Classes

There were three main social classes. The first included the warriors, who were the aristocracy. The second included the priests, and the third included herdsmen and farmers. The king came from the warrior class.

Justice

Darius reformed taxation to be more just.

One law that had seemed unjust said that conquered people were required to pay taxes on their land as a type of rent since conquered land was considered the king's property. The Persians were not required to pay taxes on their land because they were not a conquered people. Darius did not change this law.

However, Darius changed tax laws on crops to be more just. He no longer charged a high tax on crop production regardless of whether the yield was good or not. He surveyed the land to determine an average yield. He then instituted a fixed rate of tax based on a percentage of the average yield.

Power

The Persians divided their vast territory into provinces called *satrapies* that were overseen by a satrap. A secretary and a military leader kept the satrap from having too much control.

Religion

The main religion was Zoroastrianism. The Achaemenid kings believed Ahura Mazda gave them their kingdoms and was responsible for their accomplishments. There were many religions in Persia because Cyrus and Darius permitted conquered people to retain their own religious practices.

Environment

Persia bordered bodies of water that maximized trade. It had a rugged semi-desert region with mountain ranges forming natural barriers. Between the mountains was a plateau used for farming. There were also cities on the plateau. Persepolis was in the cooler mountain region and was used as the capital during the spring and summer months. But the rainy season made the roads so muddy that it was difficult to reach the city during winter months.

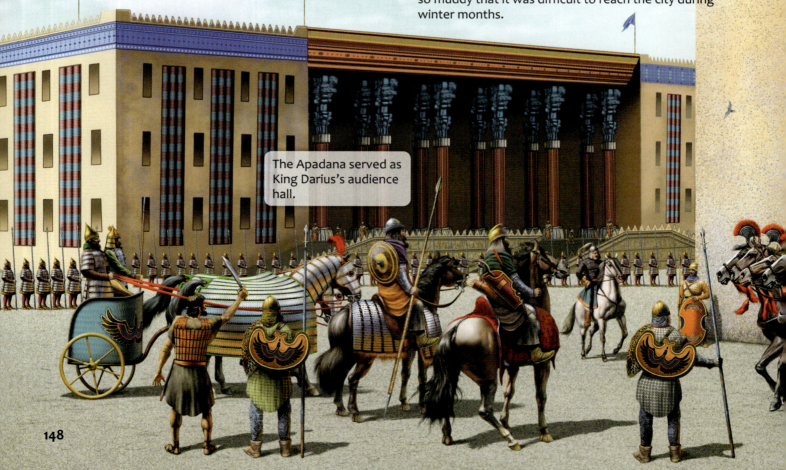

The Apadana served as King Darius's audience hall.

OLIS

Job Specialization
Farmers grew food for the empire. Weavers wove cloth and rugs. Craftsmen made weaponry, pottery, jewelry, and seals. Traders promoted commerce. Coinmakers struck coins. Bankers loaned money and acted as tax collectors. Wealthy property owners rented land and shops to others. Men served in the military. The government paid builders to dig canals, build roads, and construct buildings.

Arts, Sciences, and Written Language
The Persians sculpted, carved, and cast works of art. They also wove colorful rugs.

The Persians developed the composite bow for warfare. They practiced medicine and used the earliest batteries to lessen pain at a surgery site. The Persians studied astronomy. The government invested in developing irrigation and cultivating crops.

There was not a written Persian language until Cyrus commanded that script be created to document his rise to power.

Key Themes of Civilization
- Justice
- Power
- Citizenship
- Environment

Features of a Civilization
- Organized cities and government
- Social classes
- Job specialization
- Arts, sciences, and written language
- Religion

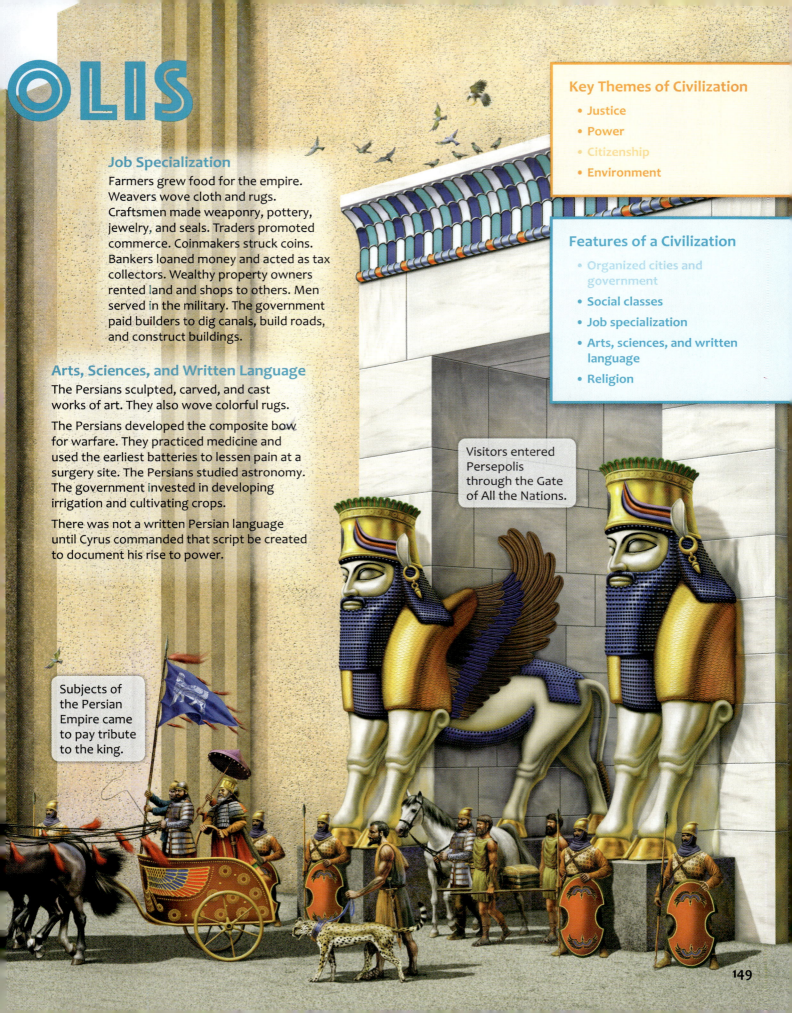

Visitors entered Persepolis through the Gate of All the Nations.

Subjects of the Persian Empire came to pay tribute to the king.

Art

Darius built the city of Persepolis on a terrace with a huge stairway leading up to it. The city had splendid palaces, a royal treasury, and the Hall of a Hundred Columns. Parts of these buildings are still standing today.

Darius filled the city with glorious works of art. Ornate carvings decorated the steps, entrances, and walls of buildings. Columns adorned the halls. Doors and furnishings were beautified with gold, silver, or bronze. Floors were often paved with brick or stone and covered with carpets. The carpets were likely woven of wool with intricate patterns and beautiful colors.

The Persians had great wealth, and they loved beautiful things. Archaeologists have found many Persian carvings that show people wearing bracelets, necklaces, earrings, and elaborate headdresses. Bowls carved with intricate patterns have been found. Jars, jugs, utensils, and drinking vessels called *rhytons* often had animal-shaped handles. Persian kings and nobles were buried with jewelry and other valuables.

Solid gold bracelet with winged-griffins

What might this gold rhyton have been used for during the Achaemenid period?

This carpet from the 17th century AD is an example of the beautiful carpets made in Persia.

Religion

During the sixth century BC, **Zoroaster** founded the main religion of ancient Persia, **Zoroastrianism**. Through this religion, Zoroaster tried to explain the existence of good and evil. He taught that a good god, Ahura Mazda, struggled with an equally powerful evil being, Angra Mainyu. Ahura Mazda was believed to be the creator.

Zoroaster Founder of Zoroastrianism in ancient Persia.
Zoroastrianism The main religion of ancient Persia.

ZOROASTRIANISM

Zoroastrianism teaches that there are two uncreated spirits. The entirely good spirit is Ahura Mazda, and the entirely evil spirit is Angra Mainyu. They are equal in power and are in battle against each other. Ahura Mazda created the world to be a place for good and evil to fight each other. He used six gods who came from him to create the world.

Three days after a person dies, the soul ascends to cross the bridge into heaven. If the good deeds outweigh the evil, that person crosses the bridge and ascends to heaven. If the evil deeds outweigh the good, the person plunges off the bridge into hell. In the last day, both the good and the evil will be resurrected to pass through a last judgment by fire. The wicked will be consumed by the fire along with Angra Mainyu and the other evil spirits. The good will become immortal and live forever with Ahura Mazda in a garden paradise.

Christianity also teaches that there is a battle between good and evil, but it does not teach that God and Satan are equal, uncreated spirits. God is the only eternal being. God created Satan as a good creature, but Satan rebelled and became evil.

The Bible also teaches that there will be a last judgment in which everyone will be raised from the dead and judged. But people will not be judged by whether their good works outweigh their bad works. No one is good enough to earn eternity with God. People will be judged by whether they have accepted Jesus Christ as their Savior. The Bible teaches that people must have the righteousness of Christ credited to them to have eternal life.

Zoroaster claimed that he had seen visions sent from Ahura Mazda. Zoroaster taught that each person must choose between good and evil. He also taught that a person could have eternal happiness if he did more good than evil in this life. The holy writings of Zoroastrianism are called the **Avesta**. The Avesta is made up of myths, rules, and hymns.

ZOROASTER

What: founder of Zoroastrianism
When: sixth century BC
Where: ancient Persia

Zoroaster was a religious teacher who may have been a priest. He claimed that there was one god, Ahura Mazda, who had shown him visions about what to teach. Based on these visions, he developed the Zoroastrian religion. The beliefs and teachings of Zoroaster are found in the Avesta.

The Zoroastrians believed that Ahura Mazda was represented by fire. The priests kept fires burning continually on altars in the temples. The priests in the Persian Empire were called **magi**. Some sources suggest that kings relied on the magi to interpret dreams and tell the future by the stars. Historical records are not clear on whether all the magi followed Zoroastrianism.

Zoroastrianism was the official religion of Persia. But like Cyrus, Darius tolerated other religions in his empire. He even played an important role in the rebuilding of the Jewish temple.

Some people in modern Iran and India still follow Zoroastrianism. They call themselves *Parsis*, another word for Persians.

Avesta The sacred writings of Zoroastrianism.
magi The name for Zoroastrian priests in ancient Persia.

What language was common among the Persian people?

What was learned by deciphering the Behistun Inscription?

Why is Zoroastrianism unbiblical?

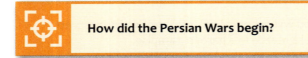

How did the Persian Wars begin?

War with Greece
The Battle of Marathon

Persia wanted to expand its empire into the mainland of Greece. This expansion would be a direct threat to the future of Greek culture and its political structures. In 499 BC, the Greek city-states in Asia Minor rebelled against the Persians. Athens and a few other city-states on the mainland of Greece sent an army to help the Greeks in Asia Minor. Persia put down the rebellion, but Darius was angry with the Greeks for banding together to rebel. In 490 BC, Darius and his army sailed to the plain of **Marathon** near Athens.

The Persian army had about twenty thousand soldiers spread out on the plain, while the Athenian army had only about ten thousand men. The Athenians stayed hidden and planned their strategy. They would wait in the hills and attack the Persians the next day.

In the morning, one of the Athenian generals ordered his men to attack the Persians. He placed the army in a long line and had them run full speed toward the Persians. It looked like a foolish plan to the Persians, but it worked.

The Persians forced back the center of the Athenian line. But the soldiers who were out on the wings of the line were stronger. They attacked both sides of the Persian army, trapping them and then drawing together like giant pincers. The Persians lost the battle of Marathon.

According to legend, a Greek runner named Pheidippides ran back to Athens, a distance of more than twenty-five miles, to report the good news. When he got there, he could breathe out only one word, "Victory." Then he collapsed and died. The name for the modern marathon, a race of 26.2 miles, comes from this legend.

Marathon An ancient plain in Greece, the site of the battle in which the Athenian army defeated the Persian army.

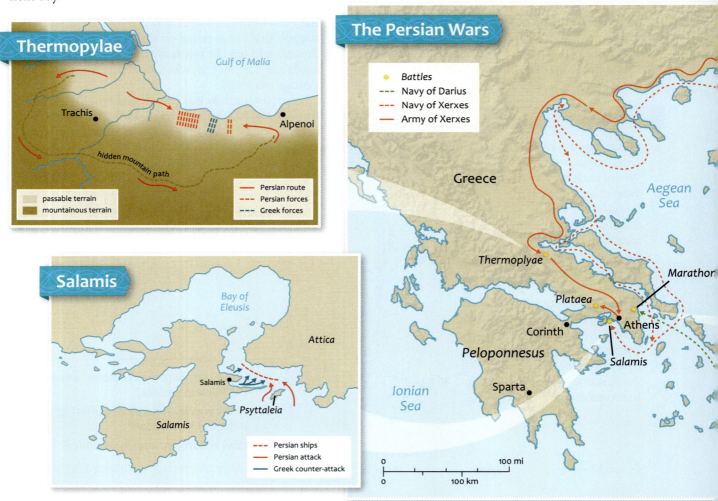

The Battle of Thermopylae

Darius died before he could take revenge on the Greeks. His son **Xerxes** became king and decided to continue the war with Greece.

In 480 BC, the Persian army attacked Greece again. They crossed from Asia Minor to Greece through a strait called the **Hellespont**. Xerxes had his men build bridges across the Hellespont. They laid planks across two long lines of Persian ships to make the bridges. But a storm destroyed the bridges before they could be completed. Xerxes was so angry that he executed the engineers who had designed the bridges. He also ordered his soldiers to beat the waters of the Hellespont with three hundred lashes. When his anger subsided, Xerxes ordered that the bridges be rebuilt. His army was finally able to march across to the coast of Greece.

Sparta, another Greek city-state, joined with Athens in fighting the Persians. Sparta had a strong army. The Greeks decided to position their forces at **Thermopylae**, a mountain pass about fifty feet wide. At first, it looked like they would be able to defend the pass and hold back the Persian army. But then a Greek traitor showed the Persians another path through the mountains.

Before long, the Greek army was surrounded. They fought to the end but lost. The Persians then marched to Athens and burned the entire city.

Xerxes King of Persia; also called Ahasuerus; son of Darius.

Hellespont The strait between Asia Minor and ancient Greece, the present-day Dardanelles; site where Xerxes and his army built bridges to reach the coast of Greece.

Thermopylae A narrow mountain pass in Greece; site where the Greeks were defeated by the Persians.

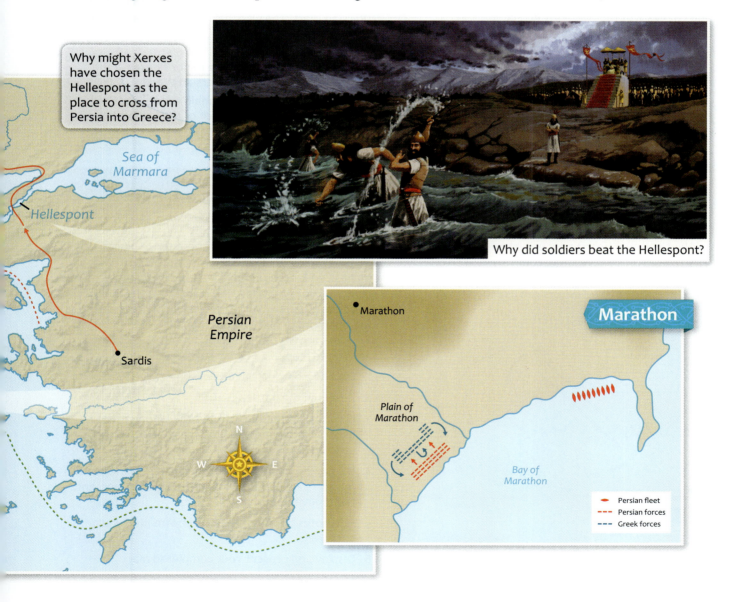

Why might Xerxes have chosen the Hellespont as the place to cross from Persia into Greece?

Why did soldiers beat the Hellespont?

Sea fight off Salamis between Ptolmey and Demetrius Poliorcetes

The Battle of Salamis

The Persians had won the battle of Thermopylae, but the Greeks were not ready to give up. An Athenian general named Themistocles had a plan to help the Greeks win the war with Persia.

Themistocles knew that the Greek ships were smaller and faster than the Persian ships. If the Greeks could trap the Persian ships in a tight space, the Greeks could win.

Themistocles decided to fight the Persians in the strait between the island of **Salamis** and the mainland of Greece. The Greeks lured the Persians into the strait with a false report that the Greek ships were trying to flee. The battle began in the morning, when sea breezes create strong waves in the strait. Once the Persian fleet had entered the strait, the sailors had a difficult time steering their large ships against the waves. Meanwhile, the Greeks launched their ships from the beach of Salamis. The small, lightweight Greek ships rammed and sank many of the Persian ships. The Greeks won the battle.

During the next year, the Greeks fought one more battle with the Persians in the city of Plataea. Many Persian soldiers were killed, and Persia had to admit defeat. Xerxes pulled the last of the Persian troops out of Greece and went home.

The wars between the Persians and the Greeks are known as the **Persian Wars**. Although Persia lost the wars, it remained a powerful empire for more than a century after the losses.

Salamis An island off the coast of Greece; site where the Greeks defeated the Persians in a naval battle.

Persian Wars The wars between the Persians and the Greeks.

Who were some major figures in the battles of the Persian Wars?

What were the main events and the outcomes of each of the key battles of the Persian Wars?

ACTIVITY

Making an Annotated Map

Have you ever been to a museum or a historical park? Such places often have large, colorful maps on display. These maps often include detailed information about the places they show. Visitors can use these maps to locate places and read notes about those places.

These kinds of maps are annotated, a term which means "with notes added." An annotated map contains notes that describe places, events, or other important features. Often an arrow connects a note to the appropriate place on the map.

In this activity, you will work together to create an annotated map of a Persian battle.

1. Choose a battle from one of the Persian Wars.
2. Research the battle.
3. Create a flat map that shows the land features, especially the ones that may have affected the outcome of the battle.
4. Display information about the militaries. Include the numbers and kinds of soldiers, their locations, and their movements.
5. Add notes of other historical information you gathered.
6. Display and present your completed map.

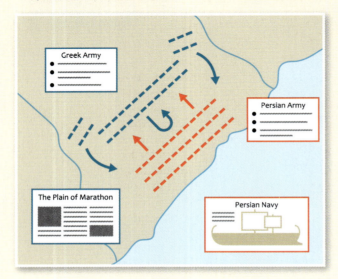

What caused the Persian Empire to weaken?

The Empire Declines

Xerxes reigned as king for twenty years. In 465 BC, Xerxes was murdered by members of the court, one of whom was Xerxes's minister Artabanus. A power struggle followed. Xerxes's son **Artaxerxes I** slew Artabanus several months later and then became king.

The Reign of Artaxerxes I

Artaxerxes I was the last of the strong Achaemenid kings. He continued the building projects his ancestors had started. He also dealt with a major Egyptian revolt and with skirmishes with the Greeks.

Artaxerxes showed kindness to the Israelites, as several other Persian kings had before him. The Bible records that during his reign, Ezra and Nehemiah returned to Jerusalem. Ezra, an Israelite priest and scribe, traveled to Jerusalem to teach the people after the temple was rebuilt. Artaxerxes paid Ezra's expenses for the journey. Nehemiah, Artaxerxes's cupbearer, later returned to lead the Israelites in rebuilding the wall around Jerusalem. Artaxerxes supplied the wood that Nehemiah needed to build the city gates and sent letters to protect Nehemiah in his travels.

Artaxerxes was one of the few Persian kings to die a natural death. Many of the Achaemenid rulers after Darius I were assassinated.

Artaxerxes I King of Persia and son of Xerxes; allowed Ezra and Nehemiah to return to Jerusalem to restore worship and rebuild its wall.

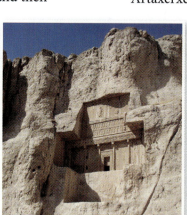
Artaxerxes I's tomb was hewn from rock.

A Weakening Kingdom

The Persian Empire had weakened since the days of Darius I. The wars with Greece had been costly and had resulted in great losses. In spite of the wars, the Persian royalty had continued their luxurious lifestyle. They placed heavier and heavier taxes on the people.

The people were discontent with both the high taxes and their rulers. As time went on, the people's loyalty decreased.

XERXES & ESTHER

The Persian king Xerxes is called Ahasuerus in the book of Esther. *Ahasuerus* is the Hebrew form of *Xerxes*. When Xerxes's queen, Vashti, refused his summons to a royal feast, he became angry and removed her from being queen. He then ordered that beautiful, young, unmarried women of his kingdom be brought to the palace. He would take a new queen from among them.

Esther was one of the women taken to the king. She was an Israelite whose parents had died. Her cousin Mordecai was caring for her as if she were his own daughter. Her Hebrew name was Hadassah.

Mordecai's great-grandfather had been taken to Babylon when Nebuchadnezzar invaded Jerusalem. Several generations later, Mordecai was living in a land that was now part of the Persian Empire. He and Esther lived in Susa, one of the capital cities of the empire. The palace at Susa was Xerxes's main residence during the winter.

Xerxes took Esther to be his queen. God had placed Esther in this important position for a special purpose. Haman, one of the king's officials, plotted to destroy the Jews. However, Esther used her influence to plead for the lives of her people.

As shown during the crossing of the Hellespont and the removal of Vashti from being queen, Xerxes sometimes demonstrated unreasonable anger. The historian Josephus claimed that men with axes guarded the king's throne from anyone who approached it without a summons from the king. It took great courage for Esther to go before Xerxes without being summoned, and God gave her favor with the king. Through Esther, God brought about deliverance for His people.

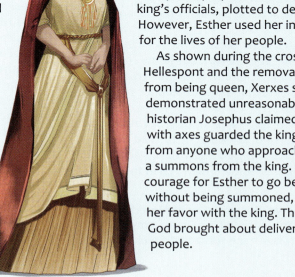

Alexander the Great battling the Persians

Alexander's Conquest

A young man named Alexander had taken the throne in Macedonia, north of Greece. Most of Greece was already under Alexander's control when he became king. He would conquer many more lands during his short life and become known as **Alexander the Great**.

The prophet Daniel had prophesied about the fall of the great Medo-Persian Empire (Daniel 8). He described Alexander the Great's rise to power in Greece, his conquest of the Persian Empire, and his death.

In 334 BC, Alexander invaded the Persian Empire. Although the Persian army was larger than Alexander's, he defeated them. In only four years' time, Alexander ruled all the lands that had once made up the Persian Empire.

Alexander destroyed many of the beautiful structures and works of art when he burned Persepolis. Yet Alexander admired many things about the Persian Empire. He continued the Persian form of centralized government, placed the Persian cavalry in his own army, and married several Persian princesses. He also kept some of the Persian customs and blended them with influences from Greek culture.

Rule by the Seleucids

Alexander's reign over Persia was short. He died in his early thirties, but the cause of his death remains uncertain. It is possible that he died from illness or by poisoning. After his death, there was a contest between Alexander's generals to decide who would rule. Four generals triumphed and declared themselves kings over parts of Alexander's empire. Each general wanted to defeat the others and bring the entire kingdom under his own rule. Dynasties developed from the families of three of the generals. The Antigonids ruled Greece and Macedonia, the Ptolemies ruled Egypt, and the Seleucids ruled Syria and Persia.

Alexander the Great Became ruler of Macedonia at the age of twenty-two; led the Greek army in conquering many lands and spreading Greek culture.

How did Artaxerxes influence Israel's history?

Whose control did Persia come under after Alexander the Great's reign?

How did Persian culture change during the period of the Parthians and Sassanians?

Persian Rule Revived

The Parthians

It was only a little more than a century before Persians controlled the Persian territory again. Parthia was a province in northeast Persia near the Caspian Sea. A tribe of nomads called the Parni moved down from central Asia, fought the Seleucid king, and took over Parthia. During the reign of Mithradates I (171–138 BC) and followed by the reign of Artabanus II (138–124 BC), the **Parthians** slowly extended their control. Toward the end of the second century BC, they had recovered nearly all the eastern part of the former Persian Empire.

The Parthians ruled for about four centuries. The art from their culture reflects their close contact with the Greeks, and the coins minted in their empire have Greek writing on them. The Parthians also had contact with the Asian peoples farther east because the Silk Road ran through their empire. For a while, the Parthians controlled the road and collected a toll from those traveling on it.

However, the Parthians lacked a strong central government like the one Darius I had established. They were further weakened by war with the Romans. In the second century AD, they were defeated by the **Sassanians**.

The Sassanians

The Sassanian dynasty came from the area around Persepolis. They ruled from AD 224 to 651. The first Sassanian king, Ardashir, defeated the last Parthian king and established himself as Persia's ruler. The Sassanian kings wanted to bring back all that was truly Persian and to rid the culture of Greek influences.

Each Sassanian ruler called himself a "king of kings." These rulers conducted their empire much the same as the Achaemenid kings had. They strengthened the central government and revived Zoroastrianism as the state religion. Under their rule, there was a strict system of social classes. The highest classes were the powerful, priestly class and a network of noblemen who ruled the provinces and collected taxes.

Parthians A nomadic people from northern Persia that began retaking part of the Persian Empire around 171 BC.

Sassanians Rulers of the Sassanian dynasty in ancient Persia; the last of the true Persian kings.

Silver drachma with the image of the Sassanian king Shapur I wearing a notched crown with earflaps

Persia achieved its greatest wealth during this period. Tribute money and trade from the Silk Road allowed Persia's economy to thrive. Persian arts and crafts flowered again. Some of the Sassanian kings built new cities, buildings, and canals. They improved irrigation and industry.

The Sassanians fought with the Romans and later with the Byzantines. The Sassanian losses from warfare brought about decline, and the power of the ruling class waned.

The end of the Sassanian period brought an end to Persian culture in its purest form. Arab invaders conquered the last Sassanian king and introduced Islam to Persia.

The Persian Empire never again reached the extent and grandeur that it had under Darius I. Yet Iran still contains traces of the Persian Empire. Ruins of the ancient palaces stand at Persepolis, and Cyrus's tomb can be seen at Pasargadae. The Persian kings and the vast kingdom they established will always be a part of Iran's heritage.

What weakened the rule of the Parthians?

Describe the Sassanian rule and its decline.

8 ANCIENT GREECE

FOCUS
The accomplishments of ancient Greece impacted the world.

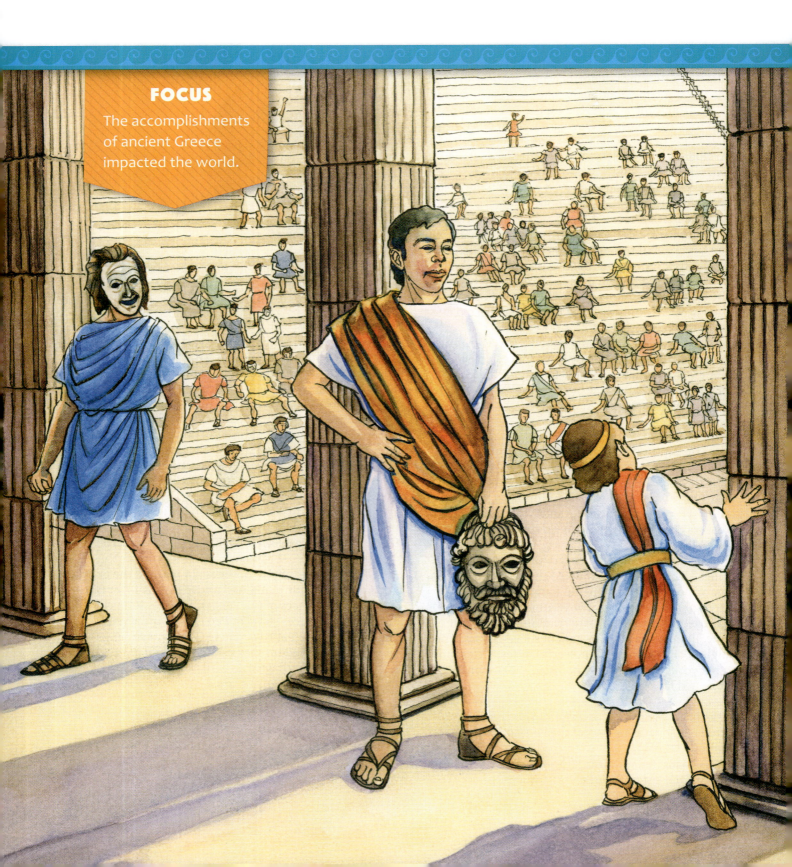

Minoan civilization
ca. 2000–1400 BC

Dark age
ca. 1150–750 BC

Peloponnesian War
431–404 BC

2000 BC | 1500 BC | 1000 BC | 500 BC | BC AD

ca. 1400–1200 BC
Mycenaean civilization

ca. 500–323 BC
Classical age

If you have ever been in a play or sung with a choir, you know the feeling of anticipation (and perhaps nervousness) as the audience begins to come in. Nicholas, the boy behind the column, has talked his older brother, Galen, into letting him see the view from the stage. They are in the famous Athens theatre, named for the Greek god Dionysus.

Galen holds one of the masks that Greek actors wore. Galen and other actors will use different masks to be different characters while a chorus narrates. Since the mask is large and its expression dramatic, even people watching from high up in the theatre will be able to recognize the characters.

People in the highest rows will also be able to hear Galen clearly. In Greek amphitheaters like this one, there were no sound systems. Instead, architects used mathematics and science to design spaces where an actor's voice could be heard from the stage all the way to the top row. Some Greek amphitheaters could hold 20,000 people. The shape of Galen's mask also will help his words carry well.

Only men acted in plays. Actors were respected in city-states like Athens.

Nicholas enjoys watching his brother perform, and he loves the colors and sounds of the theatre. Later, he and his friends will reenact the play in a less busy corner of the agora, the marketplace. Someday, Nicholas hopes to write plays of his own. Perhaps he will even compete with other playwrights in the annual festival called City Dionysia.

What period in Greece was a peak of human achievement?

The Land of Greece

Greek culture made a lasting impact on the Western world. Over the centuries, people have looked to the Greeks for patterns to follow in government, philosophy, and the arts. The classical age of Greece is often described as glorious. Many scholars believe that ancient Greece was a peak of human achievement. The Greek accomplishments were known throughout most of the ancient world.

Peloponnesus A peninsula that forms the southern portion of Greece; site of the Peloponnesian War.

Though some Greeks continue to fish for a living, fish populations are smaller in the Mediterranean Sea today.

A view of the modern seacoast of Andros Island, Greece

Geography

Greece is a land of mountains, valleys, natural harbors, and hundreds of tiny islands. It is a peninsula bordered by three seas: the Ionian, the Mediterranean, and the Aegean. The southern portion of this peninsula is called the **Peloponnesus**.

Greece's mild climate, rugged coastline, and island-strewn seas led its people to become fishermen, seafarers, and traders. It was often easier to travel on the sea than on the mountainous land.

Some Greeks were farmers, but the rocky soil in Greece made farming difficult. Nonetheless, farmers managed to grow crops such as barley, wheat, olives, and grapes.

THE REGION TODAY

Greece

Location
Greece is located in southeastern Europe. The country sits on the southern end of the Balkan Peninsula. Three seas surround Greece: the Ionian, the Mediterranean, and the Aegean.

Climate
The climate of Greece is typical for the Mediterranean region. Summers are long, and winters are mild and rainy. Temperatures range from 80°F in the summer to 48°F in the winter.

Topography
Greece is mountainous and has a narrow coastal plain. The country includes over six thousand islands. Crete is the largest of the 227 inhabited islands.

Natural Resources
Greece's natural resources include bauxite, iron ore, and small quantities of coal and oil.

Greece Then & Now

On what landform is Sparta located?

Legend:
- Ancient Greece ca. 550 BC
- Ancient city
- Modern capital
- Modern borders
- Modern Greece

161

The palace at Knossos. What made this palace unusually luxurious for its time?

Early Civilizations

The Minoans

After the Flood, some descendants of Japheth journeyed westward from Mesopotamia and settled in the "isles of the Gentiles" (Genesis 10:1–5). These islands may have been the area of Greece. The earliest known civilization from the land of Greece is the **Minoan civilization**. The Minoans lived on the island of **Crete**. Their civilization existed at the same time as the Shang dynasty in China and as the New Kingdom in Egypt.

By 2000 BC, the Minoans had built a large, beautiful palace in the city of Knossos. The palace had hundreds of rooms. It had some unusual luxuries for its time, such as bathtubs and indoor plumbing. Archaeologists have found pottery, carvings, and wall paintings in the palace that reflect a wealthy and artistic people. The Minoans gained their wealth through trading with other people from lands as far away as Egypt.

The Minoan people also traveled to other parts of the Mediterranean region and formed colonies.

Archaeologists have used pottery from Crete to guess that the Minoan civilization was more unified in its later years. Why might they think so?

Some scholars believe that the Philistines, enemies of ancient Israel, were descendants of Minoan colonists.

By 1400 BC, the Minoan civilization had come to an end. The reason for their end is not known, but some scholars believe that a volcanic eruption or an invasion took place.

Minoan civilization The earliest known civilization in Greece.

Crete An island in the Mediterranean Sea off the coast of Greece.

This gold funeral mask was found in a burial chamber at Mycenae.

Lion Gate at Mycenae. How do these walls and this gate reflect the warlike nature of the Mycenaeans?

The Mycenaeans

The **Mycenaean civilization** developed on the mainland of Greece. These people might have been the ones who brought about the fall of the Minoans in Crete.

The Mycenaean civilization was made up of many cities. Each city had its own king. Like the Minoans, the Mycenaeans built large palaces. But these palaces were not as richly adorned. Instead they were heavily fortified with thick walls and built on high hills. The Mycenaeans designed their buildings more for military strength than for artistry.

In the late 1800s, a German archaeologist named Heinrich Schliemann excavated the city of Mycenae. The Mycenaeans are named after this city. At its entrance stands a massive stone gate decorated with two carved lions. The city's central building is a great palace with walls more than fifteen feet thick. People have found many bronze weapons. They have also found a burial ground in Mycenae. One of the many artifacts found in the graves was a gold mask. Schliemann believed it belonged to Agamemnon, the famous king who led the war against the city of Troy. However, modern research shows that the mask is too old to be from Agamemnon's time. It is likely the mask of an honored warrior.

The Mycenaeans were often at war. Instead of trading peacefully, they frequently attacked other cities or pirated ships. Many scholars believe that the Mycenaeans attacked Troy and started the **Trojan War**. According to legend, this war lasted ten years. The Trojan War became a popular subject in Greek literature.

The Mycenaean civilization lasted until about 1200 BC. Around this time, invaders from the north conquered many of the Mycenaean fortresses. Many historians refer to the time that followed as the dark age of Greece.

Minoans & Mycenaeans

Minoans ca. 2000–1400 BC
Mycenaeans ca. 1250 BC

Mycenaean civilization An early civilization in Greece.
Trojan War The war between the Mycenaeans and the city of Troy.

 Contrast Minoan trade with that of the Mycenaeans.

How was life different for people in Athens compared with those in Sparta?

Athens and Sparta
The Dark Age of Greece

Few records exist to describe what life was like during the dark age of Greece. Most knowledge of this time comes from Greek literature. Stories about life in ancient Greece were passed down by word of mouth. After the Greeks developed an alphabet, these stories were written down.

The Rise of City-States

During the dark age, the Greeks were made up of many separate groups. Mountains and valleys divided the land, so the people lived in independent societies scattered throughout Greece. These societies were called city-states. The people in a city-state were like a large family. They claimed common ancestors, practiced the same customs, and spoke the same dialect. At the time, Greece did not have one central government. Instead each city-state had its own government. A city-state was sometimes ruled by a king. This type of government is called a monarchy, which comes from the Greek word for "rule by one."

Government and Life in Athens and Sparta

The two most famous city-states were **Athens** and **Sparta**. By the end of the dark age, both city-states had adopted another type of government. This new government was called an **oligarchy**. Both Athens and Sparta were ruled by small groups of nobles who owned their own land.

Athens

Although Athens and Sparta were once similar to one another, they ended up being very different.

After the dark age, many city-states branched out and formed colonies along the Mediterranean Sea. People who had gained wealth and power from trading grew discontent with having an oligarchy. Some city-states began to form new ideas about what type of government was best. In Athens, a nobleman

Athens A powerful city-state in ancient Greece, where the world's first democracy developed; capital of present-day Greece.

Sparta A powerful city-state in ancient Greece.
oligarchy A form of government in which a few people rule.

A meeting of the Assembly. What skills and strengths might have made certain men rise to power in Athens?

named Solon wrote new laws that allowed men of the lower classes to participate in government.

Individual men rose to power in Athens, supported by discontented people. These men ruled with absolute authority and were called **tyrants**. Though we today think of all tyrants as evil rulers, some tyrants ruled well.

One ruler who made important changes was Cleisthenes. Under his leadership, meetings of the **Assembly** were opened to all adult male citizens. There they could speak out on issues and vote. This was a significant step, though many Athenian residents (such as women and slaves) were still excluded from participation in government.

The Athenians voted on many types of issues. They voted for leaders. They voted on new laws and who could become a citizen. They voted on whether to go to war. Once a year, if there was someone who needed to be punished, they voted on whether to banish him from Athens for ten years. This punishment was called ostracism.

Most voting was done by a show of hands. However, it could also be done using pebbles or **potsherds**. Sometimes, during a trial, voters would place black or white pebbles in an urn to express their belief in a person's guilt or innocence. In a decision for ostracism, voters would write on a potsherd the name of the person they thought should be sent away. Many of these potsherds from the fifth century BC have been found in Athens.

The Assembly met in the **agora**, a place where citizens gathered to buy and sell. Citizens could buy fresh food that had been brought by local farmers. Since there was not enough good farmland around Athens to produce food for all the people, some foods, such as meats and cheeses, were imported. Shoppers in the agora could also find materials such as iron, copper, timber, ivory, animal hides, wool, and papyrus, as well as furniture and textiles.

The agora was more than a marketplace. Schools, governmental buildings, courts, and private businesses were also located there. Sometimes people gathered there just to meet with friends and talk. They would discuss politics, philosophy, and the latest news.

By 500 BC, new laws in Athens had greatly changed the government. Under Cleisthenes, Athens became the first known **democracy**. Democratic countries today look back to Athens as a model for how a government by the people might work. The Athenians recognized that a democratic form of government did not necessarily mean a just form of government. For instance, when the island of Melos wanted to remain neutral in a war between Athens and Sparta, the Athenians destroyed Melos. Some Athenians, such as **Thucydides**, thought that the Assembly was too easily persuaded to go to war.

The most famous leader of the Athenian democracy was **Pericles**. He is considered one of the greatest public speakers, or orators, of all time. The Greeks made him their leader because they respected his wisdom and his ability to reason.

Pericles encouraged as many people as possible to take part in the Athenian government. He even paid people to be officers in the Assembly and to serve on juries. Through his speeches, Pericles helped define the democracy of Athens.

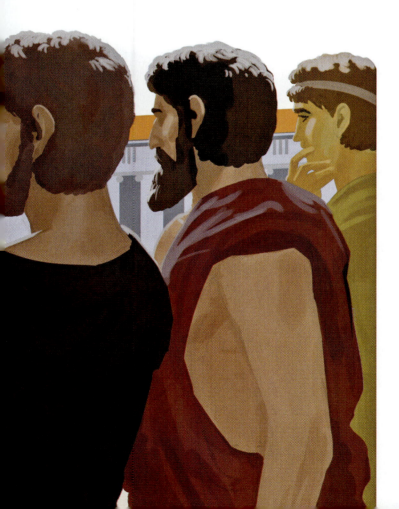

tyrant A ruler who has absolute authority.

Assembly A group of Greek citizens who met to make laws.

potsherds Pieces of broken pottery.

agora A busy marketplace in the center of Athens made up of open-air buildings.

democracy A form of government in which the citizens of the country have the power.

Thucydides Athenian historian who recorded the events of the Peloponnesian War.

Pericles One of the leaders of the democracy in Athens; considered one of the best orators of all time.

LIFE IN ATHENS

Justice
Justice was determined by a jury. Only citizens could serve on a jury. Jurors determined the punishment if they found the accused person guilty.

An acropolis is a group of buildings on a high spot. This one was best known for the Parthenon, a temple to the goddess Athena.

Arts, Sciences, and Written Language
Arts, sciences, and written language developed unhindered because Athens nurtured creativity, trade, democracy, and individualism.

Environment
Rocky terrain hindered farming, but the seas surrounding Greece provided transportation for trade.

Typically only the wealthy could afford horses. In times of peace, they used them for racing.

People used the Altar of the Twelve Gods as a base from which to measure distances from Athens.

Social Classes

Wealthy male citizens formed the upper class. They owned and managed property. The middle class was made up of farmers. The lower class included craftsmen. Women of all classes managed the home and cared for children.

Foreigners paid taxes and were required to serve in the military, but they could not own property or vote.

There were three levels of slaves. The highest level were tutors. The middle level worked in construction and property maintenance. The lowest level were mine workers.

Key Themes of Civilization
- Justice
- Power
- Citizenship
- Environment

Citizenship

Only adult Athenian-born males were considered citizens, so only about twenty percent of the population had citizenship. These citizens were expected to get an education, vote, and join the military.

Religion

Greek mythology claimed that gods and goddesses lived on Mount Olympus. They believed these deities had human characteristics, special powers, and immortality.

Features of a Civilization
- Organized cities and government
- Social classes
- Job specialization
- Arts, sciences, and written language
- Religion

Job Specialization

In the marketplace, traders made goods such as pottery and shoes, and merchants sold the goods to the public.

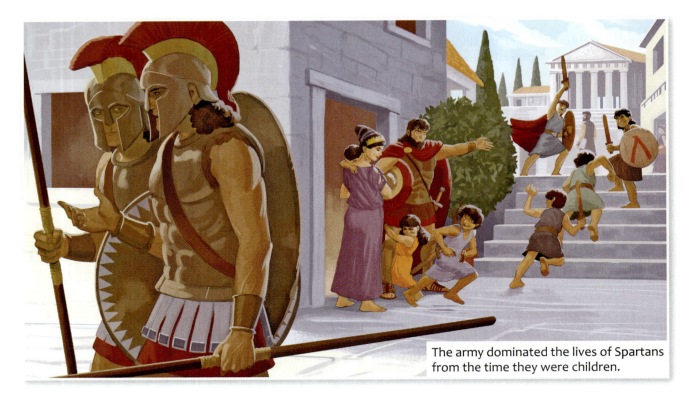

The army dominated the lives of Spartans from the time they were children.

Sparta

Unlike Athens, Sparta kept its oligarchy. Sparta's primary goal was to have a strong army. For centuries, Sparta made no significant advances in art or literature as Athens and other city-states did.

Life in Sparta was much more rigid than life in Athens. When a baby boy was born in Sparta, his parents presented him to the rulers of the city. If the rulers thought he was strong, they allowed him to live. If not, they left him in the countryside to die. The Spartans did not want any weaklings in their army. A boy who was accepted stayed at home until he was seven years old. Then the army took him and trained him to be a soldier. During most of his young adult life, a Spartan boy lived in army barracks with other boys. Life in the barracks was designed to prepare them for warfare. The boys had little to eat. They were expected to steal food from farms, but they were punished if they were caught. They were taught to live by their wits so that they would be prepared to survive during wartime. Every year, some of the boys were beaten in public as part of a ceremony to the gods. The beatings were meant to help the boys learn to endure pain.

Around age twenty, a Spartan man would marry. But he could not live at home with his wife. He had to live with the other men, training to be a soldier, for ten more years. The training a man received in the Spartan army was harsh and disciplined. The Spartans believed that learning to suffer pain and hardship would make a man a good soldier.

Women in Athens and Sparta

Athenian women spent most of their time at home. An upper-class woman was accompanied by servants when she did have to leave her house for events such as festivals. Slaves did the daily shopping and ran errands. Even lower-class women who did not have slaves rarely shopped or worked outside the home. Athenian women were skilled at spinning and weaving. A few women from wealthy families learned to read and write at home.

In Sparta, women also managed their households. But since the men were often away from home with the army, the women had more responsibilities than the women in Athens. Spartan women went out in public more than Athenian women. Some even owned property. Like the men, Spartan women received physical training. This training was designed to make them strong mothers. Mothers taught their children to be brave and loyal to Sparta. Plutarch writes that one mother handed her son his shield and instructed him to return as either a living conqueror or a dead hero. The Spartan army had no room for cowards or quitters.

 How did city-states develop in Ancient Greece?

What were the consequences of the Peloponnesian War for Greece?

War and Restoration
The Persian Wars

The Greeks clashed with the Persian Empire in the fifth century BC. The Persians were angered by the growth of the Greek city-states. They wanted to conquer Greece and make it part of the Persian Empire. But they discovered that defeating the Greeks would not be easy. For over ten years, the Greeks fought the Persians and won many battles.

After the Athenian army won the battle of Marathon, Sparta joined forces with Athens to fight the Persians in later battles. In the battle of Thermopylae, the Greeks suffered a defeat and watched Athens go up in flames.

But the Greek spirit was not defeated. One of the most decisive battles was the Battle of Salamis in 480 BC. The battle took place at sea when the Greeks met the Persian forces. The Greeks lost about forty ships, but they burned at least two hundred of the Persian ships and won the battle. The Persians tried only one more time to conquer the Greeks but were unsuccessful. Greece was victorious.

However, war had taken its toll on Greece. Many buildings lay in ruins. One of the first ways the Greeks put their new confidence to work was in restoring their cities.

Pericles, a powerful speaker and politician, loved the city of Athens. He had grown up in Athens and wanted it always to be a city that others would admire and love as much as he did. After the Persian Wars, he wanted to repair the damages caused when the Persians burned the city.

Pericles helped restore the former beauty of Athens. He encouraged the Athenians to rebuild the ruined temple and to construct other sacred buildings on the **Acropolis**. He hired talented architects, sculptors, and artists. Under his leadership, the architecture of the classical age took shape. Columns, sculptures, and the great Entrance Gate were built.

Pericles also supported the growth of manufacturing and trade, and he helped strengthen the military. Because of his influence during the fifth century BC, the period is often called the Age of Pericles.

Acropolis The center of religious life in Athens; a hill overlooking the city of Athens.

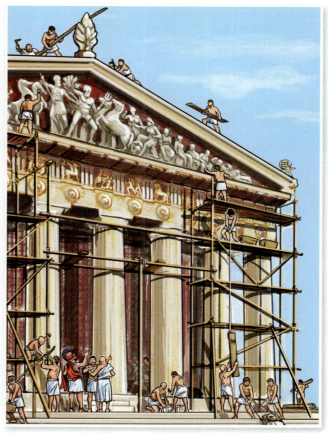

After the Parthenon was destroyed with the burning of Athens in 480 BC, Pericles ordered its reconstruction in 447 BC.

The Peloponnesian War

Growing Tension

After the Persian Wars, Athens took steps to protect itself and its trading practices. Athens had a strong navy, but the Athenians knew they were not strong enough by themselves. They wanted to be able to defend their city-state against other world powers like Persia. Athens believed that if the Greek city-states worked together, they would be stronger. Athens formed an alliance with many city-states. The alliance was called the **Delian League**. The city-states agreed to pay money into the league's treasury to help protect each other. They also contributed troops and ships.

The dominant power of the league was Athens. It had the most control over the Aegean Sea, where the Greeks traded. Taxes were paid to Athens to maintain its navy. Later, Athens also received payments for guarding the league's treasury. As a result, the city-state grew wealthier and more powerful. Sometimes Athens pressured other city-states to join or stay in the league. Many Greeks thought that Athens wanted to build an empire and control the rest of Greece.

Sparta did not join the Delian League. Athens and Sparta disagreed on many things, including their forms of government. Sparta felt that Athens was using the Delian League to gain power. Tensions grew between the two city-states. Some city-states took sides with Sparta and formed an alliance called the **Peloponnesian League**.

Finally, in 431 BC, Athens and Sparta went to war with each other. Their allies joined the fighting. Because most of the fighting took place on the Peloponnesus, the war is called the **Peloponnesian War**. It lasted more than twenty-seven years.

The Siege of Athens

The Spartan army marched to Athens and surrounded the city. The Spartans settled in for a siege, hoping that the Athenians would eventually begin to starve. There would be nothing for the Athenians to do except surrender. But even inside its city walls, Athens was not cut off from its seaport. The Athenian navy supplied the city with food and other needed items by way of the sea.

The siege lasted until a plague broke out in Athens. Many Athenians died, including Pericles. The Spartans left because they did not want to catch the disease themselves.

Battle by Land and Sea

The Athenian navy continued the war by attacking Sparta's allies on the coast. Both sides won some battles and lost others. Neither Athens nor Sparta could gain the advantage. Finally, both agreed to a truce.

Delian League The defensive alliance of Greek city-states led by Athens against the Persians.

Peloponnesian League An alliance of Greek city-states led by Sparta against Athens.

Peloponnesian War The war between Athens and Sparta that lasted over twenty-seven years.

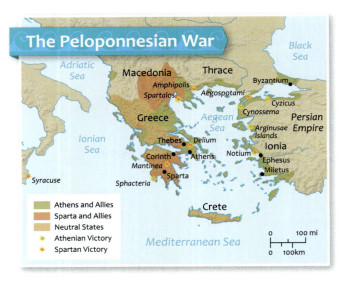

Allies and battle sites of the Peloponnesian War. Judging by the location of Athens and its allies, what would have been a primary source of military power for them?

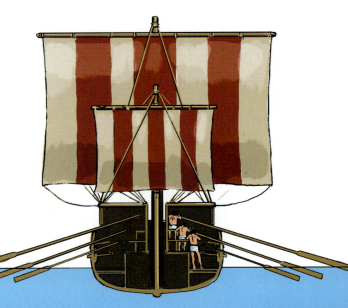

The Defeat of Athens

The truce lasted only a few years. Athens broke it by attacking Sicily, one of Sparta's allies. Sicily defeated the powerful Athenian fleet. Then Sparta joined forces with the Greeks' old enemy, the Persians. Persia began giving money to Sparta, and Sparta was able to build a navy of its own. The Spartan navy took control of the Hellespont, blocking Athenian ships from bringing food and supplies into Athens. In 404 BC, Athens was forced to surrender. Sparta had won the war.

Consequences of the War

Sparta took control of Greece for about thirty years. But neither Sparta nor Athens ever fully recovered from the effects of the war. Both city-states had been weakened by their losses. The weaker city-states had once looked to Sparta for protection, but now they found it to be an oppressor. Many people had died. Buildings lay in ruins. Farmland had been ravaged. Athens lost its democracy and found it difficult to submit to Spartan oligarchical rule. Uprisings caused Sparta to lose control over the Greek city-states, leaving disunity once again. The "glory that was Greece" would never return.

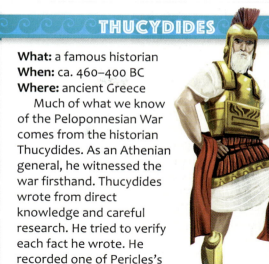

THUCYDIDES

What: a famous historian
When: ca. 460–400 BC
Where: ancient Greece

Much of what we know of the Peloponnesian War comes from the historian Thucydides. As an Athenian general, he witnessed the war firsthand. Thucydides wrote from direct knowledge and careful research. He tried to verify each fact he wrote. He recorded one of Pericles's most famous speeches during the war. The speech was given at a funeral for an Athenian soldier who had died in battle.

 How did Persia influence the outcome of the war?

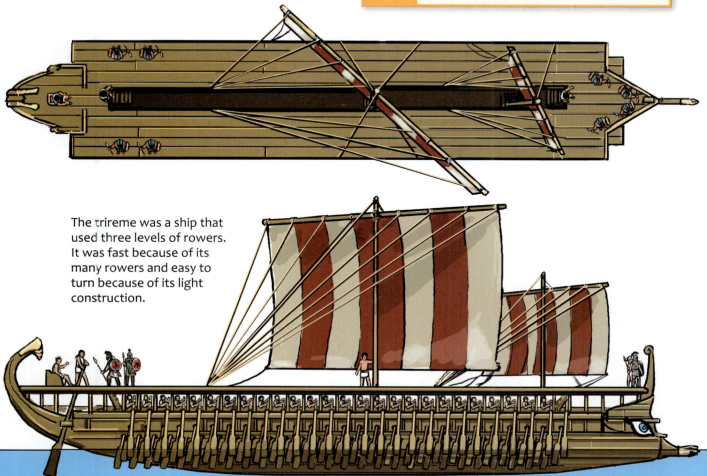

The trireme was a ship that used three levels of rowers. It was fast because of its many rowers and easy to turn because of its light construction.

How did the beliefs of Greek religion differ from those of Greek philosophy?

Religion in Greece

The Greeks believed that there were many gods. They believed these gods lived on **Mount Olympus**, the highest mountain in Greece. Although these gods were perceived as having supernatural powers, the Greeks did not believe that the gods were much different from humans. Drawings and sculptures depicted the gods as having human bodies. The gods displayed human characteristics such as jealousy, vengefulness, and immorality. They even acted childishly at times.

The Greeks made up fanciful stories about their gods and goddesses. These stories are called **myths**. They told how the actions of the gods affected events in nature or in the lives of humans. There were myths to explain sunrise and sunset, thunder and lightning, changing seasons, and constellations.

The names of many of the gods and goddesses are well-known. Stories about them became so popular that people named many things after them. The city of Athens was named after the Greek goddess Athena. The American space program had spacecraft named after the god Apollo. Athletic shoes have been named after Nike, the goddess of victory. Books of maps are named after Atlas, who carried the world on his shoulders.

 GREEK MYTHOLOGY

The Greeks worshiped gods and goddesses who were similar to humans and were just as sinful as humans. The Greeks believed that they needed the favor of the gods to accomplish the various tasks of life. To win the favor of the gods, the Greeks offered them sacrifices.

Unlike the Greek gods and goddesses, the true God is perfectly holy (Isaiah 6:3). Humans may have sinful desires and do sinful things, but God never sins. Because God is holy, He will judge sinners (Romans 2:12).

The idea of offering sacrifices to a god may have been remembered from the sacrifices that God taught people to give (Genesis 4:3–4; 8:20). But the sacrifices in the Old Testament could not solve mankind's sin problem. When Jesus died on the cross, He became the sacrifice for all people (Hebrews 10:4–14). God provided the perfect sacrifice so that people who trust Jesus for salvation can be accepted by God.

Mount Olympus The highest mountain in Greece, believed by the ancient Greeks to be the dwelling place of the gods.

myth A legend or traditional story; often about gods and goddesses.

GREEK GODS AND GODDESSES

Aphrodite	goddess of love and beauty	**Hades**	god of the underworld
Apollo	god of the sun, music, and poetry	**Hephaestus**	god of fire and metalworking
Ares	god of war	**Hera**	goddess of marriage; queen of the gods
Artemis	goddess of hunting	**Hermes**	messenger god
Athena	goddess of wisdom and war	**Hestia**	goddess of hearth and home
Demeter	goddess of harvest	**Poseidon**	god of the sea
Dionysus	god of wine, agriculture, and fertility	**Zeus**	king of the gods; god of the sky

Although there were many gods and goddesses, some were more important than others. The gods and goddesses listed here were thought to be the greatest deities. They play major roles in many of the Greek myths.

How does this illustration reflect the roles of these gods?

Philosophy in Greece

Many scholars lived in Athens during this time. They wanted to explain life by their own wisdom, not by the actions of gods. These men were called **philosophers**. The word *philosopher* comes from the Greek word *philosophos,* which means "lover of wisdom."

Socrates taught by asking his students thought-provoking questions. "What is the meaning of life?" he would ask. "What is a good man?" The questions made his students think about what they really believed. He wanted to make the government a perfect one and believed that right thinking would lead to right actions.

Socrates was eventually sentenced to death for his teachings. The government said that his ideas were too different and that they led the young men of Athens to question their beliefs about the gods. The city leaders gave Socrates poison to drink, and he calmly drank it and died.

philosopher A person who studies to gain wisdom in a particular field.
Socrates Greek philosopher who encouraged his students to seek truth through human reason.

SOCRATES

What: philosopher and teacher
When: ca. 470–399 BC
Where: Athens, Greece

Socrates was a Greek philosopher whose teaching influenced the ancient world. His father was a stonemason, and his mother was a midwife. Socrates attended school and studied music, art, literature, science, math, and politics. He learned and practiced stonemasonry like his father. Socrates served in the military as a foot soldier and fought in the Peloponnesian War. He was a teacher, not a writer. His students wrote what he taught. He was accused of corrupting the youth and of rejecting the Athenian gods. At the age of seventy, he was condemned to death.

PAUL AT THE AREOPAGUS

The ancient Greeks were well-educated, artistic, and talented people. They seemed to have everything. But although the Greeks possessed knowledge of many subjects, they had no knowledge of God.

The Areopagus

The apostle Paul ministered not only to the Jews, but also to the Greeks. During his travels, Paul visited Athens. Acts 17 tells how Paul noticed widespread idolatry in the city. He found an altar with an inscription carved on it: "To the Unknown God."

Paul preached at the Areopagus, which some translations of Acts refer to as "Mars' Hill." The location of the Areopagus is significant because it is the place where the council met in the Acropolis to discuss philosophy. When Paul spoke, he brought the gospel into contact with some of the leading philosophies of the day. He told them how the one true God is not a statue made of gold or silver or stone. Paul shared with them that God is real and that He wants people everywhere to repent and seek Him.

Many people mocked Paul's message. Some left thoughtfully, wanting to hear more. But a few men and women understood the truth of Paul's words and believed in Jesus. Paul's trip to Athens had not been in vain. Paul said,

> For the Jews require a sign, and the Greeks seek after wisdom: but we preach Christ crucified, unto the Jews a stumblingblock, and unto the Greeks foolishness; but unto them which are called, both Jews and Greeks, Christ the power of God, and the wisdom of God (1 Corinthians 1:22–24).

Raphael's famous painting *School of Athens* honors the contributions of the ancient Greeks to philosophy.

1. Deocritus
2. Pythagoras
3. Hypatia
4. Heraclitus
5. Parmenides
6. Socrates
7. Plato
8. Aristotle
9. Diogenes
10. Epicurus
11. Pyrrho
12. Euclid
13. Zoroaster
14. Ptolemy
15. Raphael (self-portrait)

GREEK PHILOSOPHY

Greek philosophers believed that wisdom was found through reason and clear thinking. The Bible says that "the fear of the Lord is the beginning of wisdom" (Proverbs 9:10). A proper view of God is necessary to be truly wise. The Bible also teaches that people should not glory or be proud in their wisdom. Rather, they should glory in knowing and understanding God (Jeremiah 9:24).

Since reason is a gift from God, the Greek philosophers were right about some things. They emphasized many of the same virtues that the Bible does, such as truth, love, wisdom, and discipline. But because they did not know God, they were wrong about many things as well. The philosopher Aristotle taught that reason controls behavior. But more is needed than reason. The Bible teaches that virtues are gained only through a true knowledge of Christ (2 Peter 1:3–8). The apostle Paul says that there are times when Christians know what is right but still choose to do wrong (Romans 7:15). The Bible says that human minds need to be renewed by the Spirit of God (Romans 8:5–6). It is impossible to live a godly life without the power of the Holy Spirit.

Plato was one of Socrates's students. Plato wrote books in the form of conversations. In these books, called *Dialogues*, he said that the ideal government was ruled by a few of the most intelligent men. He also taught that there was a spiritual world, a world of the mind and of ideas, that was superior to the physical world.

Aristotle, Plato's pupil, was a third great Greek philosopher. To Aristotle, science was the most important academic subject. He introduced the scientific method, a method of study requiring careful observation and record keeping. He also taught that reason controls behavior.

Both religion and philosophy in Greece were expressions of the human need to worship. The Greek religion encouraged the worship of imagined gods and goddesses. Greek philosophers worshiped wisdom and reason. However, neither Greece's religion nor its philosophy was the answer to the greatest human need: redemption through Jesus Christ.

Plato Greek philosopher who wrote books about government.

Aristotle Greek philosopher who devoted himself to the study of science.

> Although Greek philosophers emphasized some biblical virtues, what important truth was missing?

How are fables different from epics?

Learning and the Arts

Education

Some boys from wealthy families in Greece had servants that accompanied them to school to supervise their behavior. These servants were called pedagogues. Boys began school at age six and continued to at least age fourteen. They studied reading, writing, arithmetic, grammar, music, and sports. Boys from poorer families could not afford to go to school, and girls were not allowed to go at all.

The Greeks had an alphabet with twenty-four letters. Some English letters come from the Greek alphabet. The Greeks used no punctuation or spacing between words. Greek students wrote on wax-coated tablets with a stylus. The stylus was pointed on one end to scratch letters into the wax and blunt on the other end to rub out mistakes.

Literature

Literature in ancient Greece took many forms. Some pieces of literature were records of history or writings on philosophy. Some were speeches. Some were stories that were presented in poetry and drama. Many of these written works have been preserved and are still studied today.

Myths

During the dark age, the Greeks developed myths. Greek myths tell stories about gods and goddesses. Some myths were also about human heroes. As myths were passed down from storyteller to storyteller, they sometimes changed. These changes sometimes led to several different versions of the same myth. The story of Midas is one myth that has many versions.

HOMER

What: poet and storyteller
When: ca. 1200 BC
Where: Greece

Little is known about Homer's life. He probably lived sometime between the twelfth and eighth centuries. According to legend, Homer was a blind poet who lived during the dark age of Greece. His epic poems, *The Iliad* and *The Odyssey*, were handed down through centuries of oral storytelling. *The Iliad* tells the story of the Trojan War, and *The Odyssey* recounts the adventures of the Greek hero Odysseus. Homer is credited with having influenced ancient literature.

Epics

Greek students had to study two long poems called *The Iliad* and *The Odyssey*. These poems were created by a Greek poet named **Homer**. *The Iliad* and *The Odyssey* are epics, lengthy poems about the actions of heroes. Students of literature and history still study these two epics today. The poems provide glimpses into the life and culture of ancient Greece during the dark age. They also emphasize values every hero should have, such as dignity, strength, valor, generosity, and wisdom.

Homer Greek poet and storyteller; author of *The Iliad* and *The Odyssey*.

amphitheater A large, outdoor arena.

A stylus and wax tablets

THE GREEK ALPHABET (LETTERS, NAMES, AND ENGLISH EQUIVALENTS)

Αα	alpha	Aa	Ιι	iota	Ii	Ρρ	rho	Rr
Ββ	beta	Bb	Κκ	kappa	Kk	Σσ	sigma	Ss
Γγ	gamma	Gg	Λλ	lambda	Ll	Ττ	tau	Tt
Δδ	delta	Dd	Μμ	mu	Mm	Υυ	upsilon	Uu
Εε	epsilon	Ee	Νν	nu	Nn	Φφ	phi	Ff
Ζζ	zeta	Zz	Ξξ	xi	Xx	Χχ	chi	ch
Ηη	eta	ee	Οο	omicron	Oo	Ψψ	psi	ps
Θθ	theta	th	Ππ	pi	Pp	Ωω	omega	ô

MIDAS, THE KING WITH THE GOLDEN TOUCH: A GREEK MYTH

King Midas had a lovely palace and a beautiful rose garden. He also had a little daughter whom he loved very much. But sometimes Midas wished that he could have more.

One day Midas was granted a wish by Dionysus, the god of wine. Dionysus told Midas that he could have any gift he desired.

Midas thought for a moment. "I wish that everything I touch would turn to gold," he told the god. "Then I would have enough gold to buy anything I ever wanted."

Dionysus raised his eyebrows. "Consider carefully, King Midas," he said. "Are you certain this is the wish you desire?"

"This is my wish," said Midas.

"Very well. Your wish is granted," said Dionysus. He said goodbye with a sad expression in his eyes, and he left.

Midas looked around. Could it really be true? He saw a red rose hanging over the garden wall just above his head. He reached up and touched it, holding his breath.

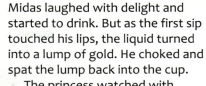

The rose turned into solid gold before his eyes! Midas looked up at the sky and laughed out loud. "It's true!" he cried. "My wish has come true! Thank you, Dionysus. You have made me the wealthiest man in the world!"

Midas leaped and danced around the palace grounds, touching trees, fountains, and benches and watching them turn to gold. Looking down, he saw that he was leaving gold footprints in the grass with every step. He hurried to the palace and entered the front hall.

"Bring me a feast to celebrate!" he called to the servants. "Bring my daughter to eat with me. I have been granted the golden touch by the gods!"

The servants bustled around, preparing a meal, and they summoned the princess to the feast.

"Watch, my dear," said King Midas. He raised his crystal goblet, and it turned to gold in his hands.

Midas laughed with delight and started to drink. But as the first sip touched his lips, the liquid turned into a lump of gold. He choked and spat the lump back into the cup.

The princess watched with frightened eyes. Midas, too, began to feel worried. "I will try eating meat," he said.

His heart pounded as he speared a piece of meat with his golden fork and raised it to his lips. Before he could even taste the savory beef, it turned to cold, hard metal in his mouth. Midas cried out in alarm and spat out the golden meat.

The princess was watching Midas with huge, fear-filled eyes. "Father," she said, "I fear you will starve. You cannot eat if all your food turns to gold before you can even swallow it."

Without thinking, Midas reached out and patted her hand to comfort her. The moment he touched her fingers, she froze into a solid gold statue.

"No!" shrieked the king. He jumped up and raced outside. Tears streamed down his face, leaving trails of liquid gold on his cheeks.

"Dionysus!" he shouted. "Please, have pity on me! I have been greedy and unwise. Please take the gift back!"

Dionysus appeared beside him. "I pity you, my friend," he said. "You have learned a hard lesson today. If you will go and wash in the river Pactolus, you will lose your golden touch. You will return, and all will be as before."

Murmuring his thanks, Midas ran to the river and leaped into it. As he bathed, streams of gold appeared in the water, and flecks of gold sparkled in the sands. But when Midas stepped out, his golden touch was gone.

But to this day, the river Pactolus gleams with the last traces of King Midas's golden touch.

Plays

The Greeks also developed another literary art form, the art of drama. Crowds would gather in **amphitheaters** where actors performed plays as part of religious festivals.

Most Greek plays were about the gods and heroes. Two types of Greek drama are *comedy* and *tragedy*. Comedies poked fun at certain people or types of people and were meant to entertain the audience and make them laugh. The most famous Greek comedies were written by the playwright Aristophanes. Tragedies left audiences feeling solemn. These plays usually ended with the downfall of the hero because of a character flaw, such as pride or jealousy. Sophocles was a popular writer of Greek tragedies. Because Greek plays shed light on human nature, many are still performed today.

The actors wore exaggerated costumes and large masks that allowed the audience to tell them apart. Some actors exchanged their masks for different ones to express the characters' feelings. The masks sometimes showed whether the characters felt happy, sad, or angry. The funnel-shaped mouthpieces inside the masks acted as megaphones that made the actors' voices carry to everyone in the crowd.

Fables

Another type of story that was passed down from the ancient Greeks by word of mouth was the **fable**. Fables did not usually involve the gods. Often the main characters in fables were animals that talked and acted as humans do. A fable usually stated its point in a brief closing statement called the moral. **Aesop** has traditionally been credited as the author of many fables.

These ruins from ancient Ephesus show the main sections of a Greek theatre: the orchestra (circular floor for the chorus), a raised stage, the skene (backstage area for actors), and the theatron (seating area for the audience).

fable A short story that teaches a lesson.
Aesop Greek author who wrote fables.

 How are comedies different from tragedies?

ACTIVITY

Making a Greek Mask

Masks used by Greek performers sometimes showed emotions. The emotional expressions on the masks helped the audience better understand the play.

Each person in your group will make a mask that shows the emotion of a character in the play. After designing and making your mask, you will act out the play.

1. Get a mirror, a copy of the play, construction paper, markers, and scissors.
2. Practice several emotions in front of the mirror. Note the facial distinctions for each emotion.
3. Read the play your teacher gives your group. Decide which character and which emotion each of you will represent with your mask.
4. Use a pencil to draw a face on construction paper. The face should show the trait or emotion you chose in step three. Trace the features with a marker.
5. Cut holes for the eyes and mouth.
6. Hold your mask in front of your face and allow the other students to guess what emotion you are illustrating.
7. Use the masks as your group performs the play.

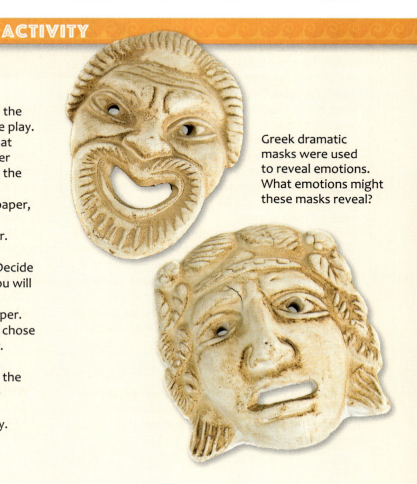

Greek dramatic masks were used to reveal emotions. What emotions might these masks reveal?

What accomplishments were made in the areas of math and science in ancient Greece?

Math and Science

Several Greek scholars contributed to math and science. **Archimedes** was a mathematician who advanced the development of pulleys, machines that make it easier to move objects. **Euclid** wrote the first known geometry book, and the entire study of geometry was built around his teachings. **Pythagoras**, another mathematician, studied geometry and came up with an important **theorem** about the side lengths of triangles.

The Greeks would sometimes use a special tool called an **abacus** to solve math problems as a calculator is used today.

Eratosthenes was the first to draw latitude and longitude lines on a map and to calculate the circumference of the earth with reasonable accuracy. He also estimated distances to the moon and sun, and he developed a method for finding prime numbers.

An astronomer named **Aristarchus** suggested that the earth revolved around the sun. Most people believed that the sun revolved around the earth.

Hippocrates is famous today for his contribution to the study of medicine. Hippocrates did not agree with the popular idea of relying on magic to treat patients. He examined them carefully and prescribed treatments. Hippocrates is called the Father of Medicine. Doctors today still take the Hippocratic Oath in honor of his wisdom and principles in the medical profession.

Athletics

The Greeks believed that developing the body was as important as developing the mind. The English word *athlete* comes from the Greek language. Schoolboys spent hours in the gymnasium running, jumping, wrestling, boxing, and throwing the javelin and the discus.

Archimedes Greek mathematician who advanced the lever and pulleys.

Euclid Greek mathematician; wrote the first known geometry book.

Pythagoras Greek mathematician who studied geometry and came up with an important theorem about the side lengths of triangles.

theorem A carefully tested idea that has been proven to be true.

abacus A frame with rows of movable beads used for calculating.

Eratosthenes Greek mathematician, astronomer, and geographer.

Aristarchus Greek astronomer who believed that the earth revolved around the sun.

Hippocrates Greek physician; called the Father of Medicine.

Boxing was introduced to the Olympics in 688 BC. How does the image of the ancient boxers compare with the photo of these boxers from the 2012 Olympic games?

The ancient Greeks were the first to hold the **Olympic Games**. These were special festivals held at the city of Olympia in honor of the gods. Athletes from all over Greece would travel to the city to compete in various events. These athletes competed in many events that Olympic athletes today compete in, such as sprints, long jumps, wrestling, and discus and javelin throwing. The ancient Greeks also had chariot races and events for younger boys. The winners were crowned with garlands of laurel leaves.

Music

The Greeks regarded music as one of the greatest of all the arts. The god Apollo was believed to be the god of music. Greek art often pictures Apollo entertaining other gods with a lyre, a type of small harp. The Greeks also believed that a group of nine goddesses called the **Muses** presided over the arts and the sciences. Each goddess had a particular specialty, such as epic poetry or religious music. The word *music* comes from their name.

During the classical age, boys from wealthy families were required to study music. They learned to play the lyre and the *aulos*, a type of flute. Singing was also an important part of musical training. Students memorized *The Iliad* and *The Odyssey*, put the words to music, and sang them. Some boys continued their studies with training in public speaking, hoping to become leaders in the democracy.

Art and Architecture

Greek artists wanted their work to be perfect. They strove to create the ideal representation of an object or a person. Important qualities of Greek art were balance, harmony, simplicity, beauty, and completeness. Their work has influenced many areas of art and architecture today.

Much of what is known about how the Greeks lived and dressed comes from their art. The work of painters adorned plates, jugs, pots, jars, cups, bowls, and perfume bottles. Craftsmen of metal decorated gold and silver cups and fashioned delicate jewelry. Sculptors created marble statues and designed coins. Greek art also flourished in wall murals, floor mosaics, and embroidery. The art portrayed human beings or gods and goddesses. It sometimes depicted mythological creatures such as Pegasus, the winged horse. Sometimes it depicted animals such as goats, deer, bulls, lions, dolphins, and cranes.

Greek women playing the lyre, the aulos, and the barbiton, another type of stringed instrument. What do these paintings reveal about the leisure activities of Greek women?

Olympic Games Special festivals originally held in the city of Olympia in Greece to honor the gods; consist of athletic contests.

Muses The goddesses who the Greeks believed presided over the arts and sciences; their father was Zeus, and their mother was Mnemosyne.

| Doric | Ionic | Corinthian |

Greek architecture expressed a love of beauty and harmony. The Greeks decorated their buildings with ornate designs. Skilled craftsmen chiseled each design into stone. Many designs included carvings of animals and gods.

The **Parthenon** is the ultimate example of Greek architecture. It stands on the Acropolis in Athens. The Parthenon is an enormous temple of white marble that originally had forty-six columns. Several optical illusions were included in its design. An optical illusion occurs when an object appears to take a shape it does not really have. The architects of the Parthenon created some clever illusions. They distorted their work on purpose to correct appearance problems. The steps leading up to the temple are humped in the center, but they appear perfectly level from a distance. The columns lean slightly inward and are thicker in the middle than at the top and the base. But they appear straight and tall.

Another great architectural contribution was the construction of columns to hold up buildings. Greek columns had carved patterns with scrolls or elaborate leafy patterns. Some of these patterns are used in modern architecture today. There were three main styles of columns. They include the Doric style (a plain pattern without a base), the Ionic style (a scroll pattern), and the Corinthian style (a leafy pattern). The columns differed in the way their tops were carved.

An artist's rendering of the ancient Parthenon...

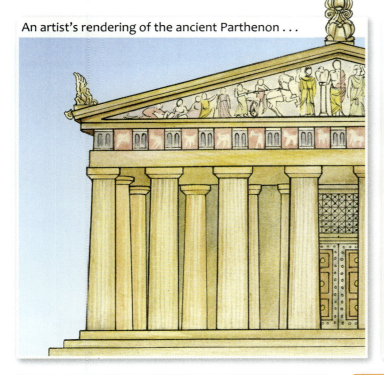

...compared to the Parthenon as it looks today.

Parthenon The ancient Greek temple on the Acropolis; known for its many columns and optical illusions in its design.

 What are some differences and similarities between ancient Olympic games and Olympic games today?

How was the Greek language important in the spread of the gospel?

The Spread of Greek Culture

After the Peloponnesian War, many quarrels broke out between the Greek city-states. The weakened condition of Greece allowed King Philip II of Macedonia to take control of it in 338 BC.

Philip died two years later. His twenty-year-old son, Alexander the Great, took the throne of Macedonia. Alexander, who had been tutored by Aristotle, loved the Greek philosophy and way of life. He took control of the Greek army and began to pursue his dream of uniting the entire world under one empire. He extended his rule eastward as far as India, spreading the Greek culture through much of the world.

After Alexander's death, the empire was divided into four parts. Most of this empire would later be conquered by Rome.

Meanwhile, people all over the Western world were becoming Hellenistic, or "like the Greeks." They adopted the ideas of Greek philosophers. They

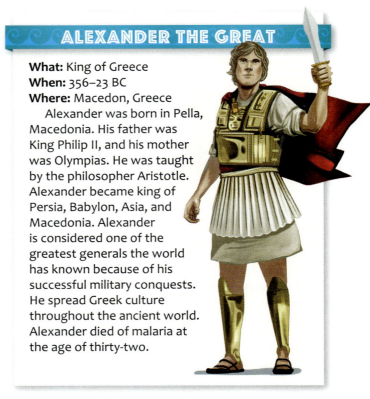

ALEXANDER THE GREAT

What: King of Greece
When: 356–23 BC
Where: Macedon, Greece

Alexander was born in Pella, Macedonia. His father was King Philip II, and his mother was Olympias. He was taught by the philosopher Aristotle. Alexander became king of Persia, Babylon, Asia, and Macedonia. Alexander is considered one of the greatest generals the world has known because of his successful military conquests. He spread Greek culture throughout the ancient world. Alexander died of malaria at the age of thirty-two.

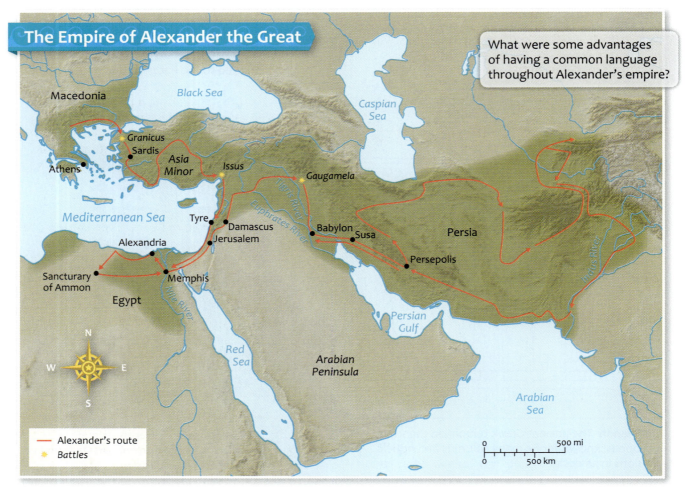

The Empire of Alexander the Great

What were some advantages of having a common language throughout Alexander's empire?

used Greek inventions and learned the teachings of Greek scholars. The works of Greek artists appeared in all parts of the empire. Most importantly, the spread of Greek culture brought a common language to the Western world.

Greek became the language of almost all scholarly writing. As Alexander the Great built his empire, he made Greek the standard language of commerce and government. People still spoke their own languages but had to learn Greek to do business with other countries. By the first century AD, people spoke Greek and understood it nearly everywhere in the empire. The Greek language made communication easier. People could travel long distances and still meet others who spoke a common language. Greek writing could be read and understood throughout the region. The spread of the Greek language paved the way for the gospel to go into all the world.

Most of the Old Testament was written in Hebrew. About 250 years before Jesus was born, people began translating the Old Testament from Hebrew to Greek. This Greek translation, the Septuagint, became commonly accepted. But Aramaic, not Greek,

The kleroterion was used to select juries. Slots were filled with tokens from potential jurors. Marbles poured in a tube next to the slots determined which rows were selected.

was the main language in Palestine during Jesus' time on earth.

Greek was the language of almost all scholarly writing during the first century AD. The New Testament was written between AD 50 and 100, so the New Testament writers wrote in Greek. Because the New Testament was written in a language that many people could read and understand, people of many backgrounds and cultures had access to God's Word.

The Greek alphabet was significant. It was the first alphabet to use symbols for vowels as well as for consonants. Written Greek represented spoken Greek more exactly than the writing of other languages.

The influence of the ancient Greeks touches lives even today. Greek columns influenced future columns, including the ones that decorate and support buildings today. Theatre today often reflects the contributions the Greeks made to drama. The appreciation of sculpture and poetry has ties to the very arts that the Greeks mastered. Literature, science, math, and history have been greatly influenced by Greek discoveries. The development of the Greek alphabet and writing skills allowed the New Testament to give a detailed history of the Lord Jesus Christ, who provides salvation for those who believe in Him.

Scholars believe that the Codex Vaticanus is one of the oldest copies of the Greek Bible. This section of the manuscript includes Second Thessalonians 3:11–18 and Hebrews 1:1–2:2.

 Why is Greek commonly found in Bible study tools?

 ANCIENT ROME

FOCUS
The Roman Empire developed after the fall of the Roman Republic.

Roman Republic
509–31 BC

Pax Romana
27 BC–AD 180

Birth of Christ ca. 4 BC

500 BC — 250 BC — BC AD — AD 250 — AD 500

Constantine legalizes Christianity AD 313

Roman Empire 31 BC–AD 476

Have you ever used an abacus? With this type of counting frame, people could add and multiply large numbers. Here Valeria is sitting at home in Rome, using an abacus to do arithmetic. Like many Roman girls of the patrician upper class, Valeria received an education but has left school to prepare for marriage.

Valeria and her sisters are dressed in the typical Roman tunic, worn by unmarried girls and peasants. When Valeria is married, she will wear a stola, a long, pleated dress encircled by a belt. Her stola will have more ribbons and decorations than the tunic she wears now.

As Valeria's sister Cara enters the home, a breeze carries in a few leaves and tosses the end of Cara's palla, a cloak worn outdoors. Cara can walk through the city streets with a sense of safety because of the peace and order provided by Octavian, Rome's first emperor. In spite of the assassinations that have darkened his rise to power, Octavian has achieved peace.

The peace allows citizens to be productive. Even the upper classes are industrious. Valeria's other sister, Julia, uses a loom to weave cloth. When the cloth is finished, perhaps it will be used to make a stola for Valeria as a gift for her upcoming wedding.

Weights made of clay or stone hold the thread straight on the loom during the weaving process.

What was the impact of the Etruscans on Rome?

The influence of Rome spread to other parts of the world. Physical evidence of Rome's influence remains in areas of Spain, France, the United Kingdom, Italy, Greece, Asia Minor, Palestine, Egypt, and North Africa. The fortresses, walls, and temples speak of Rome's impact. Rome's use of cement is found in structures in Paris and elsewhere. For example, the Arènes de Lutèce is an amphitheater in Paris where gladiators once fought. Some European laws reflect Roman law. Languages such as French and Spanish are rooted in the Latin language. Even Rome's literary works influenced literature throughout Europe.

Early Rome

The earliest inhabitants of Italy were a group of settlers from central Europe. They were called the Latins. These settlers were searching for fertile soil and a climate suitable for farming. They migrated south from across the Alps and traveled to the **Italian Peninsula**, which is now known as Italy. The early Latins settled in a region near the Tiber River. The Roman civilization rose from this region.

Italian Peninsula A boot-shaped peninsula in the Mediterranean Sea; present-day Italy.

Rome The capital city of the Roman Empire and of present-day Italy.

The Founding of Rome

The Romans told legends about the founding of their civilization. According to one legend, twin brothers were abandoned as babies in a basket on the Tiber River. A wolf spied the basket from the shore and swam out to see it. The wolf rescued the babies and cared for them. Soon a shepherd wandered by and found the two babies crying. He decided to take them home with him. The shepherd and his wife named the twins Romulus and Remus.

When the brothers were grown, they decided to build a city near the Tiber River so that they would remember the place of their rescue. However, they could not agree on where to build it. They quarreled, and Romulus killed Remus. Romulus built the city in 753 BC and named it **Rome**, after himself.

This account is only a legend. But historians do believe that Rome began near the Tiber River. They believe the Latins founded a village on the western side of the Italian Peninsula. This village was located on Palatine Hill, one of seven hills near the Tiber River. These hills were natural defenses that helped protect the people. Soon other villages sprang up on the surrounding hills. Eventually the villages developed into the city of Rome.

Roman ruins at Palatine Hill

THE REGION TODAY

Italy

Location
Italy is a boot-shaped peninsula that extends into the Mediterranean Sea. Italy includes the islands of Sardinia, Sicily, and a number of other small islands. Italy borders France, Switzerland, and Austria. To the west of Italy is the Tyrrhenian Sea, and to the east is the Adriatic Sea.

Climate
Italy's climate is mostly temperate. Temperatures in the north are cooler than in the south. Average temperatures range from about 33°F in the north to 70°F in the south.

Topography
The Italian Peninsula is mountainous and includes the Apennine Mountains and sections of the Alps. Italy also has broad plains. Most of its islands are mountainous.

Natural Resources
Italy's resources include water, natural gas, hydroelectric power, mercury, coal, zinc, potash, marble, barite, asbestos, pumice, fluorite, feldspar, pyrite (sulfur), crude oil reserves, fish, and land that is suitable for farming.

Italy Then & Now

What does the shape of the Italian Peninsula look like?

Phoenicians, Greeks, and **Etruscans** also inhabited the Italian Peninsula. The Phoenicians and the Greeks were known for sea trade and colonization.

The Latins had been living in Rome for over one hundred years when Etruscans from the north conquered Rome. During the rule of powerful Etruscan kings, Rome became the strongest and most respected city in the region. The Etruscans introduced a writing system based on the Greek alphabet. They made many improvements to the city by paving roads, building arches, draining marshes, and constructing a sewage system. But the Latins did not like having the Etruscan kings ruling over them.

EARLY ALPHABET			
Phoenician	Early Greek	Etruscan	Early Latin
ᛂ	⊟	⊟	H
✕	⋉	⋉	K
५	ና	Ⴘ	N
⊃	⊓	⊓	⌐
⊲	۹	۹	R
⊗	✕	T	T

Which ancient letters might some of the English letters have come from?

Society

A Roman family included the mother and father, all unmarried daughters and sons, and married sons with their wives and children. The father had the authority. He expected the family to show loyalty, self-control, and respect.

The Roman people were grouped into two social classes. The **patricians** made up the ruling class. They were the wealthy landowners and nobles. The **plebeians** made up the working class. They were the common people, such as farmers, traders, and craftsmen. Most people were plebeians. Both classes were hard-working people. They valued freedom and desired to have a part in governing themselves.

Small, bronze statue of an Etruscan warrior. How were Etruscan warriors fitted for battle?

Roman lictor carrying a fasces for a magistrate during a public appearance. What was the fasces a symbol of?

Early Government

The early government of Rome was a monarchy. A Roman king was also the chief priest, the commander of the army, and the administrator of justice. A group of governmental leaders advised the king.

According to legend, seven kings ruled Rome before the Etruscans invaded. When the Etruscans conquered Rome, they placed an Etruscan king on the throne. Two more Etruscan kings followed.

The fasces, a bundle of rods bound around an axe, was used as a symbol of the king's power. The fasces was carried by attendants who could salute a higher official by lowering the fasces. The axe was taken out of the fasces when it was carried in Rome to represent a citizen's right to appeal a magistrate's ruling. The axe remained in the fasces even when carried in Rome if an official was celebrating a victory.

Etruscan An ancient civilization with a Hellenistic culture on the Italian Peninsula.
patrician A member of the wealthy ruling class in ancient Rome.
plebeian A member of the working class in ancient Rome.

 Why did the Latins settle in the Italian Peninsula?
What was the role of each social class?

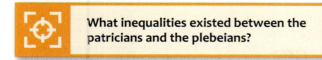

What inequalities existed between the patricians and the plebeians?

Roman Republic (509–31 BC)

The Etruscan kings ruled Rome for over a century. During that time, the Latin people did not like the policies and harsh tactics of the kings. In 509 BC, the people grew powerful enough to drive the king and the Etruscans from the city. In place of the monarchy, the Latins established a new form of government called a **republic**. The word *republic* comes from the Latin phrase *res publica*, which means "a public thing." In a republic, citizens can vote and control the power of government through officials they elect. The Latins, now called *Romans*, believed that a republic would best protect the interests of the people.

A New Government

The newly established Roman republic was divided into three governing branches: the **consuls**, the **Senate**, and the assemblies.

Two patricians were elected as consuls in place of a king. It was their responsibility to manage the affairs of the government, command the Roman army, and serve as supreme judges. Their terms lasted for one year. Both men had equal authority.

The Senate was the most powerful branch. All of its three hundred members were patricians. Senators served for life. The Senate controlled the finances, passed laws, and oversaw foreign affairs.

Several groups called assemblies existed in the early republic. The most powerful group was made up of patricians and was called the **Assembly of Centuries**. It voted on new laws, made declarations of war, and elected the consuls.

The Struggle

The consuls, the Senate, and the Assembly of Centuries were made up only of patricians. The plebeians did not have the privilege of voting. They had few social privileges and were not allowed to hold a public office. Marriage was forbidden between patricians and plebeians. Over time, more and more Romans became dissatisfied with the inequality between the two groups.

For over two hundred years, the plebeians struggled to gain political and social equality. Plebeians served as soldiers of the army, and Rome was constantly waging war against its neighbors. Since the plebeians shared in the dangers of fighting, they wanted to be represented in the government. Many threatened to leave the army. The patricians gradually began to concede, or grant, the plebeians rights.

---

republic A government ruled by representatives chosen by the people.
consul An official that was elected in the Roman Republic to serve for one year.
Senate The most powerful branch of the government in the Roman Republic.
Assembly of Centuries A powerful group of patricians in early Rome.

In this painting by Cesare Maccari, Cicero denounces Catalina, his rival who had revolutionary ideas in opposition to the Republic.

The Concessions

The plebeians were finally allowed to have their own assembly. It was known as the **Tribal Assembly**. Its members elected ten leaders, called **tribunes**. The tribunes protected the rights and the interests of the common people.

At the time, Roman laws were mostly ancient customs that were not written. The patricians often took advantage of the plebeians who were not familiar with the details of the laws. Without written laws, it was difficult to win court battles.

Eventually the plebeians pressured the Senate to write down the law. Around 450 BC, the Roman law was engraved on twelve bronze tablets. These tablets were called the **Law of the Twelve Tables**. These laws became the foundation of Roman civil law. The tablets were displayed in the **Roman Forum**, a public meeting place. The law could be understood by all and applied equally to all.

The plebeians were also given veto power. The Latin word *veto* means "I forbid." Tribunes stood in the Senate doorway during its meetings. The tribunes could stop the Senate's actions at any time by shouting, "Veto!"

Gradually, the plebeians gained more rights. They were allowed to marry patricians. They could be elected as consuls. At last, the Tribal Assembly was permitted to make laws that were as official as those the Senate made. The plebeians and the patricians had equal say in the government of Rome.

The republic worked well for several hundred years. Most people in Rome worked hard and respected the law. The majority of lawmakers wanted to help and protect the citizens of Rome.

Tribal Assembly The assembly made up of plebeians in ancient Rome.

tribune A leader of the Tribal Assembly in ancient Rome.

Law of the Twelve Tables The Roman law written on twelve bronze tablets.

Roman Forum A public meeting place in ancient Rome.

What form of government did the Romans establish after they drove out the Etruscan king?

What concessions did the patricians eventually make to the plebeians?

Why was the Law of the Twelve Tables significant?

ACTIVITY

Making a Law in the Roman Republic

A republic allows voting citizens to influence the government by electing officials. The Romans thought that a republic would be best to protect the interests of all the people. They valued a government that would keep any one person or group of people from obtaining absolute power.

Participate as a member of the Senate or of the Tribal Assembly by helping to make a new law.

1. Determine whether you will be a member of the Senate or the Tribal Assembly.
2. Work with members of the same group to choose a new rule.
3. Present the new rule to the other group and work together to find solutions to any disagreements.
4. Evaluate the decisions and determine whether this method is effective for making laws.

The Roman Forum was the place where public meetings, courts of law, and gladiatorial games took place. It also included shops and outdoor markets.

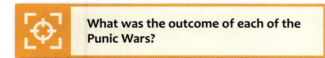

What was the outcome of each of the Punic Wars?

Growth of Rome

Rome's strength came from its military forces. Its soldiers were disciplined and well trained. The infantry was divided into legions. The soldiers in these units were called legionaries. Each legionary carried a short sword and a six-foot javelin.

In the early years of the republic, Rome fought to conquer the entire Italian Peninsula. First, Rome defeated other Latin cities and secured the central part of the peninsula. Then Rome conquered the Etruscans in the north and the Greeks in the south. By 265 BC, the peninsula was under Roman control.

Unlike many conquerors, the Romans extended mercy to those they conquered. Rome offered Roman citizenship to the Greeks, the Latins, and the Etruscans as long as they did not rebel. Rome then turned its attention to regions in the west.

Over the next 125 years, Rome battled **Carthage** for control of the Mediterranean Sea and the lands along the coast. *Punici* was the Roman word for Phoenicians, the people of Carthage. The people of Phoenicia lived in an area that is now known as Lebanon in addition to some land adjoining Syria and Israel. Phoenicians were a seafaring people. They built colonies by good harbors on trade routes. Around 800 BC, the Phoenicians chose an area along the coast of North Africa to establish Carthage. This city became an important center for commerce on the Western Mediterranean shore until it was defeated by Rome.

The Greek historian Polybius described the differences between Carthage and Rome as follows:

> With respect to military science . . . the Carthaginians . . . are more skillful than the Romans . . . . The Romans, on the other hand, are far superior in all things that belong to the establishment and discipline of armies . . . . The Carthaginians employ foreign mercenaries; . . . the Roman armies are composed of citizens, and of the people of the country. . . . The Romans place all their confidence in their own bravery, and in the assistance of their allies. From hence it happens, that the Romans, although at first defeated, are always able to renew the war; and that the Carthaginian armies never are repaired without great difficulty. Add to this, that the Romans, fighting for their country and their children, never suffer their ardor to be slackened; but persist with the same steady spirit till they become superior to their enemies. . . . Even in actions upon the sea, the Romans, though inferior to the Carthaginians, . . . in naval knowledge and experience, very frequently obtain success through the mere bravery of their forces. . . . The valor of the troops that are engaged is no less effectual to draw the victory to their side. (Oliver J. Thatcher, ed., *The Library of Original Sources*, vol. III, *The Roman World* [Milwaukee: University Research Extension Co., 1907], 187)

Carthage A city that served as a key trade center on the North African coast of the Mediterranean Sea.

Punic Wars Three major wars between Rome and Carthage.

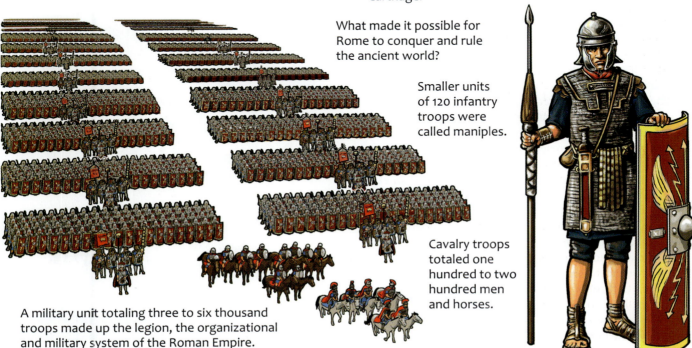

What made it possible for Rome to conquer and rule the ancient world?

Smaller units of 120 infantry troops were called maniples.

Cavalry troops totaled one hundred to two hundred men and horses.

A military unit totaling three to six thousand troops made up the legion, the organizational and military system of the Roman Empire.

THE ROMAN ROADS

Rome is famous for the system of roads it built. The roads connected the lands Rome had conquered. In a span of five hundred years, Rome constructed over fifty thousand miles of roads. The main purpose for these roads was for the armies to travel to all of Rome's provinces. Traveling to and from Rome became fast and easy.

The roads were durable. They were built in layers of sand, gravel, and concrete. The word *street* comes from the Latin word *strāta*, which means "paved road."

The Roman roads played a key part in Rome's trade and influence. Slaves, money, grain, and precious metals were taken into Rome as tribute. Many goods were taken along the Roman roads to other lands.

The roads made it easier for people to travel and exchange philosophies and ideas. Rome used and improved the inventions and discoveries of other peoples. Cultures from the East and the West blended and changed.

In 312 BC, construction began for the first and most famous Roman road, the Appian Way. This long road began in Rome and ended in the southern part of the Italian Peninsula. On his journey to Rome, the apostle Paul traveled to the Forum of Appius and the Three Inns, two locations on the Appian Way (Acts 28:14–15). Early Christians used the Roman roads to carry the gospel throughout the empire.

Many tombs and monuments line the roads leading out of Rome, similar to these burial monuments on the Appian Way.

This milestone from AD 83 on the Antioch Akko Road, Israel, credits Emperor Domitian for repairing the road.

The First Punic War (264–241 BC)

Both Rome and Carthage wanted control of **Sicily**, the largest island in the Mediterranean Sea. Sicily's central location, warm climate, fertile land, and fresh water made the island appealing to both cities. Carthage had already colonized Sicily. The Romans feared that the Carthaginians would become stronger and hinder Roman trade in the Mediterranean Sea. The Romans also feared that the Carthaginians might attack the southern region of the Italian Peninsula.

To gain control of Sicily, the Romans needed a way to defeat the powerful Carthaginian navy. Up to that time, naval battles were won by ramming and sinking enemy ships. The Romans developed an effective strategy. They designed a ship that dropped a plank with a spiked tip. The plank could attach to an enemy ship, allowing Roman soldiers to board and capture the enemy. With these newly designed ships, Rome was victorious over the Carthaginian navy. The two sides formed a peace settlement. Rome gained control of Sicily, and Carthage was forced to pay for Roman losses.

Sicily The largest island in the Mediterranean Sea; a part of Italy.

In what ways was this Roman ship made ready for battle?

The Second Punic War (218–201 BC)

The Second Punic War began when Carthage violated its treaty with Rome. While extending its borders in Spain, Carthage attacked a Spanish town that was a Roman ally.

The Second Punic War is the most famous of the three wars because of a man named **Hannibal**. He was a brilliant general of the Carthaginian army. He decided that, to defeat Rome, he would invade regions of the peninsula outside Rome. He hoped to win the support of the people in those regions. Their support would make it easier to defeat Rome. He gathered his army in Spain. To avoid having the Romans see him, he marched his soldiers across the rugged, snow-covered Alps. He hoped to surprise the Romans.

Hannibal left Spain with about forty thousand men and a herd of war elephants. The cold weather made travel difficult for the elephants and the Carthaginian soldiers. Fierce mountain tribes attacked Hannibal's army. Most of the elephants and many of Hannibal's soldiers died in the snowy Alps.

By the time Hannibal's army reached the Italian Peninsula, it was much smaller in number than the Roman army. However, Hannibal's skill at planning strategies made up for the size of his army. He won battle after battle against the Romans. But he could not completely defeat them.

One of Hannibal's strategies was to arrange his soldiers so that the front lines formed a semicircle or an arc. When the Romans attacked, the Carthaginian soldiers in the front of the arc retreated as the Romans followed them. This maneuver formed a U-shaped trap around the Romans. Using this method, Hannibal's army almost wiped out the Roman army.

HANNIBAL

What: general of Carthage
When: ca. 248–183 BC
Where: Carthage

Hannibal was the son of Hamilcar Barca, the foremost Carthaginian general of the First Punic War. Hannibal is considered one of the greatest generals in ancient history.

Hannibal was a brilliant soldier who, during the Second Punic War, tried repeatedly without success to conquer Rome. Carthage had been a thriving seaport before the First Punic War. But Carthage experienced great financial losses as a result of war with Rome. Hannibal did not have the means to completely defeat Rome. The cities of Carthage and Rome continued to fight for control of the Mediterranean area. Hannibal was forced to return to Carthage and was then defeated. He stayed in Carthage and became a statesman. Later, he chose to go into exile. He continued to oppose Rome until his death.

Hannibal General of Carthage; tried repeatedly to conquer Rome during the Second Punic War; one of the greatest generals in ancient history.

Was Hannibal's strategy of crossing the Alps effective?

The turning point of the war came when Rome sent an army to attack Carthage itself. The Roman army was led by the commander Scipio. Hannibal immediately rushed back to Carthage to protect his city. At the Battle of Zama, Scipio gained the victory. Carthage was forced to give up the territories outside Africa and pay for war damages.

The Third Punic War (149–146 BC)

Approximately fifty years after the Second Punic War, Carthage decided to fight one of Rome's allies. This action angered the Romans. As a result, Rome declared war on Carthage.

After a three-year siege, Rome captured and destroyed Carthage. The Romans sold the survivors into slavery and plowed salt into Carthage's soil to keep crops from growing.

While fighting Carthage, Rome conquered other lands. It marched eastward and conquered what was left of Alexander the Great's empire. Then it conquered Greece, made an alliance with Egypt, and gained control over the eastern Mediterranean Sea. Rome was in control of the Mediterranean world.

Ruins of an ancient Roman bath complex in Carthage. What do these baths suggest about Roman culture?

Why was Sicily important to Rome and to Carthage?

What were Rome's strengths according to the Greek historian Polybius?

How did the Roman roads benefit the empire?

How did Octavian become the ruler of Rome and the Roman world?

The Collapse of the Republic

Rome organized their conquered peoples into provinces. The Roman Senate appointed governors to the provinces to serve as chief military and civil rulers. The provinces had to pay Rome tribute of money or grain. In return, Rome provided order and protection.

Brothers Tiberius and Gaius Gracchus served as tribunes in the Assembly of Plebeians. They sought land reform whereby the government would take back property from landholders with large estates.

Problems arose from Rome's expansion. Farmers who had left their farms to be soldiers came home to find their properties ruined from neglect. Many sold their farms and moved to the city to find work. They found that many jobs had already been filled by slaves taken from conquered territories.

The wealthy profited from the wars. They bought the farms of the conquered lands, and they had slaves run those farms. The wealthy also took advantage of the poorer plebeians by buying their votes in the Tribal Assembly. This allowed the plebeians to earn money, but it also filled the government with more rich men.

The plebeians became less concerned about how the government was run. They no longer studied the governmental issues so that they could vote wisely. The plebeians cared only for what benefits they could gain by selling their votes.

The Senate increased in power and dominated the republic. Although Rome's social and economic problems were growing, the Senate was unwilling to address them. The corruption of the government soon spread throughout the Roman provinces.

Each of Rome's newly acquired provinces was required to pay taxes to Rome. Men called publicans collected these taxes. Many of the publicans and the governmental officials they worked for became greedy. They would collect a higher amount of taxes than needed. Then they kept the extra money for themselves. Publicans became despised in the Roman provinces.

Rivalry Between Commanders

The Senate's failure to deal with the poor weakened the republic. The common people found a new champion who tried to help their cause. **Marius**, a military hero, reorganized the Roman army. He allowed the poor citizens to enlist for long terms of service. In exchange, they received a share of land, money, and spoils of war. These citizens became part of a professional army that fought for financial gain rather than for patriotic causes. Generals began to use their armies for their own gain. Soldiers were more devoted to their commanders than they were to Rome.

Marius Military hero who reorganized the Roman army and allowed poor citizens to enlist for long terms of service.

Marius escaped to Carthage after being defeated by Sulla. What might he be doing or thinking about as he sits in its ruins?

The Senate appointed the general **Sulla** to command the Roman army in the war in Asia Minor. The Tribal Assembly did not like the Senate's choice and appointed Marius instead. Rivalry between the two commanders developed into civil war. After many years of battles, Sulla and the Senate emerged victorious.

Sulla declared himself the dictator, and he reorganized the Roman government. After restoring stability to the Senate, he stepped down as dictator. But the Senate was not able to maintain control of the government.

The Triumvirate

Ambitious men tried to gain control of the Senate. Three men competed with one another for fame and power. **Crassus** was a wealthy military commander. He defeated a slave revolt. **Pompey** was popular with the Senate for his accomplishments. He turned Asia Minor, Syria, and Palestine into Roman provinces. He also rid the Mediterranean Sea of pirates. **Julius Caesar** was a clever politician who could sway the common people to accomplish his goals. In 60 BC, the three men formed an alliance called a **triumvirate** to rule Rome together.

Caesar was appointed governor of Gaul. He trained a loyal army and led many campaigns. Crassus died in a war in Asia. Then Pompey became jealous of Caesar's growing strength and popularity. Pompey eventually sided with the Senate against Caesar.

Caesar's popularity threatened the power of the government leaders. They ordered him to disband his army. Instead, Caesar marched to Rome and plunged into a second civil war against Pompey and the Senate. Caesar's army fought Pompey's army for four years before defeating it. Caesar was proclaimed the dictator of Rome. His term was supposed to last only ten years, but he soon changed it so that he would be dictator for life. He made many changes in the government, hoping to solve the problems of the republic.

Sulla General appointed by the Senate to command the Roman army; declared himself dictator after winning a civil war.

Crassus A wealthy military leader; part of the triumvirate.

Pompey General who was popular with the Senate for his accomplishments of turning Asia Minor, Syria, and Palestine into Roman provinces and for ridding the Mediterranean Sea of pirates; part of the triumvirate.

Julius Caesar General who became dictator of Rome; part of the triumvirate.

triumvirate An alliance among three rulers.

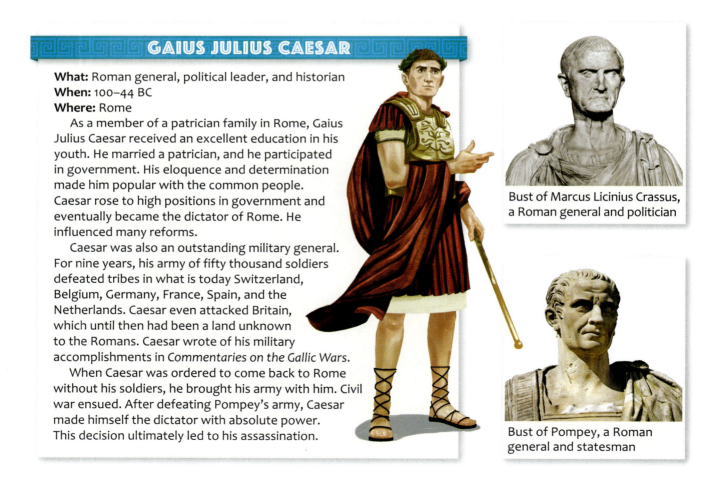

GAIUS JULIUS CAESAR

What: Roman general, political leader, and historian
When: 100–44 BC
Where: Rome

As a member of a patrician family in Rome, Gaius Julius Caesar received an excellent education in his youth. He married a patrician, and he participated in government. His eloquence and determination made him popular with the common people. Caesar rose to high positions in government and eventually became the dictator of Rome. He influenced many reforms.

Caesar was also an outstanding military general. For nine years, his army of fifty thousand soldiers defeated tribes in what is today Switzerland, Belgium, Germany, France, Spain, and the Netherlands. Caesar even attacked Britain, which until then had been a land unknown to the Romans. Caesar wrote of his military accomplishments in *Commentaries on the Gallic Wars*.

When Caesar was ordered to come back to Rome without his soldiers, he brought his army with him. Civil war ensued. After defeating Pompey's army, Caesar made himself the dictator with absolute power. This decision ultimately led to his assassination.

Bust of Marcus Licinius Crassus, a Roman general and politician

Bust of Pompey, a Roman general and statesman

JULIUS CAESAR'S CALENDAR

Early Roman calendars did not recognize that the solar year is almost six hours longer than 365 days. By the time of Julius Caesar's reign, the calendar was so inaccurate that none of the seasons fell in the right place. Caesar decided to add an extra day every four years to balance out the calendar. The fourth year is called a leap year. Since the Roman calendar started with March, the extra day was added to the last month, February.

Before putting his new idea into practice, Caesar had to bring the calendar up to date. So he made the year 46 BC last 445 days! This extra-long year was often called the "year of confusion."

Caesar's calendar, known as the Julian calendar, was used by Europeans for centuries. Today, most countries use a reformed version of this calendar, called the **Gregorian calendar**. The Gregorian calendar is based on the birth of Christ, but it is similar to the Julian calendar. It adds an extra day to February every four years to create a leap year that keeps the calendar up to date. Additionally, echoes of the Julian calendar can still be heard in the names of the months. Many of the months were named after Roman gods or rulers. Also, Julius Caesar named the month of July after himself. The names of other months come from Latin numbers.

Gregorian calendar The revised version of the Julian calendar; now used by most countries.

The month of March was named after Mars, the Roman god of war. This statue is part of a group of Roman marble statues from ca. AD 120–140.

ROMAN ORIGINS OF THE NAMES OF MONTHS

January	named after Janus, the Roman god of gates and doors	July	named after Julius Caesar
February	from the Latin word that means "to purify"	August	named after Caesar Augustus (Octavian)
March	named after Mars, the Roman god of war	September	from the Latin word for "seven"
April	from the Latin word that means "to open"	October	from the Latin word for "eight"
May	named after Maia, the goddess of spring	November	from the Latin word for "nine"
June	named after Juno, the Roman goddess of marriage	December	from the Latin word for "ten"

The Murder of Caesar oil on canvas by Karl von Piloty, 1865

Death of a Dictator

Caesar limited the power of the corrupt Senate. He granted citizenship to people from territories on the Italian Peninsula and even allowed them to be represented in the Senate. He improved the Roman calendar. He promoted colonization, schools, libraries, and public works throughout Rome and its surrounding territories. His actions helped to unify Rome and strengthen its bonds with its conquered peoples.

Although many Romans liked Caesar and respected his accomplishments, others were angry with him. They knew that as long as Caesar insisted on having absolute power, the government of Rome could no longer be a true republic. As Caesar's reign continued, angry Romans grew more and more desperate. They wanted the government of Rome to once again belong to the people.

One of Julius Caesar's weaknesses was his inability to discern who his enemies were among his associates. He placed people in his ranks that were his enemies. This would eventually cost him his life. Brutus and Cassius, two senators whom Caesar considered his friends, met with a group of other senators and plotted to kill Caesar. In 44 BC, on the fifteenth day of March (called the **Ides of March**), Caesar was assassinated.

Men eager to take Caesar's place led Rome into a third civil war. Eventually **Octavian** formed an alliance with **Mark Antony**. They divided the empire so Antony ruled the east and Octavian ruled the west. Both men, however, were too ambitious to share the power of ruling Rome. In 31 BC, at the Battle of Actium, Antony and Octavian clashed in a naval battle off the coast of Greece. Octavian defeated Antony and became the ruler of Rome and the Roman world.

Ides of March The fifteenth day of March on the Roman calendar; the day on which Julius Caesar was assassinated.

Octavian Ruled the western part of the Roman Empire after forming an alliance with Mark Antony; became the first emperor of Rome after defeating Mark Antony; also called Augustus.

Mark Antony Roman general who ruled the eastern part of the Roman Empire after forming an alliance with Octavian.

What were some of the negative results of Rome's expansion?

Why did three men form a triumvirate?

What prevented Rome from being a true republic?

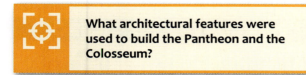

What architectural features were used to build the Pantheon and the Colosseum?

The Roman Empire (31 BC–AD 476)

Julius Caesar's death paved the way for the beginning of Rome's history as an empire. Octavian worked to restore honesty, diligence, and respect to the government of Rome. He restored power to the Senate and the Tribal Assembly, reserving the office of tribune for himself. He could propose or veto new laws. He also reorganized the army and the governments of Rome's territories. He continued to promote trade and industry and to build roads throughout the empire.

Octavian had complete control of Rome, but he did not call himself a dictator as Julius Caesar had done. He used several different titles. One of these was *princeps*, meaning "first citizen." He was also called *Augustus*, which means "revered one." His reign began a period of peace and prosperity that Rome enjoyed for the next two hundred years. This period is called the **Pax Romana**. It ended in AD 180 with the death of Emperor Marcus Aurelius, who is often referred to as the last good emperor of Rome.

During the Pax Romana, the culture of Rome was similar to Greek culture. Like the Greeks, the Romans placed importance on education, architecture, and religion.

Education and Citizenship

During the Pax Romana, fathers were responsible for the education of their children. Many wealthy families hired tutors or servants to educate their children. Some boys and girls received an education by attending school. They studied reading, writing, and mathematics. They wrote on wax tablets that could be smoothed and reused. An abacus was used for math. After mastering these basics, most girls stayed home to learn how to manage a household. Sometimes girls studied further with a private tutor. Some boys continued their education by studying Greek, Latin, history, geography, astronomy, and literature.

Roman children were citizens but did not have citizen rights. A boy was enrolled as a citizen when he turned sixteen, and a special citizenship ceremony was held at the Forum, the Roman marketplace. The boy was given an official citizen's garment, a **toga**.

Pax Romana The period of peace in the Roman Empire that began with the reign of Octavian.

toga A loose robe worn by citizens of ancient Rome.

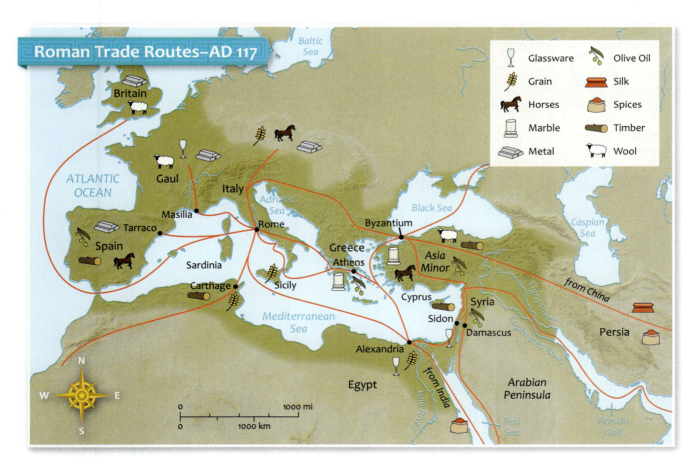

Roman Trade Routes–AD 117

After becoming citizens, young men continued their studies or entered business or the army. Women had few citizen rights.

Culture and Achievements

Many Romans loved to read. The greatest Latin literature was written during the Pax Romana. **Cicero** was a master of Latin prose, and he influenced other writers and students. He was known as the greatest orator of his day. An orator is an eloquent and skilled public speaker. **Virgil** is considered the greatest Roman poet. He wrote *The Aeneid*, an epic about Rome's glory. Another author, Livy, wrote a detailed history of Rome. He also wrote of events from the time in which he lived.

Rome came in contact with a variety of different cultures while it was expanding. As a result, many elements from these cultures were integrated into Roman culture. Roman life was especially influenced by Greek culture. The Greeks were artists and philosophers. They studied to learn about the world around them. The Romans strove to improve their lives. They learned much from Greek ideas and improved many of them. The Romans also made contributions in law and politics.

Cicero Philosopher, lawyer, and member of the Senate; considered the greatest Roman orator.

Virgil Roman poet who wrote *The Aeneid*; considered the greatest Roman poet.

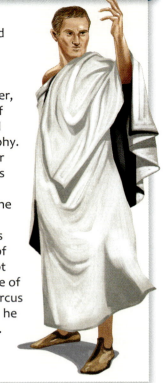

MARCUS TULLIUS CICERO

What: politician, scholar, author, lawyer, orator, and philosopher
When: 106–43 BC
Where: Rome

Cicero was a philosopher, a lawyer, and a member of the Senate. He introduced Romans to Greek philosophy. He was an excellent orator who wrote many speeches to persuade the Senate. Cicero remained loyal to the principles of the republic through the final civil wars that brought the demise of the republic. Cicero did not join the second triumvirate of Octavian, Antony, and Marcus Aemilius Lepidus. Instead, he openly criticized Octavian. Cicero was executed on December 7, 43 BC.

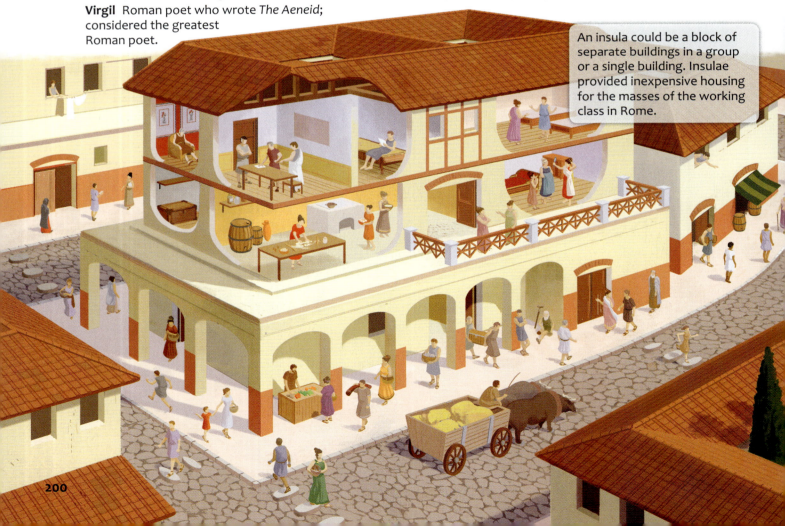

An insula could be a block of separate buildings in a group or a single building. Insulae provided inexpensive housing for the masses of the working class in Rome.

THE COLOSSEUM

The Roman Colosseum was an impressive feat of engineering and design. Architects and engineers still marvel at it today. Construction took place between AD 70 and 72. This massive arena was over 160 feet high and covered six acres of land. It was designed to hold nearly fifty thousand people.

The arena floor was made of wood and covered with sand. It had sections that could be raised and lowered. Elevators brought animals, props, and other items to the arena from rooms and tunnels beneath it. The floor could even be flooded to reenact naval scenes.

Roman emperors staged events to win public favor and to keep the people entertained. Admission was free. People were seated according to their social classes. Chariot races, gladiator contests, and wild animal fights were some of the events that spectators watched in the arena. Prisoners and war captives were also brought to fight in the arena.

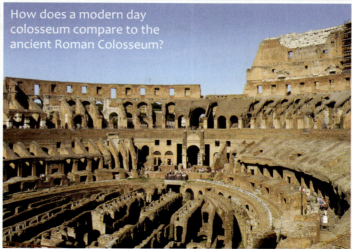

How does a modern day colosseum compare to the ancient Roman Colosseum?

Architecture in the Pax Romana

Rome's greatest artistic achievements were in its architecture. Although the Romans built for practical purposes rather than for beauty, Roman works were impressive. According to legend, Octavian claimed he had found Rome as a city of brick and left it as a city of marble.

The Romans obtained ideas from craftsmen and artists they captured during conquests. Romans used their own building techniques and improved on techniques borrowed from other civilizations. Some of the borrowed architectural ideas enhanced and strengthened Roman structures.

Romans were the first to use concrete, a mixture of gravel, sand, and mortar. Rather than using solid marble, Romans often built with concrete and covered the structure with a thin layer of marble. Not only did concrete lower building costs, but it also made Roman structures durable.

This painting, *The Interior of the Pantheon* by Giovanni Paolo Panini, depicts foreign visitors and Romans of every social class coming to the Pantheon to enjoy the architecture, to visit, and to pray.

One architectural feature the Romans improved was the dome. Since a dome does not require pillars or other supports, the room under a dome is large and open. The largest dome in Rome sits atop a temple called the **Pantheon**. Its concrete dome reaches fourteen stories above the ground.

Arches were used in many public buildings, houses, and other structures such as bridges and aqueducts (raised troughs that carried water). Arches are a main feature in the large arena known as the **Colosseum**. Both the Pantheon and the Colosseum are still standing today.

Pantheon An ancient Roman temple dedicated to all the gods.

Colosseum A large arena where events were held to entertain the Roman people.

 What was the significance of the Pax Romana on Rome's history?

LIFE IN ROME

Organized Cities and Government
Cities grew as people left farms and smaller villages to seek other work. Rome was governed primarily by the Senate in the Roman Republic. The Senate was run by patricians. Eventually, the plebeians formed the Tribal Assembly. These groups would meet at the Roman Forum.

Citizenship
A person gained Roman citizenship at birth if the parents were Romans. A person also had citizenship if only one parent was Roman as long as the parents had obtained permission to get married. Conquered people had many of the rights that citizens had.

Power
Rome's strong military made it powerful. The government exercised its power by keeping order and protecting conquered people in exchange for tribute.

Arts, Sciences, and Written Language
Rome's greatest contribution to the arts was its architecture. Romans incorporated arches, columns, and domes. The beauty of structures was enhanced by overlaying them with marble.

The Basilica Julia was an important building that was used for official business and public meetings.

Senators debated issues in the Roman Forum.

Job Specialization
Slaves and plebeians helped with household chores for the patricians, constructed roads and buildings, and worked in the army. They worked in medicine, mining, and education. Plebeians were also farmers, craftsmen, and traders. A female slave or servant might work as a hairdresser or housekeeper. Many patricians served in government. Others built and rented apartments to the plebeians or owned shipping businesses. Many patrician women managed their households, helped their husbands who worked in public office, and wrote poetry.

Religion
Romans were polytheistic. Food and drink were offered to gods at shrines in homes. Sacrifices were also made in temples. Epicureanism and Stoicism were popular beliefs. The Romans typically tolerated religions of conquered people.

Justice
Plebeians did not know the details of the law because the law was not written down. The plebeians pressured the patricians to treat them more justly. So the patricians wrote down the laws in the Law of the Twelve Tables.

Social Classes
The emperor was the only person allowed to wear a completely purple toga. The patricians were the privileged class, and the men wore white togas as a sign of their position. The plebeians wore tunics of inexpensive materials and were not allowed to wear the patrician toga.

Key Themes of Civilization
- Justice
- Power
- Citizenship
- Environment

Features of a Civilization
- Organized cities and government
- Social classes
- Job specialization
- Arts, sciences, and written language
- Religion

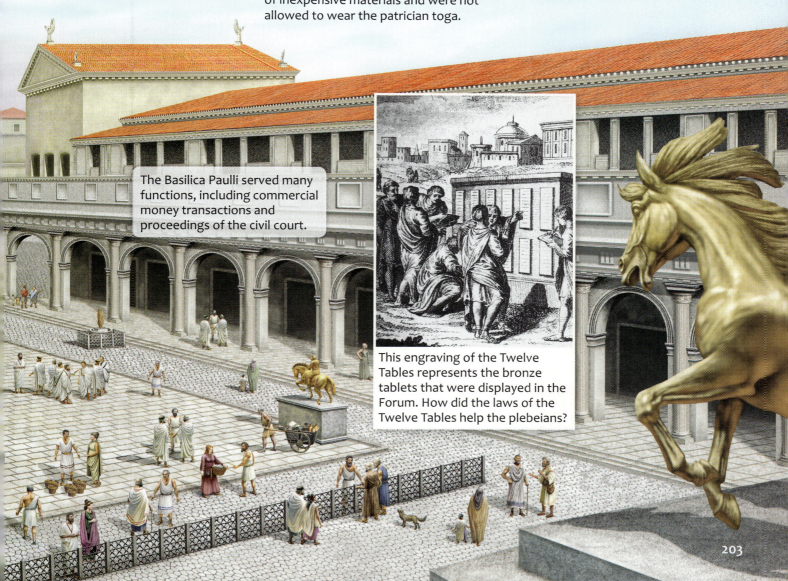

The Basilica Paulli served many functions, including commercial money transactions and proceedings of the civil court.

This engraving of the Twelve Tables represents the bronze tablets that were displayed in the Forum. How did the laws of the Twelve Tables help the plebeians?

In what ways do Epicureanism and Stoicism contrast with biblical truth?

Religion

The ancient Romans adopted gods from many of the people they conquered. As a result, the Romans were polytheistic. Some Roman gods were the same as those worshiped by the Greeks but with Roman names. For example, the Greek god Zeus, a god of sky and weather, was the same as the Roman god Jupiter. Demeter, a Greek goddess of harvest and nature, was the Roman goddess Ceres. Ares, a god of war, was the Roman god Mars. The Romans honored their gods by building temples and naming planets after them. Festivals, offerings, and prayers were part of worship. The entrance of each household had a shrine. The people worshiped their gods daily.

The Romans accepted religions from different parts of the empire. Even religions from the Far East became popular.

Epicureanism and **Stoicism** were two Greek philosophies that were practiced as religions in Rome. The followers of Epicureanism believed that everything, including gods, people's souls, and the earth, were made up of atoms. Because Epicureans believed that everything was merely physical, they thought that people did not need to fear the gods or what would happen after death. If everything was merely physical, there would not be anything after death, so they did not need to fear it.

Epicureans believed that if people are free from fear, they can find true happiness in this life. Epicureans lived for pleasure alone and tried to keep their lives happy and free from pain. Many people think that this teaching means people should pursue whatever they desire. But this is not what Epicureanism teaches. For example, Epicureans recognized that if people overate delicious food, the initial pleasure would give way to the discomfort of being over-full. If people overate often, they would suffer health problems. Epicureans thought that people should consider the future and avoid whatever would lead to pain instead of pleasure. They hoped for a quiet life that avoided the many things in this life that could lead to pain.

Another Greek philosophy was Stoicism. The Stoics believed that doing one's duty led to happiness. They emphasized virtues such as courage, justice, and obedience. Stoicism was popular among the Roman soldiers.

Epicureanism The philosophy that happiness is the most important thing.

Stoicism The philosophy that people should strive to be indifferent to pleasure and pain.

Stoicism was the most popular of the philosophies that existed during the Roman Empire. It was designed to help people handle the troubles of life. Stoics taught that the key to being happy was to accept whatever happened, to not worry about what they could not control, and to try to live an honorable life. The Stoics saw themselves as citizens of a world that required involvement in its affairs and loyalty to it. Believing that nature reveals what is right and virtuous, the Stoics sought to go along with natural laws and to accept the actions of fate.

The Stoics believed that fate is the way things will happen. Fate was not considered to be a god. The gods themselves were not all-powerful and were subject to fate. The Stoics believed that circumstances unfolded according to a chain of causes and effects with the result that the effects of events would be ultimately good. Even bad things would eventually have good come from them.

 EPICUREAN BELIEFS

Epicurus and the Epicureans who followed him believed that the chief goal of life was pleasure. Epicurus believed fear, especially fear of death, was one of the major reasons that people did not have pleasurable lives. Epicurus thought that the purpose of philosophy was to help people overcome their fears. He argued that a person's soul, as well as his body, is made up of physical atoms. When a person dies, the atoms of body and soul fall apart. There is no existence after death. Therefore, there is nothing to fear.

Epicurus did believe in gods, but they were made out of atoms like the rest of the world was. They were not persons who involved themselves in the world, so the gods did not need to be feared either.

The Christian view is much different from Epicurus's. Although God does give people pleasure in this life, the goal of life is not to avoid pain and to maintain pleasure. The goal of life is to give glory and praise to God. Jesus demonstrated that sometimes people must endure great pain in order to help others and glorify God.

In addition, God did not intend for people to get rid of all fear. For example, people should fear death and the judgment that comes after it. The way to overcome this fear is to find salvation in Christ, who has taken that judgment in the place of sinners.

ROMAN GODS AND GODDESSES

Apollo	god of music, poetry, and the sun	Mercury	god of commerce, of travelers, and of messaging
Ceres	goddess of agriculture and fertility	Minerva	goddess of wisdom and war
Diana	goddess of the hunt, of women, and of childbirth	Neptune	god of the sea
Janus	god of gates, of transitions, and of beginnings	Pluto	god of the underworld
Juno	goddess of marriage and childbirth	Venus	goddess of love and beauty
Jupiter	king of the gods and god of the sky	Vestia	goddess of hearth and home
Mars	god of war	Vulcan	god of fire and metalworking

STOIC BELIEFS

Because the Stoics believed that fate governed all things, they did not want people to worry about things they could not control. One Stoic wrote, "Ask not that events should happen as you will, but let your will be that events should happen as they do, and you shall have peace."

Although Stoics did not want people to worry about things beyond their control, they still wanted them to work on what they were able to control. They thought that people should work hard to be virtuous. For example, they taught that people should live to help others and not be greedy.

Christians can appreciate the Stoic emphasis on living a moral life. But people are not good enough to become virtuous by their own efforts. Christians can also see some truth in the Stoic teaching of accepting events that are out of their control. The apostle Paul wrote, "I have learned, in whatsoever state I am, therewith to be content" (Philippians 4:11). But it is God, not fate, who controls all things.

Christianity also disagrees with the Stoics that even the bad things in this life are actually good. Because of sin, many things that happen are truly bad. Only when Christ returns to rule the earth will all things be set right. At that time, the wicked will be judged, and justice will be upheld.

Epictetus: The Discourses and Manual Together with Fragments of His Writings, trans. P.E. Matheson (Oxford: Oxford University Press, 1916), II:216.

The goddess Diana is shown hunting as she draws an arrow from her quiver in this marble Greco-Roman statue from the first century. What are some human characteristics attributed to the goddess in this sculpture?

 Where did the Romans get their gods?

How did the Christian church influence Roman culture?

Christianity
The Life of Jesus Christ

Around 5 BC, Octavian, also known as Caesar Augustus, decreed a census of everyone in the Roman Empire. The people had to be counted in the cities their ancestors came from, so many people had to travel for the census. During that census, the most significant birth in world history occurred in Bethlehem, a small town in Judea. Jesus was born to a virgin named Mary.

At the age of thirty, Jesus began to travel throughout Galilee, teaching in the synagogues and healing all kinds of sicknesses among the people. His message was that people should repent because the kingdom of God was at hand (Mark 1:15). The kingdom of God was something the Jewish people had been waiting for. They believed that the coming of God's kingdom meant that God would send the Messiah to rule the world and to set all things right. But Jesus' teachings revealed that this kingdom was going to come in two stages. First, He would suffer and die to pay the penalty for sin. Then as people followed Him, Jesus' kingdom would grow like a small seed grows into a tall tree (Matthew 13:31–32). Later, Jesus would come to judge the world and set all things right forever.

Jesus' teaching and miracles angered and worried Jewish leaders. They rejected the charge that they were sinners who needed Jesus to provide salvation for them, and they misunderstood Jesus' teaching about His kingdom. They thought that if Jesus grew too popular and tried to set up a kingdom in Israel, the Romans would take away their positions of leadership, and the Jews would lose their nation. They decided it would be better to have Jesus killed. They took Jesus before Pontius Pilate, the Roman governor of Judea and accused Jesus of claiming to be the King of the Jews. They said that anyone who made himself a king opposed Caesar, and they insisted that the governor execute Jesus. Even though Pilate found Jesus innocent of any insurrection against Rome, he yielded to the pressure and had Jesus crucified.

Three days after His crucifixion, Jesus rose from the dead. The guards stationed at the tomb reported that a shining angel had appeared and rolled away the stone to the tomb. The Jewish leaders paid the soldiers a large amount of money to say that the disciples caught the guards napping and stole the body. However, the disciples were as surprised as the religious rulers and the Romans by the missing body. But when the resurrected Jesus appeared to them, they understood that He had come back to life.

Fifty days after Jesus was crucified, Peter, one of Jesus' disciples, preached at the feast of Pentecost that God had raised Jesus from the dead. Jesus then went to heaven to reign until He will subdue all His enemies. Peter declared the same message that Jesus had preached: people should repent of their sins before the King returns in judgment. About three thousand people repented and were baptized that day. The events at Pentecost were the beginning of the Christian church.

Ecce Homo (Behold the Man) is an oil-on-canvas painting by Antonio Ciseri (AD 1821–91) that shows a scourged and bound Christ standing quietly as Pilate addresses the masses below. What do Christ's actions and words reveal about Him and about His relationship with Roman authorities?

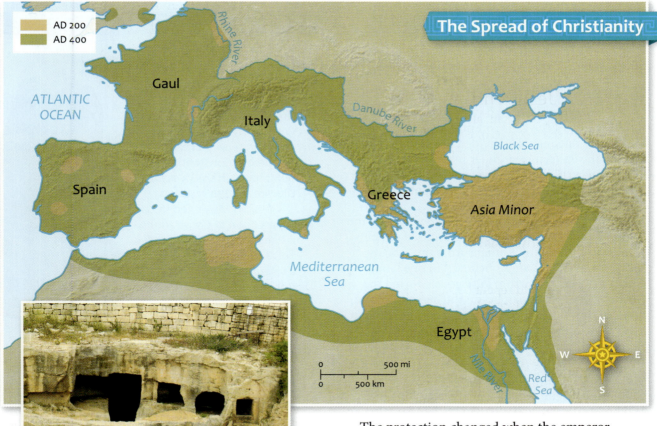

Roman catacombs, similar to these on the island of Malta, served as passageways and as burial sites.

The Spread of Christianity

The Roman roads enabled Christians to carry the gospel to many parts of the world. The spread of Christianity was greatly aided by the conversion of Paul, a Roman citizen. Paul was a well-educated Pharisee who persecuted Christians. But Acts 9:1–6 tells the story of Paul's conversion to Christ. Paul became the first missionary to the Roman world. He traveled thousands of miles on Roman roads and preached the gospel.

The earliest persecution of the Christians came from Jews. Roman leaders saw this persecution as a debate among the Jews and intervened only when the peace was disturbed. The Romans sometimes protected the Christians in order to preserve the peace.

Nero Roman emperor who ordered the death of many Christians.
gladiator An armed person who fought animals or other people in an arena such as the Colosseum.

The protection changed when the emperor, **Nero**, blamed the Christians for starting a fire that destroyed nearly two-thirds of the city of Rome. Nero ordered that many Christians be put to death by crucifixion or burning. This persecution was probably limited to the city of Rome.

By the time of the next emperor, many Gentiles had become Christians. Christianity was no longer seen as a Jewish religion. Because Christians did not worship the Roman gods or the emperor, Christianity was considered illegal. But some Romans wondered why Christians were being punished when they had committed no other crimes.

In the early second century, a Roman governor named Pliny wrote to the emperor Trajan. Pliny said he did not hunt for Christians. But if someone was accused of being a Christian and did not reject Christianity, then he would have the person executed. Trajan wrote back that this was the correct way to handle Christians.

During the second century, the persecution of Christians in the Roman Empire was up to local leaders, and it was not consistent. Nonetheless, Christianity continued to grow despite the persecution it encountered.

 Why did Jesus' teachings worry the Jewish religious leaders?

How do the key achievements of the Roman civilization contrast with those of the Greek civilization?

Collapse of the Roman Empire

The emperor Diocletian reigned from AD 284 to 305. He thought the Roman Empire was too large to be ruled by one man. He divided the empire in half, keeping the eastern part under his own control and appointing a ruler for the western part. He eventually appointed assistant rulers for each half, further dividing his power.

The division over religious beliefs weakened the kingdom further. Christians were accused of being disloyal to the empire. Romans worshiped many gods. However, Christians believed in one God, so they refused to worship false gods. During the third century, Diocletian began the harshest of the persecutions of Christians across the whole Roman empire. He ordered the destruction of Christian places of worship, the burning of the Scriptures, and the imprisonment of religious leaders. The Romans hoped that persecution would cause Christians to reject their faith in God and discourage others from converting to Christianity. Roman persecution resulted in many Christians abandoning the key teachings of Christianity for a time, but many others stayed faithful through the persecution.

After Diocletian retired, a struggle for power began. The struggle turned into civil war. **Constantine I** conquered Rome and became the ruler, unifying the empire. In 313 Constantine issued a decree to legalize Christianity.

From the church's beginning, it struggled not only against persecution but also against false teachers. One false teacher named Arius taught that Jesus was not God. This error divided the church. To resolve this dispute, Constantine called for a meeting of church leaders. These leaders met for a council in the city of Nicaea. In this meeting, the leaders rejected the false teachings of Arius and affirmed the Bible's teaching that Jesus is God.

In the fourth century AD, the Roman Empire continued to decline. Soldiers gave their allegiance to their officers rather than to the empire. Ambitious generals tried to gain control of the government but did not succeed.

Financial woes contributed to the deterioration of the Roman Empire. The high costs of keeping a large army to protect the empire's borders and the employment of a large number of governmental officials drained the empire's treasury.

CONSTANTINE

What: emperor of Rome
When: ruled AD 306–337
Where: Rome

Constantine was the first Roman emperor to convert to Christianity. The acceptance of Christianity was already on the rise before Constantine's time, but it had suffered a setback in Diocletian's persecution.

Constantine ended the official persecution of Christians by issuing the Edict of Milan. This edict made Christianity a tolerated religion in Rome. Constantine restored property and rebuilt many churches that had been destroyed. He also was the first emperor to forbid the gladiatorial games and to end public pagan sacrifices.

Tinted engraving of an ancient map of Constantinople by Konstantinos Kaldis

Roman architects and hydraulic engineers designed the plans to create The Pont du Gard in southern France. Built around 19 BC on the Gard River, it carried water to the city of Nimes and served as a bridge.

As a result, the government raised taxes to pay costs. Constantine further strained the economy by building a new capital called Constantinople. Many Romans looked to the government to provide free food and entertainment. The unemployment of the working class and the cost of supplying food and entertainment for them contributed to the failing economy.

Moral decay was another factor that weakened Rome. People demonstrated little value for human and animal life as they were entertained by brutal conflicts in the arenas. The Romans were living apart from the biblical truth that people are made in the image of God. The attitude that human life was not of value weakened social structures such as the family, government, and the military.

In 395 Emperor **Theodosius I** divided the Roman Empire for his two sons. The western part soon fell to barbarian invasions. First, the Huns moved across Asia and into Europe. Led by Attila, the Huns invaded the west. Next, the Vandals, a Germanic tribe that had established a kingdom in northern Africa, raided Rome. Then in 378, another Germanic tribe, the Visigoths, defeated the Roman army at the Battle of Adrianople.

The assault of these barbarian tribes, along with the decline of Rome's government, economy, and society, caused the collapse of the Western Roman Empire. The Roman government collapsed in AD 476. This is referred to as the **fall of the Roman Empire**. The Eastern Roman Empire endured for another thousand years and became known as the Byzantine Empire.

Rome is known for its practicality and its power. It is characterized by massive domes, arched aqueducts, grand road systems, and legionaries who lived and died for the republic. The people of Rome made advancements in education, government, and science. But the most important thing to come out of the Roman Empire was the spread of Christianity.

Constantine I Roman emperor who moved Rome's capital to Constantinople; legalized Christianity; also known as "Constantine the Great."

Theodosius I Also known as "Theodosius the Great"; joint ruler of Rome from 379 to 392 and sole ruler of Rome from 392 to 395; opposed pagan beliefs and Arianism; divided the eastern and western parts of the Roman empire under the rule of his two sons.

fall of the Roman Empire The collapse of the Roman government in AD 476.

What contributed to the spread of Christianity?

What factors contributed to the decline of the Roman Empire?

10 THE BYZANTINE EMPIRE

FOCUS

The Byzantine Empire made a lasting contribution by preserving the cultural and political thought of the classical world.

Edict of Milan 313				Fourth Crusade 1202–1204	
250	500	750	1000	1250	1500
330 Constantine founds Constantinople		1054 Roman Catholic Church and Eastern Orthodox Church split			1453 Ottoman Turks conquer Constantinople

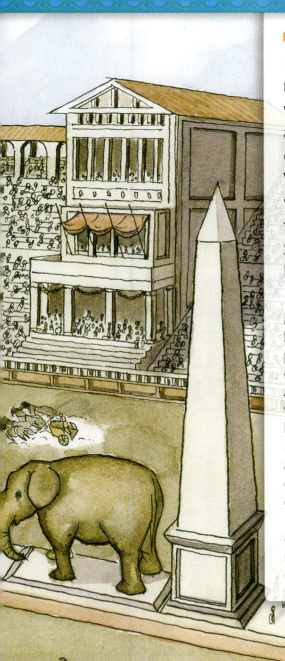

The horses gallop thunderously, and the charioteers furiously urge them on. In the stands, young Justin roars the name of his favorite driver, eyes blazing with excitement. His sister Zoe clenches her hands, anxiously watching the competitors. These Byzantine chariot races in the Hippodrome can be dangerous. With every turn, there is the risk that a chariot might veer out of control, sending driver and horses into the dust in a tangle of legs and metal and hooves. She prefers the singers and clowns who entertain between races.

The name Hippodrome comes from the Greek words for *horse* and *way*. The Imperial Hippodrome of Byzantium, the largest in the ancient world, could hold more than 60,000 people. One end of the Hippodrome was a half-circle, and the other end was square with huge bronze statues of four horses. A wall called the *spina* ran down the middle of the arena and was decorated with statues—one was of a giant woman who held a life-size horse and rider in one hand. Another was of Hercules wrestling a lion. Up to ten chariots could race at a time. Two or four horses would pull a chariot, depending on the race being held. The four-horse races were the most difficult and awarded the most prestigious prizes.

After the Roman empire's collapse, the Byzantine rulers established a sprawling empire. They built strong walls, made impressive sewage and water systems, and improved education for children like Justin and Zoe.

What did Constantine do that led to the development of the Byzantine Empire?

The Village by the Sea

The beginning of the **Byzantine Empire** can be traced to a village in southeastern Europe. This village was known as Byzantium. It is the source of the name *Byzantine*.

Byzantium was founded by Greek colonists. The site they had chosen for the village was on a peninsula. Water on both sides of the land served as protection for the colonists.

The location was ideal for trading. The nearby Bosporus Strait was a popular trading route. Merchants from India and China passed through Byzantium, selling silks and spices. A harbor to the north was another advantage. Villagers traveled around the Black Sea to trade with Asian merchants for furs and amber. The villagers could also sail west into the Aegean Sea and the Mediterranean Sea. They traded with the Greeks, the Romans, and the North Africans for grain, gold, ivory, and other goods. Eventually, Byzantium grew into a city and a center for world trade.

The Birth of Eastern Power
A New City

Rome was suffering from threats of invasion and a weakening economy. The Roman emperor Constantine decided to move the capital to another location. He saw that Byzantium would be a good site. Being on a peninsula, the city was surrounded by water and high cliffs on three sides. For several years, Constantine rebuilt and expanded Byzantium. He adorned it with many new structures. He also built walls about fifteen feet thick and nearly one hundred towers. For a thousand years, the city remained protected from foreign invaders.

Byzantine Empire The eastern part of the Roman Empire; also known as the Eastern Roman Empire.

Which of his achievements is highlighted in this mosaic of Constantine?

What does this 1422 map of Constantinople show about the city's defenses?

The Ottomans built the Rumeli Hisari fortress on the Bosporus Strait in 1452. They wanted to stop Byzantine allies from reaching Constantinople by sea.

THE REGION TODAY

Turkey

Location
Turkey is located on two continents. Most of Turkey is a large peninsula in Asia Minor. Turkey is bordered by the Black Sea and the Mediterranean Sea. The smaller part of the country is bordered by Greece in southeastern Europe.

Climate
Turkey's topography causes the climate to vary in different regions of the country. The climate is temperate along the coast and averages 48°F to 84°F. Inland, the climate is harsh and dry. Average temperatures range from 28°F to 73°F. In the mountains, it is snowy or icy in the winters. Average temperatures there reach only 63°F in the summer and dip to 9°F in the winter.

Topography
The portion of Turkey in Asia Minor is a plateau between the Taurus and the Pontic mountain ranges. Mount Ararat, traditionally considered the location where Noah's ark rested, is in eastern Turkey, where these two ranges meet.

Natural Resources
Turkey's natural resources include oil, coal, chromium, mercury, copper, boron, and gold.

Byzantine Empire Then & Now

The city of Istanbul, Turkey, has land in Europe and Asia. It is one of the world's largest cities in population.

In 330, the city became the Roman Empire's new capital and was called **Constantinople,** or Constantine's city. Constantinople was one of the richest and most powerful cities in Europe. Today this city is known as Istanbul, Turkey.

The Rise of the Roman Church

The early Christians faced many challenges. Two of these challenges were persecution and false teachers. After the passing of the Edict of Milan, which guaranteed freedom of religion in the Roman Empire, the church grew rapidly. However, not all who claimed to be Christians stayed true to Scripture. Some false teachers wrote their own gospels and changed parts of the New Testament to fit their beliefs. Others rejected key scriptural truths such as the deity of Christ.

However, there were still true believers in the church who defended the truth. They were called **orthodox**. In 325 Constantine called the bishops of the church to a meeting that came to be known as the **Council of Nicaea**. At this meeting and other meetings that followed, bishops carefully defined what true Christians should believe about the Trinity.

However, errors continued to creep into the church. Even those who were fighting to keep the purity of the church's **doctrine** made errors. Some people claimed that certain traditions that are not found in the Bible came from the apostles. They claimed that these traditions had the same authority as the Bible. This way of thinking allowed more and more errors to enter the church.

Constantinople The capital city of the Byzantine Empire; present-day Istanbul, Turkey.

orthodox Refers to those who support the traditionally accepted principles of the faith.

Council of Nicaea Defined what Christians should believe about the Trinity.

doctrine A belief or principle of a group of people.

What was the importance of the location of Byzantium?

Who founded the village of Byzantium?

What were two critical challenges that early Christians faced?

Which general led Justinian's troops in conquering lands for the empire?

Decline of the Western Roman Empire

The Roman Empire continued to decline. It had struggled with political turmoil, high taxes, and problems along its borders for years.

The city of Rome grew weaker. Constantine's attempts to strengthen the empire by building a new capital away from Rome further weakened the western part of the empire.

In 395, the Roman emperor Theodosius I permanently divided the empire into two separate parts: the Western Roman Empire and the Eastern Roman Empire. Several years after this division, the city of Rome was plundered by **barbarians**.

The Western Roman Empire was easy prey for barbarian invasions. However, the Eastern Roman Empire was stronger and more secure.

Early Years of the Byzantine Empire

Eventually, the Eastern Roman Empire became known as the Byzantine Empire.

Constantinople

The standard of living in Constantinople was extremely high. The structure and the economics of the city could support a population of a million people. In addition to the fortified walls, craftsmen constructed sewage and water systems throughout the city. Literacy and education rates among men and women far exceeded any other city at that time. Constantinople was a stronghold that attracted both invaders and merchants.

barbarian The name given by Romans to nomadic people who did not speak Greek or Latin and who did not adopt Roman culture.

Merchants and artisans sold goods in covered shopping areas along the Mese, the main street in Constantinople.

Justinian I

Justinian I, also known as Justinian the Great, reigned over the Byzantine Empire from 527 to 565. Justinian had been taught from his youth that just as there was only one God in heaven, there was only one empire here on earth. Justinian claimed that he, as the sole Christian emperor, had absolute authority. He made it his duty to fulfill this heavenly order.

Former Roman territory in the West was being controlled by barbarians. Justinian wanted to restore the greatness of the former Roman Empire. He believed the time had come to deliver the West.

Justinian sent one of his key generals, **Belisarius**, to conquer the provinces of the former Roman Empire. Belisarius marched his army across North Africa to the city of Carthage. The Vandals ruled there. They were fierce fighters, but Belisarius's army defeated them and destroyed their kingdom.

Next, Belisarius and his army built ships so that they could cross the Mediterranean Sea and invade Sicily. Before long, Belisarius led his army through the Italian Peninsula and claimed it for Justinian. As a result of Belisarius's victories, he became popular in Constantinople.

Justinian did not conquer all the former Roman Empire, but he did conquer every part he fought for. Justinian controlled land on three continents.

Political Groups

In Constantinople, almost all the people supported political groups. The two most popular groups were the Blues and the Greens. They represented different social and political views but also competed as teams in sporting events.

The people enjoyed participating in and watching sports. At sporting events, especially chariot races, the people cheered athletes from their favorite teams to victory. Sporting and social events took place in open-air stadiums called **hippodromes**. During these games, people often shouted their political views. Hostility between the groups was often hard for the authorities to control.

Justinian I Emperor of the Byzantine Empire; created a simplified code of Roman laws; also known as Justinian the Great.

Belisarius Byzantine general under Justinian I.

hippodrome An open-air stadium.

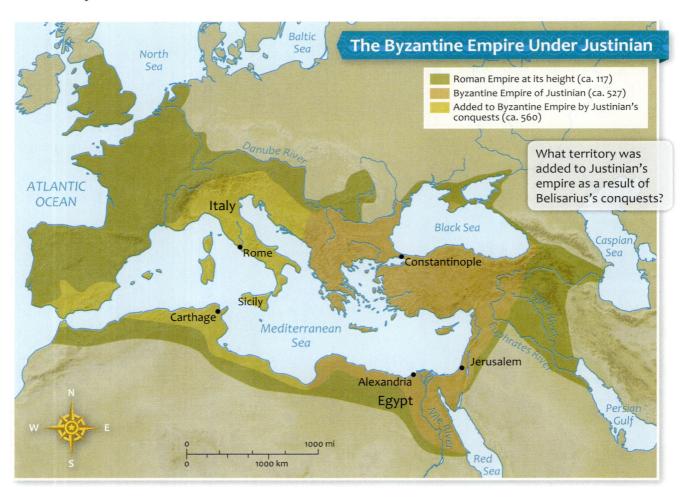

The Byzantine Empire Under Justinian

- Roman Empire at its height (ca. 117)
- Byzantine Empire of Justinian (ca. 527)
- Added to Byzantine Empire by Justinian's conquests (ca. 560)

What territory was added to Justinian's empire as a result of Belisarius's conquests?

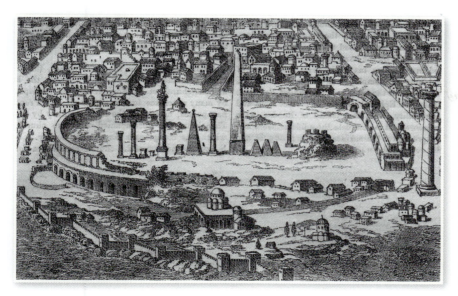

Many of the statues displayed in the Hippodrome had been taken from conquered territories.

The Nika Revolt

Not everyone in the Byzantine Empire was pleased with Justinian's rule. Justinian taxed the citizens heavily to finance building projects. He ignored the positions people held in society and the privileges many had. Tension grew as the citizens became increasingly unhappy.

Justinian's efforts to prevent an uprising failed. Early in January of 532, an enormous riot broke out at the games in the Hippodrome of Constantinople. Seven leaders of the riot were arrested and sentenced to death. Two men, one from the Blue team and one from the Green team, survived their intended executions and fled to a church for safety. The imperial guard surrounded the church.

Justinian tried to calm the situation by announcing new games, but the tension grew even worse. The Blues and the Greens had united against the emperor and cried out for mercy for the two men. Their cries went unheeded. Furious, the crowd moved through the streets, looting and burning buildings.

As the rioting continued, the nobles did not rally behind Justinian. They saw the uprising as an opportunity to take over the throne. They selected a successor for Justinian. As the situation grew out of control, Justinian was about to take a ship into exile when his wife, Theodora, convinced him to stay. She told Justinian, "May I never see the day when those who meet me do not call me empress. . . . I agree with the adage that the royal purple is the noblest shroud." Justinian decided to stay, and he sent Belisarius to fight the rioters and to end the rebellion.

Belisarius and his men killed over thirty thousand people who had gathered in the Hippodrome. Nineteen senators who plotted a takeover were executed. Their palaces were destroyed, and their bodies were thrown into the sea.

The events in Constantinople during that week became known as the **Nika Revolt** because the people shouted "Nika!" ("Conquer!") as they rioted.

Nika Revolt The Byzantine riot where half of Constantinople was destroyed and many people were killed.

JUSTINIAN I (THE GREAT) & THEODORA

What: Byzantine emperor
When: ca. 482–565
Where: ancient Turkey

Justinian was born to Slavic parents in Macedonia. He was later adopted by his uncle Justin I. Justinian was made co-emperor with Justin and given the title *Augustus*. When Justin died, Justinian became the only emperor. Justinian was married to Theodora, who was strongly influential. Theodora had been an actor before she married. She advised Justinian on building projects and offered him good advice in running the government.

 Why were the citizens of the Byzantine Empire unhappy with Justinian's rule?

LIFE IN CONSTAN

Power
The emperor held the power of rule over the government and the church. He appointed the patriarch of the church.

Religion
Constantinople was an important religious center. The Hagia Sophia was the most famous of its churches. Approximately ten thousand workers took about six years to build it. Architects Anthemius of Tralles and Isidorus of Miletus created special support structures that allowed a circular dome to sit atop a square structure. They also designed the dome to have forty windows around the circumference of its base, giving the feeling of tremendous airiness.

Job Specialization
Craftsmen, farmers, and artisans sold products to merchants who sold those goods to traders. Construction workers built roads, aqueducts, and buildings. Soldiers protected the city.

Foreign trading ships docking at Constantinople were required to pay customs duties on the goods they sold there.

TINOPLE

Arts, Sciences, and Written Language

People traded not only goods, but also information and ideas. Music, art, drama, and education were encouraged. Arts, science, and architecture advanced. There were schools for law, medicine, and philosophy.

At the founding of Constantinople, the official language was Latin, but eventually the Greek language was adopted.

Social Classes

The wealthy class included military officers, government officials, and those who owned large areas of land. The middle class included merchants, traders, and those who owned smaller areas of land. The lower class included the poor, who often did manual labor to earn a small wage. Ministers were not placed in a distinct social class but were scattered throughout all three social classes.

Key Themes of Civilization
- Justice
- Power
- Citizenship
- Environment

Features of a Civilization
- Organized cities and government
- Social classes
- Job specialization
- Arts, sciences, and written language
- Religion

Environment

Byzantium's location let the people develop a major trade center. Constantinople became the meeting place of the East and West.

The Golden Horn was a naturally sheltered spot that worked well as a harbor.

What was the Hagia Sophia like?

Rebuilding the City

During the Nika Revolt, much of Constantinople was looted and burned. Taxes increased even more to pay for the damage. Justinian took advantage of the opportunity to make the city more beautiful than it had been before. The emperor set his architects to work planning and building new public baths, governmental buildings, churches, and aqueducts and cisterns for carrying and storing water.

The Hagia Sophia was converted to a mosque by the Ottomans. What evidences do you see inside and outside the building to suggest Islamic influence?

The most famous project was the rebuilding of a church called the **Hagia Sophia**, which means "holy wisdom." The Hagia Sophia was the most important and most beautiful church in the empire. The church was built in the shape of a cross. Over the center of the church, the builders erected a magnificent dome that reached 184 feet above the floor.

The inside of the Hagia Sophia was brilliantly decorated. An image of God the Father surrounded by angels and archangels looked down from the highest part of the dome. Images of saints covered the walls of the church. Many of these images were mosaics made of thousands of pieces of colored glass, stone, or other materials.

The Final Years and Legacy

Under the command of Belisarius, the Byzantine army conquered surrounding lands, including the Italian Peninsula and parts of northern Africa. Some people believe that Justinian may have become jealous of the success Belisarius had in the Italian Peninsula. Justinian removed the general from power and imprisoned him. Without Belisarius, Justinian lost control of the Italian Peninsula. A new general led the army in conquering Spain and eventually conquered the Italian Peninsula once again.

Hagia Sophia A church in Constantinople known for its great beauty.

The Sangarius Bridge, built to give the capital better contact with its eastern provinces, was one of many public works projects during Justinian's reign. What is unusual about the shape of this bridge?

Justinian believed that a well-governed empire needed a good system of law. He adopted the laws of the former Roman Empire. Roman laws had been made over a span of five hundred years. There were so many that no one could learn them all.

Justinian Code A compilation and simplification of Roman law; ordered by Justinian for the Byzantine Empire.

Justinian appointed ten scholars to simplify the laws so they would be easier to understand. The committee finished their work in four years. The new, and much shorter, law code was called the **Justinian Code**. This code preserved the heritage of the Roman legal system. It also provided a foundation on which most modern European nations would build their political and legal systems.

Justinian's thirty-eight years on the throne marked a golden age of Byzantine culture. The Byzantine Empire experienced vast improvements in the government, the law, and the economy. He conquered every country his armies attempted to take. Leaders of surrounding nations recognized his power.

Even so, Justinian left his successors with many problems. He had neglected the defense of the empire's eastern and northern borders. He also left the empire financially drained because his military campaigns and massive building programs were extremely costly. Justinian took the Byzantine Empire to the height of glory but left it on the brink of ruin.

 Why is Justinian's reign considered a golden age of Byzantine culture?

ACTIVITY

Making a Paper Mosaic

Mosaics have been an art form since the early civilizations, such as the Mesopotamians. The Romans made mosaics of colored stones to cover floors and walkways. Artists in the Byzantine Empire expanded the use of mosaics to decorate walls as well. Many of the mosaics were made of colored Italian glass. Some of the glass had a thin layer of gold at the back.

1. Gather several sheets of colored construction paper, two sheets of black construction paper, scissors, and glue.
2. Cut the colored construction paper into small pieces of different shapes.
3. Arrange the colored pieces to form a picture on one sheet of black paper. Lay the pieces close together without letting them touch so that some of the black paper can be seen.
4. Apply a thin layer of glue to a small portion of the second sheet of black paper. Transfer the colored pieces onto the glued area.
5. Continue applying glue and transferring pieces until the picture is complete.

Justinian I

Empress Theodora

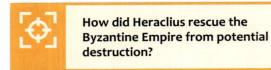

How did Heraclius rescue the Byzantine Empire from potential destruction?

The Struggle for Existence

Byzantine rulers after Justinian had difficulty holding lands that had been conquered. Financial weakness and loss of life from disease contributed to decline throughout the empire. In the West, education, commerce, and maintenance of public buildings came to a halt. In the East, merchants, industrialists, and land owners struggled as wars and uprisings disrupted trade. The growth of the arts and sciences slowed as money for building and development dwindled.

The emperors who ruled after Justinian found it impossible to keep the loyalty of conquered people in distant provinces. Each province was different from the others in culture and religious beliefs. The Byzantine army was also weaker at this time because it was made up primarily of **mercenaries**.

Persian emperors had been attacking the Byzantine Empire for several hundred years. After Justinian's death, the Persians renewed their efforts to take the province of Syria. The Persian emperor wanted Syria because it was rich from trade and could afford high taxes. The Byzantine government was not able to pay for strong mercenaries to defend Syria, so the Persians seized the territory with little difficulty.

The Byzantine Empire also faced trouble on the **Balkan Peninsula**. Two barbarian tribes, the Avars and the Bulgars, migrated into the area. They were strong enough to conquer and settle the land.

The Lombards, another tribe of barbarians, successfully invaded the Italian Peninsula. In merely one hundred years, the Byzantine Empire lost nearly all the land conquered by Justinian.

mercenary A foreign soldier hired to fight for a country.

Balkan Peninsula A peninsula in southeastern Europe bordered by the Adriatic, Black, Aegean, and Mediterranean Seas.

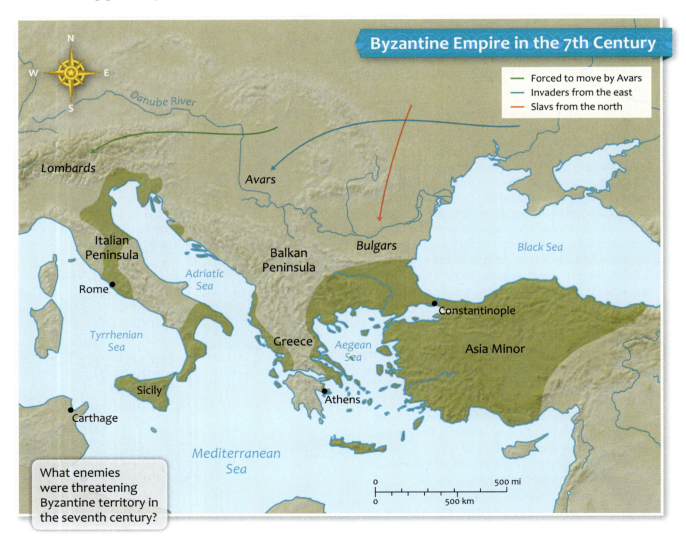

Byzantine Empire in the 7th Century

What enemies were threatening Byzantine territory in the seventh century?

Themes were governed by military leaders and protected by peasant soldiers who were given land for their service.

Heraclius

Military Success

The emperor **Heraclius** began his reign in 610. Without him, the Byzantine Empire might have disappeared. He reformed the army, reconquered the land taken by Persia and the barbarians, and made the roads safe for commerce.

Because of the empire's desperate situation, the Byzantine people often did whatever Heraclius demanded of them. He even convinced the church to provide the necessary money to fund the war against the Persians and the barbarians.

To strengthen the army, Heraclius fired the mercenary soldiers and trained Byzantine peasants for the army. It took him ten years to prepare his new soldiers. He promised to pay them by giving each one enough land to support himself and his family. With his new army, Heraclius drove the Persians from Asia Minor and conquered Syria, Palestine, and Egypt. Then he marched the army to the Balkan Peninsula and defeated the Avars and the Bulgars.

Successful Empire Leadership

Heraclius added so much land to the empire that he had to find a new way to organize it. He divided the land into provinces called *themes*. Each theme was a military zone with many peasant soldiers living in it. These soldiers were responsible for the theme's defense. This system lasted almost until the fall of the Byzantine Empire in 1453.

Trade flourished under the government of Heraclius. People who had the same skills or occupations formed special groups called *guilds*. There were many kinds of guilds. For example, there were guilds for moneychangers, goldsmiths, and notaries (legal officials whose main function was to oversee the writing and recording of official documents). In the cities, other guilds supplied meat, fish, and bread to the people.

Foreign merchants traveled throughout the Byzantine Empire selling grain, wax, leather, furs, spices, and ointments. They also sold slaves.

One of the most important items of trade was silk. Silk came all the way from China and was extremely expensive because of its complicated production process. Persians controlled much of the silk trade route. Silk was worn only by government officials. Each Byzantine official had a symbol indicating his office woven into the fabric.

Byzantine spies discovered how the Chinese made silk. The spies stole some silkworms and smuggled them out of China. Silk production became one of the most important industries in the Byzantine Empire, especially in the cities of Constantinople, Antioch, Tyre, and Beirut.

Heraclius also changed the language of the empire. Although the Byzantine people believed their empire was a continuation of the old Roman Empire, very few of them spoke Latin in the 600s. Since almost everyone spoke Greek, Heraclius decreed that the language of the empire would be Greek. He even used the Greek title *Basilius* rather than a Roman title.

Heraclius Emperor of the Byzantine Empire; reconquered land taken by the Persians and the barbarians; made roads in his empire safe for commerce.

How did Heraclius organize the new lands that he added to the empire?

Why might mercenary soldiers not be as effective as an army of citizens?

What is the significance of Mecca and Medina to Islam?

A New Religion

World Conditions

Persians and Byzantines continued to fight for the same land. Their fighting, however, made both empires weaker. Many people living in the region were not loyal to either empire.

During this time, a powerful movement was gaining strength in a remote region on the **Arabian Peninsula**. This new movement would influence history for the Persians, the Byzantines, and eventually the world.

Muhammad

Wars and pirates on the Red Sea caused merchants to open routes along the western edge of the Arabian Peninsula. The trading brought great wealth to cities there, such as **Mecca**. The trade routes also allowed the rapid spread of ideas.

A man named **Muhammad**, who lived in Mecca, made many commercial trips along the trade routes with his uncle. Muhammad's travels brought him into contact with many religions. He was particularly interested in Christianity and Judaism. These faiths were different from the polytheistic religions in the Arabian Peninsula.

Muhammad said that he had a vision when he was forty years old. In this vision, the angel Gabriel gave Muhammad a revelation. This was one of many visions Muhammad claimed to have throughout his life. Muhammad's followers compiled these revelations in a work known as the **Qur'an**. Muhammad taught that there was only one god. The Arabic word for Muhammad's god is *Allah*. The Bible also teaches that there is only

Arabian Peninsula A peninsula in southwestern Asia between the Red Sea and the Persian Gulf.

Mecca A sacred Muslim city in present-day Saudi Arabia.

Muhammad Founder of Islam.

Qur'an The Islamic book of Muhammad's visions, written by his followers.

MUHAMMAD

What: founder of Islam
When: ca. 570–632
Where: Mecca

Muhammad was born into the tribe that ruled Mecca. He was orphaned at a young age, but he grew up to be a successful merchant. At the age of twenty-five, he married the wealthy widow Khadijah. Their marriage lasted for twenty-five years. After her death, he married additional wives.

Late in life, Muhammad made a final pilgrimage to Mecca. He taught his followers to journey to Mecca once a year. A few months after making his pilgrimage and giving a farewell speech, he died from an illness.

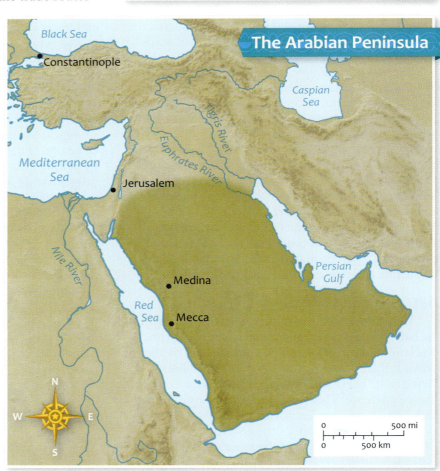

The Arabian Peninsula

ISLAM

Like Christianity and Judaism, Islam teaches there is only one god. But the god of Islam is not a triune god like the God of Christianity. Muslims insist that their god is single. Muslims also consider their god to be so far above humans that he is beyond human knowing. Allah cannot be known in his essence. Only his will, what he requires of people, can be known. His will was revealed through his prophets.

Muslims teach that Adam was the first prophet and that Muhammad was the last prophet. Jesus is viewed by Muslims as one of the prophets. Muslims do not believe that Jesus was God. In addition, Muslims do not consider Jesus to be their mediator or intercessor. Instead Muslims think that Jesus pointed people to Muhammad, who was the mediator between Allah and people.

In Islam, people are not guaranteed eternity in heaven simply because they are Muslim. Nor will their good deeds guarantee their salvation. Their eternity depends on whether Allah will be merciful to them. However, there does seem to be an expectation that faithful Muslims will get to experience paradise.

Walking around the Kaaba is one of the activities of the Hajj, a pilgrimage to Mecca that approximately two million Muslims take each year.

one God, but Muhammad's beliefs were very different from the Bible's teachings about the true God.

Muhammad began to speak out against the evils practiced by the people of Mecca. He rebuked them for their polytheism. In Mecca, there was a cube-shaped building called the *Kaaba*. It was used for pagan rituals and held many idols. Having the idols in Mecca brought some unity to the Arabian tribes as well as great prosperity to the city. However, Muhammad's message threatened this unity and the prosperity of Mecca. Lacking both support and protection from the ruling clans, Muhammad took his small group of followers and left Mecca in 622.

Muhammad and his followers traveled to **Medina**, a small oasis. The groups of Arabian tribal warriors there accepted his teachings and submitted to his leadership. During this time, Muhammad's beliefs developed into the religion known as **Islam**. Muhammad expanded his influence and increased a following among Arabian tribes. Together they raided caravans that were traveling to trade in Mecca. The attacks increased Muhammad's wealth and served as his punishment to the merchants of Mecca.

By 630, Muhammad's army took control of Mecca with little fighting. He removed the idols from the Kaaba and forced many of the people to accept Islam. Everyone who followed Islam was called a **Muslim**. Not everyone in Mecca accepted the leadership of Muhammad and his religion. Those who did not submit to him and to Islam were called *infidels*.

THE FIVE PILLARS OF ISLAM

Islam requires every Muslim to perform certain religious duties to reach heaven.
1. Sincerely believe and recite "There is no God but Allah, and Muhammad is the prophet of Allah."
2. Pray five times a day while facing Mecca.
3. Give to the poor.
4. Fast from sunrise to sunset during the month of Ramadan.
5. If able, make at least one pilgrimage to Mecca.

Medina A sacred Muslim city in present-day Saudi Arabia.
Islam The religion started by Muhammad.
Muslim A person who follows Islam.

The Dome of the Rock houses a rock that both Jews and Muslims consider to be sacred. Muslim tradition says that Muhammad went up into heaven from this spot; Jews believe that Abraham went to this spot to sacrifice Isaac.

The Conquests of the Muslims

Muhammad died in 632. One of his followers took his place to lead the Muslims. The man in this position of leadership was called a **caliph**. The first caliph was Abu-Bakr. He was a general, as were many of the caliphs that followed. Abu-Bakr led a war to conquer the entire Arabian Peninsula. His goal was to convert the people there to Islam. Muslims call a war such as this a **jihad**. Within two years, Abu-Bakr and his army reached their goal.

The word *jihad* is an Arabic word that means "to strive." Some Muslims think of a jihad as a mental struggle to become a good Muslim, not as a physical war. However, the Qur'an describes a jihad as a holy war against non-Muslims. Muslims were to fight to make sure areas under Muslim law remained under Muslim law. They could, but were not required to, fight for areas not yet under Muslim law.

Muslim Victories

The next caliph was a man named Umar. His armies moved north and threatened the territory of both the Byzantine and the Persian Empires. Important Muslim victories against the Byzantines in 636 and against the Persians in 637 opened the door for permanent gains. Umar's forces conquered the Byzantine provinces of Syria, Palestine, and Egypt and made significant advances into the Persian Empire. The Persian Empire fell completely under Umar's successor, Uthman.

The city of Jerusalem, part of the province of Palestine, surrendered to Umar in 637. The Muslims consider Jerusalem to be one of three sacred cities (along with Mecca and Medina). They believe Muhammad was taken to Jerusalem by the angel Gabriel and brought up to heaven from a rock that is on top of the Jewish Temple Mount. At the end of the seventh century, the Muslims built a shrine on the rock. The shrine, which still stands today, is called the Dome of the Rock.

Muslim Empire's Impact

The Islamic religion spread not just through military conquest but also through trade. For a time, Islamic leaders had control of the Silk Road that went from China to the Middle East. As the Muslims traded goods along the Silk Road, they spread their religion too. Islam also spread in Africa, first as Muslim armies brought the religion into North Africa and then as traders carried it further into the continent. Winning a large number of converts over a vast geographic area, the Islamic religion significantly increased its influence. In addition to religious influence, Muslims of this period made important intellectual contributions. Muslim mathematicians and physicians introduced new concepts and pioneered new treatments. Muslim philosophers aided in the preservation of the learning of the classical world.

caliph Political and religious leader of an Islamic state.
jihad A holy war fought for the cause of Islam; a spiritual striving.

 Summarize the differences between Islam and Christianity.

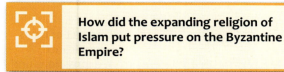

How did the expanding religion of Islam put pressure on the Byzantine Empire?

Empire in Turmoil

After Heraclius's death from a fever, the Byzantine Empire again faced a crisis. To recruit soldiers for the wars, the Byzantine emperors gave more and more land to peasants who joined the army. The nobility disliked this practice. They thought only nobles should own land. The wars also brought a rise in taxes, which angered the Byzantines. For twenty years, civil war further weakened the empire. Seven emperors tried to rule during that time. Most of them were assassinated soon after coming to power.

A New Hero

In the early 700s, **Leo III** served as an administrator and a general in the Byzantine government. He grew in power and seized the opportunity to be emperor. With his army, Leo captured the emperor and his entire household. He named himself Emperor Leo III. He was also known as Leo the Syrian.

Leo had much experience that was a benefit to his rule. He was familiar with the empire's enemies. As a boy, he had lived among the Arabs and learned their language. When he was older, he and his family moved to the Balkan Peninsula. While there, he became familiar with the barbarians and their way of life.

Muslim Invasion

Just six months after Leo III became emperor, Muslim armies camped outside the walls of Constantinople. Their navy prevented goods from coming into the port. The Muslims hoped to starve the citizens into surrendering. Leo III sent his ships out against the Muslims. The Byzantines had only a few ships, but they had a powerful weapon. This weapon was Greek fire, an explosive mixture that would burn on top of the water and was difficult to extinguish. When the Muslim ships drew close, the defenders of Constantinople threw Greek fire toward them. After the enemy ships burned, the ships with supplies for the citizens could enter the port.

The following winter was so cold that many of the Muslim soldiers who were encamped around Constantinople froze to death. The next summer, a large number of citizens and many Muslims died of a plague. Eventually, the remaining Muslims withdrew.

Leo led his army into Asia Minor and took the peninsula back from the Muslims. Although the Muslim threat had not ended, Leo had proved his ability to lead the empire.

Leo III Emperor of the Byzantine Empire; defeated the Muslims in Asia Minor.

How does the Muslim soldier compare to the Byzantine soldier on page 233?

What could have been a potential danger of Greek fire for the ones using it?

Power Struggle in the Church

A bitter rivalry developed between the leaders of the Eastern and Western churches. The bishop of Rome, later known as the **pope**, became the most important religious leader in the West. The patriarch of Constantinople was the most important religious leader in the East.

The Eastern church became the state church of the Byzantine Empire. The Byzantine emperor was the head of the state and the protector of the church and its teachings.

In 1054 the pope sent men to Constantinople. These men declared that the pope was taking authority over the churches in the southern part of the empire. These churches had been under the patriarch's authority. The patriarch refused to accept the pope's taking control of them. As a result, the pope's representatives had the patriarch excommunicated, or removed from the church. In response, the patriarch excommunicated the pope. This break between the two branches of the church has lasted for nearly one thousand years. These two branches became known as the **Roman Catholic Church** (Western church) and the **Eastern Orthodox Church** (Eastern church).

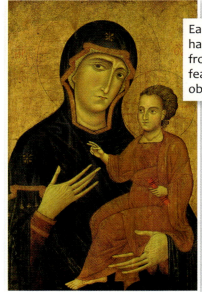

Each aspect of icons had significance, from expressions and features to colors and objects like halos.

Iconoclasm

In the Byzantine Empire, the use of **icons** became popular in churches. Most of the icons were paintings, mosaics, or frescoes. However, Leo III considered icons a type of idol. When an earthquake shook Constantinople in 726, he believed it was a judgment from God against the use of icons. Leo ordered the destruction of all the icons in the churches to prevent further judgment.

The destruction of religious icons is called *iconoclasm*. People who think icons are sinful and destroy them are called *iconoclasts*.

Throughout the empire, iconoclasts destroyed many of the icons. This action led to a division within the Eastern Orthodox Church. Leo imprisoned people who tried to protect the icons.

The controversy over icons lasted until 843. In that year, the ruler officially allowed icons back in the churches. This event is still celebrated each year in the Eastern Orthodox Church as the Feast of Orthodoxy.

---

pope The leader of the Roman Catholic Church.
Roman Catholic Church Church under the leadership of the pope.
Eastern Orthodox Church Church that developed in the Byzantine Empire.
icon A sacred image representing Christ, Mary, the saints, or other sacred objects.

> What experience did Leo III have that was beneficial to his rule?
>
> What caused the division between the Western and the Eastern branches of the church?

EASTERN ORTHODOXY

The church in the Byzantine Empire became known as the Eastern Orthodox Church. Today, many Christians and members of the Eastern Orthodox Church agree on some important truths: (1) God is a Trinity, three equal persons (the Father, the Son, and the Holy Spirit) who are one God, and (2) the Son is both fully God and fully human (not partly God, not partly human, and not a combination of the two).

But Protestants and the Eastern Orthodox Church disagree about some very important issues. Protestants argue that the Bible is the only authority for what Christians should believe and practice. Members of the Eastern Orthodox Church believe that their church's tradition is an equal authority to Scripture. Protestants and the Eastern Orthodox Church agree that Jesus' death was a victory over Satan, but Protestants point out that the emphasis in Scripture is on Jesus' dying in the place of sinners so they can be saved, whereas the Eastern Orthodox Church teaches that salvation is obtained through the sacraments of the church. These sacraments include baptism, communion, and confession. Protestants argue that salvation can be received only by faith alone in what Christ has done (Ephesians 2:8–10).

> Why was the First Crusade called?

Height of the Byzantine Empire

The Byzantine Empire had its best and most powerful years between 850 and 1050. It was strongly influenced by Hellenistic culture. Some historians consider this time a second golden age in the history of the Byzantine Empire.

During this time, the emperors successfully fought their enemies on the Balkan Peninsula and in the Middle East. Some rulers helped develop the empire's government and culture. Emperor Michael III reorganized the University of Constantinople. Basil I oversaw the revision of the law. The empire also became wealthier from its trade throughout Asia, Europe, and Africa.

Christian missionaries from Constantinople traveled throughout eastern Europe in the 860s. The missionaries helped standardize the language, ethics, laws, and political patterns of the people, including the Bulgarians and the Slavs.

Two missionaries, Cyril and Methodius, translated the Bible into Slavic. Because the Slavic people did not have a written language, the missionaries had to develop an alphabet for them. The work of these two missionaries gave thousands of people the opportunity to read the gospel for themselves.

The Bulgar Slayer

Basil II became emperor in 976. He devoted his life to making the empire stronger. His army was well trained, and he made the nobles pay their taxes.

Cyril and Methodius stand in front of the Eastern Orthodox cross, which has two or sometimes three crossbars.

BASIL II (THE BULGAR SLAYER)

What: Byzantine emperor
When: ca. 958–1025
Where: ancient Turkey

Basil II was crowned co-emperor with his brother Constantine in 960. At the time, both were too young to rule. After their father's death in 963, their stepfather, a great-uncle, and two generals ruled the empire. Later, with the help of the Russians, Basil became sole emperor.

Basil was efficient in his running of both the government and his army. He was a short, stocky man and was known for twirling his beard in his fingers when deep in thought or angry.

He kept the church from taking land from the peasants. He was one of the best managers the Byzantine government ever had.

Basil II was also a warrior. When the Bulgars attacked the empire, he led an army in defeating them. He captured fourteen thousand Bulgarian soldiers. Because of this victory and his harsh treatment of the captives, Basil II was often called the Bulgar Slayer.

Another Muslim Advance

Because Basil II never married, he had no heir. After his death in 1025, no other emperor was able to run the government the way he had. The empire had been experiencing victories and expansion. Now the empire faced new obstacles. Venice, an Italian city, took over much of the trade that used to come through Constantinople. New enemies attacked the empire. These invaders included the Normans from northern Europe, the Pechenegs from Russia, and the Seljuk Turks, a group of nomadic warriors from central Asia who had converted to Islam. The Byzantines especially feared the Seljuk Turks, who had defeated them at the Battle of Manzikert in 1071 and captured Jerusalem from the Fatimid Caliphate in 1073. Concern for the ability of their empire to withstand this new threat and worries about the safety of the holy places in Jerusalem under these new rulers prompted the Byzantines to seek help from Western Christians.

Basil II Emperor of the Byzantine Empire; strengthened the Byzantine government; known as the Bulgar Slayer.

The Crusades

The Crusades Begin

In 1095 Pope Urban II issued a call to the knights of France. He wanted them to free Jerusalem from Islamic rule. They responded with several military expeditions, known as the **Crusades**. The soldiers were called *crusaders*.

The First Three Crusades

In the First Crusade, the crusaders were able to capture Jerusalem in the summer of 1099. However, the Muslim Turks continued to invade the land of Palestine. Neither the Second Crusade nor the Third Crusade ended successfully for the Byzantines. In July of 1187, Muslims regained Jerusalem.

The Fourth Crusade

When Innocent III became the pope in 1198, he made it his primary goal to reclaim Jerusalem. Within a few years, he organized the Fourth Crusade.

At this time, the Muslim Turks controlled the Middle East from Egypt to Syria. The crusaders' planned to gain control of Egypt. They believed that their success in this wealthy center of trade would divide the Muslim power. Crusaders made an agreement with the navy of Venice. The Venetians were to supply ships, and the crusaders would supply the army and money.

The Venetians kept their part of the agreement. However, as time wore on, it became apparent that the crusaders would be unable to supply the huge army and necessary money for success.

The Venetians convinced the crusaders to attack the city of Zara, even though it was a Christian city, to capture the needed money and resources.

After they conquered Zara, the crusaders received a new proposal from a prince who claimed to be the rightful heir to the throne of the Byzantine Empire. He offered money and men for the Crusade if the crusaders would help put him on the throne. The prince wanted to take the place of the Byzantine emperor, Alexius III. The crusaders accepted the offer and headed for Constantinople with the Venetians.

Emperor Alexius III learned about the treachery. He rallied support to oppose the prince. When the Venetians and the crusaders arrived at Constantinople, the Byzantine army resisted them for several days. However, the crusaders were eventually able to take the city. Alexius fled into exile.

Crusades Religious campaigns to free Jerusalem from Islamic rule.

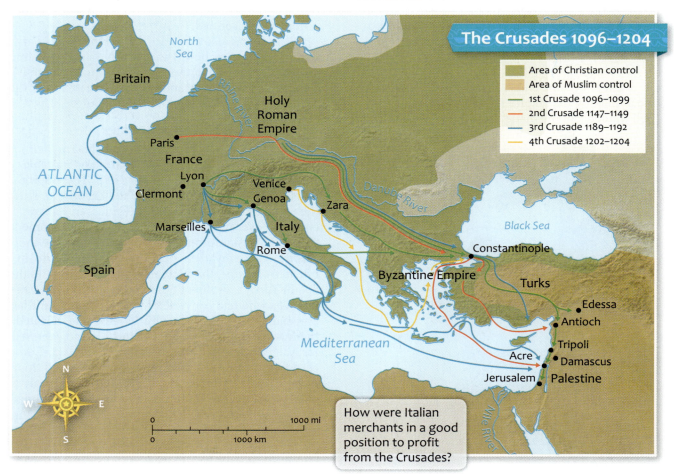

How were Italian merchants in a good position to profit from the Crusades?

LASTING CONSEQUENCES

The actions taken by the crusaders have not been forgotten. Pope John Paul II tried to mend the lasting bitterness. In June of 2004, he apologized to Patriarch Bartholomew I of the Eastern Orthodox Church for the actions of the crusaders in April 1204: "How can we not share, at a distance of eight centuries, the pain and disgust."

A group of Byzantine churchmen and senior nobles offered their submission to the crusaders. These Byzantines were hoping for a peaceful takeover. Their hopes were in vain. Over the next three days, the crusaders plundered the city, including the churches. They divided the Byzantine lands and goods among themselves and their Venetian allies.

What do these artifacts reveal about the artistic culture of the Byzantine people?

Pope Innocent III condemned the actions of the crusaders, but it was too late to prevent the destruction they caused.

The Results of the Crusades for Europe

The main result of the Crusades for Western Europe was change that helped lead to the decline of feudalism. Nobles needed large amounts of money to join Crusades. This need caused two developments. First, many serfs were allowed to buy their freedom. Second, kings gained in power as nobles became weaker financially. Many freed serfs moved to towns. Towns grew as a result of the renewed interest in trade that the Crusades had helped to prompt. Their growth helped change the focus of Western Europe's economy from agriculture to trade and industry. Stronger kings led to stronger central governments and the development of the modern nation-state.

The Recovery of the Byzantine Empire

The crusaders never did go to Egypt to fight. From 1204 to 1261, the Venetians and the crusaders ruled Constantinople. It looked as though the Byzantine Empire had come to an end. But the empire had not been completely destroyed. Some Byzantines fled to Asia Minor and organized a new empire. Its capital was Nicaea. For over fifty-seven years, the new empire fought the armies of both Constantinople and the Turks.

The emperors at Nicaea worked hard to strengthen their revived empire. One emperor, John III (1222–54), promoted political and legal reform. He helped the poor by founding hospitals and charitable institutions. His government built churches and gave land to its soldiers.

The government also encouraged the improvement of agricultural methods and raising livestock. To protect the people, John III built a system of fortifications and frontier defenses.

By 1261 the empire at Nicaea, under the leadership of Emperor Michael VIII, had strengthened its army enough to attack and recapture Constantinople. Michael entered the city on August 15, 1261, and within weeks was crowned emperor in the Hagia Sophia. He moved the capital back to Constantinople and spent vast sums of money to rebuild and beautify the city.

What was the pope's reaction to the crusaders' actions at Constantinople?

What was the real reason the crusaders plundered Constantinople?

What weakened Europe during the 1300s?

The Fall of the Byzantine Empire

After taking control of Constantinople, Emperor Michael VIII attempted to win back the land once held by the Byzantine Empire. But he faced a new enemy. A group of Turks called the **Ottomans** had invaded the Middle East. The Ottomans conquered the Seljuk Turks, adopted Islam as their religion, and headed north to attack the Byzantine Empire.

The Ottomans threatened the empire in Asia Minor. Since Michael VIII did not have enough money to go to war, he divided the empire among his family members. His hope was that each relative would protect his share, but his relatives wanted to make their parts of the empire into independent countries. They hired mercenaries and were soon fighting each other instead of protecting the empire.

Ottomans The group of Turks who conquered the Byzantine Empire.

Black Death A disease that killed one-third of the people in Europe; also called the bubonic plague.

Meanwhile, Venetian merchants gained control of Constantinople's trade. They collected the profits and taxes that had once belonged to the emperor. The emperors lacked wealth from that time on. To pay their bills, they sold their gold and silver dishes and even their palace decorations.

By 1371 the Ottomans had conquered all the Byzantine Empire except the city of Constantinople. As the conquests took place, different Byzantine emperors tried to save the empire by seeking help from European rulers. Meanwhile, the leaders of the Eastern Orthodox Church begged the pope in Rome to help the empire.

However, conditions in Europe hindered the Europeans from helping the Byzantines. England and France had been at war with each other for over one hundred years and had neither the soldiers nor the money to help. Additionally, all Europe was weakened from the **Black Death** in the 1300s. This terrible disease was also called the bubonic plague. The disease was caused by fleas that had bitten rats and other rodents infected with bacteria. Then the fleas bit humans, passing on the bacteria. A high fever and aching limbs were early symptoms of the

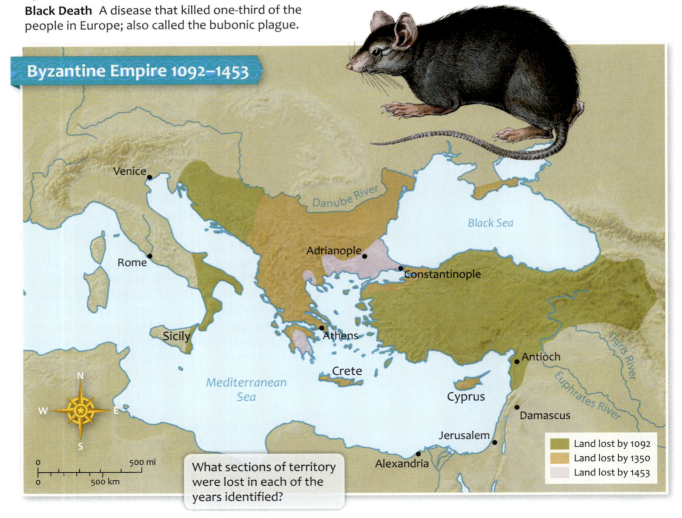

Byzantine Empire 1092–1453

Land lost by 1092
Land lost by 1350
Land lost by 1453

What sections of territory were lost in each of the years identified?

Byzantine soldiers were greatly outnumbered by Ottomans but held out as long as they could behind their thick walls.

This cannon, dating to around the time of the Ottoman siege, could fire a ball weighing more than 600 pounds but was very slow to reload.

disease. The most characteristic symptom was the swelling of spots on the neck, armpits, and legs. These spots turned blackish in color, which gave the disease its name.

The Black Death began in the Gobi Desert in China in the late 1320s and spread west along the Silk Road and other trade routes. The disease also spread with merchant ships. Within two years, one-third of the people in Europe died from the disease. Some cities suffered very little. Others suffered greatly.

After the Ottomans completed their conquest of Asia Minor, they crossed into the Balkan Peninsula. The city of Adrianople and the country of Bulgaria fell to them. The Ottomans then went on to conquer Greece.

By March of 1453, the Ottomans surrounded Constantinople. They used cannons to fire on the city's walls. The Byzantine emperor, Constantine XI, did not have many cannons for his army. The Byzantines defended their positions and spent time each night repairing the damages the Ottoman cannons had made. But after a few days, the Ottomans entered the city. Constantine XI died in the fighting.

During the invasion of Constantinople, the Ottomans stole or destroyed priceless works of art, icons, and manuscripts. The **sultan** entered the city and made it the capital of the Ottoman Empire. The Ottomans even turned the Hagia Sophia into an Islamic mosque. The Byzantine Empire had come to an end.

The Importance of the Byzantine Empire

Like all empires before it, the Byzantine Empire rose and fell. While it existed, the Byzantine Empire made many important achievements. It kept Roman law from disappearing, and its scholars preserved Greek literature, learning, and philosophy. Without the Byzantine Empire, much of what is known of the ancient world would have been lost.

What impact did the Black Death have on Europe?

How did Byzantine emperors try to save their empire from the Ottoman Turks?

sultan A ruler of a Muslim country.

11 MESOAMERICA

FOCUS
Mesoamericans made great advancements in architecture, science, and mathematics.

| 1500 BC | 1000 BC | 500 BC | BC AD | AD 500 | AD 1000 | AD 1500 |

ca. 1200–400 BC
Olmec civilization

Classic Period of the
Mayan civilization
ca. 250–900

ca. 1325–1521
Aztec civilization

Do you like milk chocolate or dark chocolate? The Mayas liked chocolate, but not even the darkest baking chocolate today compares to the bitter drink they made from crushed cacao beans, chili peppers, and water. They used no sugar or honey. Our word *chocolate* may come from the Mayan word *xocolatl*, which means "bitter water."

Ikal uses a machete to cut bean pods from the trunk and branches of the cacao tree. Later he and his younger brother Kabil will help their father scoop out the seeds when he cracks the pods open with a club. Their father also grows tomatoes, maize, onions, sweet potatoes, squash, and avocados. He and other farmers supply food not only for their own families but also for the nobility, priests, and king.

Every day, Mayan families gather and enjoy a meal the women and girls have made. They might have roasted deer or pig, tamales, spicy stews, or black and red beans. Later, after everyone has had a bath, the girls may check beehives for honey with their mothers or weave, and the boys may sharpen tools with their fathers.

Ikal and Kabil will be farmers because their father is a farmer. At fifteen, they will become adults, get married, and grow and gather their own food.

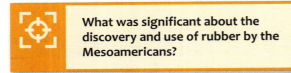

What was significant about the discovery and use of rubber by the Mesoamericans?

Hidden Civilizations in the Americas

Vast oceans separate the continents of North and South America from the other continents. These oceans isolated the ancient American civilizations from the rest of the world. There is much that people today do not know about these early civilizations. Scholars try to learn where these civilizations originated, how the ancient people got to the Americas, and why they may have migrated.

So far, archaeological findings vary on where these people came from. Some **anthropologists** think that they migrated from Africa. Others link together evidence that early Americans may have come from Asia, particularly from India or China. The most popular theory suggests that migration to North America started as people crossed over the Bering Strait into what is now Alaska and then continued southward, and many people settled in a region that researchers call **Mesoamerica**.

The Bible reveals that God created Adam and Eve, the first man and woman. All people descended from them. The Bible also says that the Flood covered the whole world, and Noah and his family were the only survivors. Some of their descendants came to the Americas. Archaeologists continue to study, trying to piece together information about these early people.

Once people arrived, they developed great civilizations. The geography of the areas where they settled was ideal for human life. Ancient people found bodies of water, mountains, rainforests, and coastal plains that provided resources for them to thrive through fishing and agriculture. Their environment provided obsidian, onyx, jade, gold, and silver that allowed items to be crafted for personal use as well as for trade.

anthropologist A scientist who studies human origins and behavior.
Mesoamerica The region stretching south from central Mexico; includes Guatemala, Belize, Honduras, and Nicaragua.

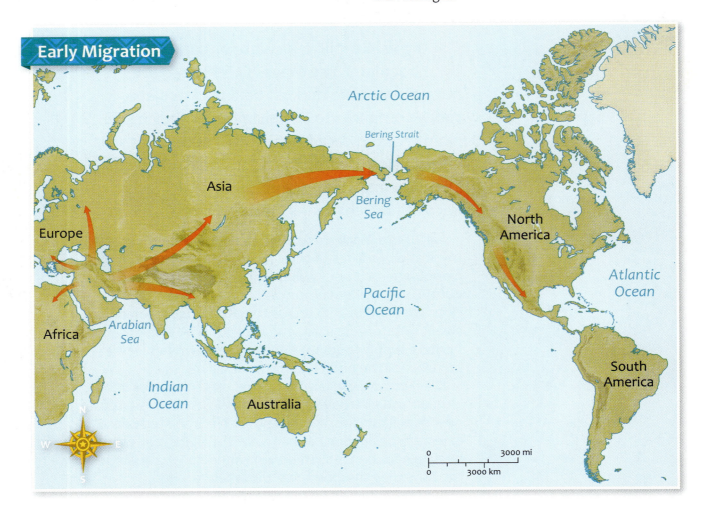

Early Migration

THE REGION TODAY

Mesoamerica

Location
Mesoamerica extends from near the middle of Mexico to the central part of Central America. It includes the Yucatán Peninsula, which is the landmass extending into the Gulf of Mexico in present-day southern Mexico.

Climate
The northern part of the Yucatán Peninsula is dry, receiving only 20–40 inches of rain per year. The southern part receives more rain. The temperatures in the peninsula range from 68°F to over 86°F. Lands south of the peninsula have temperatures averaging around 80°F and receive almost daily rain. The mountains in the southernmost region of Mesoamerica have a mild climate and receive 20–30 inches of rain per year.

Topography
The peninsula is a lowland with thin soil. The central lands are mainly rainforest. The southernmost land rises into mountains and plateaus.

Natural Resources
The rainforest and highlands offer rich sources of lumber and good places to grow coffee, cotton, rubber trees, spices, and bananas. The northern region provides the right conditions for growing cacao beans and sugar cane. Many minerals, natural lakes, and rivers can be found throughout the region.

Mesoamerica Then & Now

What modern countries are located on the Yucatán Peninsula?

Legend:
- Ancient city
- Modern capital
- Modern borders
- Aztec
- Maya
- Mesoamerica
- Olmec

Olmecs

The ancient **Olmec civilization** was one of the earliest large civilizations in Mesoamerica. It developed around 1200 BC and declined around 400 BC.

The Olmecs lived in the lowlands along the coast of the Gulf of Mexico where the climate was hot and humid. The area where they settled is known today as the Veracruz and Tabasco states in southern Mexico.

The major center of the Olmec civilization included the cities of Tenochtitlán, San Lorenzo, and Potrero Nuevo. Historians call this urban center **San Lorenzo Tenochtitlán**. San Lorenzo Tenochtitlán had water and drainage systems. The people there constructed houses out of wood, clay, and palm leaves. Another city, **La Venta**, was one of the largest and most famous Olmec cities. La Venta was located in Mexico on the northeastern coast of Mesoamerica.

Very few written records exist about the Olmec culture and its everyday life. Archaeological evidence indicates that the Olmecs lived near rivers and were hunters and fishers as well as farmers.

The most famous findings from the Olmec civilization are gigantic stone heads. The Olmecs carved these heads from stone, jade, and **basalt**. Some of the stones weigh over forty tons. People today are amazed that the Olmecs accomplished the seemingly impossible feat of transporting these huge stones, sometimes from as far away as sixty miles. Some archaeologists suggest that the Olmecs floated the stone heads down rivers on rafts, but they do not know for sure. Stone carving continued in later Mesoamerican civilizations.

The calendar used for centuries in Mexico may have originated with the Olmecs. Astronomy was important to them, and later peoples continued to study the heavenly bodies.

Olmec civilization One of the earliest known Mesoamerican civilizations.

San Lorenzo Tenochtitlán An urban center of the Olmec civilization; included the cities of Tenochtitlán, San Lorenzo, and Potrero Nuevo.

La Venta One of the largest and most famous Olmec cities; located on the northeastern coast of Mexico.

basalt A type of dark, dense volcanic rock.

This large basalt statue is one of at least seventeen stone heads sculpted by the Olmecs that range from about five to eleven feet tall. What are some possible reasons that the Olmecs made these sculptures?

MAKING RUBBER

The Olmecs are believed to have been among the first people to use rubber. The name *Olmec* means "land of rubber." The Olmecs and the people of later Mesoamerican civilizations developed a method to collect sap from trees. The people called these trees *cahuchu* (weeping trees). The cahuchu sap is a milky white liquid. Today it is known as latex. Early Mesoamericans used it to make waterproof items such as containers and foot coverings. It also was used to make balls that bounced.

By the 1700s, cahuchu sap had been taken to Europe. Scientists experimented and developed new uses for it. In 1770 Joseph Priestley found that pieces of the hardened sap could be used to rub away pencil marks. Edward Nairne also discovered the erasing properties of rubber the same year. This use led to the substance being called *rubber*.

Today latex and rubber products are used every day in items such as the tires of cars, the soles of shoes, and the gloves used by surgeons.

Olmec religious beliefs influenced the beliefs of later Mesoamerican civilizations, especially in regard to rituals. Some historians believe that the Olmecs were the first to play a ritual ball game. The game was not just a sport; it was a large part of the culture of the Olmecs and of later Mesoamerican civilizations such as the Mayas and the Aztecs. The game was played on a flat rectangular area between two stone walls. A stone ring was mounted high on each wall for players to throw the ball through. The ball game had a religious significance, and games sometimes ended with human sacrifice. The ball game likely spread as far south as Paraguay and as far north as Arizona.

 What impact did the Olmecs have on other Mesoamerican cultures?

ACTIVITY

Drawing Conclusions as an Archaeologist

Archaeologists study artifacts and other evidence to learn about people from a former time. They systematically catalog items such as jewelry, ancient tools, or pottery that they recover. They record information as they study ancient graves and buildings.

Follow the steps to draw conclusions as an archaeologist.

1. Collect ten items from home that tell about you and your life. Place the items in an unlabeled paper bag and staple it closed. Give the closed bag to your teacher.
2. Work with a partner. Get two stapled bags from your teacher. Open one bag and examine the items inside.
3. Use the questions on the Activity Manual page to help determine the habits and activities of the items' owner. Discuss your ideas with your partner and record your conclusions.
4. Repeat this process with the second bag.
5. Share your results with the class. Try to identify the owner of each bag.

Archaeologists excavate an ancient grave. What conclusions might the archaeologists come to from this site?

What was the importance of Diego de Landa's contributions in understanding the Mayas?

Mayas

Another civilization in Mesoamerica was the **Mayan civilization**. Archaeologists have found traces of Mayan-speaking villages from as far back as the time of the Olmecs. These villages contained groups of houses surrounded by fields. Some villages had public buildings, possibly for religious and governmental uses.

For about 2,500 years, the Mayas built farms and homes in the rainforests in the lowlands and on the high plateaus. The Mayas could get fresh water from deep sinkholes called **cenotes** in the rich earth of the lowlands. Mayas cleared forested land and burned the remaining vegetation in a **slash-and-burn** method of obtaining land for farming. The Mayas also built irrigation systems for their fields.

As the Mayas prospered, their population increased and their villages grew larger. By AD 250, Mayas dominated the region and built city-states. One of their great city-states was **Tikal**. Archaeologists believe its population was at least sixty thousand. Tikal covered more than forty-seven square miles.

Mayan Achievements

Arts and Architecture

Between AD 250 and 900, the Mayas made advances in art and architecture. They used limestone to make sculptures and carvings to honor their kings and their gods. They used clay to make ceramics such as whistles in the shape of animals, pots for cooking, and vessels for drinking. They built public buildings, ball courts, limestone palaces, and pyramid-shaped temples with massive stairways.

Writing and Books

Mayan writing was a combination of words and units of sound. Thus, anything that could be spoken could also be written. It was not until the 1970s that the Mayan hieroglyphics were understood. Today, 85 percent of known Mayan texts have been translated.

Mayan civilization A Mesoamerican civilization ca. AD 250–900.

cenote The name given to a deep sinkhole filled with water that formed when water eroded limestone.

slash-and-burn A practice used in agriculture where a forest is cut and burned before the land is planted.

Tikal The largest and most powerful Mayan city-state; located in northern Guatemala.

Ancient city of Tikal located in a Guatemalan rainforest. What may have been some purposes for the highest structure?

Icons of Mayan hieroglyphic writing and phonetic signs that represent syllables on a stone stele in Honduras. Why are the Mayan writing icons considered pictorial?

240

The Mayas made books of their writings. They wrote on long strips of paper made of the inner bark of fig trees. To make this paper, the Mayas pulled bark off the fig trees and soaked it in water. Then they boiled the bark in water for hours until the fibers were soft enough to separate and be manipulated. The fibers were pounded together with wooden mallets until the material was wide and flat. The paper was then stretched in the sun to dry. The dried material was cut into strips. Each strip was coated with a thin layer of a gummy substance for strength. Then the strip was painted with lime to make its surface white.

Scribes wrote and drew on the paper with paints made from vegetables and minerals. When the strips were dry, they were folded in an accordion fashion and bound between wooden covers. The type of book that the Mayas made is called a **codex**. A Mayan codex was usually about eight inches high and several yards long when unfolded.

Today only four Mayan books are known to exist. One contains observations about the planet Venus and charts used to predict solar eclipses. Some contain prophecies based on the stars and planets, calendars, and rituals. The books do not tell anything about Mayan history, nor do they give any clues to the fate of the Mayan civilization.

In the mid-1500s, a Spanish priest named **Diego de Landa** tried to force the Mayas to accept Roman Catholicism. When the Mayas refused, de Landa had some of them stretched on pulleys, burned with candles, or tortured in other ways. He wrote in his book *Yucatan: Before and After the Conquest* that he had burned an entire library of Mayan books in 1562

Page from the Dresden codex from the Mayan civilization. How were the numbers on this codex used?

"since they contained nothing but superstitions and falsehoods of the devil."

Afterward, de Landa realized that converting the Mayas would be easier if he knew more about them. He became a careful student of the Mayas and tried to translate their writing into Spanish. Much of the information known today about the Mayas of the 1500s and their ancestors comes from de Landa's writings. The rest of the information has been gathered from the artifacts in Mayan lands.

Math and Astronomy

The ancient Mayas were one of the early civilizations that developed the idea of zero. With zero, the Mayas were able to do difficult calculations and keep detailed records. Their math system was based on the number 20, unlike the decimal system today which is based on the number 10.

The Mayas made calendars similar to the calendar developed by the Olmecs. The Mayan calendar was based on the cycles of the moon and the sun. Their solar year had 365 days. The calendar was made after years of careful observations of the sky. These observations were so accurate that the Mayas were able to figure out the orbits of the planets and could predict a solar eclipse. The Sacred Round calendar included a cycle of 260 days of ritual which ran along with the cycle of 365 days. These cycles comprised a larger cycle of 18,980 days or 52 years of 365 days.

codex Mayan folding book recorded on paper made from the inner bark of fig trees.

Diego de Landa Spanish priest who tried to make the Mayas accept Roman Catholicism; much information about the Mayas is found in his writings.

MAYAN NUMBERS 0-24

0	𝟎	1	•	2	••	3	•••	4	••••
5	—	6	•/—	7	••/—	8	•••/—	9	••••/—
10	=	11	•/=	12	••/=	13	•••/=	14	••••/=
15	≡	16	•/≡	17	••/≡	18	•••/≡	19	••••/≡
20	•/𝟎	21	:	22	∴	23	•••:	24	••••

How does this image of a Mayan man reflect his culture?

This Mayan vase found in Tikal, Guatemala, depicts a Mayan man in a processional. How might his dress relate to his social status?

Mayan People
Physical Appearance

Historians today can use sculptures and paintings to infer how the ancient Mayas possibly looked.

According to Diego de Landa, the Mayan people were about five feet tall and had thick, dark hair. The men wore their long hair in braids around the tops of their heads with one braid down the back. Women also wore braids, usually coiled around their heads and held in place with ribbons.

The ancient Mayas appeared to have preferred long noses and sloping foreheads. Some used clay to create a ridge from the top of the forehead to the bridge of the nose. The sloping head had to be formed early in life, so parents bound newborns' heads between boards until the soft bones grew into a slanted, almost cone shape.

Historical evidence indicates that Mayas also preferred crossed eyes, perhaps because one of their gods was cross-eyed. To achieve this look, parents hung a bead between the baby's eyes. After the baby looked at the bead for months, his eyes grew permanently crossed.

When they were older, the Mayas made other changes to their appearances. Most young men shaved the hair above their foreheads to show off their slanting foreheads and brows. They also tattooed symbols on their arms, legs, and faces. Many had their ears pierced. The men wore plugs in holes sliced into their lobes. They kept adding bigger and bigger plugs until the holes were several inches across. In these holes, they placed disks of jade or shell. Both men and women would file their teeth to points and inlay them with jade.

Mayas took frequent baths, a practice shunned and feared in Europe at the time. They liked perfume, which they made from flowers and herbs. Many men carried mirrors to check their appearance.

 What was the purpose of the Mayan codex?

What was trade like in the Mayan civilization?

Social Classes

Classes of Mayan society had several levels. At the top was the ruler. Like the Egyptians, the Mayas believed that their kings were descended from the gods and that they should be obeyed without question. The kings, in return, claimed to speak to the gods on behalf of the people. Many kings took advantage of this absolute authority and mistreated the people.

Each city-state had unique hieroglyphics to represent it and its king. From these hieroglyphics, scholars have been able to identify thirty-three rulers of the city-state Tikal. At least one ruler was a queen. One notable king was **Jasaw Chan K'awiil I**. When he came to power, Tikal had been weak and struggling. Under his leadership, it became strong once again. Many steles and other carvings tell of this king.

Just below the kings in power were the priests. There were at least four classes of priests. The highest-ranking priests were in charge of the others. They taught writing, astronomy, mathematics, and religious rituals. Lower ranks included priests who treated sickness. Other priests were fortunetellers. The priests also offered sacrifices to the gods.

In the same social class as the priests were the nobles. All the priests came from the nobility. The nobles, both men and women, were educated, and they held important positions in the government.

Lesser nobles included artists, architects, traders, scribes, advisors, and engineers. Although they did not have the high positions of the first class of nobles, they had many of the same privileges. No nobleman or noblewoman had to do manual work, such as planting crops, grinding corn, or cleaning. Such labor was left to the common people.

The peasants did the hard manual work of the Mayan society. They grew, harvested, and processed the food. The peasants grew cotton and produced fabrics. They tended the buildings. Some were soldiers in the armies or laborers for the construction of monuments and temples.

At the bottom of Mayan society were the slaves. People who were in debt or who had committed a crime often became slaves. Sometimes prisoners of war were kept as slaves as well. Important prisoners were sacrificed to the gods. Other prisoners were made to work.

This vessel was used by Mayan nobility at banquets during the Classic Mayan period. The host often presented it as a gift to a guest to hold beverages, mainly ones made from cacao. What do people use today to hold beverages?

JASAW CHAN K'AWIIL I

What: ruler of the Mayas
When: ruled AD 682–734
Where: ancient Guatemala

Jasaw Chan K'awiil I took the throne three years after his father was defeated in 679. Jasaw was considered the first great king of the Classic Period. He ruled the Mayas from the city-state of Tikal. When Jasaw defeated a rival city-state, Tikal began to prosper. He completed new construction in Tikal. Unlike other rulers who were harsh to their people, Jasaw tried to help his people make their civilization strong. Jasaw is depicted as a heroic leader in reliefs at temple monuments. Many people believe that he died from an abscess in his jaw. He was buried in the Temple of the Jaguar in ancient Tikal.

Jasaw Chan K'awiil I Mayan ruler from AD 682–734 in the royal line of Tikal during the Classic Period.

Mayan Dress

Most Mayas wore simple cotton clothes. The men wore tunics and loincloths, sometimes with a short cape. The women wore straight, plain dresses or wraparound skirts and long blouses. The Mayas either went barefoot or wore sandals made of straw and rope. Both men and women wore a lot of jewelry, including earrings, rings, armbands, and necklaces. They made jewelry from jade, shells, volcanic rock, or animal teeth and bones.

Wealthy people dressed the same as the common people, only with more embellishments such as feathers woven into the fabric. They wore shoes made of deerskin.

The kings wore jaguar skins and jade breastplates. The three-foot plumes in their headdresses and on their clothes came from the *quetzal*, a beautiful bird of the rainforest. Kings also wore jade bands on their wrists and ankles as well as gold rings on their toes.

Mayan Homes

The classes of Mayan society were reflected not only in people's jobs and dress but also in the places they lived. Kings lived in palaces that covered many acres. Nobles lived in impressive, large houses near the center of the cities. These houses had many airy rooms and walls covered with **stucco**. Embroidered cotton draperies divided large rooms. Some houses had fireplaces, ovens, and possibly plumbing. Most peasant families lived in small wooden houses with grass-thatched roofs.

Daily Life

While the kings, priests, and nobility participated in ceremonies, waged wars on neighbors, and planned huge building projects, the average Maya led a far quieter and simpler life. Before four o'clock in the morning, women were awake and building fires to prepare breakfast. By five o'clock, the men had eaten breakfast and were tending to the crops. Family life was an important part of the Mayan civilization.

Farmers

Farmers grew many crops. Their crops included beans, squash, avocados, and **maize**. When planting maize in swampy places or on riverbanks, farmers made ridges in the soil and poked holes into the ridges with a planting stick. Another person came behind, dropping the kernels of maize into the holes and covering them.

In the dry seasons, farmers went into the rainforests and cut down trees. They burned the stumps and the underbrush. They planted maize in the ashes. The maize grew well for a year or two, but this type of soil quickly lost the nutrients the maize needed to grow well. The remedy was to move to a new place to slash and burn again. Farmers gave part of all they grew to the upper classes.

---

stucco A decorative plaster.
maize Corn.

THE DESIRE FOR CHOCOLATE

People all over the world enjoy a variety of chocolate products made from cacao beans. The Spanish brought cacao beans from Mesoamerica back to Spain, and the use of cacao beans spread throughout Europe and across the world.

Cacao was first used to make ritual beverages in early Mayan cultures. The Mayas scooped the seeds from the pods and placed the beans in containers to ferment. The beans were then dried and roasted. The dried beans were ground with a pestle in a grinding bowl. The powder was made into a chocolate paste, then mixed with water and chili peppers to make a drink. The Mayas used the bitter drink in marriage ceremonies or in rituals of kings and nobles.

The Mayas also used the cacao beans as gifts and as money. Cacao beans were traded for food, clothing, ceremonial feathers, obsidian, jade, and even slaves. In the Mayan society, a slave was typically valued at one hundred cacao beans. Because cacao beans were so valuable, counterfeiters sometimes filled empty bean pods with dirt and traded them as real beans. If caught, the counterfeiter was made a slave.

An opened cacao pod reveals the beans covered in a white pulp that is removed before processing the beans to make cacao butter and cocoa powder.

Women

Mayan women made cotton thread for use on looms. They wove cloth, made clothing, and cared for the children. They would also grind grain in stone bowls. Little girls helped make *tortillas* and other food. The big meal of the day came in the late afternoon and usually included beans, fruit, and *tamales*. Occasionally, this meal also included meat. A favorite drink, *pozole,* was made from corn paste and water, sometimes mixed with honey. Women and girls made the meal, served it to the men and boys, and ate afterward.

Burial mask made in sixth to seventh century AD from obsidian, jadeite, and pearl shell; found in a tomb under the Temple of the Inscriptions at Palenque, Chiapas, Mexico. Who would require this type of burial mask?

Trade

Mayan cities in the highlands traded with those in the lowlands. In this way, people were able to get what they needed. The lowlands produced cotton, rubber, and cacao beans. The highlands had valuable stones such as jade and **obsidian**. Mayas used obsidian to make the blades of tools and weapons.

People came to the cities for festivals and games and to buy and sell goods. The markets were busy places where people traded salt, vegetables, animals, jewelry, jade, pottery, honey, fabrics, and, of course, cacao beans.

A chert stone (a silica found in limestone that contains crystalline) blade from 300 BC–AD 200. What did Mayas have to consider when choosing material to make weapons and tools?

obsidian A glass-like volcanic rock.

> What was the relationship between social classes in the Mayan culture?
>
> What was the significance of the cacao bean to the Mayas?

LIFE IN TIKAL

Social Classes
The lowest class, the slaves, labored in construction and in the fields. Peasants, people skilled in crafts, and merchants made up the next class. The highest level included the governing priests and nobles.

Justice
There were no prisons, and justice was quickly executed. Legal decisions were final, without the chance of appeal. However, if a victim or his family pardoned the offender, a lesser punishment was given.

Environment
Tikal was in the rainforests of the Yucatán Peninsula. The thick tropical rainforests in the lowlands discouraged attacks by other Mayan city-states. The rainforest held a variety of animals and fruit that provided food. Cenotes provided freshwater. Mayas turned some wetlands into farmland.

Religion
All Mayan life was affected by religion. The pursuit of math and science helped plan religious ceremonies to honor the heavenly bodies. Taxes were seen as sacred offerings. Laws were seen as principles of the religion. Priests performed human sacrifice.

The architecture of Tikal included pyramid complexes. Mayas built two types of pyramids. One type was for sacrificial purposes with stairs that could be climbed. The other type was for sacred rituals and was not meant to be climbed. The pyramids rose above the rain forest and served as landmarks.

Arts, Sciences, and Written Language

Mayas developed a solar calendar of eighteen months with each month having 20 days. At the end of the year, there were five extra days. They also used a system of mathematics for astronomy and for keeping precise records of past events.

The Mayan advanced system of agriculture included terraces, irrigation methods, and the practice of draining swampy fields for planting.

Mayas used limestone to build palaces and pyramids. They constructed observatories and ball courts. They made sculptures, painted artistic murals, practiced weaving, created jewelry, and fired ceramics. The trumpets used in battle and rituals were made from shells of marine animals.

Key Themes of Civilization
- Justice
- Power
- Citizenship
- Environment

Features of a Civilization
- Organized cities and government
- Social classes
- Job specialization
- Arts, sciences, and written language
- Religion

Organized Cities and Government

The Mayan civilization consisted of many independent city-states. Each was ruled by a priest-king or sometimes a ruling queen. Priests and nobles formed councils to assist the ruler in matters such as charging taxes and overseeing justice.

Power

The king held power over the Mayan city-state and was believed to be a descendant of the gods. Mayas warred with other states to get honor for themselves. Captured kings and nobles were sacrificed during victory ceremonies.

Tikal stood as a Mayan political, military, and economic center. What type of commerce took place in Tikal?

The city included palaces, ceremonial platforms, temples, ball courts, residences, terraces, and roads.

247

What are possible reasons for the decline of the Mayan civilization?

Mayan Religion

Mayas were animists who believed everything had a spiritual essence. Whether it was a living tree or animal or a nonliving object such as a rock, everything was to be honored. Each Maya had a spiritual guide called a Wayob. The Wayob was thought to appear in a dream or as an animal to assist a Maya through his life.

The role of the priests was tied to the calendar and the stars and planets. They oversaw the rituals, learning, time calculation, ceremonies, written records, cures for diseases, and more. Mayan rituals were based on the 260-day Sacred Round calendar. Ritual bloodletting was a key part of all important calendar events and was done to sustain and satisfy the gods.

The supreme deity referenced in some Mayan writings was called Itzamná. He was associated with writing, the arts, and the sciences. His wife, Ixchel, was the goddess of the moon.

The main clergy of the Yucatec Maya were the *Ah Kin*. This name means, "He of the Sun." The Ah Kin performed ritual sacrifices. The Ah Kin Mai was the chief priest and held a variety of roles including astronomer, teacher, advisor to other priests, and overall administrator. Before two Mayas would marry, they would consult with the Ah Kin for approval. The position of the Ah Kin was passed from father to son.

The Mayas believed the world was flat with four gods holding up each corner. Heaven had thirteen layers, each with its own god. The cold, dismal underworld was below. There were nine layers in the underworld, and each layer had a lord of the night. Mayas who died went to the underworld and had to work their way up through the layers to get to the highest heaven. The Mayas believed that people who

During the spring and autumn equinoxes, a shadow in the shape of a serpent falls on the pyramid, El Castillo. During sunset, the shadow descends the steps to meet a stone serpent's head at the base of the staircase. How did Mayas know how to align the pyramid to make this happen?

A GAME OF LIFE AND DEATH

A ball game was played throughout the ancient Mayan civilization. Every Mayan city had at least one ball court. One city had seven ball courts. The I-shaped courts measured 100–150 feet long and 25–50 feet wide. The players' goal was to hit a small rubber ball through a vertical hoop or onto a marker on the side of the wall. However, the players were allowed to use only their padded wrists, elbows, and hips.

Only the nobles could play the ball game, but everyone in the city could watch. Many nobles placed bets on the outcome, losing much property or many slaves when they lost.

The ball game was more than a sport. The Mayan game had religious significance. Some scholars believe that members of the losing team may have been sacrificed to the gods in a ceremony after the game.

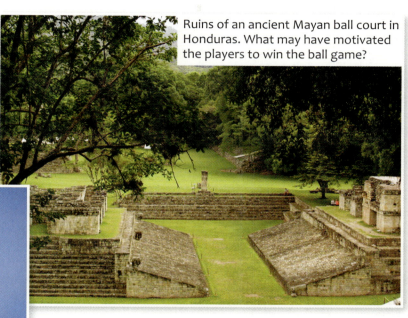

Ruins of an ancient Mayan ball court in Honduras. What may have motivated the players to win the ball game?

Ball hoop with decoration at the ball court at Chichen Itza, Yucatán, Mexico. Is there a similar game that is played today?

died from being sacrificed and women who died in childbirth went straight to the supreme heaven.

Mayas believed people went to the underworld through a cenote. Kings followed the sun's path when they died and eventually fell to the underworld. They entered the Sky World after being reborn as gods.

People who died were mourned for days. Their bodies were buried according to social class. The common people were often buried under their houses, which were then abandoned by the others who lived there. The rich could afford tombs with heavy stone coverings that were elaborately engraved. Almost everyone, regardless of social class, had a piece of valuable jade placed in his mouth so that he would have it for money in the next life.

Kings were buried with great ceremony and wealth. One king, Pacal, was buried in a large room under a Mayan pyramid. Buried with him were six other people and a huge supply of jade jewelry and other treasures. This king had a jade mask over his face, perhaps to show his power in the afterlife.

Decline of the Mayan Civilization

Archaeologists have found a stele in the city of Tikal dated at 869. This appears to have been the last record of the Mayas in that location. The Mayas seem to have left their major cities after that time. No one knows what happened. In many places, the Mayas seem to have departed suddenly. The belongings left behind suggest that the people meant to return, but never did. Or, at least, they never returned to rebuild. For the next six hundred years, they lived in other cities and parts of Mesoamerica, never regaining their former power.

Some archaeologists believe that the people moved away because of famine. Others think that war may have ended the great civilization. Still others think that the way of life in Mayan cities, full of rituals and religious superstitions, may have caused the people to rebel. Perhaps a combination of all these reasons ended the society. Nonetheless, forms of the Mayan civilization continued in smaller towns and in the cultures of other peoples.

 What are the major beliefs of the Mayan religion?

In what ways were the Aztecs treated unjustly by the Spaniards?

Aztecs

By the 1400s, people in the area known today as Mexico had become an advanced society known as the **Aztec civilization**. They had developed a complete language along with some significant technological advances.

According to legend, the Aztecs believed the sun god would lead them to a place where they were to settle and build a city. The Aztecs eventually settled on a swampy island in **Lake Texcoco**. Rather than be discouraged by this location, the Aztecs accepted it as the ideal location for them and built one of the largest cities in the world at that time.

The Aztecs began building their unusual city on two small islands on the lake. The city was called **Tenochtitlán**. Part of modern Mexico City is built on the land where Tenochtitlán existed.

The Aztecs created additional garden islands called **chinampas**. The Aztecs made strategic **causeways** to connect the islands to the mainland. Specially designed canals separated fresh water from salt water. Canoes could easily travel in these canals.

The Aztecs were a united people. As their population grew, they formed alliances with neighboring city-states. As their military power grew, they began to conquer peoples in the surrounding areas.

As early as the beginning of the 1500s, Tenochtitlán dominated all other cities. Its power was feared and its splendor was well-known. At one point, this city had a population of about two hundred thousand people. There was an abundance of religious buildings and activities. The **Templo Mayor** was the primary location for religious ceremonies and rituals.

Aztec civilization A Mesoamerican society; around 1325–1521.
Lake Texcoco Lake in Mexico; location of Tenochtitlán.
Tenochtitlán An ancient Aztec city built on Lake Texcoco; one of the largest cities of its time; a different city from the Olmec city of San Lorenzo Tenochtitlán; part of present-day Mexico City is built on this site.
chinampa A floating garden island made of twigs, limbs, sticks, and silt; created by the Aztecs.
causeway A land bridge.
Templo Mayor The primary location for the Aztecs' religious ceremonies and rituals; also called the Great Pyramid.

The Aztec empire extended to include what city in the far southeast?

Aztecs placed the 12-foot wide, 24-ton basalt calendar stone in the Aztec capital.

Aztec Religion

The religion of the Aztecs ruled every aspect of their lives. Before making decisions about anything, the Aztecs considered the religious significance. A diviner was consulted before naming a child to see which name would align with the child's fate. The religious calendar was consulted before scheduling events. Aztecs performed rituals and ceremonies for the hundreds of gods they worshiped. Aztecs believed the gods sacrificed themselves to create people and the world. Because of this belief, they attempted to repay the gods with human sacrifice and blood offerings. The Aztecs believed the sun god had a tremendous appetite for blood and human hearts. They needed to constantly appease him, or the very existence of their world was at risk.

Some historians believe the Aztecs may have sacrificed thousands of people each year. In war, their objective was not merely to gain territory or kill the enemy but to capture prisoners to sacrifice.

Hernando Cortés, a Spanish **conquistador**, arrived at Tenochtitlán in 1519. Cortés and his army were horrified by the extent of human sacrifices. Human sacrifice in religion demonstrates how sinful people can distort the truth into extreme acts of wickedness.

Hernando Cortés Commander of the Spanish conquistadors who entered Tenochtitlán in 1519.
conquistador A Spanish conqueror.

MESOAMERICAN BELIEFS

Mesoamericans believed in many gods. Some of these gods were local deities who ensured that crops grew or that other parts of daily life went well. Other gods were more powerful. Like the gods of other ancient civilizations, these gods were not necessarily good beings.

Both the Mayas and the Aztecs believed that previous worlds had existed and been destroyed. The Aztecs believed the creator god of this world destroyed a previous world. Blood sacrifices were necessary for people to preserve the world from destruction. Sometimes blood sacrifices involved wounding a person so that his or her blood could be used. Other times, the sacrifice involved killing a person.

These human sacrifices may have been the result of a distorted truth about the necessity of a blood sacrifice to God. But the true God firmly rejected the sacrifice of humans. Each person is precious to God, and the death of one sinner cannot atone for another. Only Jesus, who was completely sinless, could be an effective sacrifice for the sins of all people (Hebrews 7:26–28).

HOW DO THEY KNOW?

Many Christians wonder about what happens to people who never hear the gospel. For example, the ancient Mesoamericans were thousands of miles from any other civilization, and they followed false beliefs. What happened to them when they died?

The Bible teaches that all people who do not worship the one true God will experience eternal condemnation. God has revealed Himself to all people through nature and through His image in each person. This revelation communicates God's existence and moral character, but it is insufficient for salvation. It provides enough information to make people accountable for doing evil when they know to do good (Romans 1:19–23). Romans 2:15 states that the "law [is] written in their hearts." This statement means that their conscience lets them know when they violate God's law. Every culture in the world has chosen to violate God's law.

Christians must take the gospel to every culture on earth (Romans 10:14–17). The gospel provides people with the hope that they can know God and worship God. Through the gospel, God shows His power to bring salvation to people.

Social Classes

The social classes of the Aztecs were similar to other Mesoamerican civilizations. The nobility lived in brick or stone homes while the common people lived in homes made of interwoven twigs and mud.

Tenochtitlán and the Aztec Empire had the same ruler. All other governing officials were expected to pay tribute to this supreme ruler. As in the Mayan society, he was considered to be a descendant of the gods. Also as in the Mayan society, Aztec nobles, warriors, and priests were responsible for supporting the ruler.

The common people, which included artisans, soldiers, laborers, farmers, and merchants, were expected to support the nobles. Women worked hard at home, where they were expected to take care of their families. Commoners had little opportunity to change their lives and leave their social classes.

Economy

The Aztec culture was built on hard work by everyone. Citizens were expected to help in the building of **dikes**, temples, roads, and aqueducts.

dike A wall that prevents flooding.

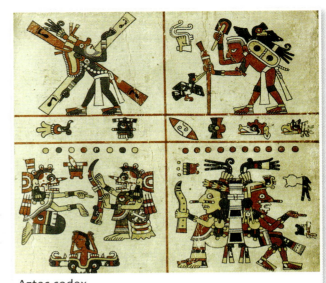

Aztec codex
The top left panel of the Codex Fejervary Mayer depicts Yacatecuhtli, Lord Nose, the patron god of merchants. He is carrying the symbol of the crossroads with merchant footprints on it.

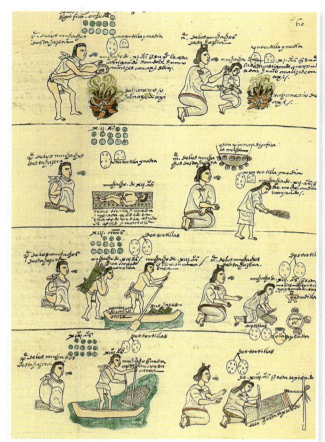

The Mendoza codex shows strict parental training and discipline of children. What goals did parents have for their children in spite of their inappropriate methods?

The Aztec economy was specialized and highly structured. A variety of goods were produced within the Aztec Empire. These included tools, pottery, figurines, jewelry, cloth, and baskets. The goods were sometimes made specifically for the ruler, and sometimes they were made to be sold in the local markets. As in other Mesoamerican civilizations, farming was important for the Aztec people.

Trade occurred along the lowlands of the Gulf Coast. The Aztecs sought goods such as gold ornaments, salt, and garments made of fine cloth. In return, the Aztecs offered goods such as jaguar skins, tropical-bird feathers, rubber, cotton, and cacao beans.

Language and Technology

The development of a written language played an important role in the Aztec civilization. Like the Mayas, the Aztecs used hieroglyphics to represent their spoken language. This written language was used while conducting business and trade. They also recorded their customs and beliefs to be passed on to future generations. This unified their culture for many years. The knowledge gained from contact with the Mayas helped the Aztecs develop their own technology. The Aztec number system and knowledge of the solar system were very advanced compared to other cultures of that time. They developed many forms of helpful medicines, such as ointments and tonics. The Aztecs did not have access to iron or bronze but still made excellent tools and weapons. These included drills made of reeds or bones.

The Aztecs did not have horses, mules, or other animals for carrying trade goods. They made dugout canoes for travel through the many canals, lakes, and waterways found in the Valley of Mexico.

WARRIORS

Aztec warriors began training at an early age. By going to war, they believed they were showing service and respect to the gods. Men were expected to prove their worth on the battlefield. As warriors, they were to be brave and noble.

The bravest Aztec warriors achieved the rank of jaguar warrior or eagle warrior. They were the most feared of all the Aztec warriors.

Most Aztec weapons were designed to stun and capture enemies rather than to kill them. This way the captured enemy could walk and not have to be carried to the temple to be sacrificed.

Warriors descended from Aztec nobility. They fought neighboring states in support of their ruler and to promote their religious beliefs.

MONTEZUMA II

What: emperor of the Aztecs
When: ca. 1466–1520
Where: ancient Mexico

Montezuma was one of the best Aztec warriors before becoming the ruler of the Aztec empire in 1502. He lived lavishly in a huge palace at Tenochtitlán, the Aztec capital. During his eighteen-year rule, he expanded the Aztec borders to include what is known today as Mexico and Guatemala. He improved the Aztec way of life by building many temples, canals, and hospitals. But his subjects did not like paying the taxes he imposed on them. After his death, the empire remained under Spanish control.

Spanish Invasion

Montezuma II was the emperor of the Aztecs when Spanish conquistadors landed on the shores of Mesoamerica in 1519. Cortés forced his way into Central Mexico with about 500 European soldiers. The soldiers were fitted with European weaponry consisting of firearms, crossbows, steel swords, and armor to protect their bodies. Horses and dogs trained for battle accompanied them. In less than a year, Hernando Cortés and the Spanish conquistadors entered Tenochtitlán. Montezuma was not certain of how to respond to the Spanish force. Some historians believe Montezuma thought Cortés might be the Aztec god-king who was supposed to return from the east. The white skin of Cortés fit the description the Aztecs had of the god-king.

Montezuma eventually welcomed Cortés with elaborate gold and silver gifts. Within two weeks, the Aztec leader was arrested and held hostage. Aztec warriors were no match for the Spanish soldiers. Aztec warriors wore padded cotton armor, and their shields were made of hide-covered wood or reeds. Their weapons were sharp obsidian swords that were used like clubs, bows and arrows, spears, and devices for throwing darts. The Aztec warriors and commanders were attired in feathers, animal skins, and headdresses. They stood out in battle as an easy target for the Spanish. After Cortés seized control of the city, the Aztec people revolted.

Cortés brought Montezuma before the people, expecting them to back down. However, many people had grown to hate the Aztec leader, and they did not listen to him or back down. Montezuma was struck by a stone while addressing his subjects. Some people believe he was killed by Spanish soldiers. Whatever the cause, Montezuma died three days later.

Montezuma II Aztec emperor who expanded the Aztec boundaries and built many temples, canals, and hospitals.

A frieze by Constantino Brumidi is in the Rotunda of the US Capitol. It depicts Montezuma II welcoming Cortés into the capital city of Tenochtitlán, fearing that he was the god Quetzalcóatl and had returned to rule the empire. How did Cortés take advantage of Montezuma's fear?

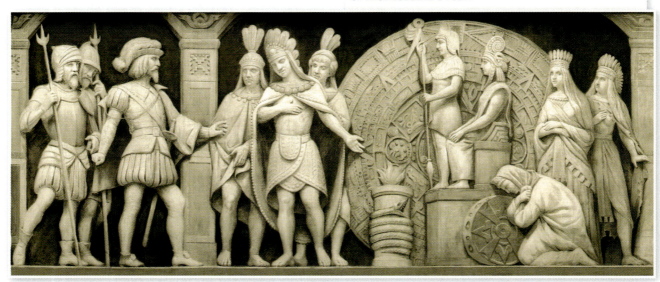

Was it likely that the Aztec warrior's cotton armor or wooden shield would protect him against Spanish firearms?

Many people died of diseases brought by the Europeans because the **indigenous** people had little immunity to these diseases.

Local groups of people hoped to see the collapse of Aztec rulership. They disliked having to pay heavy tribute and having to capture people to sacrifice at the Aztec capital.

The Spanish were able to gain control of Tenochtitlán and of many surrounding territories.

This surviving half of the world map drawn by Ottoman Admiral Piri Reis in 1513 shows the coast of Central America and South America.

The Fate of the Mesoamericans

There are several possible reasons for why the well-trained Aztec army was defeated quickly. The Aztecs used swords and daggers that required fighting at close range. They also threw javelins and used darts. But the Spanish fought with superior weapons and used advanced military tactics. Spanish military equipment included crossbows, steel pikes (long spears), swords, small cannons, guns, and horses. Additionally, the Aztecs had developed enemies who were willing to be allies with the Spanish. The Tlaxcalans were allies during the Spanish siege of the Aztec capital. Another reason the Aztecs were quickly defeated was that they had been weakened by an epidemic that reduced the size of their forces.

Not only were the Mesoamerican people defeated in battle with Europeans, but they also lost their culture. As a result of the European conquests, the Mesoamericans no longer practiced many of their traditions or forms of their native religion.

As seen throughout history, nations rise and fall. Mesoamerica rose with advancements in architecture, mathematics, and science until it fell into decline. Like all nations, Mesoamerica violated the laws God has revealed through His creation.

indigenous A native or original inhabitant of a certain place.

What was unusual about the city of Tenochtitlán?

What was the role of religion in the Aztec culture?

ANCIENT AFRICA

FOCUS: Africa's abundant resources gave rise to great civilizations.

| 1st–7th centuries Aksum Empire | Eastern African coastal trade cities established ca. 900s | | Slave trade in the West ca. 1400s–1808 |

Timeline: BC/AD — 500 — 1000 — 1500 — 2000

ca. 700–ca. 1500 Western African trade empires

Alika and Oduwa hurry to join the other children. They never miss the afternoon story.

The storyteller has just started. "The hyena was caught in a trap and wanted to get out. He called out to an elephant, 'Help me!' But the elephant said over his shoulder, 'Remember how you laughed when I could not find enough water last summer?'

"The hyena called to a black mamba, 'Help me!' The snake went on by. 'No. Remember all those times you stole my food?'

"A young monkey scampered up. The hyena said, 'Help me!' 'Oh, no,' said the monkey. 'If I set you free, you will kill me!' The hyena said, 'I promise I will not eat you if you help me!' The monkey thought a moment. He said, 'Your reputation is not very good.' The hyena said, 'I give you my word as a fellow creature of this world.' So the monkey let the hyena out of the trap. Immediately, the hyena jumped on the monkey to kill him.

"At that moment, a great eagle swooped down and snatched up the hyena. He set him on a rock. 'What happened here?' the eagle asked. The monkey said, 'I helped the hyena, and as thanks, he tried to kill me!' 'That's a lie!' said the hyena. 'The monkey attacked me! I was defending myself!'

"The eagle, who had seen it all from above, said, 'Show me what happened. Each of you act out your story.'

"'Well,' said the monkey, 'the hyena was in this trap when I came along.' The eagle said to the hyena, 'Show me how it was.' The hyena got into the trap, and the eagle immediately snapped it shut. He said to the monkey, 'Run home.' And to the hyena the eagle said, 'You are where you deserve to be.' And he flew away."

Alika and Oduwa smile at the end. They are expected to learn from this teller, their grandfather, because only a child in his family may become the next official village storyteller.

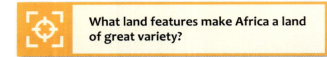

What land features make Africa a land of great variety?

The Continent of Africa

Africa is the second largest continent. Geographers often divide it into regions (northern, western, central, eastern, and southern) to better study its land and people. It has large lakes, grand mountain ranges, mighty rivers, vast deserts, and lush rainforests. Though the people of Europe, Asia, and the Americas knew little about the interior of Africa for hundreds of years, ancient Africa was a land of thriving civilizations.

Africa's Geography

Africa is surrounded by four bodies of water: the Mediterranean Sea, the Red Sea, the Indian Ocean, and the Atlantic Ocean. The equator runs through the middle of the continent. Africa is the only continent to have deserts both north and south of the equator. The main deserts of Africa are the Sahara in the north and the Kalahari and the Namib Desert in the south.

The Sahara is the largest desert in Africa. It covers most of the northern half of the continent. The Sahara is made up of sand, rocky plains, and stony plateaus. Winds blow the sand and create ridges and hills called sand dunes. The dunes continually

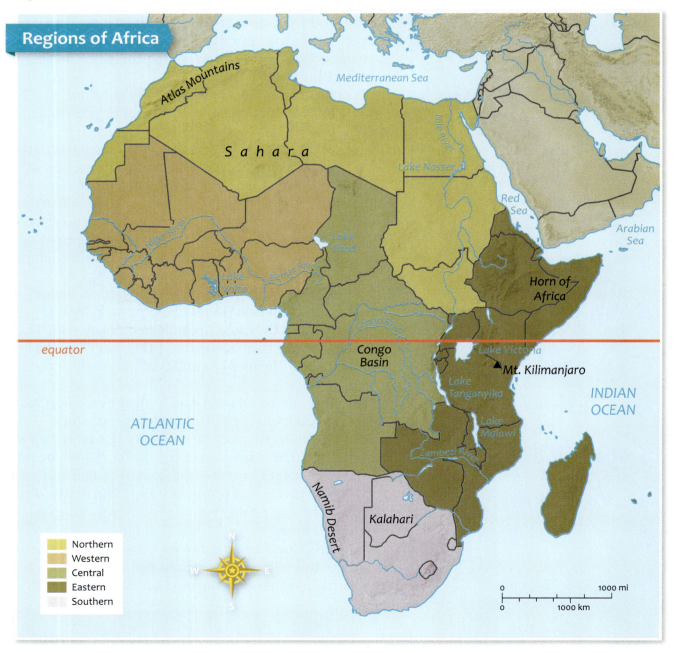

Regions of Africa

THE REGION TODAY

Africa

Location
Africa, the second largest continent, lies to the southwest of Asia. It includes the islands of Madagascar, Comoros, Réunion, Mauritius, Mayotte, and Seychelles. Africa is divided almost in half by the equator.

Climate
Much of the land has a tropical climate, with warm temperatures during the day and cool temperatures at night. Other parts have a dry, desert climate.

Temperatures in the Sahara range from 50°F in the winter to 100°F in the summer. In northern Somalia, summer temperatures of 115°F or higher are common.

Topography
Deserts cover about two-fifths of Africa's land. Africa also has mountain ranges, rivers, rainforests, large lakes, and savannas.

Natural Resources
Rich in mineral resources, Africa has deposits of gold, petroleum, oil, copper, diamonds, and natural gas.

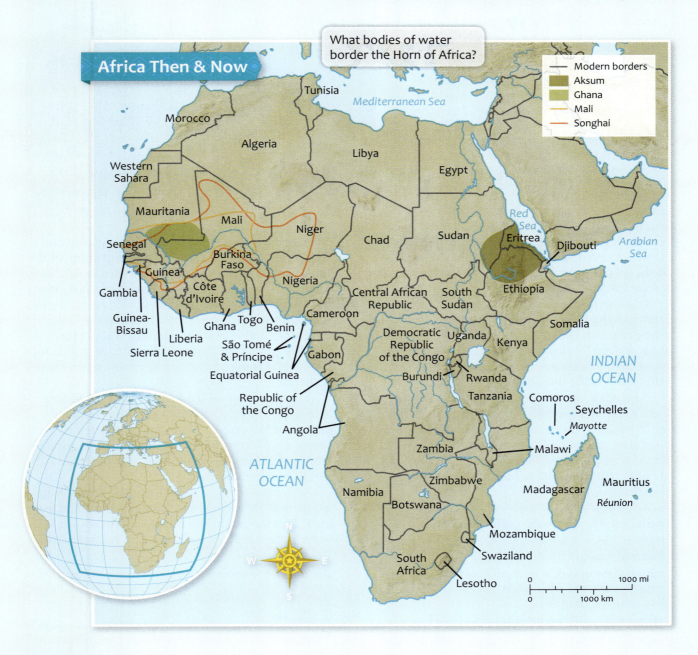

Africa Then & Now

What bodies of water border the Horn of Africa?

Above: Ergs, areas of concentrated sand, cover around fifteen percent of the entire Sahara.

Above, right: The Niari River runs through the Republic of the Congo. Unlike many parts of the rainforest, the region that the Niari flows through has good soil that is useful for farming.

Right: As the largest land animals in the world, adult African bush elephants are usually left alone by other animals of the savanna.

change shape and size. Some dunes rise to over four hundred feet high. Most of the Sahara receives less than three inches of rainfall per year. However, people can live there if they live near an **oasis**. An oasis can support animals and crops. Oases are scattered throughout the desert.

In eastern Africa, Somalia is part of a peninsula known as the **Horn of Africa**. The land of Somalia is a type of desert called a **rain shadow desert**. A rain shadow desert forms when the wind blows water vapor high into nearby mountains without allowing rain to fall on the lowlands.

Africa is also home to many lakes and rivers. Lake Victoria is generally considered the source of the White Nile River, one of the tributaries of the Nile River. Lake Chad supplies water to four different African countries. Lake Nasser and Lake Volta are both man-made lakes that are used to generate electricity.

Africa has the largest tropical area of any continent. The tropics are just north and just south of the equator. Rainforests cover much of the tropics. Some parts of Africa's rainforests receive as much as one hundred inches of rainfall per year. These rainforests are filled with huge trees and vines and the largest variety of wildlife in the world. The soil in rainforests is not fertile. Farmers cannot raise good crops because the frequent rain washes many nutrients out of the soil.

The area between the Kalahari and the Sahara (except for the rainforest) is a **savanna**. With tall grasses and few trees, the savanna is where the people raise crops and cattle. Wild antelope, giraffes, zebras, elephants, leopards, lions, and other animals also live on the savanna.

Africa has many mountain ranges. Mount Kilimanjaro in Tanzania is over nineteen thousand feet high. This mountain and others in Africa, such as some in the Sahara, were formed by volcanic activity.

oasis A fertile area in the desert with water.
Horn of Africa A peninsula in northeastern Africa that projects into the Arabian Sea.
rain shadow desert A lowland area that receives little rain; formed when wind blows water vapor high into nearby mountains.
savanna A region with tall grass and few trees.

 Describe an African rainforest.

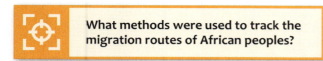

What methods were used to track the migration routes of African peoples?

Keys to Africa's Past

The ancient Egyptians left written records on both stone and papyrus. But most of the people of ancient Africa did not have a written language. However, historians can study these people because there are many ways of learning about people other than by reading written records.

Linguistics

One way to learn about ancient people is to study the spread of languages. Long ago, the **Bantu** left their homes on the Benue River and migrated into central and eventually eastern and southern Africa. This migration took place over hundreds of years. As the Bantu migrated and settled in a new area, they learned how to speak with the people already living there. Both groups shared and borrowed bits of language. Slowly, each language changed.

Linguists study words and grammar to learn of people's migration routes. Linguists helped trace the migration route of the Bantu.

Botany

While linguists follow people through changes in their language, **botanists** can trace the movements of people by their crops. Botanists can also make assumptions about why people moved or spread out and how their methods of food gathering and production changed.

When the Bantu farmers moved, they took seeds with them so that they could plant crops to feed their families. By tracking the spread of crops, botanists helped trace the Bantu migration routes.

Archaeology

Another important source of information comes from archaeology. Discoveries of ancient ruins show where people lived and sometimes reveal their manner of life.

Bantu An early African people.
botanist A scientist who studies plants.
oral history Stories about the past that are spoken instead of written down.
griot An African oral storyteller.

In some areas of Africa, archaeologists have found caves with paintings on the walls. From these drawings, they know about the weapons the early African people used for fighting and hunting, as well as what animals they hunted. Some of the paintings are accompanied by symbols that may have been part of a written language. Unfortunately, so far no one has discovered what these symbols mean.

Oral History

Another way of learning about ancient people is through **oral history.** Oral history spreads the traditions of a culture from one generation to the next by the spoken word.

Many African villages had at least one official **griot**. It was the job of a griot to learn the village's history. Griots did not write history down; instead they passed it on by word of mouth. Griots taught the children and reminded the adults of their past. They described the journeys of their ancestors when they looked for new farmland. They told of the deeds of past leaders and heroes, and they reminded the villagers about their ancient traditions.

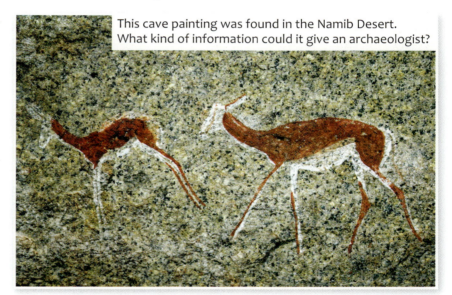

This cave painting was found in the Namib Desert. What kind of information could it give an archaeologist?

Village griots told their stories at every opportunity to keep their history from being forgotten. Modern historians know that oral history is important in learning about the past. They often try to evaluate the truth of a story by comparing it with stories from different areas. If many different parts of Africa have stories of the same past event, modern historians can assume that the event really happened.

 What was the significance of the African griot in preserving people's history?

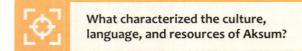

What characterized the culture, language, and resources of Aksum?

Africa's Empires
Aksum

On the eastern side of Africa lies the modern nation of Ethiopia. Long before the birth of Christ, farmers settled in this area and built the empire of **Aksum**. Aksum was a wealthy and powerful kingdom. It supplied precious stones, incense, gold, ivory, ebony, myrrh, and elephants to the Egyptian pharaohs, and it traded with Arabs and Europeans as well. It is the kingdom that eventually conquered Kush in AD 330.

Archaeologists who have studied the ruins of Aksum say that walled castles dominated the capital city. Stone inscriptions found among the ruins indicate that Aksum's educated people knew Greek. Linguists believe that the Aksumites visited the Greek city of Byzantium often, perhaps to trade. Eventually Aksum developed a written language called *Ge'ez*.

A system of social classes developed in Aksum. The king and the nobles were the highest class, followed by merchants, then artisans and traders, and then servants.

Ezana ruled the empire of Aksum in the AD 300s. He had great wealth and built many beautiful palaces, temples, and monuments. At least one of his

Aksum An ancient civilization in eastern Africa; a town in present-day Ethiopia.

Ezana King of the Aksum Empire in the AD 300s who made Christianity the official religion.

A stele is a large stone monument that may have marked the location of a tomb. At sixty-nine feet, King Ezana's Stele is the largest one still standing in the Northern Stelae Park in Aksum, Ethiopia.

What clues indicate that Aksum was involved in trade?

EZANA

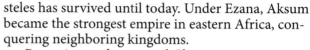

What: king of Aksum Empire
When: ruled AD 300s
Where: eastern Africa

Ezana was young when his father died, and his mother ruled the country for him. Influenced by his tutor, Frumentius, Ezana became a Christian and was baptized. Frumentius became the first Bishop of Aksum, and Ezana made Christianity the official religion of Aksum. He was the first to issue coins with a Christian cross on them.

Ezana was also known for his strong army. He waged wars to gain wealth and expand the kingdom of Aksum.

steles has survived until today. Under Ezana, Aksum became the strongest empire in eastern Africa, conquering neighboring kingdoms.

Byzantine traders spread Christianity into eastern Africa in the 300s. After Ezana conquered the people of Kush, he gave thanks to God for the victory with an inscription on a large stone slab. A Syrian Christian named Frumentius became a tutor to Ezana. It was probably through his influence that Ezana became a Christian. With Ezana's conversion, Christianity became Aksum's official religion.

Justin I of the Byzantine Empire, who ruled from AD 518 to 527, viewed the people of Aksum as fellow Christians. He asked King Kaleb of Aksum to help Christians in South Arabia (now Yemen) who were facing persecution from a Jewish prince. The region became part of the Aksumite Empire until the end of the sixth century.

After the fall of Rome, Aksum's trade dwindled. Then in the 600s, Muslim armies conquered Egypt and cut Aksum off from its trade with the Mediterranean world. The power of the rulers declined as the empire grew poorer. Yet even after the empire disappeared, the civilization continued. It formed the basis for the modern state of Ethiopia.

THE QUEEN OF SHEBA

First Kings 10 tells how a queen from Sheba visited King Solomon during his reign over Israel. Many scholars believe that Sheba was a kingdom located in what is now Ethiopia. The descriptions of the gifts the queen brought indicate that Sheba was wealthy.

The queen of Sheba had heard of Solomon's great wealth and about the wisdom he had gained from the Lord. She wanted to see Solomon's wealth and hear his wisdom firsthand. She devised difficult questions to ask Solomon, and he answered all of them. After he showed her the treasures and richness of his lifestyle, she saw that the reports she had heard were true. She told Solomon that his riches and wisdom were even greater than the stories claimed.

Many believe that the queen of Sheba began to serve Israel's God and brought knowledge of Him back to her own people.

Later, Jesus used the queen of Sheba as an example of the eager faith with which the Jews should have welcomed Him, their Messiah. The queen had come from "the uttermost parts of the earth to hear the wisdom of Solomon." Jesus, who was much greater than Solomon, had brought the glory of God to the Jewish people, but they did not receive Him in faith (Matthew 12:42).

Why would each of these items have been valuable?

Why was Koumbi Saleh an ideal location for a trading center?

Ghana

The ancient empire of **Ghana** was located along the Niger River. It was not in present-day Ghana but in what is now Mauritania. No one knows who founded ancient Ghana, but the kingdom probably appeared about three hundred years after the birth of Christ. By AD 700, Ghana was an empire. It was governed by African kings; in fact, the word *ghana* was the title these rulers used for themselves.

Many Arabian merchants traveled back and forth to Ghana, and some lived there. They introduced the use of camels on trade routes across the Sahara. Much of what historians know about this empire is from the merchants' accounts.

Ghana became a wealthy center of trade. Its location was ideal. Ghana was situated at the edge of the Sahara and was near the only water source for miles. There were gold mines to the south, so the people of Ghana traded gold for goods from merchants from all over the world. One of the main items exchanged for gold was salt. There were no sources for salt in Ghana, so salt from the Saharan mines was valuable.

Trade for salt and gold was done in an unusual way. The traders never saw one another. This system was called silent trade. First, merchants placed their slabs of rock salt in a special place and left. Next, the traders brought their gold and left it beside the salt. Finally, the merchants returned to take the gold. If either side was not satisfied with the amount that had been left, the deal was not complete. The merchants and the traders continued to come and go, adjusting their amounts until the deal was acceptable to both. This method of trade kept both sides happy and the location of the gold mines a secret.

Along with gold, the Ghanaians traded cola nuts, honey, textiles, and slaves. In addition to salt, they traded for items such as copper, dried fruit, cowry shells, horses, cloth, swords, and books from North Africa and Europe.

The king of Ghana charged taxes on all trade with his kingdom, so he was incredibly wealthy. An Arabian geographer named al-Bakri wrote a work called the *Book of Highways and Kingdoms*. In it, he described the king of Ghana's court as reported to him by traders. Gold was lavishly displayed everywhere. The precious metal decorated everything from clothing to swords and shields. Even saddles and dog collars had gold in them.

Arabian merchants brought the religion of Islam to Ghana. The king of Ghana continued to practice traditional beliefs, but many of the traders converted to Islam. As the ancient capital city of Koumbi Saleh grew, a separate Islamic community developed there.

Ghana had a huge army that helped protect its trade. But eventually wars with the Arabs began to interrupt trade and weaken Ghana's kings. The empire's military power declined. When the army of Mali attacked, Ghana could not fight back. The empire of Ghana ended in the thirteenth century.

Ghana An ancient African empire located along the Niger River; location of present-day Mauritania; name of a modern nation in western Africa.

 What influenced Ghana's economic growth?

What were the values, culture, and economy like in ancient Mali?

Mali

The empire of **Mali** included all of Ghana as well as much more land. In the 1200s, Mali had a strong ruler named **Sundiata Keita**. After taking the throne of Mali, Sundiata and his army conquered Ghana. In just a few years, Sundiata gained control of the gold and salt trade and built his capital on the main trade route across the Sahara. Legends grew that were based on Sundiata's life, and he became the hero of an epic that was popular with West Africans.

Sundiata and his successors were called by the title *mansa*, which is the word for *ruler* in the language of Mali's people. The kings of Mali grew wealthy from the gold trade, just as the kings of Ghana had before them. Most of them adopted Islam.

Ibn Battuta, a traveler from Tangier, visited Mali in the 1300s. He described the people as loving justice and honesty.

> They are seldom unjust, and have a greater abhorrence of injustice than any other people. Their sultan shows no mercy to anyone who is guilty of the least act of it. There is complete security in their country. Neither traveller nor inhabitant in it has anything to fear from robbers or men of violence. (Ibn Battuta, *Travels in Asia and Africa, 1325–1354* trans. and ed. H. A. R. Gibb, [London: Broadway House, 1929], 329.)

Several decades after Sundiata's rule, the most famous of all the Malian kings, **Musa I**, rose to power. Musa ruled from 1312 to 1337. He was famous for his immense wealth and his devotion to Islam.

Islamic learning in Timbuktu took place in mosques that were noted throughout the Islamic world for the excellence of their scholarship.

SUNDIATA KEITA

What: founder and king of the Mali Empire
When: ruled AD 1200s
Where: western Africa

Sundiata Keita, known as the Lion King, was part of the Keita clan of the Malinke people from the West African kingdom of Kangaba. According to one account, Sundiata and his eleven brothers were heirs to the throne of Kangaba. A ruler named Sumanguru conquered Kangaba and killed all the brothers except Sundiata. People have traditionally believed that Sumanguru did not kill Sundiata because the child was sickly and likely to die anyway. But Sundiata grew stronger and eventually put together a force that defeated Sumanguru, in the process establishing the basis of the Malian empire.

In 1324 Mansa Musa made a pilgrimage to Mecca, as faithful Muslims are required to do. People who witnessed his procession wrote descriptions of the scene. Hundreds of slaves marched with him, many of them carrying golden staffs. Camels loaded with gold also traveled in the grand parade. The stories claim that he carried more than a ton of gold.

In spite of his love of pomp and extravagance, Mansa Musa was very generous. During his pilgrimage, he gave away so much gold that the price of gold went down in that region for the next several years. Upon his return to Mali, he used his wealth to build many mosques, schools, and even a university in the city of **Timbuktu**. The university became a great center of Islamic learning.

Mali An ancient empire located in northwestern Africa; a modern nation in western Africa.

Sundiata Keita King of Mali in ancient western Africa; the first mansa (ruler) of Mali; known as the Lion King.

Musa I Malian king in ancient western Africa; known for his immense wealth and devotion to Islam; most famous of the Malian kings.

Timbuktu An African city in the Malian Empire that became a center of Islamic faith and learning.

MANSA MUSA

What: king of Mali
When: ruled ca. AD 1312–37
Where: Western Africa

Mansa Musa was the emperor of the Mali Empire for approximately twenty-seven years. He was a descendant of Sundiata, who was the founder of the Mali Empire. Mansa Musa is remembered for his extravagant pilgrimage to Mecca. He was accompanied by 60,000 people, including many slaves who carried staffs topped with gold. Eighty camels carried three hundred pounds of gold each. It was this pilgrimage that made people aware of Mansa Musa's great wealth. He is also known for building mosques such as the Great Mosque at Timbuktu, which was built of burnt bricks.

This 1375 map of Africa shows Mansa Musa with a gold nugget and a scepter by the city of Timbuktu. Why would Mansa Musa be drawn with a gold nugget in his hand?

After Mansa Musa's death, there were no more strong kings in Mali. Men fought over who had the right to the throne, and the great empire weakened. The fighting inside the empire encouraged enemies on the outside to attack. Parts of the empire gradually broke away. After four hundred years, Mali was once again a small village on the banks of the Niger River.

Songhai

Songhai was an important town in the Mali Empire. Like Mali, it depended on trade and sent merchants to Europe, Asia, and other parts of Africa.

In the 1400s, under the leadership of a ruler named **Sunni Ali**, Songhai won its independence from Mali. Sunni Ali conquered the cities around him to establish the large empire called **Songhai**.

Sunni Ali was a man of war, and he was never defeated. Some people believed that he was a magician who could change himself, his horses, and his soldiers into other creatures or even make them invisible. Sunni Ali fought Mali for twenty-eight years. Eventually, he controlled all the trade routes and the best farmland. Sunni Ali built a fleet of canoes to patrol the Niger River. He also built several capital cities to better rule his empire. The ancient city of Timbuktu became Songhai's center of Islamic faith and learning.

After Sunni Ali's death, another ruler, Askia Muhammad, took control. He fought more wars and conquered more territory. Songhai became larger than either Ghana or Mali had been. It looked as though no one would ever be able to defeat Songhai.

The Songhai Empire continued for more than a hundred years. Finally Morocco, one of its neighbors to the north, attacked. The Moroccan army had muskets, and its soldiers were better trained than Songhai's. The army of Songhai was defeated, and its government was destroyed.

Other enemies attacked Songhai, and soon the empire disappeared. In its place appeared many smaller kingdoms that frequently fought each other over land and trade.

Sunni Ali African ruler who established the large empire of Songhai.

Songhai An important town in the Malian Empire that won its independence and became its own empire near the Niger River.

Who was Mali's most famous ruler? What was he famous for?

How did Songhai become an independent empire?

ACTIVITY

Making Economic Predictions

Most of the empires in ancient Africa rose to power because of the wealth they gained through trade. Each of these empires had a healthy economy. The term *economy* refers to all the economic activities that take place within a country. It includes the country's production of goods, its selling of goods, and its buying of goods.

Many countries' economies depend on principles of supply and demand. People who buy goods are called consumers. What and how much consumers are willing to buy at a given price is called demand. People who produce goods are called suppliers. What and how much suppliers are willing to produce and sell at a given price is called supply. Variations in supply and demand help determine the price of a good. Generally, suppliers can charge more for a good if the supply is low and the demand is high. They must charge less for a good if the supply is high and the demand is low.

In ancient African economies, Arabian and European traders were important consumers. Their purchase of gold and other items from African suppliers contributed to the wealth of many African empires. The suppliers tried to produce only as much gold and other items as the traders and the Africans themselves wanted. If there was a greater supply than people wanted, the prices would go down.

When Mansa Musa gave away gold on his journey to Mecca, he created a change in the economy. The demand for gold decreased because the supply of gold had increased. The decreased demand caused the price of gold to go down.

LAW OF SUPPLY AND DEMAND

	Supply goes up.	Supply goes down.	Supply stays the same.
Demand goes up.	Prices do not change.	Prices rise.	Prices rise.
Demand goes down.	Prices fall.	Prices do not change.	Prices fall.
Demand stays the same.	Prices fall.	Prices rise.	Prices do not change.

Pretend to be a citizen of an imaginary African country. The nation's resources include gold, textiles, and cola nuts. Determine the impact of the following situations on the economy.

1. New gold mines have been discovered to the north. Merchants traveling across the Sahara have been stopping to trade at those mines rather than coming south to trade here.
2. Arabian merchants bring information that West African textiles have become popular in the Byzantine Empire. Therefore, demand has increased.
3. Farmers report an infestation affecting cola trees. Half of the crop of nuts has been ruined.
4. You defeat a nation to the west and add its gold mines to those you already possess.

The designs of West African textiles symbolize important aspects of the region's history and culture.

LIFE IN TIMBUKTU

Religion
Study of the Qur'an and Islamic law flourished in Timbuktu. Its one hundred fifty Islamic schools were generously funded by the government.

Environment
The position of Timbuktu at the edge of the Sahara and within a few miles of the Niger River made it an ideal location for trade.

Social Classes
The social structure in ancient African city-states was similar to other ancient civilizations. The monarch and royal family were at the top, having the most governmental control and wealth. Under the monarch came the nobles, priests, traders, and merchants. Next came the laborers, artisans, and farmers. Last were the slaves.

The minaret, or tower, in the center of the mosque is used for calling Muslims to prayer.

Justice
A minister of justice oversaw the legal administration of the empire. Islamic law and learning flourished under Askia Muhammad.

Organized Cities and Government
City-states emerged along the western coast of Africa as trading ports. These cities became prosperous by trading and selling goods from the interior kingdoms of Africa to the Arabs and Persians. The earliest ancient African civilizations were monarchies, ruled by a king or queen.

Key Themes of Civilization
- Justice
- Power
- Citizenship
- Environment

Job Specialization
Farmers were essential as they provided food. Some people raised livestock such as cattle and sheep. Traders transported goods to other civilizations. Artisans, such as blacksmiths, weavers, and potters, provided functional items. Warriors provided security and protection against invaders.

Power
The emperor had final authority, but was aided by the governors of the empire's provinces and by officials who directed policy for the empire in important areas like finance.

Features of a Civilization
- Organized cities and government
- Social classes
- Job specialization
- Arts, sciences, and written language
- Religion

The Djinguereber Mosque was built of mud bricks, a cheap building material that requires regular upkeep.

What influence did geography and natural resources have on the nomads of northern Africa?

Africa's People

Ancient Africa was home to many different peoples. Historians divide Africa's early peoples into groups by common language. The peoples in these language groups migrated, spread out, and eventually settled in various regions. Distinct tribes formed, and many different dialects developed.

Northern Africa

More than in other African regions, the people of northern Africa were influenced by the rest of the world. The presence of gold, copper, and ivory drew traders from Europe and Asia. Some cities on Africa's northern coast, such as Carthage, were established by outside civilizations for trading. As part of the Roman Empire after the Punic Wars, the northern coast was strongly influenced by Western culture. Christianity entered northern Africa in the first century.

Tuareg

Nomads of the Sahara lived in the north. Most of these nomads belonged to a language group called the Berber. The greatest of these nomadic people were the **Tuareg**.

The Tuareg dressed in loose, flowing garments and rode swift camels. The men wrapped their heads with a long piece of dark blue cotton that acted as both a turban and a veil. It hid the man's face except for a narrow slit for his eyes. Sometimes it stained his skin, earning the Tuareg the name "blue people."

The Tuareg were farmers, herders, and traders. They knew the best ways for caravans to cross the desert and often acted as guides. But they were also feared for their skill as warriors. Bands of Tuareg frequently attacked caravans. They even attacked towns built on the edges of the desert.

The camel was valuable to the Tuareg. Camels had been introduced into northern Africa shortly after the birth of Christ. Though stubborn, the camel was a necessity because of its ability to live and work in the desert. Horses and cattle often could not survive the long distances between oases. Camels could travel much longer without water. With camels, the Tuareg could move freely across the Sahara. They also used camel hides to make tents, and they made butter and cheese from camel milk.

Tuareg people still live in the countries of Algeria, Mali, Niger, Mauritania, Burkina Faso, and Libya.

Some modern Tuareg earn money by making and selling traditional jewelry.

Tuareg A nomadic people of the Sahara in northern Africa.

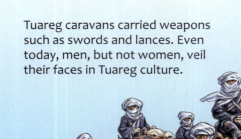
Tuareg caravans carried weapons such as swords and lances. Even today, men, but not women, veil their faces in Tuareg culture.

Central Africa

The area known as Central Africa lies south of the Sahara and on both sides of the equator. This region is sometimes referred to as Middle Africa. It is characterized by smooth plateaus which extend into rugged terrain with high peaks as well as deep gorges. The Congo River flows through Central Africa. In the Congo basin, volcanoes form mountain ranges.

Central Africa has been inhabited for a long time. There are no written records of the earliest people who lived there, but ancient stone tools and knives from the region indicate that people arrived there early in human history. In some areas in Central Africa, people used sophisticated metalworking methods soon after 1000 BC.

The first known writing in Central Africa is from around 3000 BC with an alphabet of between 22 and 30 sounds. The first people to live in the region included Dravidians (people who spoke the language of southern India and northern Sri Lanka), Sumerians, Egyptians, speakers of Niger-Congo languages, and Elamite language speakers.

Copper and salt became important to Central Africa's commerce in the 1500s. People formed small empires to protect themselves and their trade routes.

Sao

The Sao were one of the earliest people groups in Central Africa, dating back to about the sixth century BC. Their civilization was located near the Chari River in what today is part of Cameroon and Chad. Archaeologists have found evidence that the Sao were skilled in metalworking and advanced in the arts.

Pygmies

One prominent feature of the Congo basin is its tropical rainforest, the second largest in the world. **Pygmies**, a people of small stature, lived deep in the rainforest. Moving from place to place, they lived off the land, hunting, fishing, and gathering vegetation. Pygmy tribes still live in Central Africa today. They are often referred to by their specific ethnic names (e.g., Mbuti and Twa). Serious abuses of the human rights of these people have plagued Central Africa into modern times.

Pygmies An African people of small stature who live in the rainforest of the Congo basin.

Today the Mbuti people make beautiful cloth from hand-beaten tree bark and paint it with various designs.

Southern Africa

Bantu

Much of the rest of Africa was settled by the Bantu, who migrated from the Benue River area. They wandered east and south and settled in the Congo basin. The Bantu prospered and their numbers grew. Eventually, the land could support no more villages. Some of the Bantu packed their belongings and moved south once more, all the way to the southern tip of Africa.

Bantu Migration

What route did the Bantu take as they left the Benue River?

The San gather water from the pulp of tubers during the dry season.

The Great Enclosure is the largest structure remaining from the ancient world in southern Africa.

San and Khoikhoi

The Bantu were not the only ones living in Southern Africa. The **San** and Khoikhoi also lived there. When these two groups lost their land to the Bantu, they moved south and west, where they formed small family groups of hunters and gatherers.

Both the San and the Khoikhoi spoke click languages. Click languages have a large number of consonants, many of which are clicking sounds produced by the tongue and the roof of the mouth.

Shona

Some of the first settlers in ancient Zimbabwe were of the **Shona** family. They were ancestors of the modern Shona people who still live in Zimbabwe. They settled near the Zambezi River to have more room to live and to plant crops. They organized themselves into **clans** and built big stone houses called **zimbabwes**.

One city was known as **Great Zimbabwe**. Historians believe this city could have been home to as many as twenty thousand people. All the buildings were built of stone without any mortar. Stone slabs were tightly stacked on top of one another to create a smooth surface. In some places of the ruins, the walls are more than fifteen feet thick and up to thirty-two feet tall.

In the city was a large zimbabwe that historians believe may have been the king's palace. They call it the Great Enclosure. A huge outer wall surrounds the Great Enclosure and is over eight hundred feet long.

The ancient Shona were farmers and raised cattle. They found gold along rivers and streams and traded it for textiles, glass beads, and porcelain. They moved away during the 1400s, but the reason for the move remains a mystery. Many people believe there may have been too many people for the land to support, or the center of trade may have moved farther north.

European Settlers

In the middle of the 1600s, large groups of Europeans came to live in Africa. The Dutch settled on the southern tip of Africa. They set up a station to provide water and food for ships traveling to and from India. People from Great Britain came about 150 years later. Descendants of both the Dutch and the British have lived in South Africa ever since.

San An African people living south of the Sahara.
Shona An African people living in southern Africa.
clan A group of families descended from a common ancestor.
zimbabwe A large stone house built by the Shona.
Great Zimbabwe Ancient African city built of stone by the Shona.

 How do historians divide Africa's early peoples into groups?

What were some common features of cities on Africa's eastern coast?

Eastern Africa
Coastal Cities

The Shona traded their gold on the eastern coast in cities built especially for trade. By the 900s, these cities were controlled by Arabian and Persian merchants who traded with faraway ports in Asia and India. Mogadishu and Sofala were two important trading cities.

The coastal cities were not part of any empire. They were independent. However, they still had certain things in common. For example, most of the cities were predominantly Islamic. They also used the same language, **Swahili**, when conducting trade. Swahili includes many words from Arabic. In fact, the name *Swahili* comes from the Arabic word that means coast. This language is still spoken in parts of eastern Africa today.

As the cities grew, more items became available for trade. In addition to gold, other popular products included ivory, rhinoceros horns, tortoise shells, and animal skins. A Chinese admiral, Zheng He, visited eastern Africa's coastal cities. He reportedly brought back live exotic animals to China, such as giraffes, ostriches, and zebras.

Swahili A Bantu language commonly spoken in eastern Africa.

Trading was not the only occupation along Africa's eastern coast. Fishers, farmers, masons, and builders also lived there. Because so many traders needed boats, boat building was a profitable business. In some of the cities, masons built houses out of coral. Coral could easily be found in reefs along the coast. When it was brought from the ocean and exposed to air, it hardened into a sturdy building material. Only wealthy people could afford to have coral houses.

East African Coastal Trade

What island also had a part in eastern African coastal trade?

What types of goods might these people be loading onto the ships?

What contributed to the development of the Shona civilization in ancient Zimbabwe?

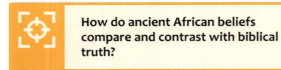

How do ancient African beliefs compare and contrast with biblical truth?

Africa and the Outside World
The Slave Trade

One practice that harmed Africa was the slave trade. Slaves became one of the most prominent exports from Africa. Slavery had long been practiced within Africa itself, and Africans had sometimes traded slaves to Europe and Asia. Yet the international trade of African slaves did not become widespread until the 1600s. As Europeans settled and formed colonies on the continents of North and South America, their desire for slaves increased.

The slave trade had many negative cultural effects on Africa. For example, the African population declined. More than ten million Africans were sold into slavery from the 1400s to the 1800s. Also, because European traders commonly offered guns in exchange for slaves, wars and violence increased. Families were torn apart, and fear reigned. Because the Africans fled from their cities to avoid capture, civilization and culture in many parts of Africa were hindered from growing.

However, much more important than slavery's cultural effects was its moral injustice. Humans are created in God's image (Genesis 1:26–27). Because of this unique position, they have great value. As evidence of that, anyone who committed murder or who kidnapped and sold a person in Old Testament times was to be put to death (Genesis 9:6, Exodus 21:16). In New Testament times, Jesus taught that "all things whatsoever ye would that men should do to you, do ye even so to them" (Matthew 7:12). Slave traders were not treating the Africans the way they would have wanted to be treated themselves. Instead, they chose to harm their fellow image bearers.

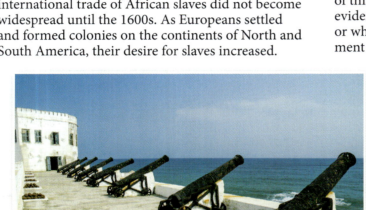

The Cape Coast Castle in Ghana was built for the trade of timber and gold and later used for the slave trade. Look at both pictures. What else was the castle used for?

TRADITIONAL AFRICAN BELIEFS

Until Christianity and Islam were introduced to Africa from other nations, African religion consisted primarily of certain traditional beliefs that varied slightly from tribe to tribe. Africans' religious beliefs influenced every area of their lives. Many Africans still hold these beliefs today.

Most Africans had a concept of a god as a supreme being, but they relied on their tradition to explain what this god was like. They believed he could be worshiped through sacrifices and offerings.

Africans had much interest in the supernatural world. One common belief was that there were spirits who controlled natural forces for good or for evil. Africans worshiped these spirits and tried to please them. They did not want the spirits to use their powers to harm them and their surroundings. Many African religions taught that spirits lived in animals or things in nature such as trees and rivers, a belief known as animism. Africans often relied on a person thought to have magical powers, such as a medicine man or a rainmaker, to connect them with the supernatural world.

Another common belief was that the spirits of departed relatives visited people and influenced their lives. The people gave offerings to these spirits and tried to stay in favor with them.

Unlike traditional African religions, the Bible teaches that there is only one God who controls all things, including the forces of nature, and who alone deserves to be praised (Psalm 107). The Bible also teaches that Christians do not need medicine men or any mediator other than Christ in order to approach God (1 Timothy 2:5).

This Turkana medicine man wears necklaces to protect himself from evil spirits.

Religion

Christianity first came to Africa in the first or second century. It spread in the coastlands and the backcountry along the Mediterranean and the Red Seas. Then in the seventh and eighth centuries, Islam was introduced to North Africa. From there, traders spread the religion to West Africa. Traders coming across the Indian Ocean also converted many in East Africa to Islam.

Despite the strong Islamic presence to the north, however, Christianity began to spread, especially in the central and southern parts of the continent, through the efforts of European missionaries. There have been charges that missionaries helped the governments of Europe exploit native peoples, and it is true that some did. For example, one missionary deliberately mistranslated a document, causing a king in northern Africa to sign away all his land to investors. In another case, a priest deceived an illiterate person into signing a note pledging his allegiance to the king of Portugal when he thought he was signing a thank-you note for a gold-backed chair. Some missionaries were harsh to the Africans or even sold them into slavery.

However, there are also many stories of missionaries who helped the native people. John Mackenzie, missionary to South Africa, helped a native chief protect his land from white settlers. John and Alice Harris, missionaries to the Belgian Congo, brought public attention to abuse of villagers by those involved in the rubber trade. Many missionaries spoke out against the slave trade. They also started schools so that native peoples, both men and women, rich and poor, could read the Bible for themselves. The influence of missionaries like these can be seen today in congregations of African believers.

 How did contact with traders and missionaries influence Africa?

13 ANCIENT JAPAN

FOCUS
Japan rose from seclusion to become a powerful nation.

Yamato period ca. 250–700			Heian period 794–1185		
250	500	750		1000	1250

ca. 645 Taika Reforms
ca. 710 Capital established in Nara

Most likely, when you learned to write, you learned how to print first, and then you began to learn cursive. Perhaps later you even learned some calligraphy, a type of decorative handwriting. In ancient Japan, there were several kinds of writing, or *shodo*, all of them a kind of calligraphy. One style was *kaisho*, a block style of writing with plain symbols. Another style was *sosho*, a sweeping cursive style.

When you write, you probably use a pen or a pencil. In ancient Japan, people wrote with a *fude* (a brush similar to a modern watercolor brush and made from rabbit or raccoon hair) or a *wayo-fude* (a thinner brush of horse or deer hair).

The paper you write on is smooth. The ancient Japanese liked textured paper. It was made by thoroughly soaking bark, husks, or bamboo in water and then draining off the water. When dried, these materials formed a rough, thick paper. The Japanese created ink by rubbing a *sumi* (a stick made of soot and glue scented with cloves or other spices) against a *suzuri* (a rough stone) and adding water.

To the ancient Japanese, writing was an art that produced music without sound. Often, however, musicians were playing actual music nearby.

Miyu is learning kaisho by watching her mother. Yumiko, the other noblewoman, is telling stories of the imperial court. Outside, Miyu's brother Ayumu is copying the moves of a master swordsman. Miyu sometimes wonders if learning to use a sword might be easier than writing. To master kaisho and sosho, she may have to practice every day for more than twenty years.

A *biwa* is a short-necked Japanese lute with silk strings that are plucked with a *bachi*.

Why is so little known about Japan's ancient history?

Located off the northeastern coast of Asia, an ancient tribal people rose to power. The civilization of Japan would help shape modern history. The name *Japan* comes from the Chinese words *jih pŭn*, which mean *origin of the sun*. Japan is an **archipelago**. The four main islands of Japan are **Hokkaido**, **Honshu**, **Shikoku**, and **Kyushu**. For centuries, Japan was isolated from the rest of the world by the Sea of Japan and the Pacific Ocean.

Early History

Little is known of Japan's early history. Like other nations, the Japanese people did not keep records during the early development of their civilization. Like the ancient Greeks and Romans, the Japanese passed down their early history through legends and myths. For centuries, these stories shaped Japan's culture.

One myth tells of how the Japanese believe life began. A god and a goddess dipped a jeweled spear into the ocean. The drops that fell from the spear formed the islands of Japan, where the god and the goddess lived. Their children were the Japanese people. Even today, some of the Japanese believe they are descendants of gods.

archipelago A large group of islands.
Hokkaido Second largest of the four major islands of Japan.
Honshu The largest of the four major islands of central Japan.
Shikoku A southern island of Japan.
Kyushu The southernmost island of the major islands of Japan.

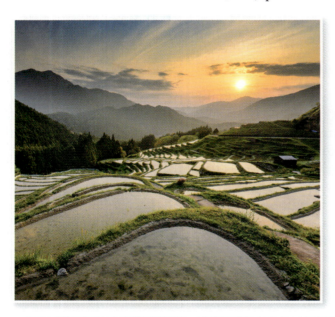

Left: Why do the Japanese sometimes grow rice in terraces?

Above: What might motivate people to hike to the summit of Mount Fuji?

Below: The Iroha Islands are part of Japan's archipelago.

THE REGION TODAY

Japan

Location
Japan is an archipelago of over 6,800 islands in the Pacific Ocean. It is to the east of China and Korea.

Climate
Northern and southern Japan vary in climate. Southern Japan is generally warmer. Average temperatures range from winter lows of 21°F in the north to summer highs of 79°F in the south. Annual precipitation is an average of fifty inches.

Topography
Japan is made up of four main islands and many smaller islands that are the peaks of submerged mountains. The Japanese Alps on the island of Honshu include Mount Fuji, Japan's highest mountain (12,388 ft). Many of Japan's mountains are volcanoes.

Natural Resources
Japan has few natural resources. The mountainous terrain leaves less than 15 percent of land that can be farmed. There are deposits of coal, zinc, copper, lead, and gold. Several short, swift rivers are used to provide electricity and to irrigate rice paddies.

Japan Then & Now

"Flame Rimmed" cooking vessel with cord pattern from the Jomon period. How could this decorative rim be useful?

Another group of immigrants also came to Japan. They mingled with the Jomon. Archaeologists call these immigrants the Yayoi. Some historians believe the Yayoi are the primary ancestors of the Japanese people.

Villages in Japan developed along freshwater sources. The Yayoi borrowed a form of irrigation from the Chinese called wet-paddy farming to grow rice.

Artifacts suggest that the Yayoi were advanced in their craftsmanship. During the middle Yayoi period, artisans continued to make pottery using a clay rope and coiling it upward. The surfaces and edges were smoothed with a tool. Then the pottery was painted red and polished until it was glossy. They also used bronze to create coins, bells, tools, weapons, and mirrors. They also cast iron objects.

Early Settlers

The earliest settlers in Japan likely migrated from northeastern Asia. People have found pieces of pottery that might have been made by these early settlers. Most of this pottery has a cord or rope design. Because there were no potter's wheels, clay was formed into a rope. As the artisan coiled the clay rope upward, the pottery took shape. Some archaeologists have named these early people the Jomon, which means "cord pattern." The Jomon were probably hunters, fishers, and gatherers of plants for food. Excavations suggest that agriculture first developed with the cultivation of rice near the end of the Jomon period.

The Yayoi cast bronze bells with no clappers like this dotaku, which has a height of 43½ inches. What may have been the purpose of a silent bell?

Jomon fishhooks and a harpoon made from bone. What food was a major part of the Japanese diet during the Jomon period?

Clans

By 200 BC, the Japanese people had divided into clans. Each clan had its own warrior chieftain who protected his people from other clans. In return for protection, the people gave part of their rice harvest to the chieftain. Each clan also had its own land and god.

 Why is Japan considered to be an archipelago?

How does Japan's creation myth compare to the Bible's account of Creation?

In what ways did Prince Shotoku shape the culture of Japan?

Yamato Period

Around AD 250, the **Yamato** clan rose to power over rival clans and formed strong military states. The Yamato clan established imperial rule. They developed organized cities, social classes, and a written language. The Yamato were influenced by the Chinese and the Koreans. As people traded, Japan borrowed Chinese and Korean concepts.

Part of the Yamato period was also known as the Kofun period, named after giant tomb mounds called **kofuns**. The aristocracy during this period built magnificent kofuns to show their wealth and power. These tombs had keyhole-shaped burial mounds. The keyhole-shaped kofun of Nintoku was longer than five football fields. From the excavation of the kofuns, scholars can learn much about the ancient Japanese culture.

Tomb of Emperor Nintoku is part of a kofun. What does the design in the center of the tomb look like?

The Imperial Rule

The Yamato chose one man to be their emperor. They claimed that their emperor was a descendant of **Jimmu Tenno**. According to legend, Jimmu Tenno was the first emperor and a descendant of the sun goddess, Amaterasu. For this reason, Tenno was to be worshiped. By claiming a relationship to Jimmu Tenno, the Yamato gained the loyalty of other clans.

The ruling family of Japan came from the Yamato clan. It remained the only imperial family for many years. The emperors continued to claim that Jimmu Tenno was their ancestor.

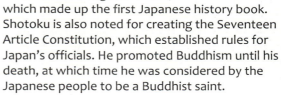

PRINCE SHOTOKU

What: crown prince
When: AD 573–622
Where: Japan

At an early age, Shotoku was schooled in Buddhism and Confucianism. Both influenced him greatly when he served as prince of Japan. During his reign, Shotoku sent ambassadors to China to learn about Chinese culture, economy, and politics. He brought Chinese artists, craftspeople, and clerks into Japan. Shotoku used the Chinese calendar. He built Buddhist temples and made a network of roads. He developed irrigation systems and was involved in the welfare of the people. Shotoku put together the chronicles of the government, which made up the first Japanese history book. Shotoku is also noted for creating the Seventeen Article Constitution, which established rules for Japan's officials. He promoted Buddhism until his death, at which time he was considered by the Japanese people to be a Buddhist saint.

The Japanese admired Chinese achievements. One of these achievements was a strong system of government. The Japanese wanted such progress in their own land. Prince **Shotoku** developed a constitution that became the basis of the imperial government of Japan. He also encouraged his people to accept the Chinese religion and way of life.

Yamato A Japanese clan that rose to power around AD 250.

kofun A giant tomb with a keyhole-shaped burial mound surrounded by a moat; built by the Japanese aristocracy during the Yamato dynasty.

Jimmu Tenno Mythical Japanese ancestor who was believed to be the first Japanese emperor.

Shotoku Became the Japanese crown prince and regent in 573.

Japanese followers of Shintoism visit a shrine like this one to pay respects to the kami and to pray for good fortune.

Buddha's image is enshrined in the Kondo, the main sanctuary of the Buddhist temple. The five-story pagoda holds relics and is used for ceremonies and as a place to give thanks.

Religion

The main religion of Japan was **Shintoism**. *Shinto* means the way of the gods. This religion is a form of nature worship. It teaches that every object or creature in nature has a spirit that should be worshiped as a god. These gods, or nature spirits, are called **kami**. The most important kami is the sun goddess, Amaterasu. A kami can be in an inanimate object such as a rock or an animate object such as a bird. The Shintoists worship these objects, called *shintai*, in a shrine. Shintoism is still practiced in Japan today.

In addition to Shintoism, Buddhism was practiced in Japan. Prince Shotoku is credited for spreading this second religion. He sent students to China to learn about Buddhism and encouraged the Japanese to practice it. Several Buddhist temples were built throughout Japan. Many Japanese practiced a mixture of both Shintoism and Buddhism.

Shintoism A form of nature worship; the main religion of Japan.

kami The gods or nature spirits of Shintoism.

SHINTO BELIEFS

Shintoism teaches that the main problem with the world is that humanity is out of harmony with nature. By practicing Shinto rituals, people can develop a connection with the kami, the spirits in nature. This connection will bring about prosperity and harmony in this life.

In contrast with Shintoism, Christianity identifies sin as the main problem with the world. Sin disrupts people's relationships with each other, with creation, and with God. In addition, the Bible teaches that there is only one God. Other spirit beings, such as angels, exist. But they are not tied to features of the natural world. They are different from the Shinto idea of kami. Christianity teaches that a truly prosperous life involves being made right with God by having sins forgiven. This may bring suffering in the present. But in eternity, God will set right all that is wrong with the world.

This torii gate is located at the Itsukushima Shrine in Hiroshima, Japan.

WRITING IN CALLIGRAPHY

Calligraphy was introduced to the Japanese by Buddhist missionaries from China. Chinese calligrapher **Wang Xizhi** is credited for being the father of this art form. The Japanese adapted the Chinese characters to the Japanese language.

Japanese calligraphy is called *shodo*. One style of shodo is called *kaisho*, which means correct writing. This is a formal block style used in most publications in Japan, such as newspapers and magazines. Another style is called *gyosho*, which means traveling writing. Students use this semicursive style to write notes. A third style, *sosho*, means grass writing. This is a flowing cursive style used in formal Japanese calligraphy.

Left: Empress Komyo's copy of Wang Xizhi's work from 744. Why is Japanese calligraphy more than just writing?

Below: A young boy wearing a yukata uses a bamboo brush and ink to practice shodo on rice paper.

Buddhist missionaries from China were sent to Japan and had a significant influence. Many were scholars and teachers. They taught the Japanese how to read and write Chinese, study Chinese literature, and create art in the Chinese style. The missionaries also brought new customs and new styles of clothing. Later, many Japanese traveled to China to study in the Buddhist schools.

This print shows a woman using a shuttle and a loom to make material. How does she operate the loom? What kind of thread might she be using?

Government

The Yamato emperor controlled the government. He chose people from the most powerful families to help him govern the many clans. Positions passed from officials to their sons. The government paid officials by giving them control over land and farmers.

About AD 645, a time of political and economic changes came to Japan and was known as the Great Change or the **Taika Reforms.** The leaders of Japan wanted to weaken the influence of the clan chieftains. They modeled their changes in the Japanese government after the strong, centralized Chinese government. The Japanese established a civil-service examination. Governmental positions were given to trained officials. Many of these officials were educated in China. New laws were established and a tax system was put in place. Clan chieftains no longer collected the taxes. Instead governmental officials gathered the taxes for the emperor.

Taika Reforms A series of changes in the Japanese political and economic structure around AD 645; known as the Great Change.
calligraphy The art of fine handwriting.
Wang Xizhi Chinese calligrapher; credited by some as the Father of Calligraphy.

 How does Shintoism contrast with biblical truth?

In what ways was the court the center of culture and learning?

Heian Period

The Japanese government established a permanent capital at **Nara** in 710. Nara had broad streets, governmental offices, and large public squares. Later, the capital was moved to **Heian-kyo**. Today Heian-kyo is the city of Kyoto.

After the capital was moved to Heian-kyo, the Heian period followed. It was named after the capital city and was a time of peace and security. Japan began to develop a culture independent of the Chinese during this time.

Life at the Court

The nobles who followed the emperor to Heian-kyo lived near him to win his favor. This group of nobles, known as the **imperial court**, served or advised the emperor. Life at the imperial court demanded strict rules of behavior. Court **etiquette** included proper actions and responses for all activities, whether accepting a piece of food or meeting the emperor. A person at the court was also supposed to have composure and not demonstrate emotions. Those who did not follow these rules were not welcome at court.

The nobles of the court loved beauty and elegance, and many supported the arts. The court became the center of culture and learning. The Heian period was the golden age of the arts in ancient Japan.

The love of beauty by the nobles included their own appearance. The nobles loved elaborate outfits. For example, the women wore long gowns of twelve layers of colored silk. As the wind blew, the various colors showed in shifting patterns. Both men and women wore makeup. They blackened their teeth because white teeth were considered ugly.

Nobles often carried decorative fans. The fans were painted with flowers, trees, and birds. Some fans had flowers and long silk cords attached to them.

Nara Japan's first capital city.
Heian-kyo The capital city of Japan after Nara; present-day Kyoto.
imperial court A group of nobles who live near, serve, and advise the ruler.
etiquette Proper actions and responses that are expected in society; manners.

The aristocracy of the Heian court sought refinement in behavior, art, and literature.

Located in Uji, Japan, this monument shows Murasaki Shikibu, the author of *The Tale of the Genji*.

This modern woodcut print shows a snow scene from *The Tale of the Genji*. A woman is brandishing a broom, and a man is carrying an umbrella.

Language

During the Heian period, the Japanese nobles were restrained in how they spoke and wrote, being careful not to offend anyone. Chinese was the official language used by the imperial court. Japanese scholars spent many years learning Chinese.

Although the Japanese had a spoken language, they did not have a written language of their own. The Japanese began to use Chinese characters to represent the pronunciation and meaning of the Japanese oral language. The Japanese began to use only phonetic syllables in their writing system. Two types of characters were developed by making some Chinese characters simpler and by abbreviating others. These scripts made it possible to write Japan's national language.

Literature

Writing was popular among the nobles, especially among the women. Since the women were not trained in Chinese writing as the men were, women wrote in the common Japanese language. They spent their leisure time writing about their experiences in the imperial court. Most of the literature that has survived the Heian period was written by women.

One of the greatest writers in early Japan was Lady **Murasaki Shikibu**. As a lady at the court, she wrote what has been called the world's first true novel. Her six-volume *The Tale of the Genji* tells the story of Prince Genji, his life at court, and his countless loves. A modern edition of the novel fills over four thousand pages.

Poetry was an important part of Japanese culture. To be accepted in Heian society, a person had to write poetry. One type of Japanese poem that is still popular today is the haiku. **Haiku** is a verse form with seventeen syllables and a *kigo*. A kigo is a word that hints at the season in which the poem takes place. The words in a haiku are chosen according to meaning and syllables. The poet tries to develop a mood and a picture with the words.

Murasaki Shikibu Japanese author who wrote what is considered to be the world's first novel; a lady of the Japanese court.

haiku A type of Japanese poem that has a verse form with seventeen syllables and an aspect of nature or seasons.

The Imperial crest of the emperor on a gate of a shrine in Tokyo, Japan. Why might the emperor have chosen the chrysanthemum for the imperial seal?

How do this modern building and its surroundings reflect Heian forms of art and architecture?

Arts and Architecture

Even though Chinese art influenced Japanese art and architecture, the Japanese still developed their own artistic patterns. One characteristic of Japanese art was its use of brilliant colors. Bright colors made paintings full of life and activity. In architecture, colors were used to decorate houses and temples. A second characteristic of Japanese art was its use of everyday objects. Artists made and painted objects such as fans, combs, boxes, baskets, and carved furniture. These objects were beautiful as well as useful.

The Japanese also liked to arrange flowers. *Ikebana* was an art form that involved flower arranging. Colors and types of flowers were chosen carefully to match the occasion and the season. For example, chrysanthemums were used in the month of May, and a chrysanthemum festival was held every year. One emperor visited the imperial flower garden during a May festival to enjoy its beauty. He adopted the chrysanthemum for his official seal and crest. This seal and crest are still official today.

The nobles of Heian-kyo worked to make their city beautiful. They admired Chinese architecture and modeled Heian-kyo after Changan, a Chinese city. They copied Chinese building styles, especially those of temples. For other buildings, the nobles liked simple, airy designs. To add beauty to these buildings, the nobles surrounded them with elegant gardens and ponds.

 What art characteristics are unique to Japan?

ACTIVITY

Writing a Haiku

The poet Matsuo Basho is credited for making haiku a popular form of poetry. He traveled the Japanese countryside to gain inspiration for his writings.

1. Go outside and look at the surroundings. Choose an object or a scene to describe in the haiku.
2. Write a haiku with five syllables in the first line, seven syllables in the second line, and five syllables in the last line. The lines of haiku are unrhymed. Include a word or an idea that lets the reader know what season the haiku is taking place in.
3. Illustrate the haiku.

Celebration
Leaves sprinkle the grass
Confetti tangled in hair
Fall hosts a party

How did the Fujiwara family rise to power?

Religion

During the Heian period, religion was a part of everyday life. The Japanese blended Shintoism with Buddhism. Often Shinto shrines were constructed near or on the property of Buddhist temples. The Japanese began combining the divine beings of Buddhism with the Shinto gods. They worshiped at Shinto shrines to obtain help for their daily lives. They worshiped in Buddhist temples to prepare for the life to come. Religion shaped Japanese culture and affected art, architecture, and education.

The Main Hall at Heian Jingu Shrine stands as part of the recreated Imperial Palace of Heian-kyo. Emperor Kanmu is enshrined here for relocating the capital from Nara to Kyoto, along with Emperor Komei, who was the last emperor to rule from Kyoto. Why did the Japanese enshrine emperors?

Government

During the Heian period, Japan's central government was strong. But it would soon be challenged. Instead of the emperor being in authority, the key posts in government came to rest in the hands of powerful families. One family, the **Fujiwara**, sought to control the government. They had their daughters marry the sons of the imperial family. The Fujiwara would then persuade the reigning emperor to give up his throne to an heir born to one of these daughters. The Fujiwara then ruled as **regents** for the child emperor. As regents, this family held much influence at court.

In addition to the regents, aristocrats helped run the country. These aristocrats were assigned a rank in order to hold an office in government. The emperor held the highest rank. Nobles who served as ministers of state were in second or third place. The fourth or fifth rank was filled by young nobles and some who governed provinces. Other government workers such as clerks, administrators, and those with specialized skills made up the lower ranks. When a political office became available, the aristocrats used various means, including bribery, to win a position in government. Women were able to receive rank but were not appointed to government positions. However, women were important and held power at court, influencing decisions on who was appointed to a government office.

These seventeenth-century Japanese screen panels depict battles during the Gempei Wars. What forms of battle are shown?

The Fujiwara family controlled the Japanese government from 794 to 1185, a large portion of the Heian period. The family became wealthy and powerful. But the Fujiwara also brought corruption to the government. By 1156, the country was in a civil war. After almost thirty years of fighting, the power struggle ended with the rule of Japan shifting to military officials who were landowners in the provinces. A warrior clan, the Genji, defeated a rival clan, the Heike. The Genji created a government run by military generals. Although the line of the imperial family continued, the emperor did not have significant power. This brought in the feudal age of Japan.

Fujiwara A Japanese family who gained power by marrying into Japan's imperial family.

regent A person who rules in place of a rightful ruler who is unable to fulfill the duties because of age, illness, or other reasons.

 How did the Japanese practice religion during the Heian period?

Evaluate the Heian period as a time of peace and security.

LIFE IN

Organized Cities and Government
During the Heian period, the court experienced an extended time of political strength and peace. After a while, the Fujiwara family began to control the imperial family. Later, political power shifted to military leaders.

Justice
Certain marriage practices led to injustice. The Fujiwara family controlled the royal line by marrying their daughters to imperial heirs. In this way, the Fujiwara family was able to attach itself to the imperial family to gain power.

Social Classes
Aristocrats were assigned a rank in society. The emperor held the highest position. The second or third ranks were made up of the highest nobles who served as ministers of state. The fourth or fifth rank were young nobles and some members of the ruling class in the country. The clerks, skilled workers, and bureaucrats comprised the lower ranks.

Environment
Heian-kyo was established on Honshu Island. It was located on a fertile plain with rivers. The area was good for rice and silk farms. Mountains in the north and several rivers were natural barriers for defense. The climate included hot summers with cold winters.

Religion
Shintoism and Buddhism became common, and some people practiced a mixture of the two religions.

Heian-kyo reflected Chinese influence in its orderly grid design that covered ten square miles.

The Heian palace was an imperial residence and administrative center.

HEIAN-KYO

Arts, Sciences, and Written Language

The Japanese practiced Chinese art but also developed their own art forms characterized by the use of brilliant colors and depictions of everyday objects. The Japanese created a special art form by arranging flowers.

The Japanese used simple, airy designs for buildings and encircled them with elegant gardens and ponds.

Most literature was written by noblewomen and was in the common Japanese language.

Citizenship

The elite made up a small part of the population and lived in luxury. Those without rank, such as peasants, merchants, and craftspeople, paid taxes to the government and taxes to the landlords.

Key Themes of Civilization
- Justice
- Power
- Citizenship
- Environment

Features of a Civilization
- Organized cities and government
- Social classes
- Job specialization
- Arts, sciences, and written language
- Religion

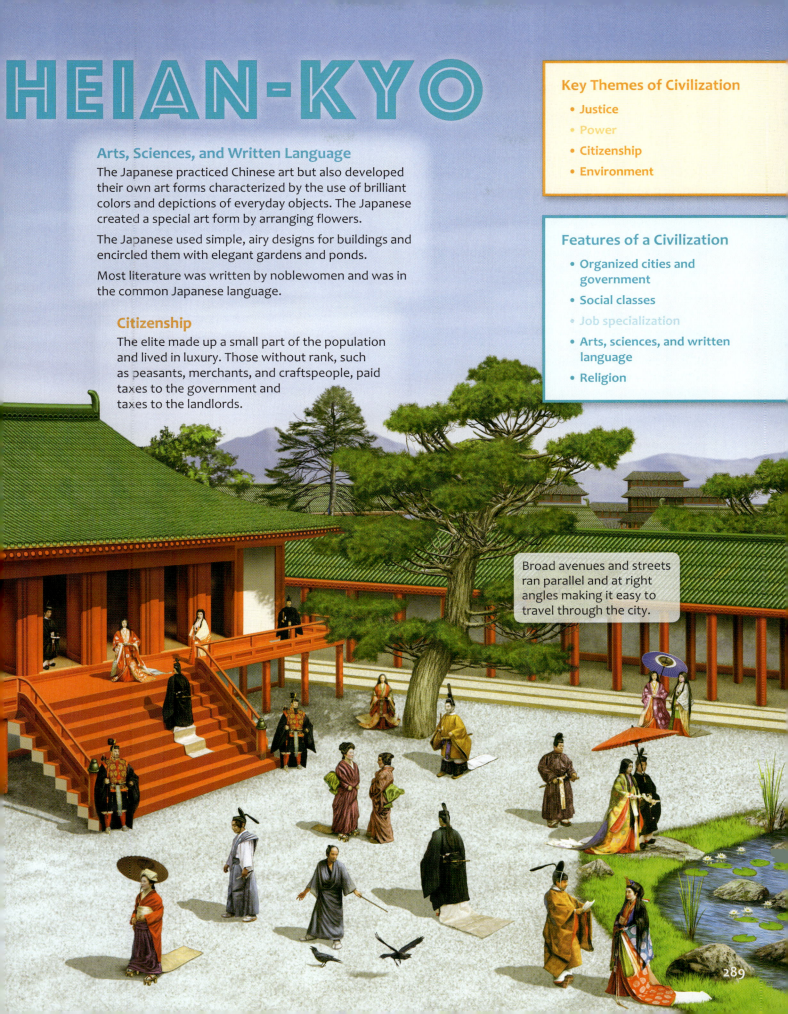

Broad avenues and streets ran parallel and at right angles making it easy to travel through the city.

What was the Japanese feudal system?

Feudal Japan

During the late Heian period, **feudalism** developed. The ruler divided the land among the nobles, who then subdivided it among the peasants, all in exchange for loyalty and allegiance.

At the top of the Japanese feudal system were the emperor, his family, and the military leader. The emperor was the religious leader but had little political power. The military leader, called the **shogun**, was chosen by the emperor and given supreme political power.

In 1192 **Yoritomo**, the leader of the Minamoto clan, was appointed as the first shogun for winning the war among the clans. He became the supreme military leader of Japan and set up his government from the city of Kamakura. This military government was known as a *shogunate*. Shoguns continued to rule for the next seven hundred years, while the imperial emperor had little power but was still the official ruler.

This copy of an 1179 hanging silk scroll, credited to Fujiwara no Takanobu, is a color portrait of Minamoto no Yoritomo, Japan's first shogun.

FEUDAL SOCIETY	
Emperor & shogun	The emperor had little governmental power. The shogun ruled in the emperor's name.
Daimyo	The daimyo were powerful warlords or chief nobles.
Samurai	The samurai were warriors who served the shogun and the daimyo.
Peasants	There were several subclasses of peasants. The farmers were the highest ranking. The artisans came next, and the merchants were last.

Next in the feudal system were the **daimyo**, the chief nobles or powerful warlords. The daimyo had military and economic power to rule their lands. They also had armies to protect their lands and the workers on them. The most powerful daimyo often became shoguns.

The daimyo's armies were made up of **samurai**, the next feudal class. The samurai warrior mastered the skills of horsemanship, fencing, archery, and *jujitsu* (a form of self-defense that uses no weapons). The samurai worked under the daimyo. It was a samurai's duty to protect the daimyo. A samurai had additional privileges that included being able to have a surname, a family crest, and the right to carry two swords. The samurai lived by a strict code of conduct called the *Bushido Code* which demanded loyalty, honor, duty, justice, courage, sincerity, and politeness.

The last class of the Japanese feudal system was the peasants. The peasants were divided into several subclasses. The highest-ranking peasants were the farmers. If a farmer owned his own land, he had a higher position than a farmer who did not own land. Farmers were highly valued because they produced the food. They paid taxes by giving a percentage of their crops to the government or to the daimyo.

The artisans were in the next peasant subclass. They made products from metal and wood for the other classes. These products included tools for the farmers, fishhooks and anchors for the fishers, and swords and other weapons for the samurai.

---

feudalism A system of organizing and governing society based on land and service.

shogun A Japanese military leader with the most political power in the government; chosen by the emperor.

Yoritomo Leader of the Minamoto clan; the first shogun, the supreme military leader of Japan; set up a military government called the shogunate.

daimyo Chief Japanese nobles or powerful warlords who had military and economic power to rule over their lands.

samurai A Japanese warrior whose duty was to protect the daimyo; a master of horsemanship, fencing, archery, and jujitsu.

Samurai were part of the warrior class.

The kabuto protected the skull while the hinged menpo attached to the helmet protected the face and looked formidable to the enemy.

The ni-mai-do, a two-pieced breastplate, had lacquered leather strips of armor that were laced together with silk.

Shoulder guards called sode were attached to sleeves called kote. Both were made of plates and mail.

The samurai carried two swords, the katana and the wakazashi. Together, the swords were called the daisho meaning "big and small."

The samurai wore haidate made of chain mail to protect the thighs along with suneate made of leather, mail, and metal plates to protect the lower legs.

In this colored woodblock print by Utagawa Kuniyoshi, a Mongol Buddhist monk calms the typhoon. How did the typhoon contribute to the defeat of the Mongols?

This Japanese scroll painting depicts farmers paying taxes to the daimyo. What method did the farmers use to pay their taxes in rice?

The last peasant subclass was made up of merchants. They were the lowest ranking because they relied on others for their livelihood. Traders and shopkeepers were part of this subclass.

The early Japanese people had been mainly fishers and hunters. Other jobs and trades developed as the needs in society increased.

The Mongols

In the late 1200s, a people from China called the Mongols tried to attack Japan twice. The shoguns were strong enough to turn back both invasions. In the second invasion, the Japanese samurai fought the Mongols, who attacked twice before a typhoon swept across the Sea of Japan. Much of the Mongol fleet was destroyed, and many Mongols drowned. Others were slain by the samurai. As a result, the Mongol invasion failed. The Japanese named the strong storm *kamikaze*, meaning "divine wind." The Japanese believed that spirits had sent the kamikaze.

The Japanese victory over the Mongols drained Japan's treasury. The samurai resented the government when they were not paid. The shoguns began to lose their power. Over the next five hundred years, power struggles continued, and the country once again isolated itself from the rest of the world.

 What determined a person's position in the peasant subclasses?

Describe the Japanese defeat of the Mongols.

14 THE MIDDLE AGES IN EUROPE

FOCUS

The fall of the Western Roman Empire in AD 476 led to a period in which nobles had much control over their local regions and kings had to rebuild their power.

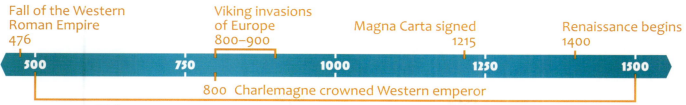

Do you have coins with you today? Even if you have only one, you have more than Bernard. Bernard's father has gotten a fair price for the goods they have brought to the village. They are usually paid in *deniers* (small silver coins similar in worth to American pennies) or in *sous*, which are equal to twelve deniers. The largest unit of money is the *livre*, equal to twenty sous—but Bernard has never seen a livre.

Bernard and his sister Emma wait while their father gives a tithe to the priest. The priest tells of Vikings burning villages to the north. Even churches are being robbed. He is taking the one book he has to hide in a sturdy chest under lock and key.

After setting aside rent for the lord of their manor, the family had just enough money to buy a chicken. They typically eat dark rye bread and pottage, a stew of vegetables and grain they grow around their cottage.

For Bernard, the future looks much the same as his father's—a life of farming in service to the lord of the land—unless he can somehow earn enough money to buy his freedom or escape and remain uncaptured for a year.

Deniers were the first Frankish coins made of silver. These deniers were minted during the time of Charles the Bald.

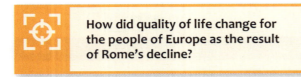

How did quality of life change for the people of Europe as the result of Rome's decline?

The Medieval Period

The Western Roman Empire began to weaken around AD 400. Northern tribes that had often challenged the empire finally prevailed and swept through the empire, conquering its cities. By 476, the great empire had been replaced by small kingdoms governed by military heroes. In that year, the first non-Roman took over as ruler of Italy.

followed a teaching called **Arianism**, a belief that God the Son is separate from and lesser than God the Father. Christian leaders had already condemned Arianism as heresy.

Once their warriors had conquered Roman lands, the Germanic rulers quickly adopted the beliefs of the Roman Catholic Church. In this way, the rulers could gain support from the local people and from the church leaders. The conquering rulers gradually added Roman law to their culture.

As the Western Roman Empire fell apart, the quality of life in most of Europe began to decline. Roads became overgrown with weeds, trade stopped, and cities stood in ruins. People built isolated

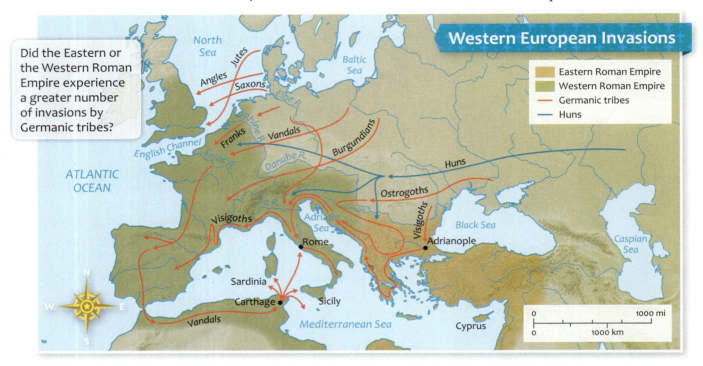

Did the Eastern or the Western Roman Empire experience a greater number of invasions by Germanic tribes?

After the fall of the Western Roman Empire, Europe entered an era known as the **medieval** period. The word *medieval* comes from two Latin words: *medius*, meaning "middle," and *aevum*, meaning "age." Many people refer to this period as the **Middle Ages**. Historians consider the medieval world as a bridge between the ancient world and the modern world.

Roman Lands in Other Hands

Even before the Western Roman Empire fell completely, the Roman Catholic Church had begun to grow more powerful in the West. It even helped negotiate the safety of Roman citizens with the invaders. In many parts of the Roman Empire, the only source of law and authority among Roman citizens was the local bishop.

Many of the invading Germanic rulers had already converted to a form of Christianity. But they

villages and worked hard to grow food for their families. Invaders brought disorder and destruction. Many people lacked time or money for education.

The people of the former Roman Empire needed a place to turn to for leadership. Without an emperor to guide them, many turned to local leaders and to the Roman Catholic Church.

medieval Of or relating to the Middle Ages.
Middle Ages The historical period beginning after the fall of the Western Roman Empire; AD 476–1400.
Arianism Belief that God the Son is separate from and lesser than God the Father.

 How did the Roman Catholic Church become influential in the Western Roman Empire?

THE REGION TODAY

Europe

Location
Europe is bordered by the Arctic Ocean to the north, the Atlantic Ocean to the west, the Mediterranean Sea to the south, and the Ural Mountains to the east.

Climate
Europe's climate has great variety. It ranges from polar conditions (harsh winters and cool summers) along the Arctic Ocean to subtropical ones (warm summers and mild winters) along the Mediterranean Sea. Western Europe is influenced by the Gulf Stream, a warm ocean current that originates in the Gulf of Mexico and moderates temperatures along the western European coast. The average annual rainfall in Europe is 20–60 inches. Average winter temperatures range from -3°F to 13°F in Ufa, Russia. Average summer temperatures range from 73°F to 89°F in Athens, Greece.

Topography
Europe includes icy tundra in the north, mountainous regions in the south, and lush farmland in the east and the west. Europe's islands include Great Britain, Ireland, Iceland, Cyprus, Crete, and Sicily. Bodies of water include the Caspian Sea, Baltic Sea, North Sea, Black Sea, and Mediterranean Sea. Mount Elbrus is Europe's highest point. The Caspian Sea is Europe's lowest elevation.

Natural Resources
Europe has large oil, coal, and natural gas reserves. Other resources include uranium deposits, timber, peat, potash, zinc, and copper. Europe also has a well-developed fishing industry.

Europe Then & Now

How did the Carolingian Empire compare in size to the Merovingian Kingdom?

295

How did the teachings of the church change during the Middle Ages?

The Roman Catholic Church

Church Leadership

The patriarch of the Roman Catholic Church was called the pope, a title that comes from the Latin word for father. He gradually extended his leadership over the church in all of Western Europe. Most Europeans followed his teachings. Underneath the pope were bishops, who acted as leaders within districts. The pope and the bishops directed the activities of the **clergy** during the Middle Ages.

Some clergymen lived among the people. They ministered as priests in the churches. They led the services and instructed people in how to live and worship. The priests preserved and developed many of the doctrines that Christians hold even today. However, over time, the priests taught that the church and its leaders had a role in salvation. Many of them began to teach that people could not receive God's grace without the help of a priest. They also taught that, to be saved, people had to participate in certain religious ceremonies called **sacraments**.

Other clergymen called **monks** lived in large **monasteries**. Many monks vowed to never marry and instead to devote their lives to serving the Roman Catholic Church. One famous monk was **Benedict**. He founded a monastery and wrote a set of rules for monks to follow. This set of rules was called the Benedictine Rule.

During the early Middle Ages, monasteries were the primary places where education and art were valued. Literature, science, mathematics, and medicine were not often taught to the common people. But some monks learned to read and write. These monks spent hours copying the Scriptures and the writings from the early centuries of the church. They bent over their desks, scratching with quill pens for hours at a time. The word *clerical*, describing office work, can be traced to this task of clergymen in the Middle Ages.

Another group of clergymen was the **friars**. *Friar* comes from a Latin word for brother. Like the monks, friars dedicated their lives to service. Neither monks nor friars owned property. However, friars were different from monks in several ways. Friars did not live in monasteries. Instead, they lived among the people and were traveling ministers. They had simple lives and often begged for food. Friars wore plain robes, and some did not wear shoes. A friar's main goal was to teach people how to live good lives.

Some women also devoted their lives to the church. These women who took religious vows were called **nuns**. Nuns lived in convents. They took vows to live lives of poverty, chastity, and obedience to the church.

clergy People ordained as religious leaders.

sacrament A religious ceremony believed to provide grace for salvation.

monk A clergyman who lives a secluded life of devotion and service to the church.

monastery A large, secluded dwelling where monks live and work.

Benedict Key monastic leader; wrote a set of rules for monks to follow.

friar A clergyman who lives among the people, lives simply, owns no property, and teaches people how to live good lives.

nun A member of a women's religious order who lives a secluded life of devotion and service to the church.

BENEDICT

What: Italian monk
When: AD 480–547
Where: Italy

Benedict grew up in a wealthy Roman family and was well educated. As a young man, he withdrew from the corruption in Roman society and began life as a hermit. A friend supplied him with food and clothing, allowing Benedict to focus on prayer and holy living.

About three years later, Benedict founded the Monte Cassino monastery in the mountains near Rome. He developed the Benedictine Rule, which provided a set of instructions for living as a monk. It became the model for most other monasteries in Western Europe. Monks were urged to vary their daily routine with prayer, work, and the study of Scripture and other writings. At this time, some monks would harm their bodies in an attempt to rid themselves of sin. But Benedict instructed monks to get enough food and sleep to live healthy lives.

ROMAN CATHOLIC BELIEFS

The Roman Catholic Church teaches that baptism is needed to remove the sin that all people have as descendants of Adam. Baptism is the means by which a person is justified. However, baptized people still are tempted to sin.

The righteousness that comes at baptism is maintained through living rightly and doing penance when one sins. Penance involves sorrow over sin, confession of that sin to a priest, and the doing of deeds that make satisfaction, or compensation, for the sin.

Also, the Eucharist (Lord's Supper) is important for maintaining the salvation begun in baptism. Medieval theologian Peter Lombard wrote, "'By baptism we are cleansed; by the Eucharist we are perfected in the good. . . . The Eucharist restores [us] spiritually.'" [Philipp W. Rosemann, *Peter Lombard*, Great Medieval Thinkers (New York: Oxford University Press, 2004), 150] The Eucharist is viewed as spiritually helpful because it is believed to be a representation of Jesus' sacrifice. People believe the bread changes into the body of Jesus and the wine changes into His blood—though outwardly they still taste and feel like bread and wine.

At the end of the medieval period, those who would later be referred to as Protestants tried to reform the Roman Catholic Church to a true biblical position but were driven out of it. At the heart of the Protestant position was the belief that the teachings of the Roman Catholic Church regarding baptism, penance, and the Eucharist were not found in the Bible. Protestants argued that the Bible teaches that justification comes through faith alone. In addition, when Christians sin, they do not need to do penance for their sin. Christ has paid for their sin already. And although Christians need to repent of their sins and confess them to God, many Protestants concluded they do not need to confess them to a priest. Many Protestants also rejected the claim that Christ's literal body and blood were present in the bread and wine of the Lord's Supper.

THE SACRAMENTS

By the 1200s, the Roman Catholic Church had developed seven sacraments it believed were necessary for receiving the grace needed for salvation.

1. Baptism removes original sin from infants and original sin and all subsequent sins from adults.
2. Confirmation gives the Holy Spirit to strengthen members of the Roman Catholic Church.
3. The Eucharist gives grace to members of the church by presenting them with the literal sacrificed body and blood of Christ in the form of bread and wine.
4. Penance enables people to merit forgiveness for sins committed after baptism.
5. Last rites are given to a seriously ill or dying person to provide forgiveness of sins.
6. Holy orders give priests the power to absolve, or pardon, sin and to conduct the Eucharist.
7. Matrimony gives grace to a husband and wife in marriage to strengthen their union and make it unbreakable.

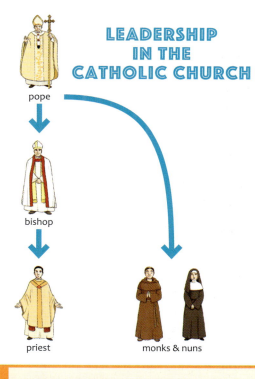

LEADERSHIP IN THE CATHOLIC CHURCH

pope → bishop → priest; bishop → monks & nuns

 Identify the types of clergy in the Roman Catholic Church.

What changes did Charlemagne make in government and learning?

The Franks

Clovis

After the fall of Rome, a people called the Franks invaded Europe. They were a Germanic tribe that came from northeast of the Rhine River. The Franks inhabited the wealthy Roman provinces in Gaul and gained the support of the Roman Catholic Church. They became the most powerful of the Germanic tribes. Over the next several centuries, the Franks formed a kingdom. Their first king was **Clovis**, who conquered the last of the Romans in Gaul. In 507 the Franks successfully drove out the Visigoths from southern Gaul. The conquests of Clovis shaped a nation that would later be called France.

Clovis divided his kingdom among his four sons before his death. His sons and their descendants were called the Merovingian kings. They struggled and plotted against one another, each wanting greater control. The authority of the Merovingians weakened until most of the governmental work was done by their palace officials.

Charles Martel

In the 700s, **Charles Martel** became mayor of the Frankish palace and united the Franks. He became famous for defeating Muslim invaders at Tours in what is now France. This victory kept the rest of Europe free from Muslim rule. Because he was powerful both as a soldier and as a leader, Charles was called *Martel*, which means "the Hammer." The empire that Charles and his descendants ruled became known as the **Carolingian Empire**.

Pepin the Short

After Charles Martel died, his son **Pepin the Short** ruled for ten years as mayor of the palace before becoming the new king of the Franks. Pepin is best known for making an alliance with the Roman Catholic Church.

Before Pepin became king, Pope Stephen II asked him to help defend Rome against the **Lombards**. In exchange for Pepin's help, the pope officially approved Pepin's taking the Frankish crown away from the Merovingians. In a public ceremony, Frankish bishops anointed Pepin with oil, and he received the pope's blessing as king of the Franks.

Pepin defeated the Lombards and gave part of the conquered lands to the church leaders. The church called these lands the **Papal States**; the Roman Catholic Church kept them until the 1800s. Pepin's alliance with the church played a major role in politics and religion for several centuries.

Clovis converted to Christianity after a battle in which he believed he received help from God.

As mayor of the palace of Austrasia, Charles Martel expanded his control over all the Merovingian kingdoms.

The pope anointed Pepin the Short with oil as the prophet Samuel had anointed Saul and David.

Clovis First king of the Franks whose conquests shaped what would later become the French nation.

Charles Martel High official of the Franks who led their army to many great military victories; he and his descendants ruled the Carolingian Empire.

Carolingian Empire The Frankish empire under the rule of Charles Martel and his descendants.

Pepin the Short King of the Franks; son of Charles Martel; gave conquered Lombard lands to leaders of the Roman Catholic Church.

Lombards A Germanic tribe from Scandinavia who migrated to the Italian Peninsula.

Papal States The conquered Lombard lands given to the Roman Catholic Church by Pepin the Short.

Charlemagne

The Carolingian Empire Grows

Pepin's son **Charlemagne** was the greatest of the Carolingian kings. His accomplishments won him the title *Charlemagne*, which means Charles the Great. He reigned for about forty-five years.

Charlemagne defeated many tribes in Europe. Among them were the Saxons and the Lombards, who had again invaded Rome. His military aid to Rome earned him favor with the pope. On Christmas Day in AD 800, Pope Leo III crowned Charlemagne emperor, reviving the Western Roman Empire.

Charlemagne extended the Frankish kingdom to be greater in size than ever before. It became an empire that included most of western Europe. Charlemagne divided his lands into small districts, each having several **manors**. Each manor was controlled by a lord and farmed by peasants. Manors sent Charlemagne yearly reports on their workers, production, and resources. Charlemagne regularly checked on local officials to make sure their methods of rule were just.

A Love for Learning

Under Charlemagne's rule, the importance of learning expanded throughout the empire. Believing in the value of education, Charlemagne invited scholars to his royal court to study and to train others. With the help of these scholars, Charlemagne started schools for boys from both noble and poor families. The students studied reading, writing, mathematics, and astronomy.

Although he enjoyed studying, Charlemagne struggled to read and write. There are accounts of him keeping a tablet and quill beneath his pillow so he could practice in his free time, but he never mastered these skills. However, he did learn how to make mathematical calculations. He was also an excellent speaker, even in the Latin language.

Charlemagne reformed handwriting in his empire. During the Middle Ages, books were

CHARLEMAGNE

What: king of the Franks and first emperor of the Western Roman Empire after the fall of Rome
When: ruled AD 768–814
Where: Frankish Empire/Western Europe

During the first thirty years, Charlemagne's reign was marked by military campaigns. His accomplishments on the battlefield caused him to be known as the Franks' warrior king.

Charlemagne's greatest challenge was a thirty-year campaign against the Saxons. This campaign resulted in the acquisition of land between the Rhine and the Elbe Rivers. Charlemagne carried out other conquests during the Saxon campaign. His military victories allowed him to extend the Frankish kingdom to its greatest size.

Charlemagne was crowned emperor by the pope in AD 800. He used diplomacy and his reputation as the warrior king to promote the Frankish empire as a leader in Europe.

In medieval universities students learned by listening to masters read the texts aloud and then discuss their meaning. Even subjects such as logic and geometry were taught like this.

rare, and those that were available were made by hand in monasteries. Scholars had difficulty reading the handwriting in the books. A church scholar named Alcuin developed a new style of writing that used both small and capital letters. This new style is the basis for many letters of the Roman alphabet, the alphabet that came from Latin and is used for most Western European languages.

Charlemagne's conduct as a ruler was not always ideal. He dealt harshly with those he captured in his military conquests. He married and divorced several wives. But in spite of his faults, Charlemagne was greatly revered by his people. Although the empire did not last long after his death, Charlemagne's accomplishments made him the most memorable of the Frankish kings.

Charlemagne King of the Franks; greatest of the Carolingian kings; extended the Frankish kingdom to its greatest size; crowned by the pope as emperor of the Western Roman Empire.

manor A large farming community during the Middle Ages.

 How did the Carolingian Empire develop?

How did European countries emerge from Charlemagne's empire?

Division of the Frankish Empire

After Charlemagne's death, his son Louis the Pious inherited the empire. But it was too large for him to rule successfully, so it weakened. Wars took place among Louis's three sons: Lothair, Charles the Bald, and Louis the German. The conflicts led to a division of the empire into three parts after the death of Louis the Pious. Each of Louis's sons received a share. Two of these parts formed the basis for two modern European countries: France and Germany. Lothair's part of the empire, located between the territories of his brothers, would be a frequent source of strife between the French and Germans.

At the time of the division, the languages of the Franks in the western and eastern parts of the empire began to change. Western Frankish was developing into French, and eastern Frankish was developing into German. Both French and German are part of the Indo-European family of languages, but French is a Romance language while German is a Germanic one. Romance languages developed out of Latin and are found generally in areas that were ruled by the Roman Empire (places like Italy and Spain). Germanic languages came from tribes who originated in northern Europe. German, Dutch, and English are Germanic languages.

The Franks were a Germanic tribe, but their empire was not consistent in language (Romance language in the west, Germanic in the east). This difference is likely because French territory was once part of the Roman Empire but most German territory was not. However, even though France speaks a Romance language, it shows Germanic influence in some of its pronunciations and words.

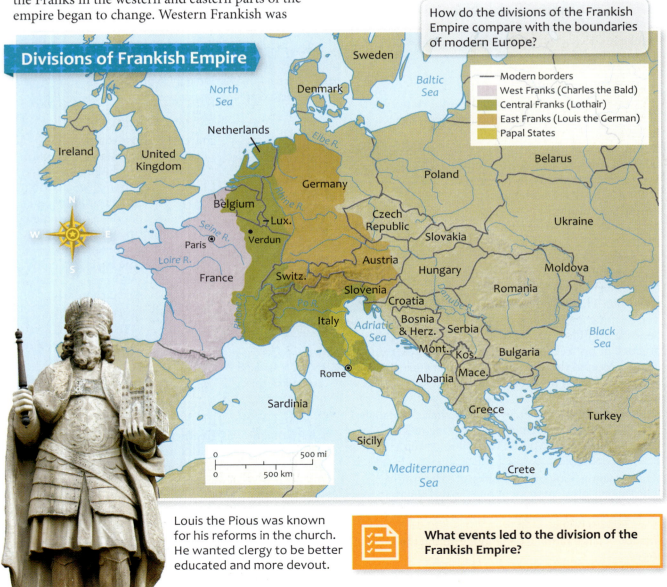

How do the divisions of the Frankish Empire compare with the boundaries of modern Europe?

Louis the Pious was known for his reforms in the church. He wanted clergy to be better educated and more devout.

What events led to the division of the Frankish Empire?

> How were Vikings viewed?

Vikings

The weakened remains of Charlemagne's empire had become prey for invaders. Many of the invaders were from modern **Scandinavia**. These invaders were called the Norse, Norsemen, Northmen, or **Vikings**. The Vikings raided various parts of Europe.

Viking raiders attacked England and then invaded the Franks in Western Europe. They attacked coastal villages, one at a time. Their attacks were sudden and merciless. They were feared by all. These attacks were swift. Armed with spears, the Vikings invaded the village. They killed people, stole gold and jewelry, and destroyed homes and buildings. Then, as quickly as they had come, they shoved offshore and were gone, leaving villages aflame, homes and crops destroyed, and churches and monasteries ransacked.

The Vikings attacked the modern-day countries of Germany, France, Spain, and the United Kingdom. Vikings were among the first Europeans to discover Iceland, Greenland, and the North American Atlantic coast.

Eventually, Viking attacks changed in purpose. Instead of attacking just to raid, they began attacking to conquer and establish new settlements. Their distinctly shaped boats and expert sailing skills allowed them to sail up inland rivers to attack small towns. One group of Vikings established a settlement near the Seine River in what is today northern France. One of the later Carolingian kings made a treaty with their chieftain in 911. This settlement gradually developed into the region that became known as Normandy (for Northmen or Norsemen). Its inhabitants were called Normans. Their descendants were warriors and conquerors and also great administrators and explorers.

Starting in the mid-800s, Danish Vikings began attacking England in order to take the land. After Viking armies won several important military victories, Danish settlers flocked to England to settle a large region that became known as the Danelaw. Though they only briefly established political control over most of England, the Danes left a distinct mark on English culture.

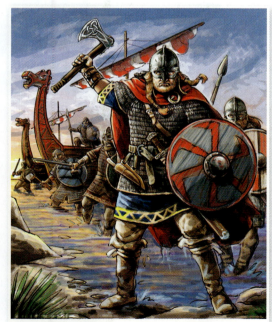

Viking ships used oars for extra speed when preparing to attack a village and used sails when moving across open waters.

NORSE MYTHOLOGY

Like the Greeks and the Romans, the Norse worshiped many gods. The chief Norse god was named Odin. He was the god of war, creation, and the dead. His appearance was that of an old man with a beard and sometimes only one eye. Odin's wife was Frigg, the goddess of the heavens. Under Odin was Thor, the god of thunder. Thor controlled the wind and rain and was the champion of the gods.

The modern names of some days of the week come from the names of Norse gods. Tuesday comes from Tiu, the Anglo-Saxon name for the Norse god of war, Tyr. Wednesday comes from the name for the chief god, Odin, which corresponds to the Anglo-Saxon god Woden (Woden's Day). Thursday is named for Thor (Thor's Day). Friday is named after Frigg.

Odin was often pictured with two wolves (Geri and Freki) and two ravens (Huginn and Muninn).

Scandinavia Region in northern Europe that includes the countries of Sweden, Denmark, and Norway.

Vikings Scandinavians who raided parts of Europe during the Middle Ages; also called Norsemen and Northmen.

> Who were the Normans?

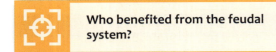

Who benefited from the feudal system?

Feudalism

The people of Europe no longer had a strong central government after Charlemagne's kingdom divided. They passed into a period of feudalism. Under this system, wealthy landowners promised protection in exchange for service. People in Europe were in constant danger of attacks from invaders such as the Vikings, the Muslims, and the Asiatic nomads.

Lords and Vassals

Under the system of feudalism, kings granted estates called **fiefs** to nobles who had performed a service to the king. These nobles were known as **lords**. A lord would then choose nobles who did not own land to manage portions of the fief. These nobles were called **vassals**. In a special ceremony, the vassal knelt before the lord and took an oath of faithfulness, promising loyal service to the lord. Being asked to become a vassal was considered a great honor.

In exchange for the vassal's service, the lord gave the vassal a piece of land. Although the fief still belonged to the lord, the vassal could use that piece of land freely. A vassal could also divide up the land and become a lord over lesser vassals. Divisions of land and loyalties often continued until the fief was the size of an average manor.

Knights

Important to the protection of life and property during the Middle Ages was the **knight**. He wore metal armor from head to foot, and his horse was also heavily armored. He wielded a sword, a lance, and sometimes a battle-axe. He carried a heavy shield to protect himself in battle.

Nearly any nobleman could become a knight if he proved himself worthy. He had to be faithful and skilled in warfare. A boy pursuing knighthood could take the first step at the age of seven by becoming a **page**. As a page, a boy went to live in the home of another noble to learn horsemanship and fighting skills. He also did chores for the lord and the lady of the castle. Around age fourteen, a page became a **squire**, a servant to a knight. His responsibilities then would include helping his master dress,

---

fief A tract of land given by a lord to a vassal.
lord A noble.
vassal A person who pledged loyalty and service to a lord and managed the lord's land in exchange for protection.
knight A soldier who defended a manor during the Middle Ages.
page A boy in the first stage of becoming a knight; lived in a noble's home to learn horsemanship and fighting skills; did chores for the lord and lady.
squire A boy in the second stage of becoming a knight; his responsibilities included helping his master dress, accompanying him on hunts or in battles, and caring for his horse.

One of a page's duties was to serve the lord and his guests at meals.

Dogs were important for protection and assistance in hunting.

accompanying him on hunts or in battles, and caring for his master's horse. A squire continued his lessons in archery, swordsmanship, and lance fighting.

When a squire turned twenty-one, he could become a knight. Sometimes a squire was knighted instantly on the battlefield in recognition of unusual bravery, but most squires received knighthood in a special religious ceremony. The squire spent the entire night praying in the church. The next morning, other knights solemnly dressed him in his armor. The knight knelt before his lord, who touched him on the shoulder with a sword and declared him a knight.

Knights of the Middle Ages promised to live by a strict code of behavior called **chivalry**. This code taught a knight to be generous, loyal to his lord, skillful and brave in battle, faithful to the Roman Catholic Church, protective of the weak and defenseless, and courteous to women.

Sometimes new knights went immediately into battle. When there were no battles going on, groups of knights might participate in **tournaments**. Jousting was one contest where pairs of rival knights met to compete. The goal of a joust was for one knight to knock the other off his horse with a blunt lance.

chivalry A special code of behavior for knights.
tournament An exercise for knights to practice and compete; often included jousting.

Depending on whether it was chain mail or full plates of metal, a knight's armor might weigh between thirty and sixty pounds.

The lady of the manor supervised the household. When the lord was away, she also managed the estate.

The kite shield was often used by cavalry because it covered most of the body but was fairly light.

The word *squire* originally referred to the one who carried the shield.

303

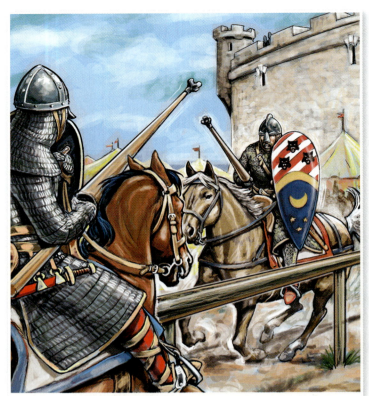

At first, tournaments were full mock battles. Later, jousts were introduced and gradually became more popular.

While a knight was fighting, the best way to identify him was by his **coat of arms**. The coat of arms was the emblem painted on his shield. Each knight had a different coat of arms.

Disadvantages of Feudalism

Although feudalism provided order and protection in a time of upheaval and weak national leadership, it had some distinct disadvantages. First, it lacked the unity of a strong central government and military. This disunity could be felt in practical ways like frequent conflicts between rival lords and their armies. Second, the feudal lords had almost total control over the residents of their manors. In many legal matters, for instance, the lord's decision was final. It could not be appealed to a higher authority. Finally, peasants, the vast majority of people living under the feudal system, had very little freedom and opportunity, although their basic needs might be met.

coat of arms A distinctive emblem that identified a knight in battle; today an emblem that can identify an individual, family, school, or organization.

ACTIVITY

Designing a Coat of Arms

A knight's coat of arms was his own distinct emblem that identified him in battle. A knight would have his coat of arms painted on his shield. Each knight's coat of arms represented him or the family he served. Its symbols and colors had special meanings.

Design a coat of arms. The Internet is a good source for finding examples of various coats of arms.

1. Gather the following materials: blank shield page, markers, paper, ruler, and glue.
2. Decide what color you want your shield to be and color it. Some shields are a solid color; others are divided into parts or checkered. The table lists some common colors in heraldry and their meanings.
3. Choose symbols or a design to include in your coat of arms and draw or glue them in place.
4. Choose a motto for the coat of arms. Design a banner over the top or at the bottom of the shield that displays this motto.

This English coat of arms was actively used during the fifteenth and sixteenth centuries.

Color	Meaning	Color	Meaning	Color	Meaning
gold	generosity	blue	truth, loyalty	purple	justice, royalty
white	peace, sincerity	green	hope, loyal love	orange	worthy ambition
red	military strength	black	constancy, grief	maroon	patience, victory

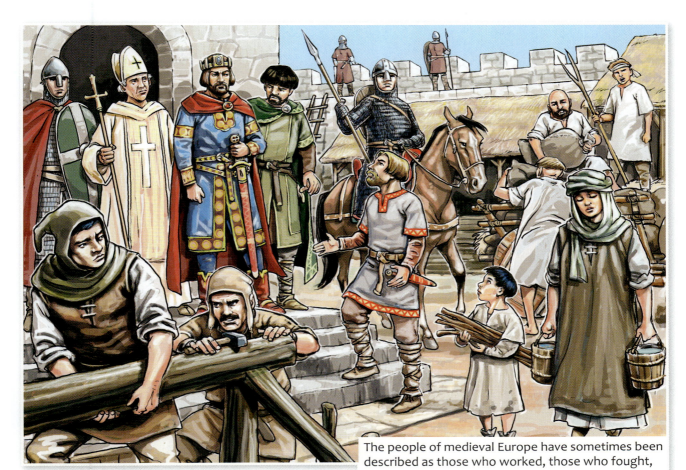

The people of medieval Europe have sometimes been described as those who worked, those who fought, and those who prayed. How would you categorize the people in this scene?

Life on the Manor

The manor was the center of daily life during the Middle Ages. The manor system allowed wealthy nobles to defend their lands and the people living on them. In the early Middle Ages, the lord who owned the manor lived in the manor house, usually a large house made of logs. From about the ninth century on, lords lived in castles. The lord's home was built to offer a place of protection during attacks.

The manor was self-sufficient. It had woods, fishing ponds, and fields for growing grain. Each manor usually had its own priest and skilled workers. Peasants produced their own food and made their own clothing. They grew crops and raised livestock. The manor had a village where the peasants lived. Every manor also had a church. Most people did not have to work on Sundays. People were also released from work on some of the special *holy days* celebrated by the church. The word *holiday* comes from this medieval term.

Most of the peasants living on a manor were **serfs**. They farmed the lord's land, cleared fields, built and repaired buildings, dug ditches, and fixed roads.

The serfs did not have many possessions. They used the lord's mill to grind their grain into flour. They baked their bread in the lord's oven. Often the lord charged them a fee to use these items.

The homes of the serfs were small. Some were only about fifteen feet long and six feet wide. Entire families ate, slept, and lived in the same room. Most serfs shared their homes with their sheep, cows, or pigs. The animals usually stayed in a separate area, partitioned off from the living area. Serfs were bound to the manor all their lives. They could leave only with the lord's permission.

Some peasants on manors were more privileged. They were the **freemen**, skilled craftsmen such as blacksmiths and carpenters. They paid less rent and worked fewer hours for the lord. They were allowed to move from the manor if they wanted to.

serf A peasant who lived on a lord's manor, paid rent to the lord, and worked part-time for him.

freeman A peasant who lived on a lord's manor and specialized in a skill.

 Why did feudalism arise during the Middle Ages?

LIFE IN FEUDAL

Organized Cities and Government
Weak kings could not protect people from invaders, so powerful lords gained control of large tracts of land and provided many of the government functions.

Justice
Manor courts tried minor crimes like property damage and disorderly conduct. Serfs were charged with crimes against the lord; serfs could also sue each other. Witnesses were an important part of the trial process. Jurors made decisions. The lord's representative determined punishments, typically a fine.

Power
Kings and popes challenged each other's authority. Kings claimed sovereignty in their national territory, but popes claimed sovereignty over all Roman Catholics.

Arts, Sciences, and Written Language
Latin was the language of scholarship and was used in church services, in official legal and government documents, and in academic pursuits. In the later Middle Ages, languages spoken by the common people developed in written form, and literature was written for the common people.

Roofs were often thatched with bundles of straw or grass. Some cottages did not have windows or a chimney. Smoke would escape through a small hole in the roof.

FRANCE

Religion
The Roman Catholic Church influenced almost every aspect of life. People were baptized into the church when they were born and were given last rites when they died. They were married by the church. They attended weekly services and paid tithes of their crops. Even leisure time was influenced by the church. Holidays celebrated important Christian events and saints. Medieval drama was designed to improve biblical knowledge. Medieval travel often included pilgrimages to holy sites.

Citizenship
National identity was weak after the breakup of Charlemagne's empire. Since lords provided for people on their lands, tenants felt greater loyalty to the lords than to a country or king.

Key Themes of Civilization
- Justice
- Power
- Citizenship
- Environment

Features of a Civilization
- Organized cities and government
- Social classes
- Job specialization
- Arts, sciences, and written language
- Religion

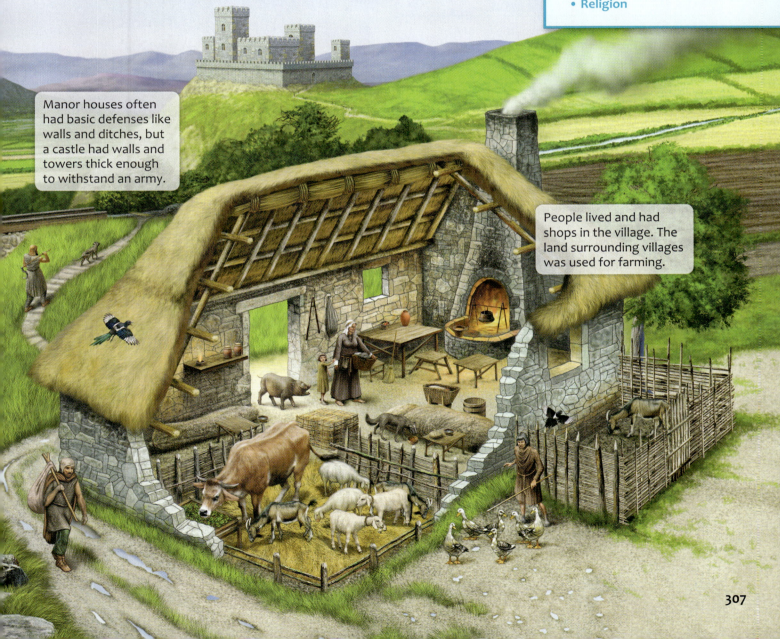

Manor houses often had basic defenses like walls and ditches, but a castle had walls and towers thick enough to withstand an army.

People lived and had shops in the village. The land surrounding villages was used for farming.

307

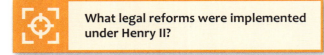

What legal reforms were implemented under Henry II?

Medieval England
The Battle of Hastings

As more nobles obtained land, their social class became more powerful. People looked to them for protection rather than to the king. In 1066 the king of England died without an heir. Two powerful nobles, Harold Godwinson and Duke William of Normandy, both claimed the throne. When Harold set himself up as the next king, William called upon his vassals to provide him with men and supplies to form an army. William and his army then met Harold's forces on a field near the town of Hastings.

Harold, wanting to force William to attack first, placed his men along the top of a hill. Standing side by side with their shields raised, Harold's men formed a wall of shields. William knew his men would have to break through this wall to win the battle.

William and the Norman army surged up the hill toward Harold's men. Shouts rang out and metal clanged as the two armies clashed. William's army attacked the wall again and again. Late in the afternoon, the Norman army finally broke through. Harold was killed in the fierce struggle, and his army fled soon afterward. This conflict became known as the **Battle of Hastings**.

William was now the king of England. He chose some of his own men to be lords, replacing the ones who were not loyal to him. All England became a feudal kingdom. William was called **William the Conqueror**. He began a new royal line called the Normans.

Battle of Hastings The English battle in 1066 in which William of Normandy was victorious over Harold Godwinson; resulted in Harold's death and the ascension of William to the throne.

William the Conqueror First king of the Norman line; defeated Harold Godwinson at the Battle of Hastings.

Right: The shield wall was a common tactic in ancient and medieval warfare. What advantage would it give soldiers?

Below: The Bayeux Tapestry depicts the Battle of Hastings and the Normans' invasion of England. It is on display in Bayeux, Normandy, France.

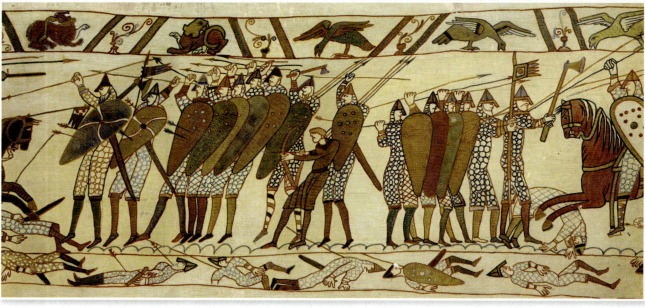

Henry's Legal System

The line of Norman kings in England lasted only through William's grandchildren. William's great-grandson, **Henry II**, came to power in 1154 after many years of civil war between his mother and her cousin Stephen of Blois. Henry II's family, the Plantagenets, ruled England until the end of the 1400s. Henry developed England's legal system, extending the king's jurisdiction over issues that had been handled previously by local officials.

During King Henry's time, the courts practiced **trial by ordeal**. A common method of trial by ordeal was to tie an accused person's hands and feet with rope and throw him into deep water. The people believed that if he floated, the pure water had rejected him because of his sin, and he was considered guilty. If he sank, he was innocent. Sadly, many innocent people lost their lives under this system.

After the civil wars, many land claims had to be settled to determine rightful ownership. Henry II developed procedures to handle these issues. He issued **writs** to the local sheriffs. The writ instructed the sheriff to decide who actually held each piece of disputed land. Even though someone else may have owned the land, the person who actually lived on it usually got to keep it. The sheriff's decision required a **trial by jury**. Jury members were made up of local people who came to the court. They told what they knew about the people who had claims to the land.

HENRY II

What: first Plantagenet king
When: ruled 1154–1189
Where: England

Henry II was the son of Geoffrey, Count of Anjou, and Matilda, the daughter of King Henry I. He was also the great-grandson of William the Conqueror. He married Eleanor of Aquitaine. Since he was a Frenchman, he owned more land outside of England than within it. He gained more land in France through inheritance and marriage. He eventually acquired more land than his feudal lord, the French king. He established legal reforms for England by reorganizing the judicial system. He also gained money for the treasury and expanded his control over the country. Henry controlled territory from Ireland to the Pyrenees Mountains.

Henry II First of the Plantagenet kings of England; came to the throne in 1154; developed England's legal system.

trial by ordeal A legal practice during the Middle Ages in which a person had to undergo difficult physical circumstances to determine guilt or innocence.

writ A royal order.

trial by jury A legal practice in which a group of local people helps decide the outcome of a court trial.

A trial by ordeal was supposed to guarantee justice by letting God decide whether a person was guilty.

Juries of Henry II's day did not decide cases like modern juries; the jury itself presented evidence.

With the help of the jury, the sheriff determined who should be the landowner. When there was a disagreement over the sheriff's decision, the case could be retried. When a particularly difficult case came up, it would be sent directly to Henry II for his decision. Over time, such decisions were written down and enforced throughout England, becoming England's common law.

Signing the Magna Carta

In 1199 Henry II's youngest son, John, became the king of England. **King John** was not popular with the people. He imposed heavy taxes to cover his military losses, and he used his power to gain money and land for himself.

John was often at odds with the church. The key religious leader in a region was called an archbishop. In England, the most important church leader was the archbishop of Canterbury. John got into a dispute with the pope over who should choose the archbishop of Canterbury, and the pope excommunicated John (removed him from membership in the church) for a time.

The Magna Carta was written in Latin. It was sealed by King John in a meadow called Runnymede near the Thames River.

King John Youngest son of Henry II; forced to put his seal on the Magna Carta.

THE LEGEND OF ROBIN HOOD

The legend of Robin Hood is about a man living in medieval England during the reigns of Richard the Lion-hearted and his brother John. He lived as an outlaw in Sherwood Forest near the town of Nottingham. Robin excelled as a swordsman and an archer. A band of merry men, who were all clad in green, lived there with him. Robin Hood and his merry men spent their days fighting injustice and robbing the rich to give to the poor.

Although it is unlikely that Robin Hood was an actual historical person, the legend raised him to the status of a national hero. Robin Hood's methods are not justified by Scripture, but many people view him as a champion who stood up for the rights of the poor during a time of tyranny.

As dissatisfaction with King John's reign increased, a group of nobles examined English laws and determined that King John's abuses of power were violating their rights. The nobles agreed that the king's power needed to be limited.

In 1215 the nobles led a revolt against King John. They captured the city of London, and John began negotiating with them in an attempt to end the conflict. One of their demands was that John sign a document called the **Magna Carta**.

The Magna Carta was based on English laws from the time of the Norman kings. The nobles designed the document to ensure that their own rights were protected. However, in time, the English people viewed the Magna Carta as a statement of the rights of all citizens. Under the Magna Carta, the king had to submit to the law. If he did not, the Magna Carta gave the nobles power to compel him to obey. This document greatly limited the king's power to tax and control his subjects.

John signed the Magna Carta, but it is doubtful that he intended to abide by it. However, he died suddenly the following year, and his nine-year-old son became king. At that time, the Magna Carta was confirmed by the king's council and approved by the pope.

When the Magna Carta was signed, the people did not know the significance it would have in the future. The document continues to be a statement of rights for free citizens. Its influence has spanned several centuries of history and has even reached other countries.

American colonists used the rights granted in the Magna Carta as the basis for their resisting unfair taxation by the king of England. The Magna Carta's legacy can be seen in the Constitution of the United States and in the Bill of Rights.

Other territories within the British Empire have also referenced the Magna Carta and its guarantee of rights. For example, British colonizers claimed economic rights because of the document, while native peoples of the regions pointed to the political and legal freedoms they should be provided under its provisions. In addition, the trial of Nelson Mandela in South Africa in 1963–64 contained one well-known appeal to the rights guaranteed by the Magna Carta.

Magna Carta An important document that limited the king's powers and guaranteed certain rights to the people.

THE MAGNA CARTA

The Magna Carta was written as if the king were addressing his subjects. Although much of it concerned matters applicable only in feudal times, some of it applied to later times as well. Here are a few of the rights granted in the Magna Carta.

(9) Neither we nor our officials will seize any land or rent in payment of a debt, so long as the debtor has movable goods sufficient to discharge the debt. . . .

(12) No 'scutage' or 'aid' [types of taxes] may be levied in our kingdom without its general consent [unless certain requirements are met]. . . .

(30) No sheriff, royal official, or other person shall take horses or carts for transport from any free man, without his consent.

(31) Neither we nor any royal official will take wood for our castle, or for any other purpose, without the consent of the owner.

(38) In future no official shall place a man on trial upon his own unsupported statement, without producing credible witnesses to the truth of it.

(G.R.C. Davis, *Magna Carta* [London: British Museum, 1963], pp. 23–33.)

Four copies remain of the 1215 Magna Carta. This copy is from the British Library.

 Why was the Magna Carta written, and what did it accomplish?

> Why did people need fortresses?

The Castle

Castles gradually began to replace large log houses as homes of medieval lords. Castles had become common in Europe by the eleventh century. The castle in the Middle Ages was both a home and a military fortress.

Castles were surrounded by strong walls. Some castles in the late Middle Ages had stone walls over thirty feet thick. Inside the walls were towers, a courtyard, living areas, kitchens, and a great hall where meetings and banquets were held.

Some castles had a strong central tower, called the **keep**, where the lord and his family lived. It was the safest place in the castle. Often the keep stood on a hill. Inside the keep were several rooms. They included the family's bedrooms and sitting rooms and a few other rooms, such as offices or a chapel. Most servants slept in the rooms where they worked, rather than having private bedrooms.

Castles were cold and dark inside. Lords tried to brighten them by painting the walls and ceilings with bright colors and placing burning torches in the rooms. They also put mats on the floors and hung woven tapestries on the walls to keep out the cold.

Early castles were made of wood. By the twelfth century, most castles were made of thick stone. Builders dug a **moat** around the castle to keep attackers from reaching it easily. A **drawbridge** crossed the moat to the castle gate. During an attack, the guards raised the drawbridge to cover the gate, cutting off the entrance to the castle.

If attackers got safely across the moat, they had to face the **gatehouse**. The gatehouse was a large stronghold in the castle wall. If the attackers entered the gatehouse, castle defenders could lower a large screen to trap them inside.

Invaders attacked castles in different ways. Sometimes they used a battering ram, a long log tipped with iron. This weapon could knock down the gate or part of the castle wall. Other soldiers rolled tall siege towers against a wall and then climbed into the castle. Sometimes the attacking army threw rocks and burning rags over the walls. The soldiers also dug tunnels under the castle and started fires there, hoping to burn away the castle's foundation to make the structure collapse.

Medieval Banquets

During the Middle Ages, wealthy people liked to host large banquets. Lords would invite many guests, and they would eat at long tables in the great hall of the castle. Pages waited on tables. Squires were often responsible for carving the meat. Court jesters provided live entertainment such as music, juggling, and acrobatics for the lord and his guests.

Many different foods were served at these banquets. A meal might have included soup, head cheese (a sausage-like dish that is made from the meat of a pig's head), puddings, fish, pork, venison, pheasants, larks, and other birds. Dessert was usually a pie filled with fish or fowl. One medieval custom was to insert live birds into a pie and release them in front of the guests when dessert was served. Many people have heard the nursery rhyme about this custom.

> Sing a song for sixpence,
> A pocket full of rye,
> Four and twenty blackbirds
> Baked in a pie.
> When the pie was opened
> The birds began to sing—
> Wasn't that a dainty dish
> To set before the king?

Banquet guests used large, flat pieces of bread as plates. Forks were not used until the 1600s, so people used their fingers to eat most foods. But they still had table manners. For example, it was considered rude to gnaw on the bones or to dip food into the common salt bowl.

keep Strong central tower in a castle where the lord and his family lived.

moat A wide trench filled with water surrounding a castle to keep out attackers.

drawbridge A bridge that can be raised or lowered to prevent or allow passage.

gatehouse A stronghold for the gatekeeper at the gate in the wall of a castle.

Medieval banquet tables were often arranged in a U shape, with the most important guests at a raised table.

Why do political and economic systems fail?

The Decline of Feudalism

There were a number of things that contributed to the weakening of feudalism in Medieval Europe.

Politics

Legal reforms such as Henry II's use of trial by jury gave more authority to royal officials. More authority for royal officials meant less power and authority for feudal lords.

Famine and Plague

Medieval Europe had grown and prospered during the 1200s, but the following century brought struggles that contributed to its decline.

A famine resulted after too much rain during planting and harvest times caused crops to spoil before they were ripe. Excessively cold winters added to the difficult environment. Disease and hunger claimed the lives of people and animals. It was during the 1300s that the Black Death spread throughout Asia and into Europe, killing more than 40 million people in Asia and about 25 million people in Europe.

The famine and the plague weakened Europe's feudal economy. Fewer people meant fewer workers. A reduced work force could demand higher wages and better conditions. Although feudal lords tried to put legal limits on these demands, they still lost much wealth and authority through the population declines of this period.

War

This century also brought a series of conflicts between England and France that together became known as the Hundred Years' War. These conflicts weakened feudalism in both countries. As a result of the conflicts, power shifted from feudal lords to monarchs and common people. English monarchs used tax money to build large, expertly trained armies skilled in the use of the longbow. They also had cannons that fired iron balls to assault castle walls. They no longer depended on feudal lords to provide knights for battle. Peasants gained a sense of national loyalty above the loyalty they had previously held for their local lords.

Development of Towns

Another important factor in the decline of feudalism was the growth of towns in the eleventh and twelfth centuries. Increased food production from new farming methods allowed the population to grow. Not all the people were needed to work the land, so many moved to towns. As trade again increased, merchants needed places to sell goods, so towns grew up at key points along trade routes.

Because they were not lords, knights, or farmers, townspeople did not fit into the traditional feudal social structure. Though many towns were originally controlled by feudal lords, townspeople began to insist on having charters. These documents gave townspeople freedom from many of the work obligations that were required of peasants on manors.

Many townspeople became part of a newly developing social class: the middle class. The middle class was composed of people such as merchants and bankers. Although they did not own large pieces of land like the feudal lords, they were becoming wealthy through business and trade. In time, members of the middle class began to surpass some of the lords in wealth. The middle class often preferred one central government over many feudal governments because there would be fewer taxes to pay on trade.

Crusaders built this island castle in the thirteenth century. Why would they have built a castle on an island?

THE RENAISSANCE

The Renaissance was a period that began in Italy about AD 1400. The word *renaissance* means "rebirth" and refers to the rebirth of learning. The growth of trade and the rise of towns and cities in the later Middle Ages led to the expansion of a professional class (people who worked as merchants, bankers, lawyers, etc.). These workers needed training. While most medieval learning had been related to the church, programs of study sprang up during the Renaissance to prepare people for secular work. These new programs looked to the classical world for examples of things such as how to draw up a contract. In the process, scholars rediscovered many works of ancient authors that inspired a period of great cultural change.

This cultural revival spread north and into other parts of Europe over the next two hundred years, greatly changing European life and culture. Classical Greek and Roman literature were widely studied, and universities developed. As a result of this revival of classical education, the arts also flourished, based on models of the classical world.

Florence, Italy, was the home of many of the artistic masters of the Renaissance.

The Crusades

By the late 1000s, most of the Byzantine Empire had fallen to Muslim invaders. The pope called for Western Europeans to join the Byzantines in a crusade to recapture the Holy Land from the Turks. This crusade was the first in a series of religious wars between the Christians and the Muslim Turks.

During the Crusades, Western Europeans were exposed to many new ideas. They came in contact with other civilizations and cultures. Western Europeans returned with a broader knowledge and richer culture. They began to implement what they had seen and learned. The Crusaders brought back goods such as spices, cloth, and sugar. Their world was made bigger with the knowledge of how to build better ships, a development that contributed to the coming age of world exploration. Trade with other civilizations grew.

The Crusades did much to weaken the system of feudalism. Fighting was expensive. Most of the money was provided by individual lords. Some lords had to sell or mortgage their properties to pay for their Crusade expenses. Many serfs left their manors to fight in the Crusades. Most who left, having experienced freedom, never returned.

The Great Schism

During the late 1300s, a disagreement called the Great Schism divided the Western church. The argument was about who was the true pope. The Council of Pisa's failed attempt at resolving the problem resulted in the election of three popes. Eventually, the Council of Constance met to find a solution. The bishops elected a pope that the members of the church would approve of, ending the Great Schism. But the church faced other problems. European kings grew powerful and started to question the pope's authority, and people became intolerant of the riches and dishonesty of the clergy. Some longed for a truer form of Christianity.

A Time of Transition

By the year 1500, central governments all over Europe were run by kings. England and France were becoming strong nations. More and more people were living in towns and cities rather than on manors. Most of the medieval world's culture had faded into something different.

Changes were taking place that would usher in a new era in Europe. Universities began to form in cities where prominent teachers lived. Scholars were no longer confined to monasteries or church-sponsored schools. A revival of learning was beginning that would sweep across Europe and result in new discoveries and accomplishments. The modern era of history was about to begin with a cultural revival known as the Renaissance. Scholars and thinkers were also beginning to question the teachings and practices of the Roman Catholic Church. Their efforts to return to the teachings and practices of Scripture would eventually lead to the Protestant Reformation.

 How did famine and plague affect the economy?

15 A KINGDOM FROM SHORE TO SHORE

FOCUS
Christ's kingdom has spread across the globe.

Protestant Reformation
1517–1648

Robert Morrison to China
1807

1500 1600 1700 1800 1900 2000

1500s
Early Protestant missions
to South America

1792
William Carey to India,
beginning the modern
mission movement

1817
Robert Moffat
to Africa

How many languages do you think are spoken in the world right now? Most experts agree that there are more than 7,000 distinct languages. In Papua New Guinea alone, there are more than 800 native languages. In the United States, there are about 150 native languages, including Navajo, Cherokee, and Dakota. The 200 languages introduced by immigrants include languages such as Spanish, French, German, Chinese, and Italian.

The number of languages changes from year to year. Some are used by only a few people; when those people die, so will the languages. A couple of Native American languages, for example, are now spoken by fewer than one hundred people. But occasionally a language is brought back. Hebrew was not spoken for hundreds of years, but now a million people in Israel and elsewhere are fluent in it.

In New York City, it is possible to hear nearly 200 different languages. New York City is often thought of as a symbol of the blending of many cultures and people groups. Christians can look at this city and see a reflection of God's kingdom. Though there is great variety among people, each person has equal value before God. As people of many backgrounds blend as Americans in New York City, many diverse types of people unite as citizens of the kindgom of God.

Here, Kendra and Madison enjoy a day in Central Park while their mothers visit. Kendra and her mother are fluent in English and Spanish. Kendra's mother even translates the sermon into Spanish at their church. Madison's mother speaks English and Mandarin, but she follows the teachings of Buddhism. Kendra hopes to soon be able to invite Madison home for *sopa de fideo*.

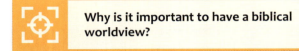

Why is it important to have a biblical worldview?

God's Master Plan

Creation

Genesis 1:26–28 explains that God created people as His image bearers. Because humans are made in God's likeness, they are able to carry out God's command to have dominion in the earth. God created Adam and Eve and all people with a purpose and a job to do. God's first words to humanity have been marvelously fulfilled in many ways. Civilizations have developed in Egypt, Persia, Japan, Mesoamerica, Africa, Europe, and other places. People truly have filled the earth.

Mankind has exercised dominion over the earth. The Egyptians harnessed the Nile. They built pyramids that still awe people today. The Romans built a vast empire that filled Europe and the Middle East with roads, new cities, and systems of government that still exist. The Greeks and the Persians developed philosophies that lived on even after their countries were conquered.

Although the people may not have realized it, the greatness of civilizations resulted from people using the abilities they had, which came from being made in God's image. Each person bears the image of God.

Historians with an evolutionary worldview marvel at the intelligence on display in ancient civilizations. Ancient people built impressive structures, developed languages, and wrote beautiful poetry. Historians with a biblical worldview also admire and marvel at what these civilizations accomplished, but they recognize that people do creative, intelligent things because an intelligent God created them to be like Himself.

In early civilizations, people also had a sense of right and wrong. They organized governments to protect people and to establish rules of conduct. People desire justice because they are God's image bearers. God is just and is the perfect Lawgiver. God deserves praise and glory for the greatness and contributions of civilizations.

The Fall

The perfect world God created fell into sin. The abilities that God gave men and women when He created them in His image were damaged, though not completely destroyed, by the Fall. By God's grace, history records many wonderful events because His image bearers still do what He created them to do, though imperfectly. But history also records many unjust and ungodly events, clear evidence of people's sinfulness.

The Egyptians built their magnificent buildings on the backs of slaves. The Japanese developed fine literature, including the first novel, but some of their stories praised behavior that God condemns. Mesoamericans developed a complex calendar, but their civilizations practiced human sacrifice.

People used the abilities God gave them to rebel against Him. This is most clearly seen in the religions of each culture.

On the surface, false religions seem to have elements of worth in them. Religious myths often contain creative stories. Religious structures such as pyramids or cathedrals are some of the most impressive ever built.

Philosophies also contain elements of worth. Philosophers have tackled difficult problems and beliefs. Sometimes their thoughts have been studied for thousands of years by people from many other cultures.

Yet each false religion or worldly philosophy has formed because people rejected God's truth. Often people had a concept of God, but they accepted only the features of His character that they liked or feared. They then used this flawed knowledge to create their own religious systems.

When God told Adam and Eve to subdue the earth and rule over it, He was telling them to build a civilization. Later, Scripture would describe Jerusalem as the city of God.

GOD'S MERCY ON DISPLAY

After the Fall, God told Eve He would put hatred between her offspring and Satan's offspring. History has been the struggle between Eve's seed (God's people) and the serpent's seed (Satan's people). Genesis records that the descendants of Cain rebelled against God. The descendants of Seth, Cain's brother, worshiped God for a while but soon also turned to wickedness. God destroyed the world's first civilization with a universal flood. Only Noah and his family accepted God's grace and survived the destruction.

In the rise and fall of civilizations, it has been God's mercy that has kept the human race from complete self-destruction. For example, at the tower of Babel, God divided the people into different language groups that forced them to scatter over the earth. In addition, as civilizations have grown powerful around the world, He brought down their power as their wickedness increased. God also preserved the Israelites as His chosen people through whom the Messiah would come. Throughout ancient history, God was preparing the world for the Redeemer.

Since the whole world is God's, all cities in it should be His cities. So, in a sense, when God told Adam and Eve to build civilizations, He was telling humanity to build cities for Him, to build Jerusalems. But instead of building Jerusalems, people have built and continue to build Babels, cities of rebellion against God.

Redemption

God's plan has always been to redeem mankind from sin and sin's effects in the world. History is important to God's plan of redemption.

From the beginning, God intended for people to rule the world wisely. But by giving in to temptation, Adam failed to rule wisely, and all his descendants could no longer perfectly exercise righteous dominion over the earth. Even the Israelites, whom God had chosen to be His special people, did not rule their small nation according to God's law.

Yet God's plan of redemption was underway in the Israelites' history. God had given them His law, and He continued to give them promises of a savior and king. This king would rule over Israel and over the entire world. He would save Jews as well as people from every nation in the world.

That king is Jesus, the Son of God, who came as a man to redeem the world. Jesus lived a perfect life as a man. When He died, He paid the penalty for sinful people in all times and in all places. Those who turn from their sin to trust Him for salvation receive His righteousness. They are brought out of the kingdom of darkness and placed into the kingdom of light (Colossians 1:12–14).

When Jesus rose from the dead and ascended to heaven, He rose as a king. All authority was given to Him in heaven and on earth. His kingdom is not like the empires of Persia or Rome. Today, as in the past, Jesus' kingdom spreads as more and more people enter it by placing their faith in Him.

One day Jesus will return to rule over the earth from Jerusalem. He will judge those who reject God and live contrary to His good law. This coming judgment is good news because Jesus will be a righteous judge who will end all injustice and oppression. In the end, all the Babels that humans have built will be swept away. The new Jerusalem will descend from heaven, and the earth will be made new. It will be a place full of righteousness, just as God intended from the beginning.

Identifying One's Own Worldview

The chapters in this book discuss mighty empires that spread over vast portions of the earth. This book details many cultures with their language, architecture, and styles of dress. It describes world-changing events, including important battles or new inventions. Descriptions of false religions show how people have been led away from truth.

It is important to look deeper than the surface of these civilizations. Is there a world of chaos that has no purpose? Is there a world guided by an impersonal, unknown power? Or is there a God with a master plan who controls all things to accomplish His purposes?

The way a person answers these questions reflects his or her worldview. The people who study and write about history have many different viewpoints. Some historians and archaeologists look at past civilizations and reject the account of history in the Bible. However, Christians look at the past and see how the plan of God has unfolded. The Bible teaches a Christian not only what happened in history but also how to think about what happened. Knowing what God says in His Word is the key to developing a biblical worldview.

The Ascension by Gustave Doré

 How does the kingship of Christ relate to God's plan of redemption?

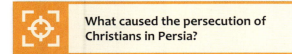 **What caused the persecution of Christians in Persia?**

The Spread of Christ's Kingdom

Each civilization in this book had religious beliefs. As Christ's followers spread the gospel, they encountered people who held false beliefs. Often the early Christians faced persecution, but this difficulty did not stop Christianity from spreading. Sometimes persecution had the opposite effect. Believers carried the gospel with them as they fled to other parts of the world to escape imprisonment, torture, or death. By the Middle Ages, Christianity had spread into nations such as Egypt, Israel, Greece, Rome, and Byzantium.

After the period of history covered in this book, the world has continued to change. Christianity is rapidly growing today in many regions that previously had little Christian influence. Some of these regions include Mesoamerica, Asia, and Africa. However, there are also regions that previously had strong Christian influence but no longer do. Such regions include Egypt, Turkey, and parts of Europe.

The spread of Christ's kingdom is not evenly distributed in all places and at all times. In the book of Revelation, Jesus warned believers that if they were not faithful, their churches would be removed. However, He had previously promised that His kingdom would continue to grow, just as yeast gradually spreads through every part of a piece of dough (Matthew 13:33). As churches have become unfaithful to God, He has removed them. As areas where the gospel once thrived become hardened to its message, areas unfamiliar with the gospel soften to it and flourish as they receive God's grace.

Egypt

The ancient Egyptians believed that Ra, the sun god, created and ruled the world. They believed the dead traveled by boat to Osiris, the god of the underworld, for judgment. The Egyptians treated their pharaohs as gods and counted on priests to tell them how to worship. The pharaohs often ruled harshly and took the people's wealth to support their own lavish living. The Egyptians also enslaved the Israelites for four hundred years.

In spite of all that was wrong in ancient Egypt, the prophet Isaiah made a surprising prediction. He foretold that one day Egyptians would be considered God's people, just as Israel had been in Old Testament times.

The Christian Martyrs' Last Prayer by Jean-Léon Gérôme. What can be inferred about the Christian martyrs based on the picture?

GOING INTO ALL

Arts, Sciences, and Written Language

The development of science and technology can help promote the gospel. Shortly before Martin Luther's time, the movable-type printing press was invented. Before this invention, books were copied by hand. It took a long time to copy a book, and books were expensive. But with the printing press, Luther's books spread quickly throughout Europe.

Justice

Christians around the world have faced injustices. For example, Christians lost property and suffered significant restrictions when Islam spread over northern Africa. Jesus said His followers should rejoice when persecuted, because the kingdom of heaven was theirs. When Jesus returns to rule over the earth, He will establish justice in the world.

Citizenship

Christians ought to be the best citizens because they should be loyal and obedient except when told to do something against God's Word (Romans 13:1-7). Sometimes the protection that citizens of certain nations experience helps the gospel to advance.

Christians in Persia benefited for a time from the tolerance of the Persian rulers. However, when Roman emperors identified as Christians, Persian rulers thought their own Christian citizens might be disloyal. Persian rulers began to persecute Christians.

THE WORLD

Key Themes of Civilization
- Justice
- Power
- Citizenship
- Environment

Environment
China's geography hindered the gospel's influence for centuries. But the gospel has spread over the entire world, regardless of geographical or environmental barriers. Today there are millions of Chinese who follow Christ.

Features of a Civilization
- Organized cities and government
- Social classes
- Job specialization
- Arts, sciences, and written language
- Religion

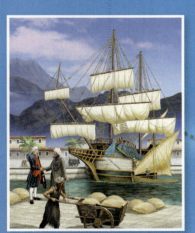

Power
The kingdom of Christ does not spread like other kingdoms. Christians often have very little power, while those who oppose them have great power. The Dutch East India Company and the British East India Company were powerful organizations that prohibited missionary work in parts of India. But no power is greater than God's. In 1813 a law required the British East India Company to permit missionary work.

Religion
When another religion has a strong hold on a culture, it is difficult for the gospel to reach people. For instance, Roman Catholicism became an influential part of Latin American culture. This made it difficult for Protestant missionaries to communicate the truth. But the gospel message has taken root in many cultures with strong attachments to other religions.

ATHANASIUS

What: theologian
When: ca. AD 293–373
Where: Egypt

Athanasius was an important Christian leader in the early church in Egypt. He defended the deity of Christ against false teachers who believed that Jesus was not equal with God the Father. Sometimes the Roman emperors sided with these false teachers. Persecuted for his beliefs, Athanasius had to hide in the Egyptian desert, sometimes for years, to carry on his fight for truth.

Athanasius probably felt as if he were the only one standing for truth, with the whole world opposed to him. But in the end, true Christians embraced the right teaching that he had spent his life defending.

The gospel may have been taken to Egypt shortly after Christ's resurrection. Some historians believe that Mark, who wrote the Gospel of Mark, was the first missionary to that area. The Egyptian city of Alexandria grew to be one of the most important places for early Christianity. Some of the church's most influential teachers came from Egypt.

Over time, the church in Egypt developed errors. Some followers of Christianity embraced false views held by the Eastern Orthodox Church or by the Roman Catholic Church. Later, Muslims conquered Egypt and placed restrictions on Christians. Muslim leaders seized church property and threatened to kill Christians who did not convert to Islam.

Today, Christianity does not have the same strength in Egypt as it once had. However, Isaiah's prophecy will still come to pass. One day the Lord will say, "Blessed be Egypt my people" (Isaiah 19:25).

Athanasius Bishop of Alexandria who defended Christian doctrine against the false teaching of Arius.

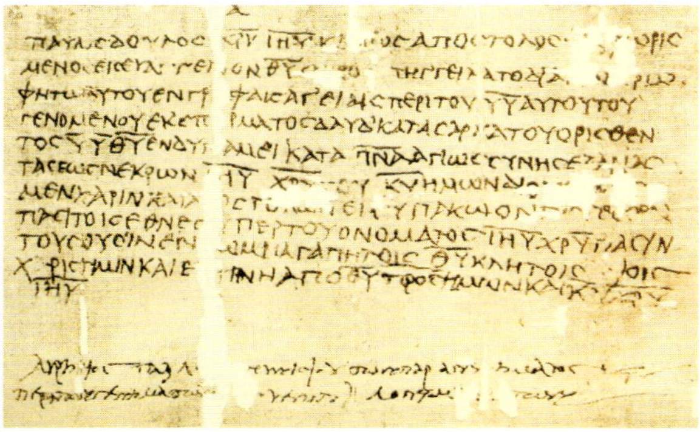

In the late 1800s and early 1900s, archaeologists discovered a large number of papyrus documents, some of which contained Scripture, in a trash pile outside the ancient Egyptian city of Oxyrhynchus. This papyrus contains Romans 1:1–7.

At least ninety percent of Egyptians are Muslims. Of those who identify themselves as Christians, most are members of the Coptic Orthodox Church. Copts have regularly faced persecution and discrimination.

CONSTANTINE AND THE CHURCH

In AD 313, Constantine declared that Christianity would be tolerated in the Roman Empire. The freedoms and privileges he granted furthered the rapid growth of the church in the Roman Empire. It increased both in members and in material prosperity. Although some members were not genuine Christians, there were still many true believers who taught and defended the truth. Many scholars believe Constantine's protection of the church kept it from being stamped out by persecution—a fate that almost happened to the church east of the Roman Empire.

Ephrem the Syrian lived during the fourth century. Archaeologists have found copies of his sermons, poetry, and hymns. The following is one of his hymns.

> The One who said that by light
> darkness was defeated, and death by life,
> taught that envy is conquered by love,
> and by his scripture deceit is transformed into wisdom.
> Blessed is the one who arms the tongue with Your word,
> who quotes from what is Yours to Your adversary.
> Our Lord, let us gaze upon You,
> Who from Moses quoted to the evil one in Your temptation.

McVey, Kathleen E., trans., *Ephrem the Syrian Hymns* (Mahwah: Paulist Press, 1989), 321.

Ephrem the Syrian, a key leader in the early Eastern Church, was an influential writer. Sermons like the one pictured here taught important doctrinal truths so that people would not be deceived by false teaching.

Mesopotamia and Persia

Mesopotamia did not seem to be a likely place for Christ's kingdom to spread. Both the Assyrian Empire and the Chaldean Empire rose out of the region of Mesopotamia. The Assyrians were known for their fierceness and cruelty. God used them to judge many sinful nations, including His own people. Even though the Assyrian people repented and turned to God in the days of Jonah, they eventually returned to their evil ways. The Chaldean Empire, which conquered the Assyrians, was also used as God's tool of judgment on His people. One Chaldean king, Nebuchadnezzar, humbled himself and worshiped the true God, but later rulers continued living wickedly.

The Persian Empire rose to power after the fall of the Chaldean Empire. The Persians introduced the false religion of Zoroastrianism, and their rulers tolerated many other religions. However, God used several pagan Persian kings to protect and provide for His people. These rulers were an important part in God's plan for the Israelites to return to their land and rebuild their nation.

Christ's kingdom spread into the regions of Mesopotamia and Persia and beyond as Christians traveled east of the Roman Empire. Christians benefited from the tolerance of Persian rulers at the time of the early church. Some Christians fled to Persia to escape Roman persecution. Archaeologists have discovered an ancient Christian hymnal in the Mesopotamian city of Edessa, located in modern Turkey. After the Roman emperor Constantine converted to Christianity, the Persians feared that the Christians would side with Rome and fight against them. Since that time, Persian Christians have endured persecution during various periods of history. Some people in that region today are Roman Catholic. In Iran, there are still true Christians who make up about two-tenths of a percent of the population.

 What was significant about Athanasius's work?

Who pioneered missionary work in Africa?

Greece, Rome, and Europe

In Greek and Roman cultures, people worshiped many different gods. These cultures also brought many new ideas and philosophies to the world. Yet their religions and ideas were unsatisfying. The gods they worshiped were unholy and spiteful, and human philosophies could not resolve the problem of human sin.

During the period of the Roman Empire, the apostle Paul traveled throughout Asia Minor and Greece, sharing the gospel and planting churches. He led many people to become followers of Christ. Eventually the Romans arrested him and sent him to Rome to await trial. As a prisoner there, he continued to write letters and encourage people and churches. Many of his letters are part of the New Testament.

Emperors and officials in the Roman Empire persecuted Christians for hundreds of years. But the persecutions were unable to stop the church. Christians multiplied, and as the empire spread

Luther's Ninety-Five Theses, being posted here to the door of the church at Wittenberg, was an important starting point for the Protestant Reformation. The theses stated concerns about selling indulgences.

north, Christianity also spread. Under Constantine's protection in the fourth century, the number of those who called themselves Christians grew.

Many errors in doctrine and practice had crept into the church by the Middle Ages. Nevertheless, the Bible and Christian books were copied in monasteries, and many priests and monks studied and taught the Bible and theology. Some of these men understood Scripture better than others. It was in a monastery in Germany that **Martin Luther** grasped the truth of how a person can be right with God. Luther realized that it is by faith that a person is justified, or declared righteous, by God. A person receives righteousness from Christ by believing God's promise that Christ paid the penalty for sinners. Justification cannot be earned by good works. However, those who are justified by God are changed by God so that they live lives of good works.

Luther and many others wanted the Roman Catholic Church to reform its teachings. The movement known as the **Protestant Reformation** resulted from their efforts. During the Reformation, many citizens of European nations separated from

Martin Luther German monk who helped start the Protestant Reformation.

Protestant Reformation The religious movement that led to the forming of Protestant churches when people separated from the Roman Catholic Church and trusted in Christ alone for salvation.

MARTIN LUTHER

What: a key leader of the Reformation
When: 1483–1546
Where: Europe

Martin Luther was pursuing a law degree when he encountered a terrible storm. He promised that he would become a monk if he survived. About six weeks later, Luther entered a German monastery.

While studying the Bible as a monk, Martin Luther discovered that no amount of good works could justify a sinner before God. Luther's teaching on justification only by faith began the Reformation in Europe.

Luther is well known for his writings, especially for his Ninety-Five Theses. These theses helped spark the Protestant Reformation. He also wrote hymns and translated the Bible into German.

the Roman Catholic Church and placed their trust in Christ alone for the forgiveness of sins. One of these European nations was England. The English planted colonies in North America that later became the United States. Eventually, missionaries from Europe and the United States would continue the spread of the gospel across the globe.

The Reformation is still viewed as one of the most important events in history. Unfortunately, many Europeans today have rejected Christ. There are still faithful churches in Europe, but not as many as there were one hundred years ago. Many old church buildings stand empty, and some have been turned into apartments, bars, or mosques. Because many European churches did not remain faithful to Christ, God removed them just as He had warned.

India

Ancient India was the birthplace of two major world religions. Hinduism, India's earliest major religion, placed people in the caste system. A person's behavior, relationships, and practices were controlled by this religion. Siddhartha Gautama saw his people suffering under the Hindu caste system. He responded by forming a new religion called Buddhism. This religion gave people the false hope that they could end their suffering by following a path of good works. Even though Buddhism never became the dominant religion of India, it spread throughout Asia.

According to tradition, the apostle Thomas brought the gospel to India. Travel between the Roman Empire and India was common in the first century. The church historian Eusebius recorded that an early believer named Pantaenus traveled as a missionary to India. When Pantaenus arrived, he found Christians there already, and they had copies of the Gospel of Matthew. By the fourth century, Persian Christians had made contact with Christians in India. The Indians sent their church leaders to schools in Persia until the Muslims conquered Persia.

Scattered communities of Christians still existed in India when Portuguese traders arrived there in the 1600s. The Portuguese brought Roman Catholic priests with them. The priests tried to force the Indian Christians to adopt some Catholic traditions, and confusion developed among Christians in India.

By the end of the 1700s, Protestants arrived in India through two trading companies, the Dutch East India Company and the British East India Company. These companies were more concerned with making money than they were with the eternal future of the Indians. The Dutch and the English forbade evangelism of the Indians for fear of upsetting the Hindus and hindering trade.

Despite the opposition from the trading companies, missionaries still came to India. **William Carey** went to India in 1792. He and his coworkers knew that they needed Indian evangelists if the gospel were to spread throughout the vast region. However, it took many years for them to lead only a handful of Indians to Christ.

In 1813 England passed a law that required the British East India Company to permit missionary work in the areas the company controlled. This opened the way for more missionaries. More and more Indians became Christians. Eventually Carey and the other missionaries were able to train Indian pastors and evangelists.

By the mid-1850s, the United Kingdom had gained complete governmental control of India and maintained control until 1947 when India gained its independence. Hinduism remained the dominant religion of India. Today, Christians in some parts of India experience persecution. Nevertheless, the number of Christians has grown to millions. Although this is a large number, it represents only a small percentage of India's vast population.

William Carey British missionary to India; began missionary work there in 1792; trained Indian pastors and evangelists.

Under William Carey's direction, all or parts of the Bible were translated into Bengali, Sanskrit, and several other Indian languages and dialects.

Africa

Africa contains many different countries and geographic regions. Much of ancient Africa was dominated by traditional beliefs involving the spirit world. Christianity entered different parts of the continent at different times.

After Christ's time on earth, the gospel quickly spread from Israel to Egypt and other parts of northern Africa. At the time of the apostles, northern Africa was part of the Roman Empire. Some of Africa's Christian teachers, such as Tertullian and Augustine, greatly influenced Christianity. In northern Africa, Christianity was strongly influential until the Muslim conquest in the seventh century.

Before the Muslims arrived, Christianity had spread south into Nubia, which is now Sudan and Ethiopia. In ancient times, this area was home to the official with whom Philip shared the gospel in Acts 8. No doubt the official shared the gospel with others in Nubia. But it was not until Byzantine missionaries came in the sixth century that Christianity really took hold in Nubia. Later, the Nubians fought the Muslims who invaded Africa, and Nubian victory stopped the spread of Islam in Nubia and Aksum for several centuries.

The gospel had come to Aksum, present-day Ethiopia, as early as the fourth century. Aksum was never conquered by Muslims, but Christianity's influence there was weakened through false teaching.

Portuguese explorers attempted missionary work among the people of Africa's interior. The king of the Congo converted and asked that priests come to teach his people. However, many priests who came did not care for the people's souls. Instead, they played a part in enslaving the people of the Congo.

The United Kingdom and Germany established trade and built colonies in Africa. Their presence in Africa opened the way for missionaries to come. In the nineteenth century, **Robert Moffat** and **Mary Moffat** served in southern Africa. They provided an example that many later missionaries followed. The Moffats set up a mission station, translated the Bible into the local language, and began a church. Throughout the 1800s and early 1900s, many mission stations were established and churches were formed.

By the mid-1900s many Africans were seeking independence from European rulers. African Christians wished to provide the leadership of their churches themselves rather than have foreign missionaries lead them. Today foreign missionaries

---

Robert Moffat Scottish missionary to Africa; began missionary work there in 1817; helped set up mission stations and translated the Bible into the local language.

Mary Moffat Scottish missionary to Africa in the 1800s; helped set up mission stations.

ROBERT AND MARY MOFFAT

What: Scottish missionaries
When: Mary 1795–1871; Robert 1795–1883
Where: South Africa

In 1817 Robert Moffat arrived in Cape Town, South Africa. He had left Mary Smith, the woman he hoped to marry, in England. Her parents refused to allow her to go away to a foreign land.

Robert Moffat worked in Africa for nearly three years before Mary's parents changed their minds. During this time, he shared the gospel with a chief named Afrikaner, who eventually trusted Christ along with many of his people.

Robert and Mary were married in Cape Town. They set up mission stations, first in the village of Lattakoo, and later in the town of Kuruman. Progress in both stations was slow. Years went by with the African people showing little interest in the gospel. Mary became sick and nearly died before the birth of their first child. A time of drought came, and the water supply ran low. In addition, their mission station was threatened by tribal warfare.

A friend in England wrote to Mary and asked her if there was anything she needed. "Send us a communion service," Mary wrote back, knowing that goods shipped from England could take a long time to arrive. "We shall want it some day."

The Lord rewarded Mary's faith. A few years later, the Moffats held a baptism for six African converts. Afterward, they had a communion service, using the communion set that had arrived from England only the day before.

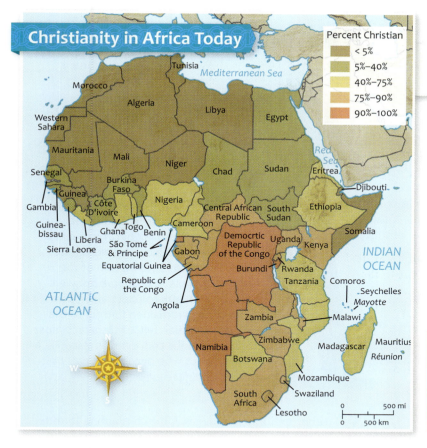

Christianity in Africa Today

Which areas of Africa contain the most people who identify themselves as Christians? Which areas contain the least?

still come to Africa, but many churches there are now led by African Christians.

Christianity is now growing faster in sub-Saharan Africa than it is in Europe and in North America. Research shows that twenty-six percent of people in the world who identify themselves as Christians are African. Researchers project that by 2050 this number will reach nearly forty percent as sub-Saharan Africans continue to embrace Christianity.

How did Martin Luther defend the Christian faith?
How did the British East India Company affect missionary work in India?

ACTIVITY

Writing a Compare-and-Contrast Essay

A compare-and-contrast essay tells how things are alike and how they are different. Compare-and-contrast essays can be organized in various ways. Two common ways to organize this type of essay are by subject or by similarities and differences. You will write an essay that compares and contrasts the same topic from two different civilizations that you have studied in this book.

1. Choose a topic from two civilizations to compare and contrast. Gather information by reviewing the appropriate chapters in this book and taking notes. Use the Venn diagram in the Activity Manual to help you organize the information you have collected.
2. Write a brief outline to put your ideas in order. Remember that your essay should have an introduction and a conclusion.
3. Follow the writing process to draft, revise, and proofread your essay.
4. Share your completed essay.

Japanese samurai

What topic for comparison is illustrated by the pictures on the page?

Roman legionary

How did Robert Morrison break the barrier to missions in China?

Latin America

In the early 1500s, Hernando Cortés was subduing the Aztec people in Mesoamerica. The Spaniards brought with them the Spanish and Portuguese languages. They also brought Roman Catholicism. This religion soon had a strong grip on all Mesoamerica. Spanish and Portuguese exploration and colonization reached from Mexico through South America. These lands became known as Latin America. As leaders of the Roman Catholic Church saw people in Europe turning to Protestant Christianity, they became determined that Latin America would remain Catholic.

In the 1500s, missionaries from Geneva, Switzerland, were some of the first Protestant missionaries to come to a French colony in Brazil. They hoped to preach the gospel, but French colonists drove them away. Three hundred years later, Spanish and Portuguese rule in Latin America ended, and Latin American nations became more open to Protestant missionaries and invited them to their lands.

Immigrants sometimes helped with the missionary efforts to Latin America. African Americans from the United States moved to Haiti and the Dominican Republic in the early 1800s. Many of them worked diligently to spread the gospel. Some immigrants from Europe and the United States started churches in Latin America. At first, they used their own languages with little success. But after living in the Latin American culture for a time, they learned to speak Spanish and Portuguese and were better able to minister to those around them.

The British Bible Society and the American Bible Society also sent missionaries to Latin America. They distributed Bibles in Portuguese, Spanish, and other national languages. Church planters founded many churches that shaped Christianity in Latin America for much of the twentieth century.

Just as in Africa, the leadership of these churches has gradually shifted from missionaries to the Latin Americans themselves. Although some churches mix the gospel with false teaching, many preach the truth and continue the spread of Christ's kingdom.

Spanish is one of more than six hundred languages that have a complete copy of the Bible thanks to the work of Bible translators. Why is it valuable for people to have the Bible in their own language?

ROBERT MORRISON

What: minister, missionary, and translator
When: 1782–1834
Where: China

Robert Morrison was one of the first English missionaries to China. Once in China, his main focus was his translation work. Some of his first translations were tracts in the Chinese language. He remained in China for twenty-seven years, long enough to publish a translation of the Bible. Morrison had only ten converts to Christianity, but they remained faithful to the Christian faith. Morrison's most famous convert was Liang Fa, a man who became China's first Chinese evangelist.

China

China's isolation kept Christianity outside its borders for centuries. The earliest known instance of Christianity in China was in the 600s, during the Tang dynasty. This dynasty began almost four hundred years after the Han dynasty. One of the Tang emperors loved books and had a library with thousands of volumes. When Christian missionaries from Persia arrived with a religion that had a holy book, the emperor was very interested. He asked the missionaries to translate the Bible into Chinese. Evidence found in 1908 shows that parts of the Bible were translated during that period.

By the 900s, the Tang dynasty had ended. Foreign religions in China came under attack, and Christianity was suppressed.

Under the Mongol rule in the thirteenth century, Persian Christians again brought the gospel into China. But once again, with the rise of the Ming dynasty, foreign religions were no longer welcome.

HUDSON TAYLOR

What: English missionary
When: 1832–1905
Where: China

Hudson Taylor desired to take the gospel to the interior of China. He began to pray for laborers. At first he prayed for twenty-four, then for seventy more, then for a hundred more, then for a thousand more. God answered his prayers by multitudes of Chinese people coming to faith in Christ. Many of the new converts worked closely with Hudson Taylor's China Inland Mission. He insisted, however, that the workers support themselves rather than be paid with foreign funds. This way, the Chinese church could stand on its own even if the foreigners were driven out.

After the Reformation, Protestant missionaries began to arrive in China. In 1642, Dutch Reformed missionaries arrived in Taiwan, an island off the coast of China. They lived in the villages among the people, learned their languages, taught the people, and began to translate the Bible. Many people of Taiwan were converted to Christ. However, the Chinese drove the missionaries away after more than twenty years of missionary work.

China remained closed to missionaries, but a British missionary named **Robert Morrison** was determined to break through the barriers. In 1807 he sailed to China. Once there, he dressed like the Chinese and sought to avoid attention. He did not openly evangelize, knowing he would be forced to leave China if he were caught. Instead, he spent his time learning Chinese and translating the entire Bible. This Chinese Bible had a tremendous impact on the evangelization of China that would follow.

Morrison counseled other missionaries to go to Chinese-speaking areas just outside China. There, on the borders of the country, they could learn Chinese, evangelize, and prepare Chinese evangelists to travel through their own country with the gospel. Missionaries followed this strategy until 1858, when China began opening certain port cities to the Europeans for trade. Missionaries moved to these port cities.

As a result of the Boxer Rebellion (1899–1900), many foreigners were driven from the Chinese empire. Some missionaries and Chinese Christians were killed. Later, all the missionaries were forced to leave when the Communists took over China after World War II. But Chinese Christians continued to worship God and spread the gospel.

Although Christians in China have experienced much persecution and often have to meet in secret, Christianity has not been stamped out. Researchers estimate that there are between twenty-five and eighty million Christians in China today.

Japan

Like China, Japan was closed to outside influences for centuries. Shintoism and Buddhism held sway over its people. But in 1853, four American naval ships sailed into Tokyo Bay. The Americans asked for permission to use certain Japanese ports on a regular basis, and the Japanese government agreed. An American diplomat worked to negotiate a trade agreement with Japan, and he also helped open Japan to missionary work. Christianity's spread in Japan has been slow, and Christians are still a very small part of the population. But God is still calling people to spread His kingdom in Japan.

Personal Role in Christ's Kingdom

In Matthew 13, Jesus describes His kingdom as a tiny mustard seed that grows into a large plant. His kingdom started small with only a few people in the Roman provinces on the eastern shore of the Mediterranean Sea. But this kingdom has spread over the entire globe. Revelation declares that the kingdom of Christ will include people from every tribe and nation who will sing His praises continually before His throne.

Christ's kingdom spreads one person at a time. Each person who places his or her faith in Christ becomes a member of His kingdom. Part of God's plan for Christians is to carry the message of salvation to all the world. Christians can accomplish this through the power of the Holy Spirit in any walk of life.

Robert Morrison British missionary to China; began missionary work there in 1807; dressed like the Chinese; translated the Bible into Chinese.

Hudson Taylor British missionary to the interior of China; began missionary work there in 1854; founded the China Inland Mission.

 What different groups of people helped spread the gospel in Latin America?

RESOURCE TREASURY

Atlas — 334
- World: Physical — 334
- World: Political — 336
- Africa: Physical — 338
- Africa: Political — 339
- Europe & Asia: Physical — 340
- Europe & Asia: Political — 342
- Western Hemisphere: Physical — 344
- Western Hemisphere: Political — 345
- World Religions — 346
- World Languages — 346
- World Climates — 347
- World Land Use — 347

Primary Source Documents — 348

Biographical Dictionary — 369

Gazetteer — 372

Glossary — 374

ATLAS

World: Physical

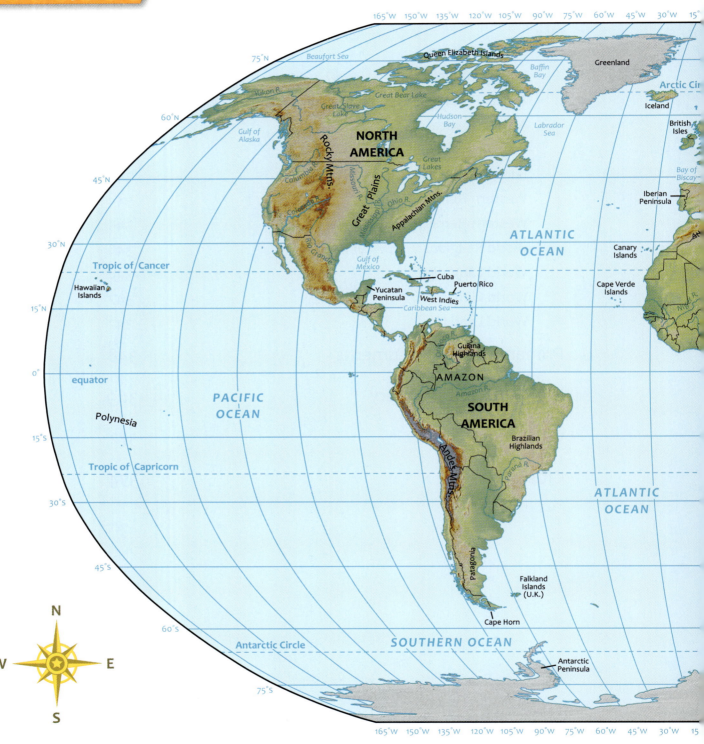

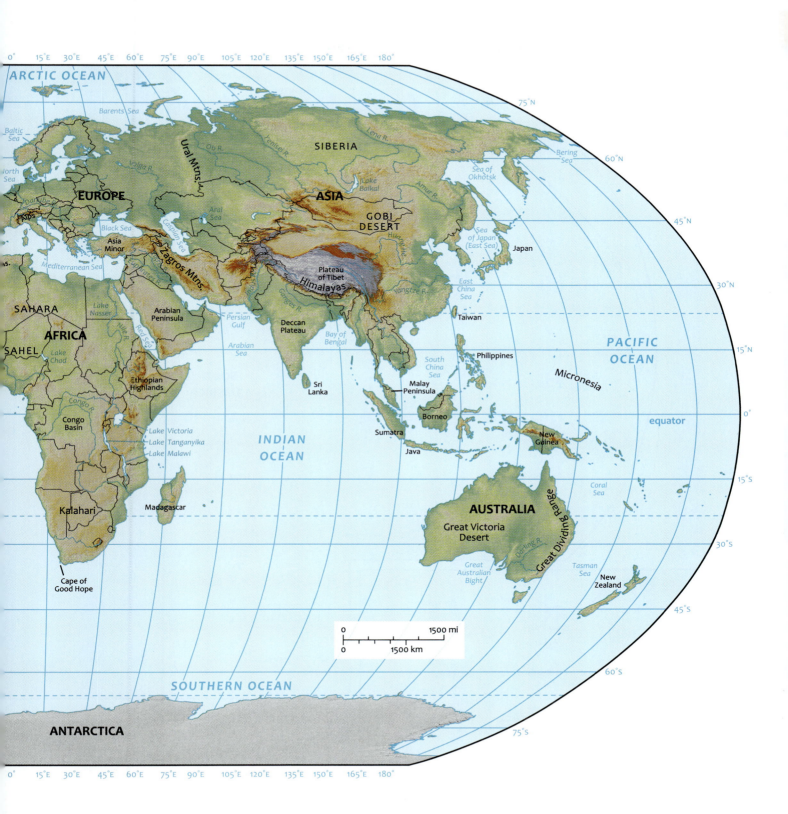

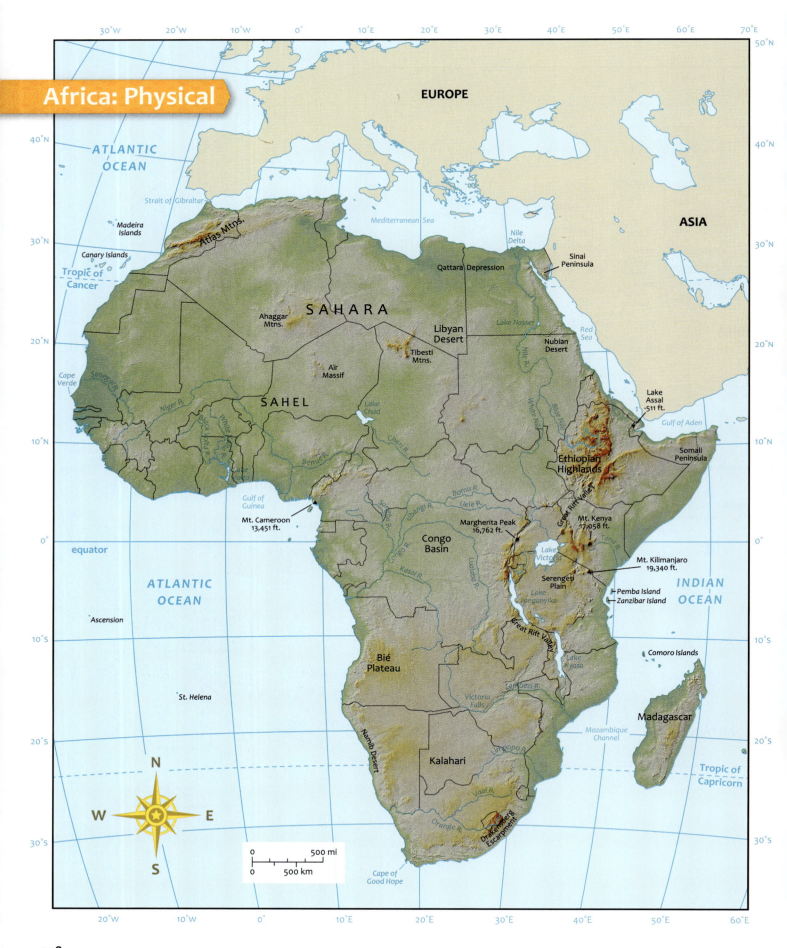

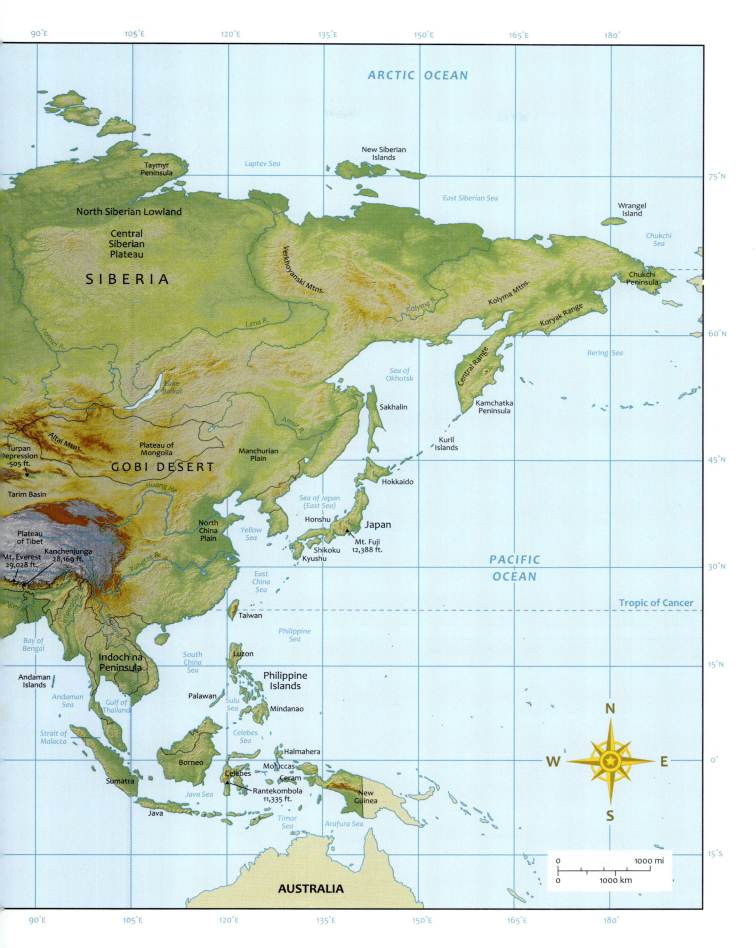

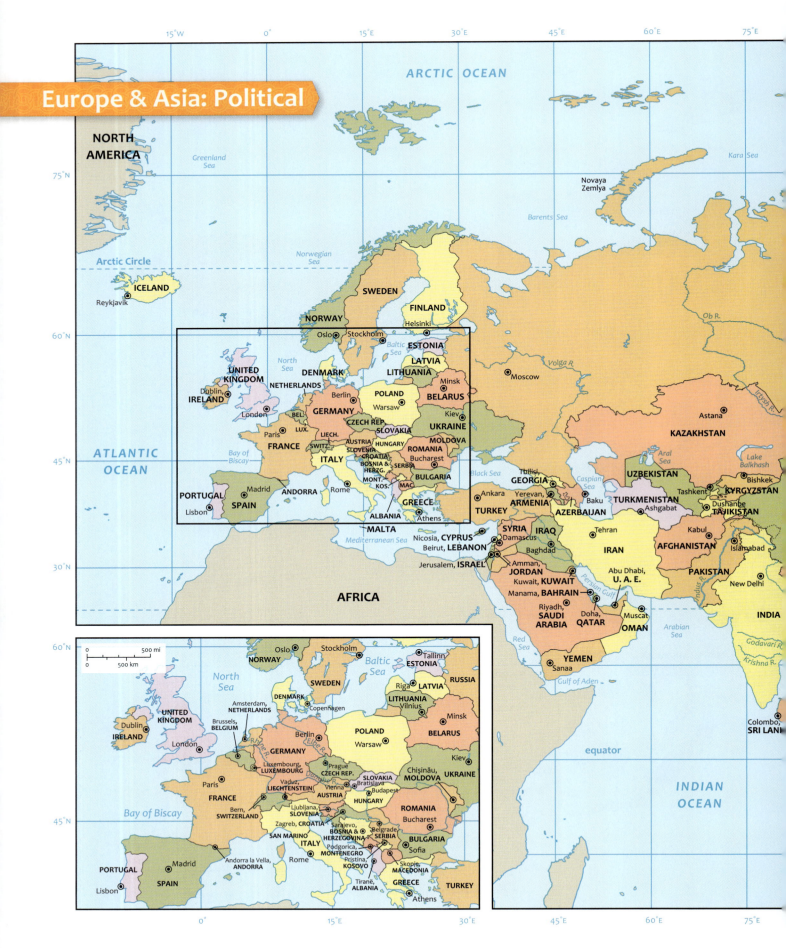

World Religions

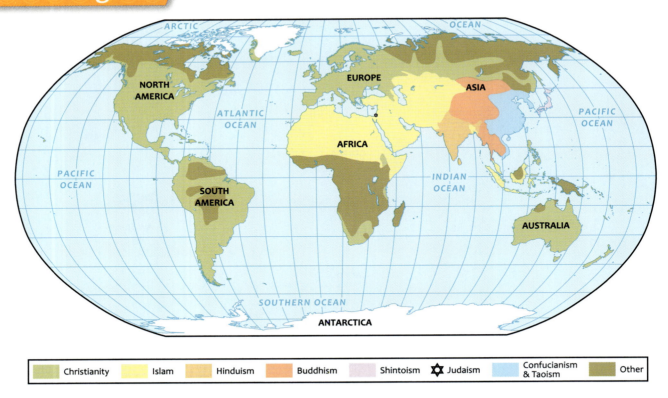

World Languages

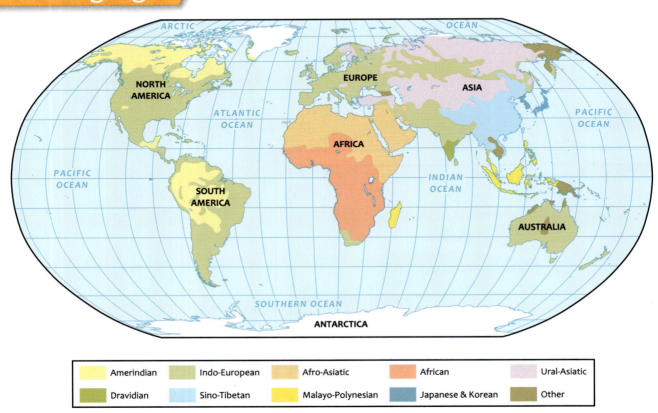

World Climates

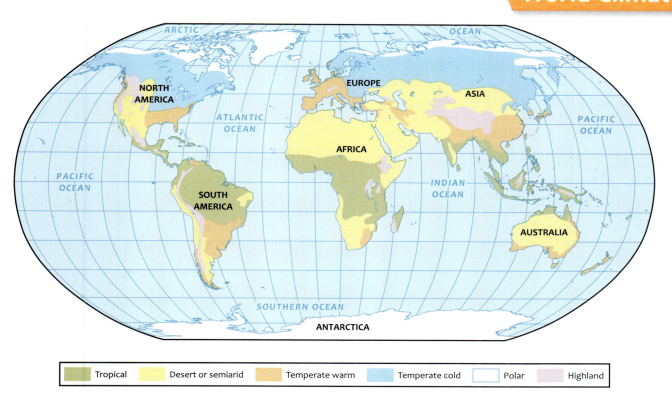

World Land Use

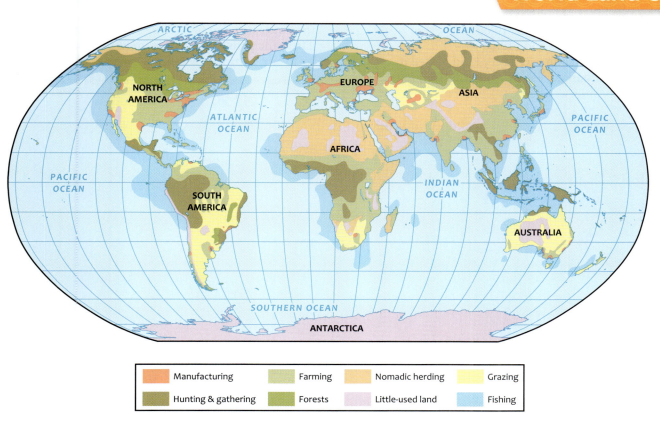

PRIMARY SOURCE DOCUMENTS

Epic of Gilgamesh

The following excerpts are from Tablet 11 of the Epic of Gilgamesh *and give an account of a great flood.*

. . . [From the shore Per-napishtim, the favourite of the gods, now relates the story of the deluge to the hero, who, sitting in his ship, is listening to him.]
Per-napishtim then said unto Gilgamesh:
"I will reveal unto thee, O Gilgamesh, the mysterious story, and the mystery of the gods I will tell thee.
The city of Shurippak, a city which, as thou knowest, is situated on the bank of the river Euphrates.
That city was corrupt, so that the gods within it decided to bring about a deluge. . . .
'Build a house, construct a ship;
Forsake thy possessions, take heed for thy life!
Abandon thy goods, save (thy) life,
and bring living seed of every kind into the ship.
As for the ship, which thou shalt build,
let its proportions be well measured:
Its breadth and its length shall bear proportion each to each, and into the sea then launch it.'
. . . the ship was completed.
. . . heavy was the work, and
I added tackling above and below, [and after all was finished],
The ship sank into water two thirds of its height.
With all that I possessed I filled it;
with all the silver I had I filled it;
with all the gold I had I filled it;
with living creatures of every kind I filled it.
Then I embarked also all my family and my relatives, cattle of the field, beasts of the field, and the uprighteous people —all them I embarked. . . .
I entered the ship and shut the door.
I intrusted the guidance of the ship to Purur-bel, the boatman,
the great house, and the contents thereof.
As soon as early dawn appeared,
there rose up from the horizon a black cloud,
within which the weather god (Adad) thundered,
and Nabu and the king of the gods (Marduk) went before.
The destroyers passed across mountain and dale (literally, country). . . .
The storm brought on by Adad swept even up to the heavens,
and all light was turned into darkness.
[   ] overflooded the land like . . .
It blew with violence and in one day (?) it rose above the mountains (??).
Like an onslaught in battle it rushed in on the people.
Not could brother look after brother.
Not were recognised the people from heaven.
The gods even were afraid of the storm;
they retreated and took refuge in the heaven of Anu.
There the gods crouched down like dogs, on the inclosure of heaven they sat cowering.

Assyrian and Babylonian Literature: Selected Translations, Introduction by Robert Francis Harper (New York: D. Appleton and Company, 1904), 351–55.

Nebuchadnezzar's Letter

These excerpts from Daniel 4 record portions of Nebuchadnezzar's letter that explain how God humbled Nebuchadnezzar by driving him from his kingdom. Once Nebuchadnezzar began to praise the Lord, he was honored and his kingdom was restored to him.

Nebuchadnezzar greets those for whom the letter was written.

1 Nebuchadnezzar the king, unto all people, nations, and languages, that dwell in all the earth; Peace be multiplied unto you.

The king praises God.

2 I thought it good to shew the signs and wonders that the high God hath wrought toward me.

3 How great are his signs! and how mighty are his wonders! his kingdom is an everlasting kingdom, and his dominion is from generation to generation.

Nebuchadnezzar describes his second dream to Daniel.

10 Thus were the visions of mine head in my bed; I saw, and behold a tree in the midst of the earth, and the height thereof was great.

11 The tree grew, and was strong, and the height thereof reached unto heaven, and the sight thereof to the end of all the earth:

12 The leaves thereof were fair, and the fruit thereof much, and in it was meat for all: the beasts of the field had shadow under it, and the fowls of the heaven dwelt in the boughs thereof, and all flesh was fed of it.

13 I saw in the visions of my head upon my bed, and, behold, a watcher and an holy one came down from heaven;

14 He cried aloud, and said thus, Hew down the tree, and cut off his branches, shake off his leaves, and scatter his fruit: let the beasts get away from under it, and the fowls from his branches:

15 Nevertheless leave the stump of his roots in the earth, even with a band of iron and brass, in the tender grass of the field; and let it be wet with the dew of heaven, and let his portion be with the beasts in the grass of the earth:

16 Let his heart be changed from man's, and let a beast's heart be given unto him; and let seven times pass over him.

17 This matter is by the decree of the watchers [observant angels], and the demand by the word of the holy ones [holy angels]: to the intent that the living may know that the most High ruleth in the kingdom of men, and giveth it to whomsoever he will, and setteth up over it the basest [most humble] of men.

18 This dream I king Nebuchadnezzar have seen. Now thou, O Belteshazzar, declare the interpretation thereof, forasmuch as all the wise men of my kingdom are not able to make known unto me the interpretation: but thou art able; for the spirit of the holy gods is in thee.

Daniel interprets Nebuchadnezzar's dream.

19 Then Daniel, whose name was Belteshazzar, was astonied [astonished] for one hour, and his thoughts troubled him. The king spake, and said, Belteshazzar, let not the dream, or the interpretation thereof, trouble thee. Belteshazzar answered and said, My lord, the dream be to them that hate thee, and the interpretation thereof to thine enemies.

20 The tree that thou sawest, which grew, and was strong, whose height reached unto the heaven, and the sight thereof to all the earth;

21 Whose leaves were fair, and the fruit thereof much, and in it was meat for all; under which the beasts of the field dwelt, and upon whose branches the fowls of the heaven had their habitation:

22 It is thou, O king, that art grown and become strong: for thy greatness is grown, and reacheth unto heaven, and thy dominion to the end of the earth.

23 And whereas the king saw a watcher [angel] and an holy one [angel] coming down from heaven, and saying, Hew the tree down, and destroy it; yet leave the stump of the roots thereof in the earth, even with a band of iron and brass, in the tender grass of the field; and let it be wet with the dew of heaven, and let his portion be with the beasts of the field, till seven times [years] pass over him;

24 This is the interpretation, O king, and this is the decree of the most High, which is come upon my lord the king:

25 That they shall drive thee from men, and thy dwelling shall be with the beasts of the field, and they shall make thee to eat grass as oxen, and they shall wet thee with the dew of heaven, and seven times shall pass over thee, till thou know that the most High ruleth in the kingdom of men, and giveth it to whomsoever he will.

26 And whereas they commanded to leave the stump of the tree roots; thy kingdom shall be sure unto thee, after that thou shalt have known that the heavens do rule.

27 Wherefore, O king, let my counsel be acceptable unto thee, and break off thy sins by righteousness, and thine iniquities by shewing mercy to the poor; if it may be a lengthening of thy tranquillity.

God chastens Nebuchadnezzar.

28 All this came upon the king Nebuchadnezzar.

29 At the end of twelve months he walked in the palace of the kingdom of Babylon.

30 The king spake, and said, Is not this great Babylon, that I have built for the house of the kingdom by the might of my power, and for the honour [honor] of my majesty?

31 While the word was in the king's mouth, there fell a voice from heaven, saying, O king Nebuchadnezzar, to thee it is spoken; The kingdom is departed from thee.

32 And they shall drive thee from men, and thy dwelling shall be with the beasts of the field: they shall make thee to eat grass as oxen, and seven times shall pass over thee, until thou know that the most High ruleth in the kingdom of men, and giveth it to whomsoever he will.

33 The same hour was the thing fulfilled upon Nebuchadnezzar: and he was driven from men, and did eat grass as oxen, and his body was wet with the dew of heaven, till his hairs were grown like eagles' feathers, and his nails like birds' claws.

Nebuchadnezzar is restored and brings glory to God.

34 And at the end of the days I Nebuchadnezzar lifted up mine eyes unto heaven, and mine understanding returned unto me, and I blessed the most High, and I praised and honoured him that liveth for ever, whose dominion is an everlasting dominion, and his kingdom is from generation to generation:

35 And all the inhabitants of the earth are reputed as nothing: and he doeth according to his will in the army of heaven, and among the inhabitants of the earth: and none can stay his hand, or say unto him, What doest thou?

36 At the same time my reason returned unto me; and for the glory of my kingdom, mine honour and brightness returned unto me; and my counsellors and my lords sought unto me; and I was established in my kingdom, and excellent majesty was added unto me.

37 Now I Nebuchadnezzar praise and extol and honour the King of heaven, all whose works are truth, and his ways judgment: and those that walk in pride he is able to abase [humble].

Pyramid Texts

The Pyramid Texts are inscribed on the interior walls of certain pyramids. The texts include prayers, hymns, and spells on behalf of the dead pharaoh for his passage to his new celestial abode.

Thy two wings are spread out like a falcon with thick plumage, like the hawk seen in the evening traversing the sky (Pyr. 1048).

Thy bones are falconesses, goddesses dwelling in the sky. . . . Thou ascendest to the sky as a falcon, thy feathers are (those of) geese (Pyr. 913).

King Unis goes to the sky, king Unis goes to the sky! On the wind! On the wind! (Pyr. 309)

[S]tairs to the sky are laid for him that he may ascend thereon to the sky (Pyr. 365).

King Unis ascends upon the ladder which his father Re (the Sun-god) made for him (Pyr. 390).

Atum has done that which he said he would do for this king Pepi II, binding for him the rope-ladder, joining together the (wooden) ladder for this king Pepi II; (thus) this king is far from the abomination of men (Pyr. 2083).

"How beautiful to see, how satisfying to behold," say the gods, "when this god (meaning the king) ascends to the sky. His fearfulness is on his head, his terror is at his side, his magical charms are before him." Geb has done for him as was done for himself (Geb). The gods and souls of Buto, the gods and souls of Hierakonpolis, the gods in the sky and the gods on earth come to him. They make supports for king Unis on their arm(s). Thou ascendest, O King Unis, to the sky. Ascend upon it in this its name "Ladder" (Pyr. 476–9).

Opened are the double doors of the horizon; unlocked are its bolts (Pyr. 194).

Thy messengers go, thy swift messengers run, thy heralds make haste. They announce to Re that thou hast come, (even) this king Pepi (Pyr. 1539–40).

This king Pepi found the gods standing, wrapped in their garments, their white sandals on their feet. They cast off their white sandals to the earth, they throw off their garments. "Our heart was not glad until thy coming," say they (Pyr. 1197).

Unis comes indeed, an imperishable spirit, adorned with the jackal on the sceptre before the western height. He numbers the hearts, he takes possession of the hearts. When he desires that he live, he lives; when he desires that he die, he dies. . . . This king Unis comes indeed, an imperishable spirit. . . . O Re-Atum! Thy son comes to thee, Unis comes to thee. Lift him up to thee, enfold thou him in thy embrace. He is thy bodily son forever (Pyr. 217).

The king ascends to the sky among the gods dwelling in the sky. He stands on the great [dais], he hears (in judicial session) the (legal) affairs of men. . . . become thou a spirit dwelling in Dewat. Live thou this pleasant life which the lord of the horizon lives (Pyr. 1169–72).

James Henry Breasted, *Development of Religion and Thought in Ancient Egypt: Lectures Delivered on the Morse Foundation at Union Theological Seminary*, (New York: Charles Scribner's Sons, 1912), 109–11, 113–14, 118, 120, 136.

The Second Book of Maccabees

The following verses are excerpts from the second book of Maccabees. This book highlights the Jewish rebellion against Antiochus. It ends with Judas Maccabeus's defeat of the Syrian general Nicanor in 161 BC.

2 Maccabees 8

16 But Maccabeus, calling together seven thousand who were with him, asked them not to be reconciled to the enemies. . . .

19 Moreover, he reminded them also of the assistance of God which their parents had received; and how, under Sennacherib, one hundred and eighty-five thousand had perished;

21 By these words, they were brought to constancy and were prepared to die for the laws and their nation.

24 And, with the Almighty as their helper, they slew over nine thousand men. Furthermore, having wounded and disabled the greater part of the army of Nicanor, they forced them to take flight.

29 And so, when these things were done, and supplication was made by all in common, they asked the merciful Lord to be reconciled to his servants unto the end.

36 And he who had promised to pay a tribute to the Romans from the captives of Jerusalem, now professed that the Jews had God as their protector, and, for this reason, they were invulnerable, because they followed the laws established by him.

2 Maccabees 10

2 Then he demolished the altars, which the foreigners had constructed in the streets, and likewise the shrines.

3 And, having purged the temple, they made another altar. And, taking glowing stones from the fire, they began to offer sacrifices again after two years, and they set out incense, and lamps, and the bread of the Presence.

5 Then, on the day that the temple had been polluted by the foreigners, it happened on the same day that the purification was accomplished, on the twenty-fifth day of the month, which was Kislev.

6 And they celebrated for eight days with joy, . . .

7 Because of this, they now preferred to carry boughs and green branches and palms, for him who had prospered the cleansing of his place.

8 And they decreed a common precept and decree, that all the people of the Jews should keep those days every year.

The Sacred Bible: The Second Book of Maccabees, Catholic Public Domain Version, Original Edition, trans. and ed. Ronald L. Conte Jr.

The Laws of Manu

Manu was a mythical character. Because of his ability to protect the people, the god Brahma transformed him into a king. The ancient Indians credited the beginnings of kings and social classes to Manu, who they believed was the first man. These ancient laws discuss the Indian social structure.

I.3. . . . The Brahmin is the lord of all castes.

I.31. But for the sake of the prosperity of the worlds, [the Creator] caused the Brahmin, the Kshatriya, the Vaisya, and the Sudra to proceed from his mouth, his arms, his thighs, and his feet.

I.87. But in order to protect this universe He, the most resplendent one, assigned separate duties and occupations to those who sprang from his mouth, arms, thighs, and feet.

Duties of a Brahmin

X.75. Teaching, studying, sacrificing for himself, sacrificing for others, making gifts and receiving them are the six acts prescribed for a Brahmin.

X.76. But among the six acts ordained for him three are his means of subsistence, sacrificing for others, teaching, and accepting gifts from pure men.
Duties of a Kshatriya
VII.2. A Kshatriya . . . must duly protect this whole world.

VII.3. . . . The Lord created a king for the protection of this whole creation.

VII.20. If the king did not, without tiring, inflict punishment on those worthy to be punished, the stronger would roast the weaker, like fish on a spit.

VII.35. The king has been created to be the protector of the castes and orders, who, all according to their rank, discharge their several duties.

Duties of a Vaisya

IX.326. After a Vaisya has received the sacraments and has taken a wife, he shall be always attentive to the business whereby he may subsist and to that of tending cattle.

IX.327. For when the Lord of creatures . . . created cattle, he made them over to the Vaisya; to the Brahmins and to the king he entrusted all created beings.

IX.332. He must be acquainted with the proper wages of servants, with the various languages of men, with the manner of keeping goods, and the rules of purchase and sale.

Duties of a Sudra

IX.334. [T]o serve Brahmins who are learned in the Vedas, householders, and famous for virtue is the highest duty of a Sudra, which leads to beatitude.

IX.335. A Sudra who is pure, the servant of his betters, gentle in his speech, and free from pride, and always seeks a refuge with Brahmins, attains . . . a higher caste.

IX.336. The excellent law for the conduct of the (four) castes (varna), when they are not in distress, has been thus promulgated.

The Laws of Manu, ed. G. Buhler (Oxford: Clarendon Press, 1886).

The Analects by Confucius

The following excerpts are from Section 1 of The Analects. *The Analects are sayings of Confucius that were written by his disciples after his death.*

Book I—Concerning Fundamental Principles

I. The Master said; "Is it not indeed a pleasure to acquire knowledge and constantly to exercise oneself therein?"

***

VIII. The Master said; "A Scholar who is not grave will not inspire respect, and his learning will therefore lack stability. His chief principles should be conscientiousness and sincerity. Let him have no friends unequal to himself. And when in the wrong let him not hesitate to amend."

***

XI. The Master said: "While a man's father lives mark his tendencies; when his father is dead mark his conduct."

Book II—Concerning Government

X. The Master said: "Observe what he does; look into his motives; find out in what he rests. Can a man hide himself! Can a man hide himself!"

***

XV. The Master said: "Learning without thought is useless. Thought without learning is dangerous."

***

XXIV. "To see the right and not do it is cowardice."

Book IV—Concerning Virtue

III. The Master said: "Only the Virtuous are competent to love or to hate men."

***

V. The Master said: "Wealth and rank are what men desire, but unless they be obtained in the right way they are not to be possessed. Poverty and obscurity are what men detest; but unless it can be brought about in the right way, they are not to be abandoned."

***

XI. The Master said: "The man of honour thinks of his character, the inferior man of his position. The man of honour desires justice, the inferior man favour."

***

XXIII. The Master said: "The self-restrained seldom err."

***

XXIV. The Master said: "The wise man desires to be slow to speak but quick to act."

***

XXV. The Master said: "Virtue never dwells alone; it always has neighbours."

Book V—Concerning Certain Disciples and Others

XI. Tzŭ Kung said: "What I do not wish others to do to me, that also I wish not to do to them."

The Analects of Confucius, trans. William Edward Soothill (Yokohama: Fleming H. Revell, 1910).

God's Writing on the Wall

Scripture records how Daniel interpreted the writing for Belshazzar.

Daniel 5

1 Belshazzar the king made a great feast to a thousand of his lords, and drank wine before the thousand.

2 Belshazzar, whiles he tasted the wine, commanded to bring the golden and silver vessels which his father Nebuchadnezzar had taken out of the temple which was in Jerusalem; that the king, and his princes, his wives, and his concubines, might drink therein.

3 Then they brought the golden vessels that were taken out of the temple of the house of God which was at Jerusalem; and the king, and his princes, his wives, and his concubines, drank in them.

4 They drank wine, and praised the gods of gold, and of silver, of brass, of iron, of wood, and of stone.

5 In the same hour came forth fingers of a man's hand, and wrote over against the candlestick upon the plaister of the wall of the king's palace: and the king saw the part of the hand that wrote.

6 Then the king's countenance was changed, and his thoughts troubled him, so that the joints of his loins were loosed, and his knees smote one against another.

7 The king cried aloud to bring in the astrologers, the Chaldeans, and the soothsayers. And the king spake, and said to the wise men of Babylon, Whosoever shall read this writing, and shew me the interpretation thereof, shall be clothed with scarlet, and have a chain of gold about his neck, and shall be the third ruler in the kingdom.

8 Then came in all the king's wise men: but they could not read the writing, nor make known to the king the interpretation thereof.

9 Then was king Belshazzar greatly troubled, and his countenance was changed in him, and his lords were astonied.

10 Now the queen, by reason of the words of the king and his lords, came into the banquet house: and the queen spake and said, O king, live for ever: let not thy thoughts trouble thee, nor let thy countenance be changed:

11 There is a man in thy kingdom, in whom is the spirit of the holy gods; and in the days of thy father light and understanding and wisdom, like the wisdom of the gods, was found in him; whom the king Nebuchadnezzar thy father, the king, I say, thy father, made master of the magicians, astrologers, Chaldeans, and soothsayers;

12 Forasmuch as an excellent spirit, and knowledge, and understanding, interpreting of dreams, and shewing of hard sentences, and dissolving of doubts, were found in the same Daniel, whom the king named Belteshazzar: now let Daniel be called, and he will shew the interpretation.

13 Then was Daniel brought in before the king. And the king spake and said unto Daniel, Art thou that Daniel, which art of the children of the captivity of Judah, whom the king my father brought out of Jewry?

14 I have even heard of thee, that the spirit of the gods is in thee, and that light and understanding and excellent wisdom is found in thee.

15 And now the wise men, the astrologers, have been brought in before me, that they should read this writing, and make known unto me the interpretation thereof: but they could not shew the interpretation of the thing:

16 And I have heard of thee, that thou canst make interpretations, and dissolve doubts: now if thou canst read the writing, and make known to me the interpretation thereof, thou shalt be clothed with scarlet, and have a chain of gold about thy neck, and shalt be the third ruler in the kingdom.

17 Then Daniel answered and said before the king, Let thy gifts be to thyself, and give thy rewards to another; yet I will read the writing unto the king, and make known to him the interpretation.

18 O thou king, the most high God gave Nebuchadnezzar thy father a kingdom, and majesty, and glory, and honour:

19 And for the majesty that he gave him, all people, nations, and languages, trembled and feared before him: whom he would he slew; and whom he would he kept alive; and whom he would he set up; and whom he would he put down.

20 But when his heart was lifted up, and his mind hardened in pride, he was deposed from his kingly throne, and they took his glory from him:

21 And he was driven from the sons of men; and his heart was made like the beasts, and his dwelling was with the wild asses: they fed him with grass like oxen, and his body was wet with the dew of heaven; till he knew that the most high God ruled in the kingdom of men, and that he appointeth over it whomsoever he will.

22 And thou his son, O Belshazzar, hast not humbled thine heart, though thou knewest all this;

23 But hast lifted up thyself against the Lord of heaven; and they have brought the vessels of his house before thee, and thou, and thy lords, thy wives,

and thy concubines, have drunk wine in them; and thou hast praised the gods of silver, and gold, of brass, iron, wood, and stone, which see not, nor hear, nor know: and the God in whose hand thy breath is, and whose are all thy ways, hast thou not glorified:

24 Then was the part of the hand sent from him; and this writing was written.

25 And this is the writing that was written, MENE, MENE, TEKEL, UPHARSIN.

26 This is the interpretation of the thing: MENE; God hath numbered thy kingdom, and finished it.

27 TEKEL; Thou art weighed in the balances, and art found wanting.

28 PERES; Thy kingdom is divided, and given to the Medes and Persians.

29 Then commanded Belshazzar, and they clothed Daniel with scarlet, and put a chain of gold about his neck, and made a proclamation concerning him, that he should be the third ruler in the kingdom.

30 In that night was Belshazzar the king of the Chaldeans slain.

31 And Darius the Median took the kingdom, being about threescore and two years old.

The History of Herodotus

The following is an excerpt from a history book about Persian judges. It is written by the historian Herodotus.

Now the royal judges are certain picked men among the Persians, who hold their office for life, or until they are found guilty of some misconduct. By them justice is administered in Persia, and they are the interpreters of the old laws, all disputes being referred to their decision. When Cambyses, therefore, put his question to these judges, they gave him an answer which was at once true and safe—"they did not find any law," they said, "allowing a brother to take his sister to wife, but they found a law, that the king of the Persians might do whatever he pleased." And so they neither warped the law through fear of Cambyses, nor ruined themselves by over stiffly maintaining the law; but they brought another quite distinct law to the king's help, which allowed him to have his wish. Cambyses, therefore, married the object of his love.

The History of Herodotus, trans. George Rawlinson, vol. II (New York: D. Appleton and Co., 1880), 358–59.

The King Dethrones Queen Vashti

The book of Esther was written to explain the origin of the Feast of Purim. This excerpt tells of the first step in moving Esther into a position of power before the threat of Haman emerges.

Esther 1

3 In the third year of his [Ahasuerus] reign, he made a feast unto all his princes and his servants; the power of Persia and Media, . . .

10 On the seventh day, when the heart of the king was merry with wine, he commanded . . .

11 To bring Vashti the queen before the king with the crown royal, to shew the people and the princes her beauty: for she was fair to look on.

12 But the queen Vashti refused to come at the king's commandment by his chamberlains: therefore was the king very wroth, and his anger burned in him.

13 Then the king said to the wise men . . . What shall we do unto the queen Vashti according to law . . . ?

16 And Memucan answered before the king and the princes, Vashti the queen hath not done wrong to the king only, but also to all the princes, and to all the people that are in all the provinces of the king Ahasuerus.

17 For this deed of the queen shall come abroad unto all women, so that they shall despise their husbands . . . .

19 If it please the king, let there go a royal commandment from him, and let it be written among the laws of the Persians and the Medes, that it be not altered, That Vashti come no more before king Ahasuerus; and let the king give her royal estate unto another that is better than she.

Pericles's Funeral Oration

Pericles gave this speech at a funeral after the beginning of the Peloponnesian War. He used this public occasion to state the values of democracy.

I shall begin with our ancestors: it is both just and proper that they should have the honour of the first mention on an occasion like the present. They dwelt in the country without break in the succession from generation to generation, and handed it down free to the present time by their valour. . . .

Our constitution does not copy the laws of neighbouring states; but we are rather a pattern to others than imitators ourselves. Its administration favours the many instead of the few; this is why it is called a democracy. If we look to the laws, they afford equal justice to all in their private differences; if to social standing, advancement in public life falls to reputation for capacity, class considerations not being allowed to interfere with merit; while as to poverty, if a man is able to serve the state, he is not hindered by the obscurity of his condition. The freedom which we enjoy in our government extends also to our ordinary life. . . . But all this ease in our private relations does not make us lawless as citizens. . . .

. . . We throw open our city to the world, and never by alien acts exclude foreigners from any opportunity of learning or observing, although the eyes of an enemy may occasionally profit by our liberality. . . .

. . . And it is only the Athenians, who, fearless of consequences, confer their benefits not from calculations of expediency, but in the confidence of liberality.

. . . Such is the Athens for which these men, in the assertion of their resolve not to lose her, nobly fought and died; and well may every one of their survivors be ready to suffer in her cause.

. . . [Y]ou must yourselves realize the power of Athens, and feed your eyes upon her from day to day, till love of her fills your hearts; and then, when all her greatness shall break upon you, you must reflect that it was by courage, sense of duty, and a keen feeling of honour in action that men were enabled to win all this. . . .

Comfort, therefore, not condolence, is what I have to offer to the parents of the dead who may be here. . . . [F]ortunate indeed are they who draw for their lot a death so glorious as that which has caused your mourning. . . . Still I know that this is a hard saying, especially when those are in question of whom you will constantly be reminded by seeing in the homes of others blessings of which once you also boasted: for grief is felt not so much for the want of what we have never known, as for the loss of that to which we have been long accustomed.

. . . The state thus offers a valuable prize, as the garland of victory in this race of valour, for the reward both of those who have fallen and their survivors. And where the rewards for merit are greatest, there are found the best citizens.

Thucydides' Peloponnesian War, Book 2.34–46, trans. Richard Crawley (London: J.M. Dent and Co., 1903).

"Pallanteum—the Site of Rome"

Excerpt from The Aeneid Book VIII

Then they all returned to the city, the sacred rites complete.
The king walked clothed with years, and kept Aeneas and his son
near him for company, lightening the road with various talk.
Aeneas marvelled, and scanned his eyes about
eagerly, captivated by the place, and delighted
to enquire about and learn each tale of the men of old.
So King Evander, founder of Rome's citadel, said:
'The local Nymphs and Fauns once lived in these groves,
and a race of men born of trees with tough timber,
who had no laws or culture, and didn't know how
to yoke oxen or gather wealth, or lay aside a store,
but the branches fed them, and the hunter's wild fare.
Saturn was the first to come down from heavenly Olympus,
fleeing Jove's weapons, and exiled from his lost realm.
He gathered together the untaught race, scattered among
the hills, and gave them laws, and chose to call it Latium,
from *latere*, 'to hide', since he had hidden in safety on these shores.
Under his reign was the Golden Age men speak of:
in such tranquil peace did he rule the nations,
until little by little an inferior, tarnished age succeeded,
with war's madness, and desire for possessions.
Then the Ausonian bands came, and the Siconian tribes,
while Saturn's land of Latium often laid aside her name:
then the kings, and savage Thybris, of vast bulk,
after whom we Italians call our river by the name
of Tiber: the ancient Albula has lost her true name.
As for me, exiled from my country and seeking
the limits of the ocean, all-powerful Chance,
and inescapable fate, settled me in this place,
driven on by my mother the Nymph Carmentis's
dire warnings, and my guardian god Apollo.'
He had scarcely spoken when advancing he pointed out
the altar and what the Romans call the Carmental Gate,
in ancient tribute to the Nymph Carmentis,
the far-seeing prophetess, who first foretold
the greatness of Aeneas's sons, the glory of Pallanteum.

Reprinted with permission from Tony Kline, "Pallanteum—the Site of Rome," *The Aeneid*, Book VIII, trans. A. S. Kline. http://www.poetryintranslation.com/PITBR/Latin/VirgilAeneidVIII.htm#_Toc3637703 (accessed July 14, 2017).

An Excerpt from Peter's Sermon at Pentecost
Acts 2:22–47

22 Ye men of Israel, hear these words; Jesus of Nazareth, a man approved of God among you by miracles and wonders and signs, which God did by him in the midst of you, as ye yourselves also know:

23 Him, being delivered by the determinate counsel and foreknowledge of God, ye have taken, and by wicked hands have crucified and slain:

24 Whom God hath raised up, having loosed the pains of death: because it was not possible that he should be holden of it.

25 For David speaketh concerning him, I foresaw the Lord always before my face, for he is on my right hand, that I should not be moved:

26 Therefore did my heart rejoice, and my tongue was glad; moreover also my flesh shall rest in hope:

27 Because thou wilt not leave my soul in hell, neither wilt thou suffer thine Holy One to see corruption.

28 Thou hast made known to me the ways of life; thou shalt make me full of joy with thy countenance.

29 Men and brethren, let me freely speak unto you of the patriarch David, that he is both dead and buried, and his sepulchre is with us unto this day.

30 Therefore being a prophet, and knowing that God had sworn with an oath to him, that of the fruit of his loins, according to the flesh, he would raise up Christ to sit on his throne;

31 He seeing this before spake of the resurrection of Christ, that his soul was not left in hell, neither his flesh did see corruption.

32 This Jesus hath God raised up, whereof we all are witnesses.

33 Therefore being by the right hand of God exalted, and having received of the Father the promise of the Holy Ghost, he hath shed forth this, which ye now see and hear.

34 For David is not ascended into the heavens: but he saith himself, The Lord said unto my Lord, Sit thou on my right hand,

35 Until I make thy foes thy footstool.

36 Therefore let all the house of Israel know assuredly, that God hath made that same Jesus, whom ye have crucified, both Lord and Christ.

37 Now when they heard this, they were pricked in their heart, and said unto Peter and to the rest of the apostles, Men and brethren, what shall we do?

38 Then Peter said unto them, Repent, and be baptized every one of you in the name of Jesus Christ for the remission of sins, and ye shall receive the gift of the Holy Ghost.

39 For the promise is unto you, and to your children, and to all that are afar off, even as many as the Lord our God shall call.

40 And with many other words did he testify and exhort, saying, Save yourselves from this untoward generation.

41 Then they that gladly received his word were baptized: and the same day there were added unto them about three thousand souls.

42 And they continued stedfastly in the apostles' doctrine and fellowship, and in breaking of bread, and in prayers.

43 And fear came upon every soul: and many wonders and signs were done by the apostles.

44 And all that believed were together, and had all things common;

45 And sold their possessions and goods, and parted them to all men, as every man had need.

46 And they, continuing daily with one accord in the temple, and breaking bread from house to house, did eat their meat with gladness and singleness of heart,

47 Praising God, and having favour with all the people. And the Lord added to the church daily such as should be saved.

Letters of Pliny the Younger and Trajan

Letters of Pliny the Younger and Trajan, XCVI [XCVII]

Pliny to the Emperor Trajan

It is my custom, my lord, to refer to you all things concerning which I am in doubt. For who is better able to guide my indecision or enlighten my ignorance? I have never taken part in the trials of Christians, hence I do not know for what crime or to what extent it is customary to punish or investigate. I have been in no little doubt as to whether any discrimination is made for age, or whether the treatment of the young does not differ from that of the more mature; whether pardon is granted in case of repentance, or whether he who has ever been a Christian gains nothing by having ceased to be one; whether the name itself, without regard to crimes, or the crimes attributed to the name are punished.

In the meantime, I have followed this procedure in the case of those who have been brought before me as Christians. I asked them whether they were Christians. If they confessed I repeated the question a second and a third time with threats of punishment; those who were obstinate I ordered to be executed. For I did not doubt that, whatever it was that they confessed, their stubbornness and inflexible obstinacy ought certainly to be punished. There were others of similar madness, who, because they were Roman citizens, I have noted for sending to the city [Rome].

Soon, the crime spreading, as is usual, because of this very treatment, more cases arose. An anonymous accusation containing many names was presented. Those who denied that they were or had been Christians ought, I thought, to be dismissed, since they repeated after me an invocation to the gods and made supplication with incense and wine to your image, which I had ordered to be brought for the purpose together with the statues of the gods, and since besides they reviled [cursed] Christ, not one of which things, they say, those who are really Christians can be compelled to do. Others accused by the informer said that they were Christians and then denied it; in fact they had been but had ceased to be, some three years before, some many years before, several even twenty. All of these both worshiped your image and the statues of the gods and reviled [cursed] Christ.

They continued to maintain that this was the amount of their fault or error, that on a fixed day they were accustomed to come together before daylight and to sing by turns a hymn to Christ as a god, and that they bound themselves by oath, not for some crime, but that they would not commit theft, robbery, or adultery, that they would not betray a trust, nor deny a deposit when called upon. After this it was their custom to disperse and to come together again to partake of food, of an ordinary and harmless variety, however. Even this they ceased to do after the publication of my edict in which, according to your command, I had forbidden associations. Hence I believed it the more necessary even to put to torture two female slaves, who were called deaconesses, in order to find out what was true. I found nothing but a vicious, extravagant superstition.

Consequently I postponed the examination and made haste to consult you. For it seemed to me a subject worthy of consultation, especially on account of the number of those in peril. For many of all ages, of every rank, and even of both sexes are and will be called into danger. The infection of this superstition has spread not alone to the cities, but even to the villages and country districts. It seems possible to check it and bring about a reform. It is certainly evident that the temples, recently deserted, have begun to be frequented, that the sacred rites, long neglected, have begun to be restored, and that fodder for victims, for which until now there was scarcely a purchaser, is sold. From which one may readily judge how great a number of men can be reclaimed if repentance is permitted.

Trajan to Pliny

You have followed the correct procedure, my Secundus, in conducting the cases of those who were accused before you as Christians. For no general rule can be laid down as a set form. They ought not to be sought out; if they are brought before you and the case is proven, they should be punished; provided that he who denies that he is a Christian, and proves this by making supplication to our gods, however much he may have been suspected in the past, shall secure pardon on repentance. Anonymous accusations, however, are inadmissible for any crime, for they afford a very bad precedent and are not worthy of our age.

Studies in History, Economics and Public Law: The Early Persecutions of the Christians, ed. faculty of Political Science of Columbia University, Vol. LV, Number 2, by Leon Hardy Canfield (Columbia University: Longmans, Green & Co., Agents, 1913), 183–85.

The Edict of Milan

In 313 the Roman emperors Constantine I and Licinius proclaimed the Edict of Milan, which established a policy of religious freedom. This ended the persecution of Christians in the Roman Empire. The following is an English translation of an excerpt from the edict.

When I, Constantine Augustus, as well as I, Licinius Augustus, had fortunately met near Mediolanurn (Milan), and were considering everything that pertained to the public welfare and security, we thought that, among other things which we saw would be for the good of many, those regulations pertaining to the reverence of the Divinity ought certainly to be made first, so that we might grant to the Christians and to all others full authority to observe that religion which each preferred; whence any Divinity whatsoever in the seat of the heavens may be propitious and kindly disposed to us and all who are placed under our rule. And thus by this wholesome counsel and most upright provision we thought to arrange that no one whatsoever should be denied the opportunity to give his heart to the observance of the Christian religion, or of that religion which he should think best for himself, so that the supreme Deity, to whose worship we freely yield our hearts, may show in all things His usual favor and benevolence. Therefore, your Worship should know that it has pleased us to remove all conditions whatsoever, which were in the rescripts formerly given to you officially, concerning the Christians, and now any one of these who wishes to observe the Christian religion may do so freely and openly, without any disturbance or molestation. We thought it fit to commend these things most fully to your care that you may know that we have given to those Christians free and unrestricted opportunity of religious worship. When you see that this has been granted to them by us, your Worship will know that we have also conceded to other religions the right of open and free observance of their worship for the sake of the peace of our times, that each one may have the free opportunity to worship as he pleases; this regulation is made that we may not seem to detract aught [anything] from any dignity or any religion.

Edict of Milan (AD 313), in *Translations and Reprints from the Original Sources of European History*, vol. 4, no. 1 (Philadelphia: University of Pennsylvania Press, 1897), 29.

Excerpts from the Qur'an

These excerpts are translations from the Qur'an (Koran).

Selections on Good Works

101.001 The Calamity!

101.002 What is the Calamity?

101.003 Ah, what will convey unto thee what the Calamity is!

101.004 A day wherein mankind will be as thickly-scattered moths

101.005 And the mountains will become as carded wool.

101.006 Then, as for him whose scales are heavy (with good works),

101.007 He will live a pleasant life.

101.008 But as for him whose scales are light,

101.009 The Bereft and Hungry One will be his mother.

101.010 Ah, what will convey unto thee what she is!—

101.011 Raging fire.

Selections on Jihad

002.190–191 Fight in the way of Allah against those who fight against you, but begin not hostilities. Lo! Allah loveth not aggressors. And slay them wherever ye find them, and drive them out of the places whence they drove you out, for persecution is worse than slaughter. And fight not with them at the Inviolable Place of Worship until they first attack you there, but if they attack you (there) then slay them. Such is the reward of disbelievers.

003.169 Think not of those, who are slain in the way of Allah, as dead. Nay, they are living. With their Lord they have provision.

005.082 Thou wilt find the most vehement of mankind in hostility to those who believe (to be) the Jews and the idolaters. And thou wilt find the nearest of them in affection to those who believe (to be) those who say: Lo! We are Christians. That is because there are among them priests and monks, and because they are not proud.

009.029 Fight against such of those who have been given the Scripture as believe not in Allah nor the Last Day, and forbid not that which Allah hath forbidden by His messenger, and follow not the religion of truth, until they pay the tribute readily, being brought low.

The Quran, trans. Marmaduke Pickthall, (New York: Alfred A Knopf, 1930).

Offensive and Defensive Arms

The following narrative contains firsthand accounts of the offensive and defensive weapons used in ancient Mesoamerican cities.

Their weapons of offense are bows and arrows, and darts which they throw with a machine made of another stick. . . . They use slings which carry very far, and ordinarily carry all these weapons. It is one of the finest things in the world to see them in war in their squadrons, because they move with perfect order, and are splendidly attired, and make such a fine appearance that nothing could be better. Among them are very resolute men who affront death with determination. I saw one of them defending himself most valiantly against two light-horsemen, and another against three or four. The Spaniards seeing that they could not kill him, one of them lost patience, and darted his lance at him, but the Indian, before it reached him, caught it in the air, and with it fought for more than an hour until two foot-soldiers arrived who wounded him with one or two successful arrows. One of them got in front of him, and the other grabbed him from behind and stabbed him. While they are fighting they sing and dance, and from time to time utter the most frightful whoopings and whistlings in the world, especially when they see that they are gaining the advantage, and it is a certain fact that, to any one who had never seen them fight before, their yells and manly appearance would be intimidating. . . . They are not permitted to kill Lords, but they made them their prisoners, and carried them off well guarded. Soon afterwards they prepared a festival, in anticipation of which there are in the middle of the squares of the cities certain massive platforms of masonry, . . . and in the middle of this place is fixed a round stone, having a hole in the center. The Lord prisoner mounted, and was tied to the stone by the narrow part of the foot with a long thin cord. They gave him one of their swords and a buckler, and soon the same man who took him prisoner came to fight with him. If he again succeeded in the combat he was esteemed a most valiant man, and was given some insignia of feats of arms, and the Lord in whose service he was gave him other rewards. But if the prisoner conquered him and six others, making in all seven vanquished, he was restored to liberty, and every one who had taken anything from him was compelled to restore it.

"Narrative of Some Things of New Spain and of the Great City of Temestitan, Mexico" in *Documents and Narratives Concerning the Discovery and Conquest of Latin America*, trans. Marshall Saville (New York: The Cortes Society, 1917), 22–27.

An African Creation Myth

This is a retelling of an African creation myth. The story comes from the San (formerly called Bushmen [now considered a derogatory term]), a native people of South Africa. The story offers an explanation for the relationship between people and animals.

Some of the tribes living in the regions around the lower portion of the Gariep have another version of a primitive state of friendship between Bushmen and the lower animals, and their subsequent dispersion. According to this myth their remote forefathers came out of a hole in the ground, at the roots of an enormous tree, which covered a wide extent of country. Immediately afterwards all kinds of animals came swarming out after them, some kinds by twos and threes and fours; others in great herds and flocks; and they crushed, and jostled, and pushed each other in their hurry, as if they could not get out fast enough; and they ever came out swarming thicker and thicker, and at last they came flocking out of the branches as well as the roots. But when the sun went down, fresh ones ceased making their appearance. The animals were endowed with the gift of speech, and remained quietly located under and around the big tree.

As the night came on, the men, who were still sitting at the foot of the tree, were told that during that night, until the sun rose again, they must not make a fire. Thus they remained for many hours, with all the animals sleeping peacefully around them. And the night grew not only very dark, but cold, and the cold went on increasing until it became bitterly cold, and then cold almost beyond endurance; and the men at last, not being able to withstand the extreme severity any longer, in spite of the warning that had been given to them, attempted, and at last succeeded in making a fire. As soon as the flames began to shoot up, the startled animals sprang to their feet in terror, and rushed off panic-stricken to the mountains and the plains, losing in their fright all powers of speech, and fleeing ever afterwards from the presence of man. Only a very few animals remained with the fire-makers, and these the men domesticated and kept about them for their service; but the great family of animals was broken up, and could never again be reunited.

George William Stow, *The Native Races of South Africa: A History of the Intrusion of the Hottentots and Bantu into the Hunting Grounds of the Bushmen, the Aborigines of the Country*. ed. George McCall Theal (London: Sonnenschein & Company, Limited, 1905), 130–31.

Songs of Japan

The following translation tells the origin of some traditional Japanese songs.

[The Emperor entertained the Imperial army with banquets. The common soldiers then sang this Kume song. In modern performances, they still beat out the rhythms by hand and use distinctly different voices.]

In the high castle of Uda
I set a snare for woodcock,
And waited,
But no woodcock came to it;
A valiant whale came to it.

. . .

[After eating,] the Emperor . . . first of all attacked the eighty bandits at Mount Kunimi, routed and slew them. It was in this campaign that the Emperor, fully resolved on victory, made these verses, saying:—

Like the Shitadami
Which creep around
The great rock [Hill of Kunimi]
Of the Sea of Ise
Where blows the divine wind
Like the Shitadami, My boys! my boys!
We will creep around,
And smite them utterly,
And smite them utterly.

. . .

So the Emperor privately commanded Michi no Omi no Mikoto, saying:— ". . . Prepare a copious banquet, invite the enemy to it, and then capture them." Michi no Omi no Mikoto thereupon . . . dug a muro [pit] at Osaka, and having selected his bravest soldiers . . . secretly arranged with them, saying:—" . . . Do you, when you hear the sound of my song, all at the same time stab the enemy." . . . Then Michi no Omi no Mikoto struck up the following song:—

At Osaka
In the great muro-house,
Though men in plenty
Enter and stay,
We the glorious
Sons of warriors,
Wielding our mallet-heads.
Wielding our stone-mallets,
Will smite them utterly.

Now when our troops heard this song, they all drew at the same time their mallet-headed swords, and simultanously slew the enemy, so that there were no eaters left. The Imperial army were greatly delighted; they looked up to Heaven and laughed. Therefore he made a song, saying:—

Though folk say
That one Yemishi
Is a match for one hundred men,
They do not so much as resist.

[Modern performances still follow the song with laughter.] Again he sang, saying:—

Ho! now is the time;
Ho! now is the time;
Ha! Ha! Psha!
Even now
My boys!
Even now
My boys!

All these songs were sung in accordance with the secret behest of the Emperor.

Nihongi: Chronicles of Japan from the Earliest Times to A.D. 697, trans. W. G. Aston (London: Kegan Paul, Trench, Trübner & Co., Limited, 1896), 1:118, 122–24.

Christopher Columbus: Extracts from Journal

The following is a translation of entries from the 1492 journal kept by Christopher Columbus on his voyage.

Whereas, Most Christian, High, Excellent, and Powerful Princes, King and Queen of Spain and of the Islands of the Sea, our Lords, this present year 1492, . . . Your Highnesses, as Catholic Christians, and princes who love and promote the holy Christian faith, . . . determined to send me, Christopher Columbus, to the said parts of India . . . ; and furthermore directed that I should not proceed by land to the East, as is customary, but by a Westerly route, in which direction we have hitherto no certain evidence that any one has gone. . . . Hereupon I left the city of Granada, on Saturday, the twelfth day of May, 1492, and proceeded to Palos, a seaport, where I equipped three vessels, very fit for such an enterprise, and having provided myself with abundance of stores and seamen, I set sail from the port, on Friday, the third of August, half an hour before sunrise, and steered for the Canary Islands of your Highnesses, which are in the said ocean, thence to take my departure and proceed till I arrived at the Indies, and perform the embassy of your Highnesses to the Princes there, and discharge the orders given me. For this purpose I determined to keep an account of the voyage, and to write down punctually every thing we performed or saw from day to day, as will hereafter appear. . . .

Wednesday, Oct. 10th

Steered west-southwest and sailed at times ten miles an hour, at others twelve, and at others, seven; day and night made fifty-nine leagues progress; reckoned to the crew but forty-four. Here the men lost all patience, and complained of the length of the voyage, but the Admiral encouraged them in the best manner he could, representing the profits they were about to acquire, and adding that it was to no purpose to complain, since he had come to the Indies, and that so he must continue on till, with the help of our Lord, he found them.

Thursday, Oct. 11th

Steered west-southwest; and encountered a heavier sea than they had met with before in the whole voyage. Saw sandpipers and a green rush near the vessel. The crew of the caravel Pinta saw a cane and a log; they also picked up a stick which appeared to have been carved with an iron tool, a piece of cane, another plant which grows on land, and a board. The crew of the Niña saw other signs of land, and a stalk loaded with rose-hips. These signs made them all grow cheerful again. . . .

At two o'clock in the morning, the land was discovered, at two leagues distance; . . . . The Admiral bore the royal standard, and the two captains each a banner of the Green Cross, which all the ships had carried for an ensign; this contained an F and a Y, one letter on each side of the cross, and a crown over each letter. Arrived on shore, they saw trees very green, many streams of water, and diverse sorts of fruits. . . . Numbers of the people of the island straightway collected together. Here follow the precise words of the Admiral. . . . "As I saw that they were very friendly to us, . . . I presented them with some red caps, and strings of beads to wear upon the neck, and many other trifles of small value. . . ."

Wednesday, Oct. 17th

. . . I strayed about among the groves, which present the most enchanting sight ever witnessed, a degree of verdure prevailing like that of May in Andalusia, the trees as different from those of our country as day is from night, and the same may be said of the fruit, the plants, the stones and everything else. . . .

Thursday, Oct. 18th

As soon as the sky grew clear, I sailed before the wind and went as far round the island as I could. . . .

Friday, Oct. 19th

. . . The wind being favourable, I came to the Cape, which I named Hermoso, where I am now anchored. . . . This cape is so green and beautiful, like all the other objects and lands of these islands, I know not in which course to proceed first; my eyes are never tired with viewing such delightful verdure, and of a species so new and dissimilar to that of our country, and I have no doubt there are trees and herbs here which would be of great value in Spain, as dyeing materials, medicine, spicery, etc. . . .

Sunday, Oct. 21st

. . . This island even exceeds the others in beauty and fertility. Groves of lofty and flourishing trees are abundant, as also large lakes, surrounded and overhung by the foliage, in a most enchanting manner. Every tree and plant looked as green as in April in Andalusia. The melody of the birds was so exquisite that one was never willing to part from the spot, and the flocks of parrots obscured the heavens. The birds, both large and small, are of so many sorts and so different from ours, that it is a wonder; there are also a thousand different sorts of trees, each with their fruit, and of a wonderfully delicious odour. . . . It is my wish to fill all the water casks of the ships at this place, which being executed, I shall depart immediately, if the weather serve, and sail round the island, till I succeed in meeting with the king, in order to see if I can acquire any of the gold, which I hear he possesses. . . . And according as I find gold or spices in abundance, I shall determine what to do; at all events I am determined to proceed on to the continent, and visit the city of Guisay where I shall deliver the letters of your Highnesses to the Great Can, and demand an answer, with which I shall return.

Journal of Columbus. trans. Las Casas, 1827.

On the Incarnation of the Word
Chapter 1: Creation and Fall
by Saint Athanasius

(Section 1). . . Now, Macarius, true lover of Christ, we must take a step further in the faith of our holy religion, and consider also the Word's becoming Man and His divine Appearing in our midst. That mystery the Jews traduce, the Greeks deride, but we adore; and your own love and devotion to the Word also will be the greater, because in His Manhood He seems so little worth. For it is a fact that the more unbelievers pour scorn on Him, so much the more does He make His Godhead evident. The things which they, as men, rule out as impossible, He plainly shows to be possible; that which they deride as unfitting, His goodness makes most fit; and things which these wiseacres laugh at as "human" He by His inherent might declares divine. Thus by what seems His utter poverty and weakness on the cross He overturns the pomp and parade of idols, and quietly and hiddenly wins over the mockers and unbelievers to recognize Him as God. Now in dealing with these matters it is necessary first to recall what has already been said. You must understand why it is that the Word of the Father, so great and so high, has been made manifest in bodily form. He has not assumed a body as proper to His own nature, far from it, for as the Word He is without body. He has been manifested in a human body for this reason only, out of the love and goodness of His Father, for the salvation of us men. We will begin, then, with the creation of the world and with God its Maker, for the first fact that you must grasp is this: *the renewal of creation has been wrought by the Self-same Word Who made it in the beginning.* There is thus no inconsistency between creation and salvation for the One Father has employed the same Agent for both works, effecting the salvation of the world through the same Word Who made it in the beginning.

The Incarnation of the Word of God, Being the Treatise of St. Athanasius, trans. A Religious of C.S.M.V. S.Th. (New York: The Macmillan Company, 1946), 25–26.

Teachings of Jesus

Jesus sometimes taught lessons through stories called parables.

Matthew 13:18–32, 36–43

The Parable of the Sower

18 Hear ye therefore the parable of the sower.

19 When any one heareth the word of the kingdom, and understandeth it not, then cometh the wicked one, and catcheth away that which was sown in his heart. This is he which received seed by the way side.

20 But he that received the seed into stony places, the same is he that heareth the word, and anon with joy receiveth it;

21 Yet hath he not root in himself, but dureth for a while: for when tribulation or persecution ariseth because of the word, by and by he is offended.

22 He also that received seed among the thorns is he that heareth the word; and the care of this world, and the deceitfulness of riches, choke the word, and he becometh unfruitful.

23 But he that received seed into the good ground is he that heareth the word, and understandeth it; which also beareth fruit, and bringeth forth, some an hundredfold, some sixty, some thirty.

24 Another parable put he forth unto them, saying, The kingdom of heaven is likened unto a man which sowed good seed in his field:

25 But while men slept, his enemy came and sowed tares among the wheat, and went his way.

26 But when the blade was sprung up, and brought forth fruit, then appeared the tares also.

27 So the servants of the householder came and said unto him, Sir, didst not thou sow good seed in thy field? from whence then hath it tares?

28 He said unto them, An enemy hath done this. The servants said unto him, Wilt thou then that we go and gather them up?

29 But he said, Nay; lest while ye gather up the tares, ye root up also the wheat with them.

30 Let both grow together until the harvest: and in the time of harvest I will say to the reapers, Gather ye together first the tares, and bind them in bundles to burn them: but gather the wheat into my barn.

The Mustard Seed and the Leaven

31 Another parable put he forth unto them, saying, The kingdom of heaven is like to a grain of mustard seed, which a man took, and sowed in his field:

32 Which indeed is the least of all seeds: but when it is grown, it is the greatest among herbs, and becometh a tree, so that the birds of the air come and lodge in the branches thereof.

The Parable of the Tares

36 Then Jesus sent the multitude away, and went into the house: and his disciples came unto him, saying, Declare unto us the parable of the tares of the field.

37 He answered and said unto them, He that soweth the good seed is the Son of man;

38 The field is the world; the good seed are the children of the kingdom; but the tares are the children of the wicked one;

39 The enemy that sowed them is the devil; the harvest is the end of the world; and the reapers are the angels.

40 As therefore the tares are gathered and burned in the fire; so shall it be in the end of this world.

41 The Son of man shall send forth his angels, and they shall gather out of his kingdom all things that offend, and them which do iniquity;

42 And shall cast them into a furnace of fire: there shall be wailing and gnashing of teeth.

43 Then shall the righteous shine forth as the sun in the kingdom of their Father. Who hath ears to hear, let him hear.

Jesus commissions all His followers to carry His message throughout the world.

Matthew 28:18–20

The Great Commission

18 And Jesus came and spake unto them, saying, All power is given unto me in heaven and in earth.

19 Go ye therefore, and teach all nations, baptizing them in the name of the Father, and of the Son, and of the Holy Ghost:

20 Teaching them to observe all things whatsoever I have commanded you: and, lo, I am with you alway, even unto the end of the world. Amen.

BIOGRAPHICAL DICTIONARY

A

Abraham Man whose descendants became the nation of Israel.

Aesop Greek author who wrote fables.

Akhenaten Pharaoh during the New Kingdom; tried to change the Egyptians' beliefs about many gods and believed there was only one god, Aten.

Alexander the Great Became ruler of Macedonia at the age of twenty-two; led the Greek army in conquering many lands and spreading Greek culture.

Antiochus IV Seleucid king who became ruler of Judea in 176 BC.

Archimedes Greek mathematician who advanced the lever and pulleys.

Aristarchus Greek astronomer who believed that the earth revolved around the sun.

Aristotle Greek philosopher who devoted himself to the study of science.

Artaxerxes I King of Persia and son of Xerxes; allowed Ezra and Nehemiah to return to Jerusalem to restore worship and rebuild its wall.

Asoka Ruler of the Mauryan Empire in ancient India; promoted Buddhism.

Athanasius Bishop of Alexandria who defended Christian doctrine against the false teaching of Arius.

B

Basil II Emperor of the Byzantine Empire; strengthened the Byzantine government; known as the Bulgar Slayer.

Belisarius Byzantine general under Justinian I.

Benedict Key monastic leader; wrote a set of rules for monks to follow.

C

Chandragupta Maurya Indian warrior who conquered a large part of India and began the Mauryan dynasty.

Chang Heng Inventor of the seismoscope.

Charlemagne King of the Franks; greatest of the Carolingian kings; extended the Frankish kingdom to its greatest size; crowned by the pope as emperor of the Western Roman Empire.

Charles Martel High official of the Franks who led their army to many great military victories; he and his descendants ruled the Carolingian Empire.

Cicero Philosopher, lawyer, and member of the Senate; considered the greatest Roman orator.

Clovis First king of the Franks whose conquests shaped what would later become the French nation.

Confucius Chinese philosopher whose teachings greatly influenced China's classical age.

Constantine I Roman emperor who moved Rome's capital to Constantinople; legalized Christianity; also known as "Constantine the Great."

Crassus A wealthy military leader; part of the triumvirate.

Cyrus II A Persian leader who led a successful revolt against the Medes.

D

Darius I Also known as Darius the Great; king who expanded the size and power of the Persian Empire.

David Second king of Israel; loved and obeyed God.

Diego de Landa Spanish priest who tried to make the Mayas accept Roman Catholicism; much information about the Mayas is found in his writings.

E

Eratosthenes Greek mathematician, astronomer, and geographer.

Esther A Jew who was chosen to be queen by King Xerxes (Ahasuerus) of Persia and whom God used to save the Israelites in Babylon from destruction.

Euclid Greek mathematician; wrote the first known geometry book.

Ezana King of the Aksum Empire in the AD 300s who made Christianity the official religion.

H

Ham A son of Noah; received a curse for his wickedness; his descendants founded nations in the Far East, Africa, and along the eastern coast of the Mediterranean Sea.

Hammurabi King of the Amorites and ruler of the Babylonian Empire.

Hannibal General of Carthage; tried repeatedly to conquer Rome during the Second Punic War; one of the greatest generals in ancient history.

Hatshepsut Queen of Egypt; ruled during the New Kingdom.

Henry II First of the Plantagenet kings of England; came to the throne in 1154; developed England's legal system.

Heraclius Emperor of the Byzantine Empire; reconquered land taken by the Persians and the barbarians; made roads in his empire safe for commerce.

Hernando Cortés Commander of the Spanish conquistadors who entered Tenochtitlán in 1519.

Herodotus Greek historian; known as the Father of History.

Hippocrates Greek physician; called the Father of Medicine.

Homer Greek poet and storyteller; author of *The Iliad* and *The Odyssey*.

Howard Carter Archaeologist who discovered and cataloged Tutankhamun's tomb.

Hudson Taylor British missionary to the interior of China; began missionary work there in 1854; founded the China Inland Mission.

J

Japheth A son of Noah; his descendants moved into what is now Turkey and eastern Europe.

Jasaw Chan K'awiil I Mayan ruler from AD 682–734 in the royal line of Tikal during the Classic Period.

Jean-François Champollion Egyptologist who translated the hieroglyphics on the Rosetta stone in 1822.

Jesus God's Son; second person of the Trinity; the promised Messiah; came to earth as a man and died on the cross to pay the penalty for sin; rose from the dead and ascended to heaven.

Jimmu Tenno Mythical Japanese ancestor who was believed to be the first Japanese emperor.

John Marshall British archaeologist who discovered and helped excavate Harappa and Mohenjo-Daro in the Indus Valley in the 1920s.

Jonah Prophet whom God sent to Nineveh to tell the Assyrians to repent.

Josephus Jewish historian; sided with the Romans during the destruction of Jerusalem.

Judas Maccabeus Leader of the Jewish revolt against the Seleucids in the second century BC.

Julius Caesar General who became dictator of Rome; part of the triumvirate.

Justinian I Emperor of the Byzantine Empire; created a simplified code of Roman laws; also known as Justinian the Great.

K

King John Youngest son of Henry II; forced to put his seal on the Magna Carta.

L

Leo III Emperor of the Byzantine Empire; defeated the Muslims in Asia Minor.

Leonard Woolley Archaeologist who, in the 1920s, uncovered many artifacts from Ur and the land of Sumer.

M

Marius Military hero who reorganized the Roman army and allowed poor citizens to enlist for long terms of service.

Mark Antony Roman general who ruled the eastern part of the Roman Empire after forming an alliance with Octavian.

Martin Luther German monk who helped start the Protestant Reformation.

Mary Moffat Scottish missionary to Africa in the 1800s; helped set up mission stations.

Montezuma II Aztec emperor who expanded the Aztec boundaries and built many temples, canals, and hospitals.

Moses Hebrew whom God used to lead the Israelites out of slavery; wrote the first five books of the Bible.

Muhammad Founder of Islam.

Murasaki Shikibu Japanese author who wrote what is considered to be the world's first novel; a lady of the Japanese court.

Musa I Malian king in ancient western Africa; known for his immense wealth and devotion to Islam; most famous of the Malian kings.

N

Nebuchadnezzar II The king of Babylon and the Chaldean Empire around 612 BC.

Nero Roman emperor who ordered the death of many Christians.

Noah Man whom God saved from the Flood with his wife, three sons, and his sons' wives; directed by God to build an ark and put every kind of animal in it.

O

Octavian Ruled the western part of the Roman Empire after forming an alliance with Mark Antony; became the first emperor of Rome after defeating Mark Antony; also called Augustus.

P

Pepin the Short King of the Franks; son of Charles Martel; gave conquered Lombard lands to leaders of the Roman Catholic Church.

Pericles One of the leaders of the democracy in Athens; considered one of the best orators of all time.

Plato Greek philosopher who wrote books about government.

Pompey General who was popular with the Senate for his accomplishments of turning Asia Minor, Syria, and Palestine into Roman provinces and for ridding the Mediterranean Sea of pirates; part of the triumvirate.

Pythagoras Greek mathematician who studied geometry and came up with an important theorem about triangles.

Q

Qin Shi Huang Chinese emperor who began the Qin dynasty; name means "first emperor."

R

Rameses II One of the last pharaohs of Egypt; also called Rameses the Great.

Robert Moffat Scottish missionary to Africa; began missionary work there in 1817; helped set up mission stations and translated the Bible into the local language.

Robert Morrison British missionary to China; began missionary work there in 1807; dressed like the Chinese; translated the Bible into Chinese.

S

Samuel Last judge in Israel; anointed Saul to be king.

Sargon I Ruler of the Sumerian city-state Kish around 2270 BC; established the first empire.

Saul First king of Israel.

Shem A son of Noah; his descendants include the nation of Israel.

Shotoku Became the Japanese crown prince and regent in 573.

Siddhartha Gautama Founder of Buddhism.

Socrates Greek philosopher who encouraged his students to seek truth through human reason.

Sulla General appointed by the Senate to command the Roman army; declared himself dictator after winning a civil war.

Sundiata Keita King of Mali in ancient western Africa; the first mansa (ruler) of Mali; known as the Lion King.

Sunni Ali African ruler who established the large empire of Songhai.

T

Theodosius I Also known as "Theodosius the Great"; joint ruler of Rome from 379 to 392 and sole ruler of Rome from 392 to 395; opposed pagan beliefs and Arianism; divided the eastern and western parts of the Roman Empire under the rule of his two sons.

Thucydides Athenian historian who recorded the events of the Peloponnesian War.

Thutmose III Became the ruling pharaoh of Egypt after Queen Hatshepsut's death.

Tutankhamun Pharaoh of Egypt at the age of nine; died around age eighteen or nineteen; sometimes referred to as King Tut; known for his tomb of treasures.

V

Virgil Roman poet who wrote *The Aeneid*; considered the greatest Roman poet.

W

Wang Xizhi Chinese calligrapher; credited by some as the Father of Calligraphy.

William Carey British missionary to India; began missionary work there in 1793; trained Indian pastors and evangelists.

William the Conqueror First king of the Norman line; defeated Harold Godwinson at the Battle of Hastings.

Wu Ti A Chinese emperor during the Han dynasty who greatly expanded China.

X

Xerxes King of Persia; also called Ahasuerus; son of Darius.

Y

Yahweh The Hebrew name for the one true God.

Yoritomo Leader of the Minamoto clan; the first shogun, the supreme military leader of Japan; set up a military government called the shogunate.

Z

Zoroaster Founder of Zoroastrianism in ancient Persia.

GAZETTEER

A gazetteer is a geographical dictionary or index. This gazetteer lists important places mentioned in the book. Most descriptions are followed by the page number of a map where that place is shown.

A

Arabian Peninsula A peninsula in southwestern Asia between the Red Sea and the Persian Gulf. (m. 224)

Asia Minor The peninsula between the Black Sea and the Mediterranean Sea in what is present-day Turkey. (m. 44)

Athens A powerful city-state in ancient Greece where the world's first democracy developed; capital of present-day Greece. (m. 161)

B

Babylon One of the greatest cities of the ancient world; beside the Euphrates River near present-day Baghdad. (m. 41)

Balkan Peninsula A peninsula in southeastern Europe bordered by the Adriatic, Black, Aegean, and Mediterranean Seas. (m. 222)

C

Carthage A city that served as a key trade center on the North African coast of the Mediterranean Sea. (m. 194)

Constantinople The capital city of the Byzantine Empire; present-day Istanbul, Turkey. (m. 222)

Crete An island in the Mediterranean Sea off the coast of Greece. (m. 161)

E

Egypt An ancient kingdom and later a modern country in northeastern Africa. (m. 52)

Euphrates River A river that flows from the Taurus Mountains through Turkey, Syria, and Iraq to the Persian Gulf; a border of Mesopotamia. (m. 25)

F

Fertile Crescent A curved area from the Persian Gulf to the Mediterranean Sea. (m. 23)

H

Harappa A city of one of the first civilizations in the Indus Valley; the sister city of Mohenjo-Daro. (m. 102)

Heian-kyo The capital city of Japan after Nara; present-day Kyoto. (m. 279)

Hellespont The strait between Asia Minor and ancient Greece; the present-day Dardanelles; site where Xerxes and his army built bridges to reach the coast of Greece. (m. 153)

Hokkaido Second largest of the four major islands of Japan. (m. 279)

Honshu The largest of the four major islands of central Japan. (m. 279)

Horn of Africa A peninsula in northeastern Africa that projects into the Arabian Sea. (m. 259)

Huang He One of two major river systems in China that begins in northern China and flows to the Pacific Ocean; sometimes called "China's Sorrow." (m. 119)

I

Indian subcontinent A peninsula in southern Asia that extends into the Indian Ocean, separated from neighboring countries by the Himalaya Mountains. (m. 102)

Italian Peninsula A boot-shaped peninsula in the Mediterranean Sea; present-day Italy. (m. 186)

J

Jerusalem The capital of Israel. (m. 83)

Jordan River A river east of Israel that flows through the Sea of Galilee to the Dead Sea. (m. 83)

K

Kush An ancient land along the Nile stretching from just south of Egypt to Khartoum in present-day Sudan. (m. 71)

Kyushu The southernmost island of the major islands of Japan. (m. 279)

L

Lake Nasser The manmade lake formed by the Aswan High Dam. (m. 72)

La Venta One of the largest and most famous Olmec cities; located on the northeastern coast of Mexico. (m. 237)

Lake Texcoco Lake in Mexico; location of Tenochtitlán. (m. 250)

M

Marathon An ancient plain in Greece; the site of the battle in which the Athenian army defeated the Persian army. (m. 153)

Mecca A sacred Muslim city in present-day Saudi Arabia. (m. 224)

Medina A sacred Muslim city in present-day Saudi Arabia. (m. 224)

Mediterranean Sea The sea surrounded by Europe, Asia, Asia Minor, the Near East, and Africa. (m. 25)

Mesoamerica The region stretching south from central Mexico; includes Guatemala, Belize, Honduras, and Nicaragua. (m. 237)

Mesopotamia The ancient region between the Euphrates River and the Tigris River. (m. 23)

Mohenjo-Daro A city of one of the first civilizations in the Indus Valley; the sister city of Harappa. (m. 102)

Mount Olympus The highest mountain in Greece, believed by the ancient Greeks to be the dwelling place of the gods. (described on p. 172)

N

Nara Japan's first capital city. (m. 279)

Nile River The river that flows from central Africa through Egypt; the longest river in the world. (m. 50)

Nineveh The capital city of the Assyrian Empire; beside the Tigris River. (m. 44)

P

Papal States The conquered Lombard lands given to the Roman Catholic Church by Pepin the Short. (m. 300)

Pasargadae The capital city of the Persian Empire under the rule of Cyrus II. (m. 140)

Pataliputra The city chosen by Chandragupta to be the capital of the Mauryan Empire. (m. 114)

Peloponnesus A peninsula that forms the southern portion of Greece; site of the Peloponnesian War. (m. 161)

Persepolis The capital city of Persia after Susa. (m. 140)

R

Rome The capital city of the Roman Empire and of present-day Italy. (m. 186)

S

Salamis An island off the coast of Greece; site where the Greeks defeated the Persians in a naval battle. (m. 152)

San Lorenzo Tenochtitlán An urban center of the Olmec civilization; included the cities of Tenochtitlán, San Lorenzo, and Potrero Nuevo. (m. 237)

Scandinavia Region in northern Europe that includes the countries of Sweden, Denmark, and Norway. (m. 295)

Shikoku A southern island of Japan. (m. 279)

Sicily The largest island in the Mediterranean Sea; a part of Italy. (m. 187)

Songhai An important town in the Malian Empire that won its independence and became its own empire near the Niger River. (m. 259)

Sparta A powerful city-state in ancient Greece. (m. 161)

Sumer One of the first civilizations in Mesopotamia. (m. 23)

Susa The capital city of ancient Persia after Darius I came to power. (m. 140)

T

Tenochtitlán An ancient Aztec city built on Lake Texcoco; one of the largest cities of its time; a different city from the Olmec city of San Lorenzo Tenochtitlán; part of present-day Mexico City is built on this site. (m. 250)

Thermopylae A narrow mountain pass in Greece; site where the Greeks were defeated by the Persians. (m. 152)

Tigris River A river that flows from the Taurus Mountains through Turkey, Syria, and Iraq to the Persian Gulf; a border of Mesopotamia. (m. 25)

Tikal The largest and most powerful Mayan city-state; located in northern Guatemala. (m. 237)

Timbuktu An African city in the Malian Empire that became a center of Islamic faith and learning. (m. 264)

U

Ur A powerful city-state in Sumer. (m. 23)

GLOSSARY

A

abacus A frame with rows of movable beads used for calculating.

Abrahamic Covenant The agreement in which God promised Abraham that his descendants would become a great nation and that through him all the nations of the world would be blessed.

Achaemenid The name of the Persian dynasty that began with Cyrus II.

Acropolis The center of religious life in Athens; a hill overlooking the city of Athens.

acupuncture A procedure using needles to prevent or treat pain and sickness; originated in ancient China.

AD Abbreviation for *anno Domini*, meaning "in the year of our Lord"; used before the number of a year to signify a year after the birth of Christ.

agora A busy marketplace in the center of Athens made up of open-air buildings.

Aksum An ancient civilization in eastern Africa; a town in present-day Ethiopia.

amphitheater A large, outdoor arena.

amulet A large ornament worn on a necklace and thought to protect the wearer from evil spirits.

ancestor worship A belief that the spirits of ancestors live on in the afterworld and have powers to help or punish people who are still alive.

anthropologist A scientist who studies human origins and behavior.

archipelago A large group of islands.

Arianism Belief that God the Son is separate from and lesser than God the Father.

artisan A skilled craftsman.

Aryans Nomads believed to have moved into the Indus Valley around 1500 BC; conquered the people of northwestern India.

Assembly A group of Greek citizens who met to make laws.

Assembly of Centuries A powerful group of patricians in early Rome.

assimilate To absorb.

astrology Studying the movements and position of the sun, moon, stars, and planets in the belief that they influence people's lives.

astronomy The scientific study of the stars and heavenly objects.

Aswan High Dam The manmade dam across the Nile River that formed Lake Nasser.

atonement The restoration of the broken relationship between God and people.

Avesta The sacred writings of Zoroastrianism.

Aztec civilization A Mesoamerican society; around 1325–1521.

B

Bantu An early African people.

barbarian The name given by Romans to nomadic people who did not speak Greek or Latin and who did not adopt Roman culture.

barter A system in which people exchange goods and services for other goods and services.

basalt A type of dark, dense volcanic rock.

Battle of Hastings The English battle in 1066 in which William of Normandy was victorious over Harold Godwinson; resulted in Harold's death and the ascension of William to the throne.

BC Abbreviation meaning "before Christ"; used after the number of a year to signify a year before the birth of Christ.

Black Death A disease that killed one-third of the people in Europe; also called the bubonic plague.

bodhisattva A Buddhist who has reached enlightenment but delays nirvana to help others reach enlightenment.

botanist A scientist who studies plants.

Brahman Divine being of Hinduism believed to be the cause and material of creation; also called "the great soul" or "the world soul."

Buddha The name Siddhartha Gautama took for himself after he left Hinduism; "Enlightened One."

Buddhism A religion founded by Siddhartha Gautama; Buddhists follow the Eightfold Path and the Four Noble Truths.

bureaucracy The managing of government through bureaus, or departments, with appointed officials.

Byzantine Empire The eastern part of the Roman Empire; also known as the Eastern Roman Empire.

C

ca. Abbreviation for *circa*, meaning "around"; used before the number of a year to signify the approximate year.

caliph Political and religious leader of an Islamic state.

calligraphy The art of fine handwriting.

canopic jar A special container for organs of a dead body.

Carolingian Empire The Frankish empire under the rule of Charles Martel and his descendants.

cartouche An oval shape containing hieroglyphs of a name written inside.

caste A strict social class a person is born into.

causeway A land bridge.

cenote The name given to a deep sinkhole filled with water that formed when water eroded limestone.

chinampa A floating garden island made of twigs, limbs, sticks, and silt; created by the Aztecs.

chivalry A special code of behavior for knights.

city-state A city and the surrounding land and villages it controls.

civilization A group of people who establish cities, government, social classes, specialized jobs, arts, sciences, written language, and religion.

clan A group of families descended from a common ancestor.

classical age A time in a civilization's history that is thought to be its high point of cultural development and achievement.

clergy People ordained as religious leaders.

coat of arms A distinctive emblem that identified a knight in battle; today an emblem that can identify an individual, family, school, or organization.

codex Mayan folding book recorded on paper made from the inner bark of fig trees.

Colosseum A large arena where events were held to entertain the Roman people.

conquistador A Spanish conqueror.

consul An official that was elected in the Roman Republic to serve for one year.

Council of Nicaea Defined what Christians should believe about the Trinity.

Creation Mandate The first command given by God to mankind; God's instruction to people to have children and to fill and rule over the earth.

Crusades Religious campaigns to free Jerusalem from Islamic rule.

culture A system of customs including language, religion, government, economy, and arts that groups of people use to develop their world.

cuneiform Wedge-shaped writing.

currency Money; any item of value that is exchanged for goods or services.

cylinder seal A clay cylinder used to imprint one's signature.

Cyrus Cylinder A cylinder seal found at an ancient Babylonian temple; contains an account of Cyrus's conquest of Babylon and his restoration of the city.

D

daimyo Chief Japanese nobles or powerful warlords who had military and economic power to rule over their lands.

daric The coin used in the Persian Empire; named after Darius I.

Davidic Covenant The agreement in which God promised to establish David's throne forever.

Delian League The offensive alliance of Greek city-states led by Athens against the Persians.

delta A fan-shaped area of fertile land at the mouth of a river.

democracy A form of government in which the citizens of the country have the power.

descendant A person whose family line can be traced to a certain person or group.

dharma Religious duties of a Hindu or a Buddhist.

Diaspora The scattering of the Israelites to many other nations at the time of the Babylonian captivity.

dike A wall that prevents flooding.

doctrine A belief or principle of a group of people.

dominion The authority to rule.

drawbridge A bridge that can be raised or lowered to prevent or allow passage.

dynasty A line of kings or rulers who belong to the same family.

E

Eastern Orthodox Church Church that developed in the Byzantine Empire.

empire A group of nations under one government.

enlightened Having received knowledge or understanding.

epic A long poem about the actions of a hero.

Epic of Gilgamesh A Mesopotamian poem describing the adventures and eternal life of Gilgamesh, a legendary hero.

Epicureanism The philosophy that happiness is the most important thing.

etiquette Proper actions and responses that are expected in society; manners.

Etruscan An ancient civilization with a Hellenistic culture on the Italian Peninsula.

Exodus The Israelites' departure from Egypt.

F

fable A short story that teaches a lesson.

Fall (of mankind) The breaking of God's law by Adam and Eve with the consequence of sin for them and all people.

fall of the Roman Empire The collapse of the Roman government in AD 476.

feudal A political system where the ruler or government provides protection in exchange for service.

feudalism A system of organizing and governing society based on land and service.

fief A tract of land given by a lord to a vassal.

freeman A peasant who lived on a lord's manor and specialized in a skill.

friar A clergyman who lives among the people, lives simply, owns no property, and teaches people how to live good lives.

Fujiwara A Japanese family who gained power by marrying into Japan's imperial family.

G

gatehouse A stronghold for the gatekeeper in the wall of a castle.

Gentiles A name given to Greeks and other people who are not Jews.

Ghana An ancient African empire located along the Niger River; location of present-day Mauritania; name of a modern nation in western Africa.

gladiator An armed person who fought animals or other people in an arena such as the Colosseum.

Great Pyramid The largest of the three pyramids in the valley of Giza; built for the pharaoh Khufu.

Great Wall A series of fortified barriers over fourteen hundred miles long built across northern China to keep invaders out.

Great Zimbabwe Ancient African city built of stone by the Shona.

Gregorian calendar The revised version of the Julian calendar; now used by most countries.

griot An African oral storyteller.

H

Hagia Sophia A church in Constantinople known for its great beauty.

haiku A type of Japanese poem that has a verse form with seventeen syllables and an aspect of nature or seasons.

Hammurabi's Code A collection of Mesopotamian laws written by Hammurabi.

Han The dynasty that began ruling China around 202 BC.

Hanukkah The yearly Jewish celebration of the rededication of the temple after their victory over the Seleucids.

Harappan civilization People who settled in the Indus Valley and established the ancient cities of Harappa and Mohenjo-Daro.

hemp A plant fiber used to make paper, baskets, rope, and thick fabrics.

hieroglyphics A system of writing made of picture symbols.

Hinduism A major Indian religion based on Vedic religious beliefs; belief in Brahman and reincarnation that serves as a unifying influence in India's diverse society.

hippodrome An open-air stadium.

Hyksos A people who invaded Egypt at the beginning of the New Kingdom; their technology included bronze and iron weapons and horse-drawn chariots.

I

icon A sacred image representing Christ, Mary, the saints, or other sacred objects.

Ides of March The fifteenth day of March on the Roman calendar; the day on which Julius Caesar was assassinated.

Immortals Special soldiers for the king in ancient Persia.

imperial court A group of nobles who live near, serve, and advise the ruler.

indigenous A native or original inhabitant of a certain place.

Indo-European A group of languages spoken by people of Europe and parts of Asia.

inspiration (of Scripture) God breathing out the Scriptures, using holy men to record them.

irrigation A way of supplying water to land or crops.

Islam The religion started by Muhammad.

Israel The nation God made from the descendants of Jacob; named after God's special name for Jacob; the name of the Northern Kingdom after Israel split into two kingdoms.

J

jihad A holy war fought for the cause of Islam; a spiritual striving.

Judaism The monotheistic religion of the Jews.

Justinian Code A compilation and simplification of Roman law; ordered by Justinian for the Byzantine Empire.

K

kami The gods or nature spirits of Shintoism.

karma The Hindu belief that a person's deeds, good or bad, determine his state in reincarnation.

keep Strong central tower in a castle where the lord and his family lived.

knight A soldier who defended a manor during the Middle Ages.

kofun A giant tomb with a keyhole-shaped burial mound surrounded by a moat; built by the Japanese aristocracy during the Yamato dynasty.

L

Law of the Twelve Tables The Roman law written on twelve bronze tablets.

Legalism The belief that people are evil by nature and so must be controlled by strict laws.

legion An army consisting of three to six thousand soldiers.

linguist A scholar who studies languages.

Lombards A Germanic tribe from Scandinavia who migrated to the Italian Peninsula.

lord A noble.

M

magi The name for Zoroastrian priests in ancient Persia.

Magna Carta An important document that limited the king's powers and guaranteed certain rights to the people.

Mahayana Buddhism A branch of Buddhism that believes that everything that people see is an illusion and the ultimate goal is the state of nirvana.

maize Corn.

Mali An ancient empire located in northwestern Africa; a modern nation in western Africa.

Mandate of Heaven The Zhou belief that heaven gave the king his right to rule but required him to rule righteously.

manor A large farming community during the Middle Ages.

Mayan civilization A Mesoamerican civilization ca. AD 250–900.

medieval Of or relating to the Middle Ages.

mercenary A foreign soldier hired to fight for a country.

Meroitic A script language developed by the people of Kush.

Messiah The Old Testament name for the promised Redeemer, Jesus Christ.

Middle Ages The historical period beginning after the fall of the Western Roman Empire; ca. AD 500–1500.

migrate To move from one country or region to settle in another.

Minoan civilization The earliest known civilization in Greece.

moat A wide trench filled with water surrounding a castle to keep out attackers.

monarchy A form of government with one ruler.

monastery A large, secluded dwelling where monks live and work.

monk A clergyman who lives a secluded life of devotion and service to the church.

monotheism The belief in one God.

monsoon A wind that reverses direction with the change of season.

Mosaic Covenant The agreement in which God gave the nation of Israel His law through Moses.

mummy A dead body that has been preserved from decaying.

Muses The goddesses who the Greeks believed presided over the arts and sciences; their father was Zeus, and their mother was Mnemosyne.

Muslim A person who follows Islam.

Mycenaean civilization An early civilization in Greece.

myth A legend or traditional story; often about gods and goddesses.

N

New Covenant The agreement in which God promised to give His Holy Spirit and to transform the hearts of His people to love and obey Him.

Nika Revolt The Byzantine riot where half of Constantinople was destroyed and many people were killed.

nilometer A device used to measure the Nile's water levels.

nirvana The Buddhist belief in a state of complete enlightenment where a person has peace and freedom from desire.

nun A member of a women's religious order who lives a secluded life of devotion and service to the church.

O

oasis A fertile area in the desert with water.

obsidian A glass-like volcanic rock.

oligarchy A form of government in which a few people rule.

Olmec civilization One of the earliest known Mesoamerican civilizations.

Olympic Games Special festivals originally held in the city of Olympia in Greece to honor the gods; consist of athletic contests.

oracle bones Animal bones or turtle shells used in ancient China to predict the future.

oral history Stories about the past that are spoken instead of written down.

orthodox Refers to those who support the traditionally accepted principles of the faith.

Ottomans The group of Turks who conquered the Byzantine Empire.

outcaste Anyone from outside the groups of the Hindu caste system; bound by strict social restrictions.

P

page A boy in the first stage of becoming a knight; lived in a noble's home to learn horsemanship and fighting skills; did chores for the lord and lady.

pantheism Belief that everything in the universe is part of a supreme being.

Pantheon An ancient Roman temple dedicated to all the gods.

papyrus Paper made from the stems of the papyrus plant.

Parthenon The ancient Greek temple on the Acropolis; known for its many columns and optical illusions in its design.

Parthians A nomadic people from northern Persia that began retaking part of the Persian Empire around 171 BC.

Passover A celebration that honors the Lord's deliverance of the Israelites from slavery in Egypt.

patrician A member of the wealthy ruling class in ancient Rome.

Pax Romana The period of peace in the Roman Empire that began with the reign of Octavian.

Peloponnesian League An alliance of Greek city-states led by Sparta against Athens.

Peloponnesian War The war between Athens and Sparta that lasted over twenty-seven years.

Persian Wars The wars between the Persians and the Greeks.

phalanx A group of warriors who stood close together in a formation.

pharaoh A ruler of Egypt.

philosopher A scholar who devotes himself to earthly wisdom; a person who studies to gain wisdom in a particular field.

pictograph A picture or symbol used in early writing to represent a word, a group of words, or an idea.

plebeian A member of the working class in ancient Rome.

polytheism The worship of many gods.

pope The leader of the Roman Catholic Church.

potsherds Pieces of broken pottery.

prehistory The period when humans supposedly evolved and when there were no written records.

Protestant Reformation The religious movement that led to the forming of Protestant churches when people separated from the Roman Catholic Church and trusted in Christ alone for salvation.

proverb A wise saying that expresses a simple truth.

Punic Wars Three major wars between Rome and Carthage.

Pygmies An African people of small stature who live in the rainforest of the Congo basin.

pyramid A large tomb constructed on a rectangular base with four sloping, triangular sides.

Q

Qin The dynasty that began ruling China around 221 BC.

Qur'an The Islamic book of Muhammad's visions; written by his followers.

R

rabbi Jewish religious teacher.

rain shadow desert A lowland area that receives little rain; formed when wind blows water vapor high into nearby mountains.

raja A chief, prince, or ruler in India.

redemption Christ's act of rescuing and freeing people from sin; salvation.

regent A person who rules in place of a rightful ruler who is unable to fulfill the duties because of age, illness, or other reasons.

reincarnation The belief that after a person dies, he comes back in another form.

republic A government ruled by representatives chosen by the people.

Roman Catholic Church Church under the leadership of the pope.

Roman Forum A public meeting place in ancient Rome.

Rosetta stone An ancient rock stele or monument carved with Egyptian hieroglyphics, Greek, and another script; used as a key to decipher Egyptian hieroglyphics; discovered in the Egyptian town of Rosetta in 1799.

Royal Road The longest stone road in the Persian Empire, stretching sixteen hundred miles from Susa to Sardis.

S

sacrament A religious ceremony believed to provide grace for salvation.

Samaritans A people in the Northern Kingdom of Israel; descendants of conquered peoples who intermarried with Israelites.

samurai A Japanese warrior whose duty was to protect the daimyo; a master of horsemanship, fencing, archery, and jujitsu.

San An African people living south of the Sahara.

Sanskrit Written language of the Aryans.

sarcophagus A stone coffin.

Sassanians Rulers of the Sassanian dynasty in ancient Persia; the last of the true Persian kings.

satrap A governor in Persia who ruled a particular province; was responsible for collecting tribute and reported to the king.

satrapy A province in ancient Persia.

savanna A region with tall grass and few trees.

scribe A person whose job is to record information in writing.

seismoscope A scientific instrument used to detect earthquakes.

Senate The most powerful branch of the government in the Roman Republic.

Septuagint A Greek translation of the Old Testament.

serf A peasant who lived on a lord's manor, paid rent to the lord, and worked part-time for him.

shadoof A device made from a long pole with a bucket on one end and a weight on the other; used to dip water out of the Nile River.

Shang The Chinese dynasty that began ruling around 1500 BC.

Shintoism A form of nature worship; the main religion of Japan.

shogun A Japanese military leader with the most political power in the government; chosen by the emperor.

Shona An African people living in southern Africa.

Silk Road The trade route that stretched about four thousand miles from China to the Mediterranean Sea; linked China to the nations in the West.

silt A sediment of very fine particles containing rock and minerals that is found in the bottom of bodies of water.

slash-and-burn A practice used in agriculture where a forest is cut and burned before the land is planted.

social class A group of people in society with the same social position, often determined by economic status.

social pyramid A triangle-shaped diagram that shows the social structure of a society.

squire A boy in the second stage of becoming a knight; his responsibilities included helping his master dress, accompanying him on hunts or in battles, and caring for his horse.

Stoicism The philosophy that people should strive to be indifferent to pleasure and pain.

stucco A decorative plaster.

stupa A dome-shaped Buddhist shrine.

sultan A ruler of a Muslim country.

surplus An amount that is more than what is needed.

Swahili A Bantu language commonly spoken in eastern Africa.

synagogue A place where the Jews gather for worship.

T

tabernacle The portable place of worship used by the Israelites in the wilderness; symbolized God's presence with the people.

Taika Reforms A series of changes in the Japanese political and economic structure around AD 645; known as the Great Change.

Taoism A Chinese philosophy that promotes humility and submission to *tao*, "the way."

tell A mound made up of layered dirt and the remains of buildings.

Templo Mayor The primary location for the Aztecs' religious ceremonies and rituals; also called the Great Pyramid.

theorem A carefully tested idea that has been proven to be true.

ting An ornate bronze vessel used in ancient China for cooking meat for sacrifices to the ancestors.

toga A loose robe worn by citizens of ancient Rome.

Torah The first five books of the Old Testament; the Pentateuch.

tournament An exercise for knights to practice and compete; often included jousting.

trial by jury A legal practice in which a group of local people helps decide the outcome of a court trial.

trial by ordeal A legal practice during the Middle Ages in which a person had to undergo difficult physical circumstances to determine guilt or innocence.

Tribal Assembly The assembly made up of plebeians in ancient Rome.

tribune A leader of the Tribal Assembly in ancient Rome.

triumvirate An alliance among three rulers.

Trojan War The war between the Mycenaeans and the city of Troy.

Tuareg A nomadic people of the Sahara in northern Africa.

tyrant A ruler who has absolute authority.

U

universal flood A flood in which water covers the entire earth; often used to refer to the Flood of Noah's time.

V

vassal A person who pledged loyalty and service to a lord and managed the lord's land in exchange for protection.

Vedas Collections of sacred hymn texts of Hinduism.

Vikings Scandinavians who raided parts of Europe during the Middle Ages; also called Norsemen and Northmen.

W

worldview How a person sees and interprets the universe and everything in it.

writ A royal order.

Y

Yamato A Japanese clan that rose to power around AD 250.

Z

Zhou The Chinese dynasty that began ruling around 1000 BC.

ziggurat A pyramid-like temple.

zimbabwe A large stone house built by the Shona.

Zoroastrianism The main religion of ancient Persia.

INDEX

A

abacus, 179, 185, 199
Abel, 16, 19
Abraham, 22–23, 26, 29, 40, 76–77, 93
Abrahamic Covenant, 76–77, 80, 84, 93, 94
Abu-Bakr, 226
Abu Simbel, 72
Achaemenid, 155
    Achaemenid period, 143
Acropolis, 166, 169, 174, 181
acupuncture, 132
AD, 42
Adam, 10, 15, 18, 19, 76, 80, 225, 236, 319–20
Aegean Sea, 140, 160, 170, 212
Aesop, 178
Africa, 5, 50–51, 194, 209, 275, 328–29
    Central Africa, 271, 275
    Eastern Africa, 262–63, 273, 275
    Northern Africa, 212, 216, 220, 226, 264, 270, 275
    religion of, 275
    Southern Africa, 271–72, 275
    Western Africa, 264–66
afterlife, 55, 56, 58, 65, 68, 121
agora, 165
agriculture, 15, 16, 51, 53, 121, 240, 244, 253, 261, 280
Ahasuerus. *See* Xerxes
Ah Kin, 248
Ahmose, 61
Akhenaten, 68
Akkad, 31, 40
    Akkadian, 35–36, 41
Akkadian Empire, 40–41
Aksum, 73, 263, 328
Aksumite Empire, 262–63
Alexander the Great, 88, 114, 156, 182
Alexandria, Egypt, 88, 324
Alexius III, 230
Amenhotep IV, 68–69
Ammonite, 85
Amorite, 41–42, 44
Amorite civilization (Babylonian Empire), 41–43
Amos, 86, 88
amphitheater, 159, 176–77, 186
amulet, 59, 64
ancestor worship, 121, 135, 275
anthropologist, 236
Antiochus IV, 88
Antony, Mark, 198
aqueduct, 201, 209, 218, 252
Arabia, 47, 273
Arabian Peninsula, 224, 226
arch, 30, 39, 201, 202, 209
archaeology, 6, 22, 34–35, 55, 58, 62, 72, 94, 100–101, 115, 122, 162, 163, 236, 238, 240, 249, 261, 262, 271, 280, 324–25
archbishop, 310
Archimedes, 179
archipelago, 278
Arianism, 294
Aristarchus, 179
Aristotle, 175, 182
Arius, 208–9
ark, 12–13
ark of the covenant, 80–81
Artaxerxes I, 155
Artaxerxes III, 148
artifact, 6–7, 22–23, 56, 72, 94, 103, 122, 130, 142, 163, 188, 241, 242
artisan, 28–29, 39, 63, 75, 101, 110, 117, 122, 137, 169, 180, 188, 200–201, 215, 218, 243, 246, 280, 290
Aryans, 104–5
Asia, 50, 69, 182
Asia Minor, 145, 152, 233
Asoka, 114–15
Assembly, 164–65
Assembly of Centuries, 189
assimilate, 87
Assyria, 12
    Assyrians, 44–45, 68, 73, 86, 87, 325
Assyrian Empire, 44, 86
astrologers, 46
astrology, 36–37
astronomy, 30, 36–37, 105, 108, 139, 149, 179, 199, 238, 241, 243, 299
Aswan High Dam, 72
Athanasius, 324
atheism, 19
Athens, 152, 154, 164–65, 166–67, 169, 170–71, 174, 181
atonement, 80, 94
Attila (the Hun), 209
Avars, 222–23
Avesta, 151
Aztec civilization, 250–55
    religion of, 251

B

Babel, 10, 14, 319
Babylon, 7, 34, 46–47, 87, 139, 142, 147, 182
Babylonia, 41, 43
Babylonian Captivity, 86–87
Babylonian Chronicles, 87
Balkan Peninsula, 222–23, 227, 229, 233
Bantu, 261, 271
baptism, 297
barbarian, 215, 216, 222–23, 227
barley, 24, 36, 50, 53, 64, 69, 160
barter, 27, 30, 47, 109, 124
basalt, 238, 251
Basil I, 229
Basil II, 229
Battle of Hastings, 308
BC, 42
BCE, 42
Behistun Inscription, 147
Belisarius, 216–17, 220
Belshazzar, 47, 142
Benedict, 296
Benedictine Rule, 296
Benue River, 261, 271
Bering Strait, 236
Bezaleel, 90
bishop, 214, 228, 294, 298, 314. *See also* archbishop
bitumen, 100–101
Black Death, 232–33, 314
Black Sea, 44, 212, 213
bodhisattva, 137
Book of Highways and Kingdoms, 264
Book of the Dead, 65
Bosporus Strait, 212
botanist, 261
Brahman, 106, 110
Brahmin, 111
brass, 23
bronze, 16, 18, 33, 35, 41, 61, 101, 108, 117, 121–22, 124, 132–33, 150, 211, 280
Buddha, 19, 112

Buddhism, 112–13, 114–15, 135–36, 281–83, 287, 327
    Mahayana, 114, 137
    Theravada, 114
Bulgars, 222–23, 229
bureaucracy, 128, 131, 288
Bushido Code, 290
Byzantine Empire, 209, 211, 212, 215, 216–17, 220–21, 222–23, 224–26, 227, 229, 230–31, 232–33, 315
Byzantium, 212, 219, 262

C

ca., 42
cacao, 235, 237, 243, 245
Caesar
    Augustus (*see* Octavian)
    Julius, 93, 196, 197, 198
    Tiberius (*see* Tiberius Caesar)
Caesarea, 94
Caesarea Maritima, 94
Cain, 10, 16, 19
calendar, 37, 54, 80, 197, 198, 238, 241, 247, 248, 251, 281
    Gregorian, 197
caliph, 226
calligraphy, 277, 283
    kaisho, 277, 283
    shodo, 277, 283
    sosho, 277, 283
Cambyses, 143–44, 146
camel, 23, 136, 270
Canaan, 6, 53, 61, 76, 82, 90
canopic jar, 58
Carey, William, 327
Carolingian (Frankish) Empire, 298–99, 300–301
Carter, Howard, 62
Carthage, 191, 192–94, 216, 270
cartouche, 59
caste, 108, 110–13, 327
castle, 312–13
cataracts, 50, 60, 71
causeway, 250
CE, 42
cement, 186
cenote, 240, 246, 249
Chaldean (New Babylonian) Empire, 46–47, 86
Chaldeans, 45, 86, 87
Champollion, Jean-François, 57, 59
Chang Heng, 132
chariot, 32, 44–46, 61–62, 104, 108, 114, 122, 130, 201, 211, 216
Charlemagne, 299

Charles Martel, 298
chieftain, 280, 283
China, 115, 117, 130, 212, 223
    influence on Japan, 281–83, 330–31
    religion of, 121
chinampa, 250
chivalry, 302–3
Christianity, 207, 224–25, 263, 270, 294, 315, 324–25, 326–29, 330–31
Christians, 207, 208, 214, 229
church, 214, 321, 324–25, 326–29, 330–31
Cicero, 201
circa, 42
city-state
    Africa, 269
    Canaan, 84
    Greek, 146, 152, 164–65, 168, 169, 170–71, 182
    Kish, 40
    Mayan, 240, 243, 246–47
    Sumerian, 26–27, 30, 35
civilization, 9, 318–20
    features of
        arts, science, and written language, 15, 16–17, 18, 30, 66, 90, 109, 135, 149, 166, 202, 219, 247, 289, 306
        job specialization, 15, 16–17, 26, 30, 67, 90, 108, 134, 149, 167, 203, 218, 269
        organized cities and government, 15, 66, 109, 135, 202, 247, 269, 288, 306
        religion, 5, 15, 16–17, 19, 31, 65, 90, 109, 135, 148, 167, 203, 218, 246, 268, 288, 307
        social classes, 15, 31, 90, 108, 134, 148, 167, 203, 219, 246, 268, 288
    key themes of
        citizenship, 11, 31, 66, 90, 135, 167, 202, 289, 307
        environment, 11, 16–17, 30, 67, 90, 109, 134, 148, 166, 219, 246, 268, 288
        justice, 10, 11, 16–17, 30, 66, 91, 108, 134, 148, 166, 203, 246, 269, 288, 306
        power, 11, 16–17, 30, 67, 90, 148, 202, 218, 247, 269, 306
clan, 272, 280, 281, 283, 287, 290
classical age
    of China, 123–25
    of Greece, 169, 315

    of Mayas, 243
    See also golden age
Cleisthenes, 165
clergy, 296–97, 315
click language, 272
Clovis, 298
coat of arms, 304
codex, 241, 252, 253
colonization, 188, 191, 192, 198, 212, 272, 274, 330
Colosseum, 201
column, 30, 39, 169, 181, 183, 202
commerce, 16, 18, 24, 28, 191
concrete, 201
Confucianism, 126, 127
Confucius, 125–27, 130–31, 135, 137
conquistador, 251, 254
Constantine I, 208–9, 212, 215, 325
Constantine XI, 233
Constantinople, 209, 212, 214, 215–17, 218–19, 220, 223, 227, 228, 229, 230–31, 232–33
consul, 189
continental plates, 13
copper, 16–17, 18, 27, 29, 35, 40, 69, 103, 108, 121, 141, 165, 213, 264, 271
coral, 273
Cortés, Hernando, 251, 254–55
cotton, 69, 136, 237, 243–44, 254–55
Council of Nicaea, 214
cradle of civilization, 22
Crassus, 196
Creation, 4–5, 7, 9, 19
Creation Mandate, 9–10, 84, 318–19
Crete, 115, 162–63
Crusades, 230–31, 314
culture, 9, 44
    of China, 127
    of Egypt, 49
    of Greece, 88, 156, 157, 160, 168, 180–81, 182–83
    of Hittites, 320
    of India, 104–5
    of Israel, 87
    of Kush, 69–70
    of Mesoamerica, 241, 243–45, 252–53, 255
    of Persia, 147, 157
    of Rome, 200, 215
cuneiform, 31, 36–38, 40, 47, 142, 147

currency, 105, 124, 129, 143, 145, 149, 157, 263
cylinder seal, 28, 31, 36, 47
Cyril, 229
Cyrus II, 87, 140–43, 146, 148, 157
Cyrus Cylinder, 142

D

daimyo, 290
Daniel, 46–47, 89, 139, 142, 156
daric, 145
Darius I (the Great), 47, 141, 143–50, 152, 157
dark age, 163, 165, 176
dating system, 60
David, 84, 86, 93
Davidic Covenant, 80, 84–85
de Landa, Diego, 241
Delian League, 170
delta, 51, 53
democracy, 164–65, 171, 180
denier, 293
descendant, 13–14, 41, 50, 319–20
dharma, 106
Diaspora, 87
dictator, 196, 198
dike, 252
Diocletian, 208
doctrine, 214
dome, 30, 39, 114, 201, 202, 209, 218, 220
Dome of the Rock, 226
dominion, 9
drama, 159, 177–78, 219
drawbridge, 312–13
dreidel, 92
dye, 28–29, 53, 75, 84, 91, 145
dynasty, 55, 61, 85, 114, 119, 122–23, 156

E

Eastern Orthodox Church, 228, 233
Eastern Roman Empire, 209, 212
ebony, 69, 71, 145, 262
Eden, 12, 15
Edict of Milan, 214
Egypt, 27, 44, 48, 53, 72, 77, 80, 84, 88, 100, 117, 223, 226, 230–31, 271, 321, 324
    empire of, 62
    plagues of, 61, 64, 78
    religion of, 64, 68
Eightfold Path, 112
embalmer, 58
England, 308–11, 314, 327

enlightened, 112, 137
Enoch
    city, 10, 16–17
    son of Cain, 15, 19
Ephesus, 7, 178
epic, 38, 176, 180
Epic of Gilgamesh, 38
Epicureanism, 204
equator, 258–60, 271
Eratosthenes, 179
Esther, 87, 139, 155
Ethiopia, 72, 73, 262–63
etiquette, 284–85, 312
Etruscans, 188, 189, 191
Eucharist, 297
Euclid, 174, 179
Euphrates River, 12, 22, 27, 30, 41, 42, 62
Europe, 14, 50, 117, 214, 233, 326–27
Eve, 10–11, 15, 19, 76, 80, 236, 319
evolution, 5, 7, 13, 18
excommunication, 310
exile, 79, 86, 88, 94, 193, 217, 230
Exodus, 60, 68, 78, 82
Ezana, 262–63
Ezra, 88, 142, 146, 155

F

fable, 178
Fall (of mankind), 10, 68, 318–19
fall of the Roman Empire, 209, 294
famine, 53, 73, 77, 79, 103, 105, 121, 249, 314
fasces, 188
Feather of Truth, 65
Fertile Crescent, 22, 23, 44
feudal, 128, 231, 304–5, 308
feudalism, 290, 302–5, 314–15
fief, 302–5
flax, 24, 29, 33, 64, 75, 91
Flood (great, universal, or worldwide), 3, 12–13, 15, 19, 22–23, 38, 41, 236
Florus, 96
Four Noble Truths, 112
France, 298–99, 300–301, 309, 314
Franks, 298–99
freeman, 305, 311
friar, 296
Frumentius, 263
Fujiwara, 287, 288

G

Garden of Eden, 9, 12–13, 15
gatehouse, 312–13

Gautama, Siddhartha, 112
Genji, 287
Gentiles, 88, 96
Ghana, 264, 265
    empire of, 264
Gihon River, 12
Giza, 52, 55
gladiator, 186, 201, 207
Gobi Desert, 118, 120, 123, 233
God, 4–5, 8–11, 14–15, 19, 37, 43, 45–47, 64, 68, 73, 76–80, 82, 93, 94–95, 96–97, 121, 127, 146, 151, 152, 174–75, 204, 205, 208, 251, 282, 294
gods and goddesses, 10, 39, 47, 76, 82, 85, 104, 106, 121, 168, 172–73, 174–75, 197, 207, 208, 248–49, 251, 278
    Ahura Mazda, 148, 150–51
    Allah, 224–25
    Amaterasu, 281–82
    Amun, 65, 70
    Amun-Ra, 65
    Angra Mainyu, 150–51
    Anubis, 58, 65
    Apollo, 172, 180, 205
    Ashtoreth, 86
    Aten, 68
    Athena, 166
    Baal, 86
    Brahma, 108
    Diana, 205
    Dionysus, 173, 177
    Ea, 35, 38
    Frigg, 301
    Hathor, 49, 65, 68
    Horus, 65, 68
    Isis, 65, 68
    Marduk, 142
    Mars, 197, 204
    Merodach, 47
    Muses, 180
    Odin, 301
    Osiris, 65, 68, 321
    Ra, 65, 321
    Shamash, 35
    Shiva, 108
    Thor, 301
    Tyr, 301
    Vishnu, 108
    Zeus, 173, 180, 204
gold, 262, 264, 265, 272, 273
golden age
    of Byzantines, 221, 229
    of China, 137
    of Greece, 160

of India, 115
of Japan, 284–86
gopura, 106, 109
gospel, 94, 214, 251, 318–20, 321, 324, 326–29, 330–31
government, 15
    of Egypt, 67
    of Greece, 164–65, 175
    of India, 104
    of Israel, 82, 84
    of Japan, 281, 283, 287
    of Mesopotamia, 31–32, 35
    of Persia, 156
    of Rome, 188, 189–90
Great Pyramid, 55
Great Schism, 315
Great Stupa, 115
Great Wall, 128–29
Great Zimbabwe, 272
Greece, 152–54, 156, 326
    Greek fire, 227
    Greek language, 57, 88, 145, 157, 182–83, 188, 215, 219, 223
    Greeks, 7, 68, 88, 140, 146, 154, 188, 191, 200, 211
    religion of, 167, 172–73, 174, 175
Greek Empire, 88, 170, 182–83
griot, 261
guilds, 223
Gupta, 115

H

Hagia Sophia, 218, 231, 233
haiku, 285, 286
Ham, 13–14, 50
Haman, 87
Hammurabi, 42
Hammurabi's Code, 43
Han, 131–34, 137
Hanging Gardens of Babylon, 46
Hannibal, 193–94
Hanukkah, 89, 92
Harappa, 100, 102, 103, 115
    Harappan civilization, 100–101, 104
Harris, Alice, 275
Harris, John, 275
Hatshepsut, 61–62
Havilah, 12
heaven, 94, 248
Heian-kyo, 284–86, 287, 288–89
Hellespont, 153, 155, 171
hemp, 133
Henry II, 309–10, 314

Heraclius, 223, 227
Herod, 93, 94, 96
Herodotus, 46, 144, 146
hieroglyphics, 57, 59, 66, 70
Himalayas, 102, 109, 118
Hinduism, 19, 106–7, 110, 327
Hippocrates, 179
hippodrome, 211, 216–17
historical account, 4, 5, 6–7, 8, 151
Hittite Empire, 44–45
    Hittites, 36, 62
Hokkaido, 278
holy of holies, 80–81
Holy Spirit, 93, 95
Homer, 176
Honduras, 236, 237
Honshu, 278
Horn of Africa, 260
horse, 136, 144–45, 166, 180, 211, 253, 254–55, 270, 302–3
Huang He, 118, 119, 135
Hundred Years' War, 314
Huns, 209
Hyksos, 61
"Hymn to the Nile," 50

I

Ibn Battuta, 265
icon, 228, 233
Ides of March, 198
Immortals, 146
imperial court, 284–86, 287, 288–89
India, 27, 100, 104, 114–15, 117, 212, 273, 327
    Indian subcontinent, 102
    religion of, 106
indigenous, 255
Indo-European, 104
Indus River, 102, 104, 146
Indus Valley, 24, 100, 104
infantry, 190
inspiration (of God), 4
Iran, 140, 147, 157, 325
iron, 3, 16–17, 18, 23, 44–45, 52, 61, 73, 119, 132, 141, 161, 165, 280
irrigation, 22, 24–25, 26, 30, 37, 51, 60, 69, 129, 149, 157, 240, 280, 281
Isaac, 77
Isaiah, 142, 321, 324
Islam, 157, 225–26, 229, 264, 265, 268–69, 273, 275
    Five Pillars of, 225
Israel

feasts of, 80
history of, 4, 45, 76–77, 82, 84–85, 86–87, 88–89, 93–95, 162
Israelites, 43, 53, 61, 73, 77, 80, 87, 140, 142, 325
judges of, 82, 84, 90
religion of, 80–81, 86, 88, 90, 94–95, 97
twelve tribes of, 77, 81, 86
Istanbul, 214
Italian Peninsula, 186, 191, 192–93, 216, 220, 222
ivory, 61, 69, 73, 85, 145, 165, 212, 262, 273

J

Jacob, 77
jade, 122, 124, 236, 238, 242, 244, 249
Japan, 115, 276–80, 331
    architecture of, 282, 286, 288–89
    feudal, 290–91
    government of, 281, 283, 287
    Heian, 284–86
    religion of, 282, 287
    Yamato, 281–83
Japheth, 13–14
Jasaw Chan K'awiil I, 243
Jericho, 82
Jeroboam, 86
Jerusalem, 11, 47, 80, 84, 86, 88, 91, 94, 96–97, 142, 146, 155, 226, 229, 230, 319–20
Jesus, 4, 11, 42, 76, 80, 84, 87, 93–94, 95, 96–97, 113, 115, 126, 137, 151, 174, 175, 183, 204–5, 206–7, 214, 225, 228, 251, 263, 275, (as king) 320, 326–27
Jews, 87, 88–89, 94–95, 96–97, 174, 207
jihad, 226
Jimmu Tenno, 281
John III, 231
John, King, 310–11
Jomon, 280
Jonah, 45, 325
Jordan River, 82
Joseph, 53, 60, 63, 73, 77
Josephus, 96–97, 155
Joshua, 82, 90
Jubal, 3, 17, 18
Judah, 84, 86, 87
Judaism, 94–95, 224–25
Judea, 87, 88, 89, 93, 94, 96, 206

jury, 165. *See also* trial by jury
justice, 10, 11, 16–17, 43
    of Africa, 274–75
    of Byzantines, 221
    of Egypt, 66
    of Greece, 165, 166, 174
    of India, 104
    of Israel, 79, 82, 91
    of Mali, 265
    of Mayas, 246
    of Mesopotamia, 30, 35, 42–43
    of Persia, 148
    of Rome, 188, 203, 221
    of Western Europe, 294, 299, 304
Justinian I, 216–17, 222
Justinian Code, 221

K

Kaaba, 225
Kalahari, 258
kami, 282
kamikaze, 291
karma, 107, 110–11
Karnak, 62
keep, 312
Khoikhoi, 272
Khufu, 55
kingdom of God, 206
Kish, 40, 41
knight, 302–5
kofun, 281
kohl, 64
Kush, 12, 68, 72–73, 262–63
    Kushites, 68–69
Kyushu, 278

L

Lamech, 10, 17, 18
lapis lazuli, 21, 29, 32, 39
Latin America, 330
Latin language, 215, 219, 223, 299, 300
Latins, 186, 188, 189
La Venta, 238
law, 3, 4, 21, 79, 165, 189–90, 203, 221, 226, 246, 294, 309–11. *See also* Mosaic law
Law of the Twelve Tables, 190, 203
Legalism (Chinese philosophy), 127
legend, 186, 188, 265, 278
    of Robin Hood, 310
legion, 96, 190
legionary, 191, 209
Leo III, 227–29

levee, 26
library, 44, 330
Life in
    Athens, 166–67
    Constantinople, 218–19
    Enoch, 16–17
    Feudal France, 306–7
    Han Dynasty, 134–35
    Heian-kyo, 288–89
    India, 108–9
    Jerusalem, 90–91
    Persepolis, 148–49
    Rome, 202–3
    Sumer, 30–31
    Thebes, 66–67
    Tikal, 246–47
    Timbuktu, 268–69
limestone, 240, 247
linen, 58, 64, 75
linguist, 59, 103, 105, 261
literature, 176, 200, 285, 296, 298, 315
Lombards, 222, 298–99
lord, 302–5, 312, 314, 315
Louis the Pious, 300
Louvre, 57
Lower Egypt, 55
Luther, Martin, 326–27
Lydia (formerly Phrygia), 140, 145
lyre, 3, 16, 18, 38–39, 105, 180

M

Maccabean Revolt, 89
Maccabees, 92
Maccabeus, Judas, 89
Macedonia, 156, 182, 213, 217
Mackenzie, John, 275
magi, 139, 151
Magna Carta, 310–11
Mahayana Buddhism. *See under* Buddhism
maize, 235, 244
Mali (empire of), 265–66
Mandate of Heaven, 123
manor, 299, 302–5, 314, 315
Marathon, 152, 153, 169
Marius, 195–96
Marshall, John, 100, 115
Masada, 97
mask, 159, 163, 178
mathematics, 30, 33, 36, 54, 61, 66, 159, 174, 176, 179, 199, 226, 241, 243, 299
Mattathias, 89
Maurya, Chandragupta, 114
Mauryan Empire, 114–15

Mayan civilization, 240–49, 253
    religion of, 243, 248–49, 251
Mecca, 224–25, 226, 265–66
Medes, 45–46, 139–40, 147
medicine, 21, 22, 30, 37, 67, 91, 105, 108, 115, 132, 149, 179, 219, 226, 243, 253
    medieval, 294, 308–11, 312, 314–15
Medina, 225, 226
Mediterranean Sea, 22, 44, 50–51, 136, 160, 191, 194, 212, 216
Melos, 165
Memphis, Egypt, 52, 56
Menes, 55
menorah, 92
mercenary, 222–23, 232
Meroë, 70, 73
Meroitic, 70
Merovingians, 298
Mesoamerica, 236, 237, 238–39, 240–45, 248–55
Mesopotamia, 12, 22, 24, 31, 40–42, 44, 325
    religion of, 26–28, 31, 34–35
Messiah, 93, 95, 263, 319–20
metallurgy, 16, 37
metalworking, 3, 17, 18, 22–23, 91, 121–22, 132, 180, 271
Methodius, 229
Michael III, 229, 231, 232
Midas, 176–77
Middle Ages, 56, 294, 296, 302–5, 308–11, 312, 314–15
middle class, 27, 314
Middle East, 14, 229, 230, 232
Middle Kingdom (Egypt), 60
Midian, 61, 78
migrate, 14, 77, 104, 236, 261, 270
Minoan civilization, 162
missionary, 115, 207, 229, 275, 283, 327–28, 330–31
Mizraim, 50
moat, 312–13
Moffat, Mary, 328
Moffat, Robert, 328
Mogadishu, 273
Mohenjo-Daro, 100–101, 102, 103, 115
monarchy, 15, 31, 90, 122, 164, 269
monastery, 296, 299, 326
Mongols, 291
monk, 112, 296–97, 327
monotheism, 80, 94
monsoon, 99, 105
Montezuma II, 254
Morocco, 266

385

Morrison, Robert, 330–31
mosaic, 39, 220–21, 228
Mosaic Covenant, 79, 80, 93
Mosaic law, 43, 79, 88, 94–95
Moses, 4–5, 19, 61, 73, 77–80, 90
mosque, 265, 268–69
Muhammad, 224–26
mummy, 58, 62
Murasaki Shikibu, 285
Musa I (Mansa Musa), 265–66
music, 3, 7, 15, 16–17, 30, 38, 63, 104–5, 124, 139, 174, 176, 180, 219, 312
musician, 18, 23, 63
Muslim, 91, 225–26, 227, 263, 298, 302, 328
Muslim Turks, 230, 314
Mycenaean civilization, 163
myth, 151, 172–73, 176, 278, 301

N

Nabonidus, 34, 46–47
Namib Desert, 258
Nanna, 31, 34
Napata, 70, 72
Nara, 284
Nasser, Lake, 70, 72, 260
Near East, 39
Nebuchadnezzar II, 6, 7, 46–47, 84, 86, 87, 139, 155, 325
Nehemiah, 88, 139, 155
Nero, 96, 207
New Covenant, 80, 86, 87, 93
New Kingdom (Egypt), 61, 68, 73, 162
New Testament, 88, 95, 183, 214, 326
Nicaea, 231. *See also* Council of Nicaea
Nika Revolt, 217, 220
Nile Delta, 52, 55
Nile River, 45, 50–54, 63, 69, 71, 72, 78
   source of, 260
nilometer, 54
Nimrod, 15, 41, 44
Ninety-Five Theses, 326–27
Nineveh, 44–46
nirvana, 112–13, 137
Noah, 12–13, 18–19, 23, 38, 41, 50, 236
Nod, 10, 17
nomad, 90, 104, 106, 117, 140, 157, 215, 229, 270, 302
Normans, 229, 301, 308–11

Northern Kingdom (of Israel), 86, 87
Nubia, 68, 328
   Nubians, 69
nun, 296–97

O

oasis, 260
obsidian, 236, 245, 254
oceanic plates, 13
Octavian, 185, 198, 199, 206
Old Aswan Dam, 72
Old Kingdom (Egypt), 55, 56, 60, 100
Old Testament, 44, 88, 93, 183
oligarchy, 164, 168, 171
Olmec civilization, 238–39
   religion of, 239
Olympic Games, 180
Olympus, Mount, 167, 172
oracle bones, 121, 122
oral history, 261
oratory, 165, 169, 180
orthodox, 214
ostracism, 165
Ottomans, 212, 232–33
outcaste, 108, 110–11

P

page, 302–3
Pakistan, 100
Palatine Hill, 186
Palestine, 62, 93, 223, 226
pantheism, 106
Pantheon, 201
Papal States, 298
paper, 133, 241, 277, 283
papyrus, 56, 59, 65, 165
Parthenon, 166, 169, 181
Parthians, 157
Pasargadae, 143, 157
Passover, 78, 80
Pataliputra, 114
patriarch, 218, 228
patrician, 185, 188, 189–90, 196, 202–3
Paul, 95, 174, 192, 207
Pax Romana, 199, 200–201
Peloponnesian League, 170
Peloponnesian War, 170–71, 174
Peloponnesus, 160
peninsula, 212
Pentateuch, 4, 88, 91
Pepin the Short, 298
Pericles, 165, 169, 170, 171

Persepolis, 143, 145–46, 148–49, 156, 157
Persia, 7, 117, 139, 140, 141, 170, 182, 325, 327, 330
   Persians, 47, 68, 139, 156, 169, 171, 222–23, 273
   Persian wars, 152–53, 154
   religion of, 150
Persian Empire, 88, 140, 156, 169, 226
Persian Gulf, 14, 22, 25, 40, 44
phalanx, 40
pharaoh, 49, 53, 55, 59–63, 68, 72–73, 77–78, 262, 321
Pharisees, 89, 92, 93, 94, 206
Philistines, 84, 162
philosopher, 125, 174–75, 200, 226
philosophy, 165, 174–75, 182, 204, 219, 319
Phoenicia, 84
   Phoenicians, 84, 85, 188, 191
pictograph, 101, 103, 124
Pilate, Pontius, 94, 206
pipe (musical), 3, 16, 18, 38
Pishon River, 12
plague, 170. *See also* Egypt, plagues of
Plantagenet, 309–11
Plato, 175
plebeian, 188, 189–90, 195, 202–3
Pliny, 207
plow, 24
Plutarch, 168
Polybius, 191
polytheism, 34–35, 40
polytheistic, 70, 121, 224
Pompey, 196
pope, 228, 232, 296–97, 310, 315
   Innocent III, 230–31
   Leo III, 299
   Stephen II, 298
   Urban II, 230
potsherds, 165
prehistory, 5
priest, 26, 65, 80, 81, 106, 111, 151, 241, 243, 296, 297
primary source, 6, 8
Promised Land, 76, 82
Protestant, 297, 315, 323, 326, 327, 330, 331
Protestant Reformation, 315, 326, 331
proverb, 125
Ptolemies, 88
Ptolemy V, 57

Punic Wars, 191, 192–94, 270
Purim, 87
Pygmies, 271
pyramid, 55–56, 60, 70
    Black, 60
    Great, 55
    Mayan, 240, 246–47
    step, 55
Pythagoras, 175, 179

Q

Qin, 128–30
Qin Shi Huang, 128–30, 133
Queen of Sheba, 263
Qur'an, 224, 226, 268

R

rabbi, 94–95
rainforest, 260, 271
rain shadow desert, 260
raja, 104, 108
Rameses II, 59, 62, 72
redemption, 10–11, 320
Red Sea, 52, 61, 224
Reformation. *See* Protestant Reformation
regent, 61, 287
Region Today, The
    Africa, 259
    China, 119
    Egypt, 52
    Europe, 295
    Greece, 161
    India, 102
    Iran (Persia), 141
    Israel, 83
    Italy, 187
    Japan, 279
    Mesoamerica, 237
    Mesopotamia, 25
    Sudan (Kush), 71
    Turkey (Byzantium), 213
Rehoboam, 86
reincarnation, 107, 109, 110–11
Remus, 186
Renaissance, 315
republic. *See* Roman Republic
reservoir, 72
Rig-Veda, 107
roads, 35, 45, 129, 141, 144–45, 149, 157, 188, 192, 207, 209, 218, 223, 247, 252, 281, 294
Roman Catholic Church, 214, 228, 241, 294, 296–97, 298–99, 303, 314–15, 326–27, 330
Roman Empire, 96, 185, 199, 207, 208–9, 214, 215, 216, 326
Roman Forum, 190, 202
Roman Republic, 93, 189–98, 209
Rome, 96, 182, 186, 188, 191, 192–94, 207, 209, 215, 299
    religion of, 204–5, 214
    Romans, 68, 92, 93, 96–97, 157, 189, 191, 207, 209, 212
Romulus, 186
Rosetta stone, 57
Royal Road, 144
rubber, 237, 239, 245

S

sacrament, 296–97
Sadducees, 89, 92, 93, 94
Sahara, 50, 258–60, 264, 268, 271
Salamis, 152, 154, 169
salt, 264, 265, 271
salvation, 93, 94–95, 296–97, 320
Samaria, 86, 87
    Samaritans, 87
Samuel, 82, 84
samurai, 290–91
San, 272
sand dune, 256–58
Sangarius Bridge, 221
San Lorenzo Tenochtitlán, 238
Sanskrit, 105, 107
Sao, 271
sarcophagus, 58–59
Sardis, 140, 141, 144
Sargon I, 40–41
Sassanians, 157
Satan, 10, 151, 319
satrap, 143
satrapy, 143, 148
Saul, 82, 84
savanna, 69, 71, 73, 260
Saxons, 299
Scandinavia, 301
scarab, 64
school, 165
school father, 33
science, 9, 13, 21, 22, 30, 36–37, 44, 54, 61, 132, 159, 166, 174–75, 179, 180
Scipio, 194
scribe, 28, 33, 36–37, 63, 67, 243
script, 70
secondary source, 6
seismoscope, 132
Seleucids, 88, 89, 93
Seljuk Turks, 229, 232
Senate, 189–90, 195–96, 198, 199, 202
Septuagint, 88, 183
serf, 305, 315
Seventeen Article Constitution, 281
shadoof, 51, 67, 69
Shang dynasty, 119, 121–22, 162
shell inlay, 29, 32, 34, 245
Shem, 13–14
shenu, 59
Shikoku, 278
Shintoism, 282, 287
shogun, 290–91
shogunate, 290–91
Shona, 272, 273
Shotoku, 281–82
Sicily, 192, 213, 216
siege, 170, 194
silk, 122, 132–33, 135, 136, 212, 223, 284
Silk Road, 117, 131, 134, 136, 157, 226, 233
silt, 24, 51, 72, 118
sin, 10–11, 19, 65, 79, 80–81, 82, 87, 93–94, 95, 113, 127, 206, 282
Sinai, Mount, 78, 79
Sinai wilderness, 78, 82
slash-and-burn, 240, 244
slaves, 27, 31, 33, 53, 61, 63, 73, 77, 78, 134, 142, 165, 167, 168, 194, 195, 196, 203, 223, 243, 246, 249, 264, 265
    in Africa, 274–75, 321
social class, 15, 63
    of Aksum, 262
    of Aztecs, 252
    of Byzantines, 219
    of China, 125–26, 134, 137
    of Egypt, 48, 78
    of Greece, 167
    of India, 107, 110–11
    of Israel, 90
    of Mayas, 242
    of Persia, 148, 157
    of Rome, 185, 188
    of Sumer, 27, 31, 43
    of Western Europe, 305, 308, 315
social pyramid, 63
social structure, 5, 15, 63, 104, 110, 123, 188, 209, 217
Socrates, 174–75
Sofala, 273
Solomon, 60, 84, 85, 86, 263

Solon, 165
Songhai, 266
Southern Kingdom (of Israel), 86, 87
Spain, 220, 254–55
Sparta, 153, 164, 168, 169, 170–71
Sphinx, 56
spies, 114, 223
sports, 168, 176, 179–80, 216, 239, 249
squire, 302–3, 312
Sri Lanka, 115
Standard of Ur, 32
stele, 43, 57, 68, 243, 249, 262–63
Stoicism, 204–5
Stonehenge, 8
stucco, 244
stupa, 114
stylus, 27, 176
Sulla, 195–96
sultan, 233
Sumer, 21–22, 24, 26–29, 31, 40–41, 142
    Sumerians, 21, 24, 26, 32–33, 36–37, 100, 271
sundial, 54
Sundiata Keita, 265
Sunni Ali, 266
surplus, 26, 35, 53
Susa, 140, 143–44, 155
Swahili, 273
synagogue, 94, 206
Syria, 6, 61–62, 88, 96, 222–23, 226, 227, 230
Syria-Palestine, 61

T

tabernacle, 75, 79, 80–81, 90
Table of Nations, 13
tablet-house, 33
Taika Reforms, 283
Taklamakan Desert, 118
Talmud, 95
Taoism, 127, 135
Taurus Mountains, 22, 23, 144, 213
taxation
    of Africa, 264
    of Aztecs, 254–55
    of Byzantines, 217, 220, 227, 229
    of China, 131
    of Egypt, 53–54, 66–67
    of Greece, 167, 170
    of Israel, 86
    of Japan, 283, 289, 290–91
    of Mayas, 246–47
    of Mesopotamia, 42, 45
    of Persia, 143, 149, 155, 157
    of Rome, 195, 209, 215
    of Western Europe, 310–11, 314
Taylor, Hudson, 331
Taylor, J. E., 34
tell, 22
Tell el-Muqayyer, 32
temple at Jerusalem, 80, 84, 85, 86, 88, 89, 90–91, 92, 94, 96–97
Templo Mayor, 250
Ten Commandments, 79, 91
Tenochtitlán, 250–51, 252, 254–55
Texcoco, Lake, 250
theatre, 159, 177–78, 183
Thebes, 52, 56, 62, 65, 67
themes, 223
Themistocles, 154
Theodora, 217
Theodosius I, 209, 215
theorem, 179
Thermopylae, 152, 153, 169
The Tale of the Genji, 285
Thucydides, 165, 171
Thutmose III, 61–62
Tiberius Caesar, 94
Tigris River, 12, 22, 24, 30, 44
Tikal, 240
Timbuktu, 265–66
tin, 16–17, 18, 108, 119
ting, 121–22
Titus, 96–97
toga, 199, 203
tools, 3, 5, 7, 16, 18, 22, 24, 73, 108, 117, 134
Torah, 4, 88, 89, 92, 95
tournament, 303–4
tower of Babel, 42, 319
town, 314, 315
trade, 16, 162, 163, 164, 166
    of Africa, 270–71, 272, 273, 274–75 (*see also* trade: of Aksum; trade: of Ghana)
    of Aksum, 262–63
    of Aztecs, 252–53
    of Byzantines, 212, 215, 218, 223
    of China, 131, 134
    of Egypt, 60–61, 69–70, 73
    of Ghana, 264
    of Greece, 167, 169
    of India, 101, 327
    of Kush, 69–70, 73
    of Mayas, 245
    of Mesopotamia, 21, 27–28, 35–36, 42
    of Persia, 145
    of Phoenicia, 84
    of Rome, 192
trade routes, 60, 117, 136, 143, 166, 191, 212, 224, 264, 271
trading center, 41, 71, 165, 191, 212, 219, 230, 264, 331
tradition, 6, 7, 123, 178, 214, 226, 228
tree of the knowledge of good and evil, 10
trial by jury, 309–11, 314
trial by ordeal, 309
Tribal Assembly, 190, 195–96, 199, 202
tribune, 190
Trinity, 214, 228
triumvirate, 196
Trojan War, 163
Tuareg, 270
Tubal-cain, 3, 16
Turkey, 14, 44, 213, 214
Tutankhamun, 62, 68
tyrant, 165
Tyre, 84, 213, 223

U

Umar, 226
university, 229, 265, 299, 315
Upper Egypt, 55, 61
Ur, 22, 23, 26–27, 29, 31, 32, 34–35, 40, 75
Ur-Nammu, 31, 34, 41
Utnapishtim, 38

V

Valley of the Kings, 62
Vandals, 209, 216
vassal, 302–5, 308, 314
Vedas, 107
Venice, 229, 230–31, 232
Vespasian, 96
veto, 190
Victoria, Lake, 260
Vikings, 301, 302
Virgil, 200
Visigoths, 209
vizier, 63
vote, 165, 167, 195

W

Wang Xizhi, 283
water clock, 54
water wheel, 51, 69
weaving, 21, 28, 64, 75, 109, 132, 149, 150, 168, 185, 235, 283

Western Roman Empire, 215, 294, 299
wheat, 24, 28, 53, 64, 69, 160
wheel
    use in China, 132
    use in Egypt, 51
    use in India, 104
    use in Sumer, 24, 29, 36–37
Whiston, William, 96
William the Conqueror, 308, 309
wool, 21, 29, 33, 64, 150, 165
Woolley, Leonard, 22, 31–32
worldview, 7, 318–20
writ, 309–10
written language, 5, 15, 22, 30, 36–38, 40, 70, 79, 80, 84, 90, 105, 108, 124–25, 128, 130–31, 133, 147, 149, 157, 164, 176–77, 183, 188, 229, 240, 271, 281, 283, 285, 299
written records, 4, 6, 8, 35, 56–57, 76, 88, 90, 93, 95, 133, 142, 145, 147, 151, 164, 171, 174–75, 176, 191, 196, 223, 240–41
Wu Ti, 131, 136

X

Xerxes, 87, 148, 153, 154–55

Y

Yahweh, 80, 86
Yamato, 281–83
Yangtze River, 118, 119, 135
Yayoi, 280
Yellow River. *See* Huang He
Yoritomo, 290
Yucatán Peninsula, 237, 246

Z

Zara, 230
Zealots, 96–97
zero, 36, 241
Zerubbabel, 88, 90
Zhou, 123, 135
ziggurat, 31, 34
zimbabwe, 272
Zoroaster, 148, 150
Zoroastrianism, 148, 157, 245

PHOTO CREDITS

Key:
(t) top; (c) center; (b) bottom;
(l) left; (r) right; (i) insert

Chapter 1

6 J.D. Dallet/age fotostock/SuperStock; **7t** DEA/G. NIMATALLAH/De Agostini/Getty Images; **7c** Alex Khripunov/Shutterstock.com; **7bl** "Passing lion Babylon AO21118" by Jastrow/Wikimedia Commons/Public Domain; **7br** DEA/G. DAGLI ORTI/De Agostini/Getty Images; **8** aslysun/Shutterstock.com; **9** "The Garden of Eden" by Thomas Cole/Wikimedia Commons/Public Domain; **10** "Expulsion from the Garden of Eden" by Thomas Cole/Wikimedia Commons/Public Domain; **11** "Among the Sierra Nevada Mountains, California" by Albert Bierstadt/Wikimedia Commons/Public Domain; **14, 18** both Answers in Genesis (www.AnswersinGenesis.org and www.ArkEncounter.com); **19l** Kullanart/Shutterstock.com; **19r** beboy/Shutterstock.com

Chapter 2

21l "Near Eastern - Cylinder Seal with Standing Figures and Inscriptions - Walters 42699 - Side D"/Walters Art Museum/Wikimedia Commons/Public Domain; **21r** "Near Eastern - Cylinder Seal with Standing Figures and Inscriptions - Walters 42699 - Side A"/Walters Art Museum/Wikimedia Commons/Public Domain; **24, 31t, 31br, 33c** © The Trustees of the British Museum; **28t** Hulton Archive/Getty Images; **28b** DeAgostini/SuperStock; **29** Leemage/Universal Images Group/Getty Images; **31bl** Bettmann/Getty Images; **32** all Iberfoto/SuperStock; **33l, 37** both, **38r, 47r** Courtesy of the Oriental Institute of the University of Chicago; **34** The Metropolitan Museum of Art, Fletcher Fund, 1940, www.metmuseum.org; **35** The Metropolitan Museum of Art, Rogers Fund, 1959, www.metmuseum.org; **36** "Pull toy, Khafajah, Temple Oval II, Early Dynastic period, 2900-2330 BC, baked clay - Oriental Institute Museum, University of Chicago - DSC07380"/Wikimedia Commons/CC0 1.0 Universal; **38l** Album/Oronoz/SuperStock; **41** Scala / Art Resource, NY; **43** Universal Images Group/Getty Images; **47l** BJU Photo Services

Chapter 3

50 NASA; **51t** Eye Ubiquitous/SuperStock; **51b** Universal Images Group Editorial/Getty Images; **53** Kunsthistorisches Museum, Wien; **54l** DeA Picture Library / Granger, NYC; **54r** Todd Bolen/BiblePlaces.com; **56** pius99/Bigstock.com; **57** Hulton Archive/Getty Images; **58t, 73** Granger, NYC; **58b** "Egyptian - A Complete Set of Canopic Jars - Walters 41171, 41172, 41173, 41174 - Group"/Wikimedia Commons/CC By-SA 3.0; **59** Werner Forman/Universal Images Group Editorial/Getty Images; **60** DeAgostini/SuperStock; **61t** Sergey Uryadnikov/Shutterstock.com; **61b** The Metropolitan Museum of Art, Rogers Fund, 1929, www.metmuseum.org; **62l** Apic/Hulton Archive/Getty Images; **62r** Iberfoto/SuperStock; **64** The Metropolitan Museum of Art, Gift of Helen Miller Gould, 1910, www.metmuseum.org; **65** Tuul/robertharding/SuperStock; **68, 70r** De Agostini Picture Library/Getty Images; **69** Sandro Vannini/Corbis Documentary/Getty Images; **70l** © Peter Horree / Alamy Stock Photo; **72t** Lisa S./Shutterstock.com; **72b** Earth Science and Remote Sensing Unit, NASA Johnson Space Center, http://eol.jsc.nasa.gov

Chapter 4

75 Roberto Nistri / Alamy Stock Photo; **77** © GoodSalt - Review and Herald Publishing Association; **84** diak/Shutterstock.com; **87, 94** www.BibleLandPictures.com / Alamy Stock Photo; **88** Museum of Archaeology and Anthropology, University of Pennsylvania; **89t** Bowen Collection of Antiquities, Bob Jones University Museum & Gallery; **89b** PhotoStock-Israel/age fotostock/SuperStock; **92t** flik47/iStock Editorial/Getty Images Plus; **92c** © Fotolia/Scott Maxwell; **92b** "Knesset Menorah P5200009" by Deror avi/Wikimedia Commons/CC By-SA 3.0; **93** mtcurado/iStock / Getty Images Plus; **95** "Baram ancient synagogue (26715813362)" by Yair Aronshtam/Wikimedia Commons/CC By-SA 2.0; **96** Danita Delimont/Gallo Images/Getty Images; **97** Albatross/SuperStock

Chapter 5

100bl SAM PANTHAKY/AFP/Getty Images; **100br** agf photo/SuperStock; **101** Leemage/Universal Images Group/Getty Images; **103tl** robertharding/SuperStock; **103tr** DEA / A. DAGLI ORTI/De Agostini/Getty Images; **103bl** 'Priest King' from Mohenjo-Daro, c.2500 BC (steatite), Harappan / National Museum of Karachi, Karachi, Pakistan / Photo © Luca Tettoni / Bridgeman Images; **103br** Angelo Hornak/Corbis Historical/Getty Images; **105, 113l** Exotica/SuperStock; **106l** © Stuart Atkinson | Dreamstime.com; **106r** Jupiter Images/Photos.com/Thinkstock; **107** World History Archive/SuperStock; **111** Hemis.fr/SuperStock; **112** "Sermon in the Deer Park depicted at Wat Chedi Liem-KayEss-1"/Wikipedia/CC By-SA 3.0; **113c** © Tichonj | Dreamstime.com; **113r** © sianstock/Fotolia; **115** Waj/Shutterstock.com

Chapter 6

117 Gift of Mr. and Mrs. Eric Lidow (AC1998.251.20)/www.lacma.org/Public Domain; **118t** aphotostory/Shutterstock.com; **118b, 133** robertharding/SuperStock; **120** Xiaolu Chu / Stringer/Getty Images; **121** "Liu Ding" by Mountain/Wikimedia Commons/CC By-SA 3.0; **123** CPA Media - Pictures from History /Granger, NYC; **124r** JingAiping/Shutterstock.com; **124tl** DEA / G. DAGLI ORTI/De Agostini/Getty Images; **124ct** "Knife Money Yan" by Davidhartill/Wikimedia Commons/CC By-SA 3.0; **124cb** The Metropolitan Museum of Art, Charlotte C. and John C. Weber Collection, Gift of Charlotte C. and John C. Weber through the Live Oak Foundation, 1988, www.metmuseum.org; **124b** "Bi with two dragons and grain pattern"/Wikimedia Commons/CC By-SA 3.0; **125b** Iberfoto/SuperStock; **126** © iStock.com/traveler1116; **127** "Statue of Lao Tzu in Quanzhou" by Tom@HK/Wikimedia Commons/CC By-SA 2.0; **129t** Xinhua News Agency/Getty Images; **129b** Digital Vision/Photodisc/Thinkstock; **130t** © iStock.com/fotoVoyager; **130b** studioEAST/Getty Images Entertainment/Getty Images; **132t** BJU Photo Services; **132bl** Science & Society Picture Library /Getty Images; **137** Heritage Images/Hulton Archive/Getty Images

Chapter 7

142 "Cyrus Cylinder" by Mike Peel (www.mikepeel.net), Modifications by یغنام/Wikimedia Commons/CC By-SA 4.0; **143** "Iran - Pasargad - The great Cyrus Tomb - ریپک شوروک هاگمارآ – panoramio" by Alireza Javaheri/Wikimedia Commons/CC By-SA 3.0; **145** "Double daric 330-300 obverse CdM Paris" by Marie-Lan Nguyen/Wikimedia Commons/CC By-SA 2.5; **146** Prapasri T/Shutterstock.com; **147t** © Livius.org; **147b** age fotostock/SuperStock; **150t** DeAgostini/SuperStock; **150c** www.BibleLandPictures.com / Alamy Stock Photo; **150b** The Metropolitan Museum of Art, Gift of Joseph V. McMullan, 1970, www.metmuseum.org; **154** © iStock.com/duncan1890; **155** "Tomb of Artaxerxes I" by Anatoly Terentiev/Wikimedia Commons/CC By-SA 3.0; **156** "Batalla de Gaugamela (M.A.N. Inv.1980-60-1) 03" by Luis García (Zaqarbal)/Wikimedia Commons/CC By-SA 3.0; **157** "Drachma Shapur I The Great (5447223661)" by dynamosquito from France/Wikimedia Commons/CC By-SA 2.0

Chapter 8

160t LatitudeStock - Eric Farrelly/Gallo Images/Getty Images; **160b** Milan Gonda /Shutterstock.com; **162t** "Knossos - North Portico 02" by Bernard Gagnon/Wikimedia Commons/CC-BY-SA 3.0; **162bl** Getty Images/iStockphoto/Thinkstock; **162br** Dimitris66/iStock/Getty Images Plus; **163l** "Funeral mask of Agamemnon-colorcorr" by DieBuche/Wikimedia Commons/CC By-SA 3.0; **163r** Henning Marquardt/Shutterstock.com; **174** © iStock.com/trevorbenbrook; **175** "Raffael 058" by The Yorck Project/Wikimedia Commons/Public Domain; **178t** Taesik Park/Shutterstock.com; **178c, 178b** Getty Images/Hemera/Thinkstock; **180tl** World History Archive / Alamy Stock Photo; **180cl** Scott Heavey/Staff/Getty Images Sport; **180cr** "Niobid Painter - Red-Figure Amphora with Musical Scene - Walters 482712 - Side A"/Walters Art Museum/Wikimedia Commons/Public Domain; **180b** "Woman kithara CdM 581" by Marie-Lan Nguyen/Wikimedia Commons/CC By-SA 2.5; **181t** Dorling Kindersley/Exactostock-4268/SuperStock; **181b** © iStock.com/MinistryOfJoy; **183t** "AGMA Kleroterion" by Marsyas/Wikimedia Commons/CC By-SA 2.5; **183b** Paul Fearn / Alamy Stock Photo

Chapter 9

185 Tolo Balaguer/age fotostock/SuperStock.com; **186t, 189, 203** Public Domain; **186b** K3S/Shutterstock.com; **188l** The Metropolitan Museum of Art, Bequest of Walter C. Baker, 1971, www.metmuseum.org; **188r** North Wind Picture Archives / Alamy Stock Photo; **190** © iStock.com/Nikada; **192l** Lev Levin/Shutterstock.com; **192r** "Domitianus Milestone" by Ingsoc/Wikimedia Commons/CC By-SA 3.0; **194** Richard I'Anson/Lonely Planet Images/Getty Images; **195t** Cenotaph of the Gracchi, 1853 (bronze), Guillaume, Eugene (1822–1905) / Musee d'Orsay, Paris, France/ Bridgeman Images; **195b** Chronicle / Alamy Stock Photo; **196t** Bust of Marcus Licinius Crassus (c.115–53 BC) (stone) (b/w photo), Roman (5th century AD) / Louvre, Paris, France /

390

Bridgeman Images; **196**b PLRANG ART/Shutterstock.com; **197** "Imperial group Mars Venus Louvre Ma1009 n3" by Marie-Lan Nguyen/Wikimedia Commons/CC By-SA 2.5; **198** "The Murder of Caesar" by Karl Theodor von Piloty/Wikimedia Commons/Public Domain; **201**t © Luzav10 | Dreamstime; **201**b "The Interior of the Pantheon, Rome" by Giovanni Paolo Panini/Wikimedia Commons/Public Domain; **205** © Claude Coquilleau/Fotolia; **206** Vincenzo Fontana/Corbis Historical/Getty Images; **207** "Malta - Mosta - Triq Francesco Napulun Tagliaferro - Ta' Bista Catacombs and Roman baths 06 ies" by Frank Vincentz/Wikimedia Commons/CC By-SA 3.0; **208** "Konstantinos Kaldis - View of Constantinople - 1851"/Wikimedia Commons/Public Domain; **209** xdrew/Shutterstock.com

Chapter 10

212l Public Domain; **212**tr "Costantino"/The Yorck Project/Wikimedia Commons/Public Domain; **212**br © iStock.com/HHakim; **214** © iStock.com/gece33; **217** © iStockphoto.com/Duncan Walker; **220**t Mikhail Markovskiy/Shutterstock.com; **220**b Anna Jedynak/Shutterstock.com; **221**t mgokalp/Moment/Getty Images; **221**bl DeAgostini/SuperStock; **221**br "Meister von San Vitale in Ravenna 008"/The Yorck Project/Wikimedia Commons/Public Domain; **225** Zurijeta/Shutterstock.com; **226** Ted Spiegel/Corbis Documentary/Getty Images; **227** "Greekfire-madridskylitzes1"/Wikimedia Commons/Public Domain; **228** The Metropolitan Museum of Art, Gift of Irma N. Straus, 1960, www.metmuseum.org; **229** Getty Images/Hemera/Thinkstock; **231**t ASSOCIATED PRESS; **231**cl (both earrings) The Metropolitan Museum of Art, Gift of J. Pierpont Morgan, 1917, www.metmuseum.org; **231**b The Metropolitan Museum of Art, Gift of Stephen V. Grancsay, 1942, www.metmuseum.org; **232** Photos.com/Thinkstock; **233**t Lestertair/Shutterstock.com; **233**b "Great Turkish Bombard at Fort Nelson" by Gaius Cornelius/Wikimedia Commons/Public Domain

Chapter 11

238 © iStock.com/arturogi; **239**t Hasnuddin/Shutterstock.com; **239**b robertharding/SuperStock; **240**l Luis Davilla/Photographer's Choice/Getty Images; **240**r Kyle Ellway/Shutterstock.com; **241** "Dresden Codex p09"/Wikimedia Commons/Public Domain; **242** DeAgostini/SuperStock; **243**, **245**br The Walters Art Museum; **245**t © iStock.com/dwart; **245**c © iStock.com/DianaLundin; **245**bl GRANGER / The Granger Collection; **248** "Chichen Itza 3" by Daniel Schwen/Wikimedia Commons/CC BY-SA 4.0; **249**l Diego Grandi/Shutterstock.com; **249**r "Copán Ballcourt" by Adalberto Hernandez Vega/Wikimedia Commons/CC BY-SA 2.0; **251** "Monolito de la Piedra del Sol" by El Comandante/ Wikimedia Commons/CC BY-SA 3.0; **252** Werner Forman/Universal Images Group/Getty Images; **253**t "Codex Mendoza folio 60r"/Wikimedia Commons/Public Domain; **253**b "Aztec Warriors (Florentine Codex)"/Wikimedia Commons/Public Domain; **254** "Flickr - USCapitol - Cortez and Montezuma at Mexican Temple"/Architect of the Capitol/Wikimedia Commons/Public Domain; **255** "Piri reis world map 01"/Wikimedia Commons/Public Domain

Chapter 12

260tl astudio/Shutterstock.com; **260**tr edeantoine/Shutterstock.com; **260**b Franky_Pictures/iStock/Thinkstock; **261** © iStock.com/zinnman; **262** Gilles Barbier/Media Bakery; **264**t Bjoern Wylezich/Shutterstock.com; **264**c AlenKadr/Shutterstock.com; **264**b © iStock.com/busypix; **265** © iStock.com/hanoded; **266** Pubic Domain; **267**l "Panel, Bushong people, mid-20th century, raffia palm fiber, plain weave, openwork embroidery, and wrapping, HMA" by Hiart/Wikimedia Commons/CC0 1.0; **267**r "Panel, Shoowa people, 20th century, Honolulu Museum of Art III" by Hiart/Wikimedia Commons/CC0 1.0; **270** Nico Tondini/MediaBakery; **271** Nick Greaves / Alamy Stock Photo; **272**l Eric LAFFORGUE/Gamma-Rapho/Getty Images; **272**r Werner Forman/Universal Images Group/Getty Images; **274**t Fabian Plock/Shutterstock.com; **274**b © Nicolas De Corte | Dreamstime; **275** John Warburton Lee/SuperStock

Chapter 13

278tl, **282**c Sean Pavone/Shutterstock.com; **278**tr Krishna.Wu/Shutterstock.com; **278**b siro46/Shutterstock.com; **280**t The Metropolitan Museum of Art, Mary Griggs Burke Collection, Gift of the Mary and Jackson Burke Foundation, 2015, www.metmuseum.org; **280**cr The Metropolitan Museum of Art, Rogers Fund, 1918, www.metmuseum.org; **280**cc, bl, bc, cl, br The Metropolitan Museum of Art, The Harry G. C. Packard Collection of Asian Art, Gift of Harry G. C. Packard, and Purchase, Fletcher, Rogers, Harris Brisbane Dick, and Louis V. Bell Funds, Joseph Pulitzer Bequest, and The Annenberg Fund Inc. Gift, 1975, www.metmuseum.org; **281** JTB Photo/Universal Images Group/Getty Images; **282**t © 2005 JupiterImages/Photos.com. All rights reserved; **282**b "Itsukushima Gate" by Jordy Meow/Wikimedia Commons/CC BY-SA 3.0; **283**tr Marie Dubrac/ANYONE/amana images/Getty Images; **283**tl "Gakkiron 1"/Wikimedia Commons/Public Domain; **283**b "Yōshū Chikanobu Filial Piety" by Toyohara Chikanobu/Wikimedia Commons/Public Domain; **285**l Joymsk140/Shutterstock.com; **285**r "Tale of Genji Toyokuni Utagawa print"/Wikimedia Commons/Public Domain; **286**l Photo Japan / Alamy Stock Photo; **286**r Philippe Widling / Design Pics/SuperStock; **287**l coward_lion/Bigstock.com; **287**r DeAgostini/SuperStock; **290** "Minamoto no Yoritomo"/Wikimedia Commons/Public Domain; **291**l Granger, NYC; **291**r Getty Images/Photos.com/Thinkstock

Chapter 14

293 "French denier of Charles the Bald (FindID 542511)"/The Portable Antiquities Scheme/Wikimedia Commons/CC BY-SA 2.0; **298**t, **298**c Universal Images Group/SuperStock; **298**b Pepin the Short, King of the Franks, 1789 (engraving) / Photo © Chris Hellier / Bridgeman Images; **299** "MS Laud Misc 165 fol 109 by Jacobus le Palmer"/Wikimedia Commons/Public Domain; **300** Heinz-Dieter Falkenstein/Media Bakery; **301** "Odin (Manual of Mythology)"/Wikimedia Commons/Public Domain; **304** Tim Gainey / Alamy Stock Photo; **308** Spencer Arnold/Stringer/Hulton Archive/Getty Images; **310** "A Chronicle of England - Page 226 - John Signs the Great Charter" by James William Edmund Doyle/Wikimedia Commons/Public Domain; **311** "Magna Carta (British Library Cotton MS Augustus II.106)"/Wikimedia Commons/Public Domain; **312** Christophel Fine Art/Universal Images Group/Getty Images; **313** © iStock.com/NicolasMcComber; **314** © iStock.com/dkaranouh; **315** robynmac/123RF

Chapter 15

320 Gustave Doré, The Ascension, Bob Jones University Collection, photo by Unusual Films; **321** "The Christian Martyrs' Last Prayer" by Jean-Léon Gérôme/Walters Art Museum/Wikimedia Commons/Public Domain; **324**l © iStock.com/zbruch; **324**r "Oxyrhynchus 209 (p10)"/Wikimedia Commons/Public Domain; **324**b BRIAN HARRIS / Alamy Stock Photo; **325** "Ephrem.01.incipit"/Wikimedia Commons/Public Domain; **326** Falkenstein Heinz-Dieter / Alamy Stock Photo; **327** William Carey (colour litho), English School, (19th century) / Private Collection / © Look and Learn / Elgar Collection / Bridgeman Images; **330** Daniel Sicolo/Media Bakery

All maps from Map Resources